The Anti-Samuelson

BY MARC LINDER

VOLUME ONE

Macroeconomics:

BASIC PROBLEMS OF THE CAPITALIST ECONOMY

URIZEN BOOKS / NEW YORK

A four-volume edition of this book was first published in a German translation in 1974 by Politladen, Erlangen, under the title **Der Anti-Samuelson**. The joint decision of the publisher and author to condense the work was dictated by the desire to reduce costs and thus bring its price within reach of both students and teachers. Inevitably, in so radical a scaling-down, a great deal of textual elaboration, annotation, and bibliographical data had to be sacrificed. Those who wish to pursue the author's ideas and argumentation in greater depth are referred to the unabridged German-language edition.

Library of Congress Cataloging in Publication Data

Linder, Marc.
  Anti-Samuelson.

  Bibliography.
  Includes index.
  1. Samuelson, Paul Anthony, 1915-   Economics.
I. Sensat, Julius, 1947-   joint author. II. Title.
HB119.S25L5   330   · 76-20796
ISBN 0-916354-14-8 (v. 1)
ISBN 0-916354-15-6 (v. 1) pbk.

Copyright © 1977 by Marc Linder

Manufactured in the United States of America

Preface

But many things are required to the conversation of inward peace; because many things concur . . . to its perturbation. . . . Some things there are, which dispose the minds of men to sedition, others which move and quicken them so disposed. Among those which dispose them, we have reckoned in the first place certain perverse doctrines. It is therefore the duty of those who have the chief authority, to root those out of the minds of men, not by commanding, but by teaching; not by the terror of penalties, but by the perspicuity of reasons, the laws whereby this evil may be withstood, are not to be made against the persons erring, but against the errors themselves. Those errors which . . . we affirmed were inconsistent with the quiet of the commonweal, have crept into the minds of ignorant men, partly from the pulpit, partly from the daily discourses of men, who, by reason of little employment otherwise, do find leisure enough to study; and they got into these men's minds by the teachers of their youth in public schools. Wherefore also, on the other side, if any man would introduce sound doctrine, he must begin from the *academies*. There the true and truly demonstrated foundations of civil doctrine are to be laid; wherewith young men, being once endued, they may afterward, both in private and public, instruct the vulgar. And this they will do so much the more cheerfully and powerfully, by how much themselves shall be more certainly convinced of the truth of those things they profess and teach. . . . I therefore conceive it to be the duty of supreme officers, to cause the true elements of civil doctrine to be written, and to command them to be taught in all the colleges of their several dominions.
—Thomas Hobbes, *Philosophical Rudiments Concerning Government and Society* (1651).

From his study of economics it is hoped that the typical student will get a new respect for the efficacy of our type of mixed economy—a respect not based upon rote slogans or upon ignorance of possible imperfections, but a respect based upon theoretical and factual knowledge and that will not fade at the first threat of difficult times.

—Paul A. Samuelson *et al., Instructor's Manual to Accompany Samuelson: Economics* 6th ed.), p. 150.

The need for a book such as ours may not be self-evident. After all, the *New York Times,* in its editorial comment on Paul Samuelson's receipt of the Nobel Prize for economic science in 1970, said that he "can be called the Einstein of economics for developing a unified field theory of economic activity." What, one might well ask, could be our quarrel with S and with the science he so illustriously represents?

In recent years, certain phenomena have evoked a variety of responses, "alternatives" to the "orthodox" economics of S's textbook which might be confused with our critique. As a matter of fact, even S's own book—particularly the 8th and 9th editions—reflects this new trend. The political-economic crises that have beset U.S. capitalism for the past decade have found vocal expression in the academic world, and among students in particular. The inclusion in S's textbook of such diverse topics as pollution, racial discrimination, and the military-industrial complex was essentially a commercial response to this growing awareness, designed to consolidate S's position in the lucrative textbook market.

The users of introductory economic texts by and large are a captive audience with little if any choice over the books they are forced to buy. They do, however, have a negative power; that is to say, if the traditional textbooks fail to interest the students sufficiently the desired ideological message about capitalism will not get across to them, and so new methods of presentation will have to be found. Here is where the teacher can play a crucial role, for not only is he in a position to promote sales for the publisher, he is also the social agent able to determine which books "work," which don't, and which might.

This brings us back to the matter of the new trend in introductory texts. Some years ago when thousands of students began to be critical of their society, the more obviously apologetic texts ran the danger of losing their ideological function, and hence their marketability. Thereupon a call went out for more "relevant" material. Most of the new entrants turned out to be nothing more than jazzed-up versions of S, commercial efforts to take over the market S was in danger of losing; but in fundamental theoretical terms they were not different from the old model.

The authors of the present book participated in the rise and decline of the American student movement of the 1960s and '70s. One of its chief failings, and one shared with the New Left in general, was a tendency to substitute moralizing for theoretically grounded politics. This moralizing took the form of trying to mobilize students on behalf of the struggles for others, or rather, these other struggles were made into the students' own, since they, being a privileged social stratum, had no battles of their own to fight other than the repudiation of their privileges. Although the concrete nature of these struggles changed as the orientational groups themselves—e.g., "Third World" countries, blacks and other suppressed groups, workers—changed, the structure of the strategic mechanism itself did not change significantly.

This is not to say that students are not in some significant sense a privileged group. Their temporary exemption from wage labor and the prospect of a future standard of living and conditions of work superior to those of the majority of the working class are indeed privileges (in part consciously manipulated by the ruling class to drive a wedge between "head workers" and the rest of the working class). Nor is this to say that students should not or must not be subordinated to other groups within the context of anticapitalist struggles. In point of fact the authors of this book believe that the working class must lead a socialist revolution in the United States or there will be no such revolution in this country.

Intellectuals will not be of any use in a socialist movement if they try to disavow their position as intellectuals by posing as proletarians—that is, unless they in fact cease to be intellectuals and become proletarians, in which case the problem disappears. On the other hand, they can contribute to a socialist revolution *as* intellectuals.

As far as the interests and roles of students are concerned, we must distinguish between the period in which students are students, that is, during their training, and the subsequent period of their working lives. Although the New Left student movement had developed a decided interest in programs and strategies for this subsequent period, particularly with respect to teaching professions, it hardly ever addressed itself to students as students. Whatever the reasons for this failure, the separation of the training and working phases must necessarily lead to a defective understanding of the latter and to faulty political strategies, because the content of the future "ideological labor" performed by former college students is influenced by their experiences at school. Hence if no attempt is made to break through bourgeois ideological "hegemony" while students are students, it is unlikely that their subsequent activities will be guided by consistent anticapitalist perceptions.

Under present academic conditions a built-in tendency operates to direct the student's attention toward his own subjective shortcomings as an individual; this is intimately connected with the hierarchic, competitive, atomized structure that poses such grave personal problems to many students. Another line of defense so to speak locates the root of theoretical problems in the "pure" nature of the particular theory or the "infinitely complicated" nature of reality. In other words, students are told that there is really nothing that can be done about this gap at the present time, and that any theories claiming the opposite are simplistic ideological distortions unworthy of scholarly attention. Here it is the function of Marxism to mediate to students the relationship between what appear to be personal problems and capitalist society, and to pinpoint the inability of bourgeois theory to answer these questions. Indeed, at some level bourgeois theory must be shown to be among the causes of these very problems.

This process of making all these links obvious presupposes a measure of intellectual motivation on the part of the students. Yet many U.S. students do not see themselves as intellectuals, part of the problem of the broader anti-intellectualism of the U.S. In its sounder aspects this implies a suspicion toward theories that do not benefit the masses of people; nevertheless, such semicritical traditions can degenerate into blanket rejection of all theories, including those able to help bring about the kind of society the people themselves would like to see.

Concretely this means that within the normal authority structure of the universities, left-wing teachers will initially experience the same sort of indifference and/or hostility accorded all other teachers. This is a fundamental dilemma which can be solved only collectively by organized teachers and students. No single book can overcome this problem, and ours is no exception; it may even exacerbate it because of its "heavy" theory, detail, and length. Consequently it may be suitable only for the more motived students (not to be confused with "elite" school students). But if used only for selected chapters, it can reach a much larger number.

At this point we feel an explanation of its genesis is in order. It all began with the attempts of the authors to provide critical commentaries to a lecture course on social philosphy at Princeton University in the spring of 1970. The rather encouraging, even enthusiastic student response to what was in fact an unplanned, even spontaneous effort on our part, persuaded us that a more systematic approach might lead to emulation in various courses and to an overall strategy on the university level.

We decided to focus on economics, which we believe constitutes the basis for an understanding of capitalist society. To this end we undertook a critical reading of the textbook being used in the introductory course. Our leaflets—short comments on each week's readings—appeared to evoke little student interest in the lectures. But our presence in the lectures as well as in the smaller classes caused the teaching staff—none of whom was sympathetic toward us—to pull out all the stops to fend off this "political attack."

Perhaps we would have been more successful had we

"equalized competitive conditions"—that is to say, had there been enough of us to cover all the classes. The fact that we were so few was largely responsible for the students' reactions, for particularly freshmen are impressed with authority and are easily persuaded that it would be best to steer clear of those who are not.

This sent us back to the drawing boards. We decided to gather together and read S's textbook critically; the chapter critiques grew out of the notes for these sessions. It is our objective to mediate to students the ability to think critically. To this end we have tried to dissect in exemplary fashion S's reasoning, a procedure he himself can hardly disagree with given his statement that "I feel it only just that every word, every comma, every line, every page and every chapter be subjected to the most unsparing criticism" (5th ed., p. vi).

Our approach has its advantages and disadvantages, especially insofar as it is linked with an attempt to follow S in his presentation of bourgeois theory. The chief advantage derives from the fact that the methodological chaos inherent in present-day bourgeois economics thus becomes obvious. The potential disadvantage lies in the danger of losing the overview by becoming bogged down in detail. This can be avoided if the reader heeds one of our demands—that before tackling our book he familiarize himself with S's text or one like it. In other words, the present book presupposes that the reader understand elementary bourgeois economics as academic proponents want it understood. However, this does not mean that one must have read S's book previously, although parallel reading of it will be necessary. The decision to "key" this book to S was a didactic one; it allowed us to focus on the teaching of economics. The reason we selected S's book has to do with its "originality" and "popularity" in the U.S. and its international use.

Obviously our book will be used largely by college students who have already taken an elementary economics course and by graduate students, not necessarily economics majors; in fact we hope that social scientists in general will make use of it. As to those who are currently taking an introductory course, perhaps critical teachers can work parts of this book into such a course in preparation for a future full course.

We will not deny that ours is an ambitious undertaking. At times, points in S's book become springboards for excursions into various subjects, because the theoretical and empirical background offered fails to elucidate his own subject matter, as for instance in the case of the chapters on Keynesian economics and on international economics (Chapters 8 and 23-26, respectively). But more generally, S's incredibly sloppy scholarly method has dictated the dissection of his empirical information, a task not made any easier by his failure to cite sources or offer relevant bibliographical information.

We do not mean to exaggerate the significance of this sort of empirical refutation, but we do believe it is good background material for a first critical look at an "authority" like S, for once this sort of shoddy science is showed up for what it is, it may serve to break down the reluctance of students to question theoretical statements. This brings us to the next "level" of our critique, which may be called an immanent theoretical one; here we try to show the internal contradictions in bourgeois theory by letting them unfold themselves. And finally, by developing critiques of essential concepts such as money, profit, value, price, capital, labor, etc., we provide an introduction to Marx's critique of political economy. However, this is merely an introduction, not a "complete" exposition. It is our intention to show the "relevance" of Marxism not by asserting its revolutionary character in the abstract but rather by demonstrating how it alone is capable of understanding contemporary capitalism and of explaining why bourgeois economics cannot.

Finally, we would like to thank the following comrades for their help in various ways: B.Stollberg, P.Crosser, W. Burlingham, P. Roman, C. Newlin, C. Neusüss, W. Semmler, L. Waldmann, H. Mattfeld, U. Förderreuter, J. Glombowski, and H. Fassbinder. Especially we would like to thank Wolfgang Müller for his copious critical commentaries on many chapters as well as on the overall structure of the book with particular reference to pedagogical matters.

OVERVIEW OF THE STRUCTURE OF THE BOOK

For purposes of analysis, S's text may be divided into six major sections, which to some extent overlap with the six parts into which he has divided it.

The first section, encompassing Chapters 1-9 (and also 39-40), can be regarded as an *ideological* introduction to certain fundamental macroeconomic phenomena which economic *theory* concerns itself with. The topics S deals with here are in fact significant, and, moreover, are designed to prepare the reader for the science by linking it to the prescientific knowledge a college student may reasonably be expected to possess from his reading of newspapers, watching television, or just from having gone shopping. They deal with what S considers the technological foundation of production and exchange and with the organizational forms assumed by the factors of production labor (unions) and capital (business firms), as well as the economic functions of the social organ designed to compensate for the destabilizing effects of the market: the state. In addition, S includes a chapter on income (distribution) which transcends his own framework and serves as a pedagogical advertisement for the mixed economy. For this reason we have grouped it with similar material from Chapters 39 and 40.

The second section, Chapters 10-14, reflects the seriousness with which "modern" economics has been forced to view the problem of cyclical depressions and/or stagnation. for in point of fact, the Keynesian theories that form the core of these chapters were developed in reaction to prolonged depressions and have, in turn, served as a tool in state measures to prevent or mitigate such cyclical phenomena. Since S, however, fails to discuss these essential connections, we have provided an analysis of the empirical and theoretical developments that led to the rise of Keynesianism. Similarly, we have offered some historical insights into the theory of national income and business cycles.

The third section, Chapters 15-19, deals with money and credit as well as with state intervention based on these "instruments." These topics presuppose mediating links which S does not present, and it was therefore incumbent upon us to develop a theoretical understanding of money. This is one of the more difficult parts of our book, particularly since the theory of money in turn presupposes a theory of value, which we were able to present only in very abbreviated form. A further difficulty relates to the fact that an understanding of the phenomena of credit discussed by S requires an extended analysis of the actual development of U.S. capitalism. Such an analysis is of course out of the question in an introductory theory textbook. Our efforts therefore to mediate theory and actuality in this regard are limited to selective aspects.

The fourth section, Chapters 20-26, figures as a surrogate for what in earlier times would have been classified under the heading "theory of value." We have therefore focused on the material and theoretical causes of this transformation. Our second major concern attaches to an immanent critique of the theories of utility and supply, with special attention paid to the degree to which these may be considered realistic.

The fifth section, Chapters 27-31, contains a general theory of production from which derive special theories on the incomes of each factor of production. Here our approach is straightforward: an immanent critique combined with historical and empirical explanatory and/or illustrative material.

The sixth and final section (Chapters 33-36, 38) deals with the international aspects of the capitalist mode of production: international monetary system, world trade, foreign investment, and the specific crises engendered on the world market. Considering the key role played by these international capital relations—especially manifest during the World War II period—we find S's treatment rather disappointing even within the framework of bourgeois economics. That is why we have supplemented our theoretical critique with a broad introduction to the multiple functions of the capitalist world market.

As a result of the extraordinary number of quotations from this book, we have placed the page references in the text. Unless otherwise noted, these references are to the ninth edition; they appear in parentheses and without the abbreviation "p." Thus "(89)" would mean a reference to page 89 of the ninth edition. References to the other editions appear for example as follows: "(5th ed., p.444)." Here is a list of the years in which the editions appeared (at McGraw-Hill/New York):

1st ed.	1948
2nd ed.	1952
3rd ed.	1955
4th ed.	1958
5th ed.	1961
6th ed.	1964
7th ed.	1967
8th ed.	1970
9th ed.	1973

Here in tabular form is the structure of our book in relation to S's text:

Chapter in S's text		Chapter in this book
VOLUME I:	**SECTION I: BASIC IDEOLOGICAL CONCEPTS**	
1		1
2-4		2
5, 39-40		3
6		4
7		5
8-9		6
	Section II: Crises and Keynesianism	
10		7
11-13		8
14		9
VOLUME 2:	**SECTION III: MONEY AND CREDIT**	
15		10
16		11
17-19		12
	Section IV: Value and Price Theory	
20		13
21		14
22		15
23-24		16
25-26		17
	Section V: Factors of Production	
27		18
28		19
29		20
30		21
31		22
	Section VI: The World Market	
33		23
34		24
35		25
36		26
38		27

Contents

Basic Ideological Concepts

1 Introduction
S's Chapter 1

A general introduction which I had sketched out I am
suppressing because on further reflection every anticipation of results which are first to be proved seems disturbing to me. . . .
—Karl Marx, "Foreword" to *Contribution to the Critique of Political Economy*
(Zur Kritik der Politischen Ökonomie), MEW, XIII, 7.

Our approach to S's first chapter differs sharply from our
treatment of all subsequent ones. Forgoing all detailed and
systematic analysis of his presentation, we will here focus
attention on some of the methodological factors crucial to
S's exposition of bourgeois economic theory. Our restraint
is based on the conviction that scientific method cannot be
developed in isolation, divorced from the science per se.
The reader should be afforded the opportunity to see the
method unfold in the course of a systematic scientific dis-
course (the procedure followed by Marx in *Capital*). But
S—and most bourgeois texts—by beginning with a so-
called methodological introduction, merely offers up unex-
plained, unsubstantiated assertions. Thus, although he
purports to have written a "discussion of the methodology
of science" which "introduces the modern approach bor-
rowed from the 'more exact' natural sciences" (7th ed., p.
vi), S's unproved assertions in fact violate the very basis of
scientific method.

Thus if we were to refute his arguments or attempt a systematic discussion of his claims we would willy-nilly be
playing by his ground rules—namely, put methodology
outside the realm of substance. We would involve our-

3

selves in the sort of mutual "dry assurances" which have made such methodological discussion so futile and sterile.

The decision nonetheless to touch on his methodology is based on this consideration: It is disturbing enough to have S introduce his method in the manner he does, for this predetermines the type of "theoretical spectacles we wear" (10) while reading his book without being given the opportunity to see for ourselves how the prescription was drawn up. In other words, the reader is confronted with an accomplished fact whose provenance he cannot trace. And what is even worse—and the reason for our intervention at this early point—is that S believes he can count on the reader's ready acceptance of his methodology because it appears common-sensical. Not only that, but, more important, the basis for this apparent "common sense" and S's methodology lies in, and is *objectively* produced by, the capitalist mode of production. The fact that the methodology of bourgeois economics is neither (merely) conscious demagoguery to deflect people (the nonruling classes) from the truth, nor a (mere) subjective failing of the bourgeois economists will form a crucial part of our entire discussion.

Before embarking on this methodological discussion, let us briefly consider the other major function of this chapter, the reasons for studying economics, a question closely related to that of methodology.

According to S, "Few study economics merely to judge the merits in the grand debates concerning historic capitalism, the modern mixed economy, or the collectivist economic systems of the East [!?]. We study economics to answer many, diverse questions" (1). Obviously S views such debates as academic and unpractical, and, as we shall see, the history of capitalism does not interest him at all; he divorces it completely from what he calls the mixed economy. He also makes short shrift of socialist societies. The net effect, then, is the reduction of economics (which in the 9th edition he interchangeably calls political economy) to the study of present-day capitalism (in the U.S.). In and of itself it is not inappropriate to restrict oneself to this subject; what matters is the context within which this is done. S's context may be characterized as positivist—i.e., he has accepted the existence of this society as given, without inquiring into its origins ("historic capitalism") or whether it might possibly be replaced by another society in the future (socialism). His attention is focused on the "problems" of the present and their possible solution *within* capitalism. This is S's unspoken value judgment: as a practical man, a "citizen," he supports capitalism and opposes socialism. Accordingly, he tries to foist these values on his reader. That, of course, is his prerogative, but it would be nice if he would at least warn the unwary reader. However, matters change when he disseminates these views in the guise of scientist, for this would imply that his theory is shaped by procapitalism and anticommunism, which in turn means that the scope of his study has been narrowed down to a search for solutions that will not pose a threat to capitalism.

But S's theory is not simply demagoguery. By far the more significant aspect of the ideological role of bourgeois economic theory is its unconscious refusal to recognize the possibility of the existence of problems serious enough to cause the demise of the capitalist mode of production.

We do not plan to devote much space to the obvious demagogical components of S's framework, as for example his forthright stand for U.S. capitalism ("the more advanced Western civilizations [8th ed., p. 3]) against "Moscow." The notion of "peaceful competition" between capitalism and socialism runs throughout the 8th edition, together with the implication that all good Americans ought to worry about it and root for the U.S. Although some of this has been deleted, in the spirit of Nixonian rapprochement (e.g., "what used to be called the Iron Curtain [734]), the main thrust remains (cf. the flyleaf and Chap. 43 [particularly 881-83]) in such phrases as "security is even more important for a nation than opulence" (3).

Let us now examine the unconscious ideological aspects of S's delineation of our interest in economics, which in turn will bring us to the methodological discussion. In the preface to an earlier edition, S told us that in writing his textbook originally he set himself a "quixotically ambitious goal—to bring into the elementary textbook the most important issues facing a modern nation" (7th ed., p. v). This stress on "nation" and its need to solve existing problems through the wise decisions of a "citizenry" trained in modern economics permeates the entire book. Part and parcel of this image is the belief that capitalist society (through the state) can cope with the fundamental problems of our era. Aside from the notion of the state as a neutral organ serving the interests of all, this image is important for two of its components: the denial of the existence of objective forces able to thwart "ideas"; and the notion of capitalism as a harmonious whole oriented toward the satisfaction of individual needs.

The first merges in the Keynes quote (14 f.; several editions have it as a chapter motto) denying that objective material forces are at work in capitalist society conditioning the "ideas" of bourgeois economists, philosophers, political scientists, et. al. Not only are these theories conditioned by the historical circumstances as expressed in concrete class interests, there is also the more general conditioning of the capitalist mode of production, which makes essential features of this society appear as the opposite of what they really are.

Perhaps this point can be better understood if we proceed to the notion of the harmonious whole. S states that "in an introductory survey, the economist is interested in the workings of the economy *as a whole* rather than in the viewpoint of any one group. Social and national policies rather than individual policy are his goal" (8). In an important sense this statement is misleading, for it appears to contrast introductory texts with advanced ones with respect to this point; yet all of bourgeois theory is characterized by this conception of the harmonious whole.

Upon closer inspection we find that this passage compares nonanalogous concepts: the "workings" of the whole as opposed to the "viewpoint" of groups. But the chapters on labor, business, wages, profits, interest, rent, etc., quite clearly deal with the workings of social groups within the economy. What S apparently means is that the professional economist must adopt the viewpoint "of the economy as a whole" in contradistinction to that of any particular class (capitalists, workers, landowners). This in turn presupposes the existence of such a viewpoint independent of the interests of a particular class, or, alternatively, that such an aggregate viewpoint represents the distillation of a political compromise of essentially compatible classes.

Once one has assumed the existence of a viewpoint encompassing the whole economy, it becomes impossible to understand the basic struggles that are taking place in this society, and, worse still, it becomes necessary to deny their existence. In effect, bourgeois economics identifies the interests of the entire economy with those of the class presiding over the subjective execution of the only "viewpoint" known to capitalism as a whole—namely, the production of profit. Thus the interests of capital or of the capitalist class are made into those of the economy as a whole.

This fundamental idea permeates all of S's examples of the "vital problems" facing the "citizen," for although S fails to mention it, they imply specifically capitalist social relations. S tells us that certain "decisions" (2) have to be made by "each citizen" on matters like whether married women should be allowed to hold public jobs, whether monopolies should be fought etc. Granting for the sake of argument that this process of decision-making does indeed take place, S does not tell us that such a choice between two evils should have to be made at all simply because capitalism has produced them, and the reason for his failure is that bourgeois theory itself cannot grasp this causality.

Somewhat condescendingly, S allows that "a worker thrown out of employment in the buggy industry cannot be expected to reflect that new jobs may have been created in the automobile industry. . . ." (8) Without going into what S might expect workers to reflect on, we believe that a worker may very well "reflect" that with the replacement of the buggy by the car, labor will be "displaced," and that he may even welcome this change if the new use value is highly thought of. What does not sit well with the worker is that these changes take place at his expense, that he will not be getting one of the new jobs created. And what bothers him even more is the claim put forward by S and others that all this is in keeping with the viewpoint of the economy as a whole, when he knows that it is in keeping with the "workings" of an economy in which such changes take place anarchically, that is, in an unplanned fashion, so that neither the development of the automobile nor the consequences thereof can be foreseen.

In this sphere of employment and unemployment, the terminology used by bourgeois economics in an unconscious expression of the way in which it inverts reality. S talks of "employers" as opposed to workers or employees (7). This is an example of what S calls the "tyranny of words" (10), but he sees the origin of this phenomenon in subjective human shortcomings: "The world is complicated enough without introducing further confusions and ambiguities. . . ." (ibid.). Here as elsewhere, conceptual confusion and ambiguity is merely a reflection of the "tyranny" of capitalist reality, that is, of the strange manner in which social relations become inverted on the surface of capitalist society.

In the instance of "employers" and "employees," it is clear that the former are the active and the latter the passive agents, those who use and those who are used. This terminology indeed reflects the appearance of capitalism in which the capitalist "provides" or "offers" work which the worker gratefully accepts.

If, however, we look beneath this surface appearance, we find that the "secret" of capitalism is the unpaid labor the capitalist appropriates from the worker; this unpaid labor—embodied in the commodities produced by the worker which are transformed into money by being sold— permits the capitalist to buy more capital in the form of machines, etc., and "employ" more "employees." In fact, all capital is unpaid labor, and since the capitalist can "give work" only on the basis of his ownership of the means of production—in this case, capital—he is able to do so only because in the past generations of workers have given part of their labor free.

Thus, in fact, the terms "employer" and "employee" invert what is taking place in capitalism, for in reality the workers are giving their labor (free) to the capitalists, and it is this gift which enables the capitalists to "employ" workers. Here we have an example of the "neutral manner" (10) in which bourgeois economics creates concepts to fit reality.

Let us now turn to the philosophy of science and the methodology of economics. S's discussion is marked by two trains of thought which in the last analysis are incompatible and contradictory. The first, which we shall call *positivist*, concentrates on so-called value judgments:

Basic questions concerning right and wrong goals to be pursued cannot be settled by mere science as such. They belong in the realm of ethics and "value judgments." The citizenry must ultimately decide such issues. What the expert can do is point out the feasible alternatives and the true costs that may be involved in the different decisions [7-8].

This statement prompts the following question: If science can indeed reveal the feasible possibilities and the "true" costs involved in executing them, what else remains to be done before we decide on goals? S would have to have a strange notion of "truth" if once he found it he would not choose it over nontruth. A major problem with this approach is that it is at best built on half-truths, because bourgeois economics cannot concede that these various "decisions" are being made within a mode of production that creates the very constraints necessitating these "choices." In other words, it does not understand that capitalism itself produces objectively a set of "value judgments" that form the basis for the relatively peripheral "decisions" bourgeois economics allows into its field of vision. Thus, for instance, the "modern" preoccupaion with "trade-offs" between various "evils" (e.g., unemployment and inflation, efficiency and equity) has become the focal point in discussions of value judgments. But the basis for all these concrete situations—namely the fact that independent and private producers own the means of production and exploit the workers—is overlooked. Rather, only the questioning of this basis itself—that is, of the forces inherent in capitalism leading to its destruction and replacement by another mode of production—is considered a value judgment and relegated to the sphere of ethical irrelevancies.

Thus it has become apparent that S's positivism is marked by internal incoherence. And he adds to this ambiguity when he goes on to say that "there is only one valid reality in a given economic situation, however hard it may be to recognize and isolate it" (7th ed., p. 6; in the 8th and 9th editions this assertion has been weakened to "there are elements of valid reality. . . [7]). In other words, the expert can detect and isolate this "valid reality" and give us the "value-free" facts for our evaluation.

On the other hand—and here we get the second train of thought—S contends that the "modern approach" to the methodology of science "insists on the irreducibly subjective element of our perception of facts depending upon the theoretive system *through* which we look at those facts" (7th ed., p. vi). And again: "Which questions we ask, and from what perspective we photograph the 'objective reality'—these are themselves at bottom subjective in nature" (8 n.2).

The contradiction in this position becomes evident when we pose the question of how the expert will be able to arrive at an objective, value-free set of facts (or a value-free, objectively valid theory) when confronted with this allegedly irreducible element of subjectivity; for although S is right when he says that "how we *perceive* the observed facts depends on the theoretical spectacles we wear" (10), his positivism fails to tell us how to deal with this truth. In fact, this truth refutes his positivism and transforms objectively valid theory into an impossibility.

The problem at this point would appear to boil down to how to grind our theoretical spectacles in order to perceive the one valid reality. But merely posing this question predetermines the answer, because it is couched in subjective terms. It severs the connection between the development of a science and the development of the society and the subject matter of that science. This severing is given very clear expression by S even when he explicitly touches on the history of economic theory for the first time. (Actually this is not correct; the 5th edition [1961] already contained a "Thumbnail Sketch of History of Economic Doctrines" [pp. 833-36]):

> The brand new chapter "Winds of Change: Evolution of Economic Doctrines" brings into the elementary course—at long last—a view of where political economy fits into the history of ideas and the intellectual history of our times. . . . Political economy is about the economic system, not about economists. . . . At the end of a long book, though, we may perhaps indulge ourselves with a brief excursion into the history and present status of economics as a scholarly discipline and as a chapter in the intellectual history of mankind [ix, 839].

In other words, S considers such a history as a discipline unto itself with which we may amuse ourselves or leave to the specialists, as is our pleasure. Yet, unwittingly to be sure, he himself provides the evidence that an understanding of the connection between the development of theory and reality is essential to an understanding of contemporary economics. On the one hand he says that at any given time there cannot be one theory for workers and one for "employers" (7), and on the other, he seems to admit that true economic theory will change *over time* in accordance with changes in the underlying economic structure. (A note of caution must be entered here: This is our reading of what he means, for at times S's ahistoricity goes so far as to claim that the "neo-classical synthesis" would actually have been adequate to the Middle Ages *if* the proper institutions had existed.) Thus in speaking of the transition from mercantilism to industrial capitalism (though not explicitly in these terms), S points out that "in a real sense, the rising bourgeois class needed a spokesman for their interests. Smith provided them with the ideology that served their purpose" (841).

Now the point is that the reason the mercantilist period

did not bring forth an Adam Smith is that it was not an industrial capitalism. Mercantilist theory served the purposes of the ruling class in a given situation; when new socioeconomic relations arose which changed the interests of the ruling class, the old theory became obsolete along with the reality. (It must not be thought that theories are mechanically replaced on orders of the ruling class; the struggle between theories is a highly complex process that cannot be summed up by a vulgar-materialistic reference to "sordid interests" [8]).

If it is indeed true that in the past valid theories lost their validity with the change of the reality upon which they developed and were supplanted by other theories, then it is puzzling why S claims universal and sole validity for his theory. It is not clear why he fails to entertain the possibility that his own theory may be superseded, just as capitalism itself may be superseded.

Instead of coming to grips with this possibility, S takes refuge in witticisms: "Careful critics of all political complexions generally think this (i.e., Marxism) a sterile analysis both of capitalism and socialism. But try to persuade a billion people of that" (5th ed., p. 836n. 1).

Those "billions" who see Karl Marx as their "ideological hero" (847) are largely beyond S's reach. In writing his textbook, S hoped to "persuade" millions of students to refrain from joining that vast mass.

2 Central Ideological Problems of all Economic Theories of Capitalism Based on Nonfundamental Relations of the Capitalist Mode of Production: the "Market" Approach
S's Chapters 2-4

> ... GM long ago recognized that it wasn't in the auto business; rather, its business is making money, using products as the means.
> —*Wall Street Journal*, September 1, 1971

Although we believe that the material touched on in Part I of S's book merits attention, its organization is somewhat ambiguous. One might claim some pedagogic justification for beginning with matters familiar to the student from everyday life, and gradually going on to theory. The problem with this approach, however, is the way in which it uses, or rather exploits, that familiarity. Instead of transcending the prescientific notions the student brings with him, S in fact reproduces that superficiality, but this time more perniciously, lending it a scientific gloss.

Not only does S's discussion in these early chapters fail to deal with the student's prescientific notions about capitalism, but the theoretical elaborations of the later chapters are also inadequate to that task. Thus, for instance, the discussion of money in Chapter 3 rests and builds on the most superficial views imposed on all agents of the capitalist sphere of circulation. Having giving scientific sanction to these views, S thus wins the reader over for their subsequent elaboration in national-income theories

(Chapter 10), banking and credit (Chapters 15-18), and the international monetary system (Chapters 33 and 36). Or again, unquestioning and convenient presuppositions are made about certain widespread notions about the autonomy, equality, and dominant position of "consumers" in capitalist societies in order to prepare the reader for accepting theories of demand, price, and production factors offered in later chapters (22-32).

Even within the methodological framework of bourgeois economics, S's discussion of supply and demand remains meaningless unless the factors "lying behind the supply and demand curves" (consumer preferences and production factors) have been explained. But the students who only take a "macro course" will never be given this basic explanation. They will have to make do with the slighly more polished version of their own circulation-sphere notions of the opening section, chapters which only strengthen existing prejudices by reinforcing beliefs about the alleged freedom, equality, and democracy of consumer sovereignty, etc.

For those who do go on to the "micro analysis," the implausible theories of Chapters 22-23 are made more palatable by the beliefs cultivated in the early chapters. (For what else could be the purpose of Chapter 4 on supply and demand and its recapitulation in Chapters 20 and 22? Interestingly enough, the first edition did not have an introductory chapter on supply and demand.)

The chapter sequence of S's textbook has confronted the authors of this critique with a difficult procedural problem. For just as supply and demand make little sense by themselves, an introductory critique of supply and demand by itself, without a prior analysis of the theoretical base, also is inadequate. Unfortunately, however, the critiques of demand theory and production factors belong to the more difficult theoretical parts of our critique, and at any earlier stage would most likely prove a hindrance rather than a help. For this reason we have decided to retain the chapter-by-chapter format and have combined the relevant material from Chapters 2-4 into this one. We have tried to restrict ourselves as much as possible to an analysis of the primarily ideological function of these early chapters, leaving the basic theoretical critique to Chapters 22-32. But we have also tried to anticipate the later discussion by pointing out where the assumption and conclusions of the introductory ideology foreshadow later arguments.

In brief, we have structured our critique thus: We begin by analyzing those factors which S presents as the ultimate determinants of economic activity in all societies. We do so not because of the intrinsic merit of the material but rather with a view toward the basis S is trying to lay for the jump to the specific capitalist determinants of economic activity. We then proceed to an examination of S's definition of the specific capitalist response to the "economic problems"; we will emphasize the superficiality and distortion growing out of the ambiguous attempt to reduce the complicated mediations between consumption and production in a society characterized by class relations of wage labor and capital to a "market economy" oriented toward the satisfaction of consumer needs.

I / THE SUPRAHISTORICAL DETERMINANTS OF ECONOMIC ACTIVITY

Chapter 2 is largely devoted to spelling out the purported fundamental constrictions valid for all forms of economic activity. The ostensible reason for this description relates to the light it will shed on the specific manner in which the mixed economy copes with these constrictions. Although later on, in Chapter 4, S contends that this discussion responds to the "basic problems of economic organization" alternative to that of a "system of markets and prices," they are merely referred to as "extremes" ("custom, instinct, command"; 18) without further comment. This gives the impression that the "market" is not an extreme but the normal way of life, an impression or suspicion strengthened by the fact that neoclassical economics singles out the "market system" as the most, or perhaps, only rational economic approach.

In large part, the methodological restrictions we imposed on ourselves in the first chapter also apply here; that is to say, the insubstantial nature of S's discussion make a plausible critique very difficult without engaging in the same sort of sterile, insubstantial methodologizing.

The connection to Chapter 1 becomes obvious when we look at the use to which its "definition" of economics is put here. Leaving a fuller discussion to Chapter 7, we notice that the central terms from that definition, as far as the present context is concerned, are "choice" and "scarcity." For S, these two notions are very tightly bound up with each other. Since in this conception causality appears to run from scarcity to choice, we will start with scarcity.

The most significant aspect of S's notion of scarcity—and one it shares with most other points of this chapter—is that he constructs it without reference to historical or societal development. It appears to arise from the human condition of constantly discovering new needs once old ones have been satisfied. Thus S's notion of scarcity might be called absolute. At first glance it cannot, strictly speaking, be considered totally ahistorical, since S explicitly asserts the existence of scarcity and its consequences in all known economic formations. Ironically, it is precisely this superficial sprinkling of history which gives us the key to an awareness of the profound ahistoricity of S's conception.

In constrast to what we have just called the absolute aspect of scarcity (namely, in the sense of its application to all societies at all times), S also offers a relative concept, apparently valid at any given time. In general, scarcity is relative in the sense that there is not enough of something for the purpose of, or relative to, something else. S defines this something else as "prescribed ends" (15). But we find no completely unambiguous answer to the question of what precisely these "prescribed ends" are. On one level, S tells us that these ends are society's desired volume and pattern of consumption as determined by people's needs and wants; and on another level, it becomes obvious that even within S's own framework the only needs or wants economically relevant in a "market economy" are those mediated by "effective demand."

S, and bourgeois economics in general, never succeeds in overcoming this basic ambiguity, which can be reduced to the inability to understand the relation between use value and value. The source of this ambiguity can be found in the attempt to explain the specific capitalist mediation of consumption needs by categories which in the abstract do not provide adequate explanations for any economic formation. What is even more pernicious is that these suprahistorical categories are not developed by drawing out what is general or common to each particular society, but rather a fictitious technological base is constructed which is then imposed on each of these societies.

Although at this point S pays lip service to the distinction between capitalism and other economic formations, he later on attempts to derive specifically capitalist relations such as interest and rent directly from the notion of scarcity. There is nothing to stop him from doing this, but he at least owes the reader an explanation why "scarcity" did not produce these relations in earlier societies.

S's ambivalent stance on scarcity becomes more clearly apparent when we consider his vacillations on the natural and social causes of scarcity. Thus in the broadside against the "famous 'labor theory of value' " which adorns the 7th edition he argues that "the 'law of increasing (relative) costs' " derives from the scarcity of land (pp. 27 f.). Without going into a detailed discussion of this "law" here, we wish to note that one might plausibly speak of natural scarcity if natural-climatic-meteorological conditions were to destroy a society's food crop, so that its total food supply became deficient compared to its customary level of consumption, or even reached a starvation level. (Even here, however, the "natural" aspect cannot be made into an absolute, for what may turn into a natural catastrophe in one society, may possibly be averted in another at a higher state of development.) But something can also be scarce relative to people's "needs," as for example, a diminished supply of "available" land in the case of private-property relations.

Now S argues on the one hand that the disappearance of "unlimited free land" underlies "the law of increasing (relative) costs.' " This would appear to be an acknowledgment of social causation inasmuch as "free" would appear to refer to a state of affairs predating private property. Yet on the very next page, when stating that "fertile land . . . *has grown scarce enough to have become private property* (7th ed., p. 29), he seems to be saying that causality runs in the opposite direction, from a natural condition to a specific social structure.

In another context S introduces the distinction between "natural" and "contrived" scarcity (622-24). The latter, supposedly the result of monopolistic behavior, would appear to be an example of social scarcity. Yet here, too, the so-called natural scarcity—the limited amount of God-given fertile Iowa farmland—becomes the direct source of capitalist land rent. S fails to explain why there was no rent on the limited amount of God-given buffalo grazing lands before Columbus landed here. The ahistorical weaknesses of S's reasoning are revealed in two important points. First, the reference to scarcity as the basis of private property implies that private property came into being in the midst of poverty caused by diminishing returns in the context of a land shortage. (The same image of overcrowding underlies the marginal-productivity theory.) In fact, however, private property arose not out of "scarcity" but rather out of a surplus of the means of subsistence above the level necessary to maintain reproduction in accordance with some traditional level of consumption. Since this surplus makes possible the existence of a class of owners who do not have to work, property relations are bound up with class relations. This important point must be kept in mind, since S's discussion of scarcity and choice is based on the assumption that social classes do not exist, which leads to an undifferentiated view of these two questions.

Second, if we look at a later stage of development, namely the period of so-called primitive capital accumulation in Western Europe, we see that the direct (and often violent) expropriation of peasants was not the results of scarcity but rather that it led to the [absolute] scarcity of land, and hence to the scarcity of the means of subsistence of those who had lost their land. Hence the relation between people's "needs" and the abundance or scarcity of natural endowments cannot be understood without a study of historico-social conditions.

Let us now proceed to examining the consequences which flow from the use of the term scarcity. For S, the most significant consequence of scarcity is the necessity for making choices about what and how much should be produced in what way for which people (18). In view of the ambiguities attaching to S's notion of scarcity we find it difficult to accept this statement at face value. Yet there is something to it—namely, that "if an *infinite* amount of every good could be produced, or if human wants were *fully* satisfied," then these "economic problems" would not arise.

But what exactly is accurate about this statement? When S says that if "everyone could have as much as he pleased" (18) there would be no relative scarcity (?) and hence no "economic goods" he is basing himself on the definition of economics given in the first chapter, namely that consumption represents the sole end of economic activity; thus once this end has been attained for all members of a society, economic activity ceases.

However, when we look at different societies, we find that the satisfaction of the consumption needs of all its members is not a universal end, and therefore scarcity and the "economic problem" lose the universal validity ascribed to them by S. To be sure, there have been societies in history in which this was a conscious and direct goal, but these so-called primitive societies by and large had very low and unchanging levels of productivity. Thus, given the low and unchanging levels of consumption plus the traditionally or ritualistically determined division of labor and methods of production, one can hardly speak of "the economic problem" with respect to these societies, for where there is no conception of the possibility of change, there cannot be any problem. (In general, one cannot tell whether S uses the term "problem" objectively, as something posed by historical development, or subjectively, in the sense of a society's conscious formulation. Since S himself stresses the unconscious operation of the "market system," it would seem that the objective meaning is the one he has in mind. Yet even a cursory glance at S's scattered references to science would seem to indicate that he would pin the label of "metaphysics" on this type of objectivity. This distinction is relevant insofar as it points up the basic difference between a society in which economic science is limited to a contemplation of objective progress [or lack of it] in the direction of satisfying needs, and one in which it is actively applied in a conscious manner. This is one way of formulating the difference between capitalism and socialism.) When we proceed to societies characterized by higher levels of productivity we find that we are dealing with societies divided into classes. For our purposes here we may speak of three such societies—slave, feudal, and capitalist. Although all three share the existence of a producing and a nonproducing (owning) class, the first two, unlike capitalism, are further characterized by production for the personal consumption of the nonworking class, and this consumption is the goal of economic activity in these social structures.

For the operation of the feudal economy the needs of the exploited class are irrelevant; in fact, given a sufficiently abundant supply of slaves, even the minimum subsistence consumption needs can be disregarded with impunity. Similarly on the production side: given fixed dividing lines between classes that primarily produce and classes that primarily consume, the ruling class faces no production problem since the entire burden has been shifted onto the other class.

The refusal to incorporate the class structure of a particular society into the study of the operation of the economic sphere must necessarily lead to a distorted and hence basically flawed theory of "economic activity," since it cannot explain the consumption differential for each social class of a particular society. Although S is similarly unable to locate the functional importance of consumption within various modes of production, even within the context of a discussion of consumption, he cannot overcome the almost universal tendency of bourgeois economists to view an "economy" or society or nation as a unified whole. Although each society is a whole in the sense that fundamental forces bring about regularity in the form of economic laws, this regularity is not immediately perceivable; and, furthermore, this "wholeness" does not involve the homogeneity of interests posited both objectively and subjectively by S. To view a society composed of antagonistic classes as a whole is to adopt a "speculative" stance which ignores and hence distorts the all-important mediating links between production and consumption in general and the forms they assume in particular modes of production.

Now if S's error in regard to precapitalist societies centers on his neglect of classes, once we proceed to capitalist society he compounds his error by adding to it an inadequate determination of the function of fulfilling consumption needs. Not only is capitalism, like slave and feudal societies, a class society, it is also, unlike them, not oriented toward the satisfaction of the personal consumption needs of the ruling class. In fact, the objective forces within capitalism which force the ruling class to use the "surplus" which it is able to appropriate at the expense of the immediate producers for the purpose of expanding production are, to use S's terminology, the turning point in "economic organization."

But this does not represent production for production's sake; for what further characterizes capitalist production is not the mere production of use values for consumption, but rather the necessity of producing values, and above all surplus value, which can be accumulated to prevent one capital from being crushed by the competition. In this sense the ruling class remains the ruling class only to the extent it subjects itself to the needs of capital to expand. (This does not mean that capitalists are necessarily frugal, for once their wealth has reached a certain level they can both accumulate and consume; what it does mean is that capitalists are not capitalists in their role of consumers—but rather that they can consume only insofar as they have fulfilled their function as the agents of accumulation.)

Once we leave the sphere of production of use values and surplus-value "carriers," a crucial transformation takes place with respect to the notion of scarcity. Use values, as it were, represent a concrete, qualitative relation between man or society and nature, whereas value and surplus value as the embodiment of human labor-time are abstract, quantitative relations among people in a society. At any given time it is theoretically possible for the needs for use values to be satisfied inasmuch as the need for specific objects of consumptoin (houses, meat, clothes, nails, radios, etc.) is quantitatively limited. Not so with value and surplus value: the "need" on the part of capital to expand, to create and appropriate and accumulate value is unlimited in partial analogy to the "Sisyphean labor of accumulation" on the part of the hoarder or miser.[1]

In this sense a relative scarcity of surplus value can be said always to prevail under capitalism; since the drive to expand capital is unlimited there can never be a superabundance of surplus value. Thus this is also the only relevant "law of scarcity" for capitalism.

This, of course, differs essentially from S's "scarcity," namely that of consumption "goods" for the mass of the population. At this point an objection might perhaps be raised along these lines: Despite the Marxist emphasis on "surplus value, and all that" (x), is S's analysis of scarcity not plausible inasmuch as the satisfaction of workers' consumption needs by capitalism could lead to the end of economic society?

Let us look at the likely conclusions of this line of reasoning. Assuming that a state of material and general satiety would destroy the impersonal work compulsion upon which capitalism rests, these further questions arise: 1. In concrete terms, what would this state of satisfaction and the disappearance of the work compulsion mean? 2. What has prevented the transformation of capitalism into a "postscarcity" society? S himself hints at the answers to both these questions. In the closing pages of the 8th and 9th editions he entertains the possibility of the end of scarcity in the form of a long quote from Keynes (813-15). A careful reading of that quotation shows that the situation described by Keynes applies only to a society in which capitalist relations of domination have been eliminated. Although such a society is generally called "communist" both by its supporters and its opponents, neither S nor Keynes does, and S explicitly includes "a totally collectivized communistic state" among those societies forced to cope with the What, How, and Whom of "economic organization" (17). The reason for this may well be that S is not really talking about social relations but about technology, for as far as one can make out from the text, production possibilities by themselves, apart from all social relations, are the only block to achieving the end of scarcity. Again, there is "something" to this, for a certain level of technological development is necessary if one is to produce enough to satisfy given needs. But this technological development takes place within, is fostered or hindered by, or assumes the form of, definite social relations.

This brings us to the second of the two questions—namely, why the transformation of capitalism into postscarcity still has not taken place. Here we may take our cue from S's minor disagreement with Galbraith. The significance of S's remark lies in its implicit refutation of social-democratic demands for the redistribution of income within capitalism; but, at the same time, by pointing out that such a redistribution would still leave the average American less than "well-off" (19), S unwittingly concedes the very point his book seeks to disprove—namely, that (U.S.) capitalist production is not oriented toward satisfying the needs of the mass of the working population; for nowhere does he show that the barriers to that higher total product which would raise the average standard of living to the level of those now "well-off" are technological in nature. Until that comes to pass, scarcity will remain a social problem, and it will be solved only by changing the social structure responsible for it.

Let us now consider the second of the two related points referred to above: "choice."

As we have seen, choice plays a key role in S's definition of economics, and its significance allegedly stems from the existence of scarcity. This line of reasoning is not without some validity, although not what S ascribes to it. His argument is exceedingly simple: from the circumstance that "every economy must somehow solve the three fundamental economic problems" (38) he jumps to the conclusion that society "does . . . choose to end up" somewhere in line with the various *technological* possibilities open to it (22). Without involving ourselves in any sophisticated philosophical dispute, we maintain that S has adopted a rather curious definition of "choosing." The term "choice" would appear inappropriate even for those precapitalist societies characterized by some form of aggregate planning (however unscientific) in light of the static nature of those modes of production. And in capitalist society, praised by its economists precisely for the absence of such planning, "choice" would appear to be a direct inversion of reality.

Let us look at this inversion more closely. In neoclassical reasoning "society's choice" ultimately rests on the (complicated) aggregation of individual choices. Assuming for the sake of argument that such individual choices exist, it is not clear why S believes one can transfer this notion to the aggregate social level. To speak of choice on a social level in capitalism might be considered an example of the very "fallacy of composition" against which S warns the reader—namely, ascribing to the whole what is true of the part (14). Yet a closer look will reveal that S's own fallacy is more profound, for he has compounded the fallacy of composition by positing the existence of a whole which is merely the fiction of bourgeois ideology, for in any unperverted meaning of "choice" capitalist society has no social organ able to exercise it.

The notion that choice underlies society's economic activity on a social plane is all the more astonishing in light of S's subsequent admission that "in a system of free private enterprise, no individual or organization is *consciously* concerned with the triad of economic problems. . ." (41). This is not so much an admission as it is a glorification of the unconscious manner in which capitalism functions. But the important point here is that despite this emphasis on the unconscious, the use of such distorted and hence loaded terms as "choice" tends to eradicate the distinction between societies which do in fact make conscious aggregate decisions based on comprehensive social planning (socialism-communism) and those in which the results of "economic activity" are unpredictable, unintended, and which can be construed as representing choices or decisions only by the most ingenious a posteriori reasoning.

By confusing and/or identifying the results of an unplanned yet *self-reproducing* ("It works" [427]) society with those of a planned society, S begins to lay the foundation for the crucial ideological negation of the difference between capitalism and socialism; that is to say, by co-opting the more obvious virtues of socialism (such as planning) for capitalism, he is able to assert that to the extent that there is anything positive in socialism, capitalism *is* socialist, thereby rendering a socialist revolution superfluous and/or irrational.

Our critique of the notions of "scarcity" and "choice" has focused on their ideological significance, with particular stress on the internal inconsistencies of S's presentation which form the basis of theories formulated in later chapters. We do not wish to deny altogether the possible usefulness of these notions, although they certainly cannot fulfill the function attributed to them by bourgeois economics. In trying to find the rational kernel of the elaborate discussion on these topics by bourgeois economics, we will center on the "trio of *basic problems of economic organization*" (17) which plays a central role in S's introductory material. It is obvious that every past society has had to expend its total disposable labor to produce certain goods in certain quantities so that they could be distributed to and consumed by its members in order to assure its reproduction.[2] What is not so obvious is what sort of theory can be constructed on this basis.

Marx, too, was aware of the "basic economic problems," but he approached them from a different theoretical vantage point. In a letter to a political friend, Ludwig Kugelmann, dealing with a critique of the value theory spelled out in the just-published *Kapital,* Marx noted that "every child knows"

> that the masses of products corresponding to the various masses of needs require various and quantitatively determined masses of the social aggregate labor. That this *necessity* of the *distribution* of the social labor in certain proportions cannot at all be eliminated by the *certain form* of social production, but rather can only change its *mode of appearance,* is selfevident. Laws of nature cannot be eliminated altogether. What can change in historically different conditions is only the form in which those laws assert themselves.[3]

Although Marx goes even further than S in emphasizing the suprahistorical foundation of production, distribution, and consumption, he also stresses that every child knows this. Marx looked toward the science of political economy for an explanation of how these laws assert themselves in a particular society. More specifically, he concerned himself with the form assumed by these "laws of nature" in the capitalist mode of production.

At first glance it might seem that we have come upon another similarity between Marx and S, for S too is restricting himself to capitalism. But is he? For Marx, "the point of bourgeois society"[4] consists in the fact that what appears on the surface is not identical with the underlying essential processes; it is the task of the science of political economy to mediate the surface phenomena with these processes which they often appear to contradict.

S, on the other hand, deals almost exclusively with these superficial phenomena; when he goes beyond supply and demand, he takes refuge in technology or tastes, both of which are "external" in the sense that they are not shown to be aspects of a self-reproducing whole. In other words, despite the formal commitment to specifying the working of economic laws in capitalism (this formulation is, of course, in itself too generous), S in these chapters establishes the framework that will serve him throughout the book: eternal technological laws mediated by "the market." Ironically, however, the market, while presumably typifying the peculiarly capitalist aspect of the "modern" economy, fails in this task, whereas the technological side, while supposedly suprahistorical in character, frequently is covertly based on factors peculiar to the capitalist production process. It is thus not surprising that all previous societies appear as inferior earlier stages of a "rationality" that culminates in capitalism. What Marx said of the vulgar economists of his day is even more pertinent today: "It is thus here the absolute interest of the ruling classes to eternalize this thoughtless confusion. And what else are the sycophantic windbags paid for. . . !"[5]

TECHNOLOGY AND THE FORCES OF PRODUCTION

Having focused on general ideological considerations of "economic organization," let us shift our attention to what we might call the underlying factors of production of "every economic society." These comprise the dead and live means of production ("technology" and "population"). We might "translate" these terms into Marx's notion of the forces of production; however, the difficulty with this is that Marx does not study the forces of production in isolation from the social relations of production which together determine the nature of the mode of production. And they cannot be studied in isolation because they do not develop independently of the social relations of production in which they are imbedded. Thus, certain social relations of production militate against the development of a certain "technology": for example, the use of machinery is incompatible with slave labor, "economies of scale and mass production" are incompatible with the scattered distribution of the means of production and the largely self-sufficient nature of production characteristic of feudalism.

Thus we can say that a given development of the forces of production is possible only under given social relations of production. Similarly, the full development of certain modes of production presupposes the development of the forces of production in certain directions, or fosters or even compels such a development. For instance, the full development of capitalist relations of production created the need for a production process which reduced qualitatively different types of labor to a real abstraction from these—namely the expenditure of human labor power per se—and which allowed for the greatest possible reduction of the share of the total product going to the laborer.

Without elaborating on this point we may conclude that the elevation of technological development above and beyond, or its placement outside, the totality of social relations that make up a mode of production is tantamount to saying that it transcends human social development; as such, this view treats a result of human activity as lying outside of human activity. But this *fetishistic* theory is not a mere figment of S's imagination; it is a product of a mode of production devoid of conscious social aggregate planning.

Here as earlier, the abstractness of S's presentation makes it difficult to pin him down. Therefore, we will by and large continue the procedure we have adopted and postpone a substantive critique of the material until it re-emerges in applied form in later chapters, and will restrict ourselves to a few general comments and/or anticipatory remarks.

To begin with the "production-possibility frontiers" and the "basic concepts" they are supposed to "illustrate": first, as with most of S's "technological" relations, there is "something" to them, although not exactly what he would have us believe. In the abstract one could, of course, at any time make an inventory of all the disposable labor, natural resources, and means of production a society can utilize for the production of certain goods, and determine the proportions in which these goods could be produced in accordance with a given level of "technological" development. A society that planned its reproduction process would have to keep track of all these factors in order to satisfy the needs of its members as producers and consumers. But the question arises of how relevant such a method would be for a society without aggregate planning. (Something on this order does take place in a capitalist factory because there limited planning is both possible and necessary.) For although in theory it is true that no society can produce more than it is able to, it is not immediately obvious how the awareness of this constraint will affect the actual operation of a capitalist economy, or its theories.

In this context it is certainly no coincidence that S selects as his example "choosing" between guns and butter, for wartime situations do bring an unusual degree of planning into the aggregate capitalist economy. Although his graphs can be and are drawn up to illustrate "trade-offs" between purely "civilian goods," the "pedagogical" advantages of focusing on exmples where an aggregate choice does seem to be taking place are not to be ignored, not to mention the bonus of claiming that "society" does "really decide" on "war goods" as the "best goals" on "society's menu of choices" (20-22).

Now what claims does S make for his production-possibility frontiers? Their function seems to be chiefly pedagogical—namely, to "help make clear" the What, How, and For Whom problems (23). First of all, as Alfred Marshall has pointed out, and as S so often seems to forget, "graphical illustrations are not proofs."[6] Applied to our example this means that the production-possibility frontiers do not "prove" that these "three problems" are in fact problems for capitalist production in the form in which S presents them; they are merely a restatement of his previous assertions.

Second, these graphs are indicative of a static approach, for they refer to what is "possible" under given conditions. This point takes on added significance because it leads directly to the artificial and hence distorted presuppositions that underlie diminishing returns. But the static nature of the graphs has still another, ahistorical dimension: they cannot tell us what is "possible" (or impossible or even necessary) in given historical conditions and social relations. Thus with respect to the "what," they cannot tell us why railroads were built under capitalism but not under slavery. They can perhaps tell us how many hospitals may have to be sacrificed, "all other things being equal," in order to build x-number of ICBMs, but they cannot tell us why the ICBMs are being built at all. In other words, even granting the relevance of the notion of choice, the graphs cannot explain how and why the possible choices come into being.

These weakness of the graphs are revealed even more plainly in the "how" problem, for as Marx noted: "Not what is made, but rather how . . . distinguishes the economic epochs."[7]

S takes "how" to mean "efficient choice of methods and proper assignment of . . . limited resources. . ." (23). He makes the distinction between economic and engineering efficiency; the former apparently relates to whether resources have been allocated so as to maximize production, while the latter refers to the choice of methods once the allocation has taken place. But here again this approach fails to consider such historic changes in production as from handicrafts to manufacture to large-scale capitalist industry. And even within (say) the capitalist mode of production, changes in methods of production cannot be adequately explained by these graphs since they presuppose the greatest possible consumption as the end of all economic activity in all societies.

Not only does S fail to demonstrate that this production for profit in capitalism does not interfere with this goal, but his approach also implies that to eschew certain allocations of labor resources (i.e., to train a worker for one "job" exlusively in order to increase "efficiency") in favor of a less crippling division of labor would be "a crime of . . . inefficiency" (23); to reject certain production methods on the grounds of safety or health hazards would also be a "crime." And in fact this would indeed be a crime for a capitalist economy, for such consideration of the interests of the immediate producers would reduce profits. (Some concession on this point is made in the new sections on "Net Economic Welfare" in the 9th edition [3-5, 195-97], but this relates to reducing production in order to improve social life *outside* the production process; furthermore, its sees the causes of the problems in technology itself, not in social relations.) Theoretically, S could include such "choices" or "trade-offs" as well, but since elsewhere he has admitted that this "freedom in choosing" does not exist in the "modern industrial regime"[8] it is no coincidence that he does not include them. As to the "For Whom" problems, S himself admits that they cannot be explained by graphs alone (23). This again is no coincidence, for forms of distribution are the most definite expression of the social relations among agents of production.[9] On the other hand, since S's interest is confined to the quantitative differences in income distribution (as opposed to the forms assumed by the participation of various classes in the social product in various modes of production—such as wages and profit), and since all class societies harbor these inequalities, his graphs could not illustrate very much anyway. But what S fails to make clear is that the graphs are drawn up on the basis not of needs but of so-called demand. However, demand is not a fixed element of every economic society, and hence here the shortcoming of S's suprahistorical approach become patently obvious. The relations of distribution are determined by the social relations of production and not, as S contends, by the physical aspect of the production process.

THE "LAW" OF DIMINISHING RETURNS

The static approach, which forms the basis of the "law of diminishing returns," is unrealistic, for it assumes unchanging productivity. Although under certain short-run conditions there is some validity to the notion of diminishing returns (which is not identical with the marginal productivity conclusions drawn from this reasoning), S's grandiose claims for "this basic technical truth" are totally unwarranted. In the classic example cited by bourgeois economists, we are offered the picture of increasing numbers of workers "crowded" onto a fixed amount of land; in S's words, this explains why living standards "in crowded China or India" (27) are low. But if we descend from the lofty heights of "basic technical truth" to sober facts, we discover that the Netherlands is more than four times as "crowded" as China and more than twice as "crowded" as India; similarly, Belgium, West Germany, Italy, and the U.K. are also more "crowded" than either India or China.[10] Not only can we see that there is no correlation between population density and "standards of living," but more importantly, we gain insight into S's sovereign disregard for essential differences between social systems and the reduction of such differences to technological features.

ECONOMIES OF SCALE

With regard to "economies of scale," here again S seeks to reduce a specific social process to a suprahistorical "technological" phenomenon. He "associates" this phenomenon with such "technological factors" as nonhuman power sources, automatic mechanisms, division of labor involving the breaking-down of labor processes into simple repetitive operations, etc. (28). Up to the 9th edition he was content to claim that "economies of scale are very important in explaining why so many of the goods we buy are produced by large companies" (29). But in the 9th edition, which comes up with the new insight that "Marxism may be too valuable to leave to the Marxists" (866)—which means that from time to time S throws in Marx's name in a seemingly positive fashion—he finds it necessary to tack on the phrase "as Karl Marx emphasized a century ago" (29).

Now it is one thing if S wants to adhere to a view which explains social processes in terms of so-called technological phenomena, but it is quite another matter when he attributes this view to, or rather sees it in the spirit of, the "new Weltanschauung that permeates the ninth edition" (ix), when he claims the authority as it were of Marx. What makes this particularly important is that precisely this same distorted, fetishistic misinterpretation of Marx underlies the spate of articles on Marx that have flowed from S's pen in recent years. Marx, in fact, said that the development of capitalist production relations was responsible for the development of the so-called technological factors mentioned above, for all of them are the expression of a mode of production in which the qualitative aspect of the labor process is increasingly subjected to quantification in terms of abstraction from the concrete labor activities and their transformation into the expenditure of a homogeneous labor power. All of this serves the end of producing as much profit as possible, so that this process may take place on an expanded scale. This also requires the expropriation of the owners of the means of production, so that they will be forced to offer their labor power to produce the means of subsistence. This process welds the vast number of people who had been largely independent of the "market" for their means of subsistence into a new social group, and it is this process which is largely responsible for the fact that it has become "worth while" (28) to produce on a large scale. It also presupposes the increasing concentration of the means of production in a few hands.

But it is not the economies of scale that lead to capitalism ("large companies"), but rather the objective socialization of the productive process brought about by the massing of ever larger numbers of workers without means of production, and hence without direct access to means of subsistence that leads to these changes in methods of producing.

POPULATION

Having presented us with the technology of any society, S proceeds to offer us "the underlying population basis of any economy" (30). His analysis is inherently inconsistent, for on the one hand he follows the Malthusian tradition of treating population growth as a natural phenomenon (paralleling the supposed natural growth of agricultural means of subsistence), while on the other, he concedes that the controlling factors are after all social, not biological. He apparently fails to realize that in doing so he has toppled his own construction of "the underlying population basis of any economy."

S sees his theory of population as an application of the law of diminishing returns (30). His description of the fate suffered by Malthus' theory turns out to be rather ironic: first he praises Malthus for fruitfully applying the powers of diminishing returns, and then he says that "false prophecies" evolved because "Malthus never fully anticipated the miracles of the Industrial Revolution" (31), a gross distortion of the actual situation. Of course, an artificial, ahistorical approach like diminishing returns lends itself easily to refutation, since it posits conditions that deny those which had led to the rapid rise in productivity characteristic of capitalism. Without going into Malthus' population theory at this juncture, we merely wish to note that the acclamation with which capitalist society greeted it (e.g., the Poor Laws of 1834) was no coincidence, for at about that time the contradictions inherent in capitalism were first manifesting themselves in the form of explosive cyclical crises, clear expressions of the tendency of capitalism to create productive forces that exceed its ability to utilize them without violating capitalist social relations. More specifically, this meant that overproduction of capitalist wealth (i.e., commodities that could be sold to the masses of workers and of capital that could profitably be set in motion) turned a corresponding segment of the labor force into supernumeraries. Once these workers (and their families) were barred from access to their sole source of subsistence, they became part of the "overpopulation." Instead of admitting that capitalism was marked by this inherent contradiction, the English bourgeoisie simply shrugged this off with the explanation of a universal and suprahistorical population theory.

S never presents a very clear account of what in his opinion a theory of population for "Western nations" should be in light of the failure of Malthusianism. He mentions a few "social factors" that influence birth rates (33 n. 11) and labor-market participation (35 f.), but still he does not seem able to rid himself of the notion that what counts are absolute numbers.[11]

Even on a rather simplistic level it is evident that under different patterns of income distribution and during different phases of the industrial cycle the same population will take on a different economic meaning. As far as labor-participation rates are concerned, the process of capital accumulation has its own methods of creating "overpopulation" independent of "nature" and of overcoming temporary shortages. When S says "that for the advanced nations, there may be an optimum population size, not too large and not too small" (37), it should be kept in mind that processes inherent in capitalism tend to keep the size optimal for capital. If any "danger" does exist, it is rather that the mechanism is too "efficient" in the sense of creating so large a premanently available reserve army of unemployed (notably in the U.S.) as to become "politically intolerable."

In contrast to "Western nations," where Malthus has outlived his usefulness, "the germs of truth in his doctrines are still important for understanding the population behavior of India, Haiti, China, and other parts of the globe where the balance of numbers and food supply is a vital factor" (32). What is significant here is S's image of a class-undifferentiated mass of poor peasants living on the brink of starvation because of a niggardly nature and their own prolific reproduction.

In fact, however, the so-called Third World is characterized by a variety of class relations that form the mediating links between nature and poverty and overpopulation. Since these class relations are not "pure types" but rather peculiar mixtures, no general theory of overpopulation to match the simplicity and universality of neo-Malthusianism can be developed. However, if we look at English colonial rule in India, by no means an atypical example, we find that it was characterized by the destruction of the traditional communal-village societies, in part the result of enormous tax burdens which forced the villages to sell their land in order to meet the payments. Ultimately the land fell into the hands of English capitalists, and the former direct producers were displaced. For a variety of reasons, this process of expropriation did not lead to the same development of capitalist accumulation and of an industrial proletariat as in Western Europe. This meant that the majority of those driven from the land did not find access to means of subsistence through wage labor; because of their "pressing on the means of employment," the result of the pecul-

iar relations of production in these societies, huge numbers
of people became a "population problem."

II / "THE MARKET"

It is the function of Chapters 2 and 3 to prepare the reader
to accept the general framework of contemporary bourgeois
economics which ascribes a central role to the "marketplace." In this conception, the "market" figures as the
"place" which economic decision-making takes place. And
since the "data" that are fed into the "market" are basically
of two kinds, either individual desires or natural-
technological givens, the "market" must bear the brunt of
sociality for our economic system. In other words, the essence of social relations, as far as economic science is concerned, finds expression in the sphere of market relations.

There was a time when relations of production played a
central role in bourgeois economics. But a number of factors, particularly the rise of marginal-utility theory, made
for a shift in focus. Thus an influential English turn-of-
the-century economist, Philip H. Wicksteed, wrote: *"The
market is the characteristic phenomenon of the economic life and it
presents the central problem of Economics."*[12]

There is of course some validity to this emphasis on market relations, since capitalism, unlike all previous modes of
production, is characterized by the massive and predominant existence of all economic resources as capable of being
bought and sold. But this is a superficial characteristic insofar as social relations on the market are not identical
with, and in fact dissimulate, the underlying relations that
distinguish capitalism from other modes of production—or
rather, this very dissimulation characterizes capitalism as a
peculiar *form* of social production. As long as this aspect of
the "market" remains obscure, it can be said to have existed in many precapitalist societies and we have not been
told anything that is specific to capitalism alone.

The massive and predominant nature of market relations
furnishes a clue to the correct approach to the role of the

market as a defining characteristic of capitalism. By transforming all economic relations into relations mediated by the market, we have established the presupposition that the worker's ability to produce useful objects can be bought and sold. In orthodox terms, there must be a labor market. Though S apparently understands this, he does not quite know how to explain it. Thus he says: *"Everything has a price*—each commodity and service. Even the different kinds of human labor have prices, namely, wage rate" (43 f.). In saying "even," S acknowledges that there is something special involved in the sale of labor, and he describes this more fully: "Interestingly enough, most of society's economic income *cannot* be capitalized into private property. Since slavery was abolished, human earning power is forbidden by law to be capitalized. A man is not even free to sell himself: he must *rent* himself at a wage" (52). To begin with, the worker does not rent himself, but rather—to use S's terminology—sells his services. Secondly, even according to bourgeois notions of "human capital," such capitalization of human earning power does in fact take place. (S implicitly admits this [50 n. 4].) Thirdly and most importantly, S does not explain this development historically. He gives the impression that with the Emancipation Proclamation the freedom to sell oneself (doubtless said tongue in cheek) ceased, to be replaced by the labor market. But such laws merely reflect economic forces pushing toward the replacement of one social form of labor by another. These changes in the social form of labor were protracted processes, the expression of the most important class struggles and transitions from one mode of production to another.

COERCION

The importance of finding out what "freedom" is involved in these world-historical transformations has been stressed by one Marxist author. In discussing the widespread tendency to accept unquestioningly the present form of social labor, John Strachey wrote:

In order that a labour market may arise, it is necessary that there should appear in the community a category of persons who will, and who habitually do, hire themselves out to work in return for wages. It is significant of the degree to which the characteristics of capitalism are taken for granted that to-day most of us simply assume the existence of such persons. The very idea that it might be impossible to establish industry or commerce, not because of any technical reasons, but because no workers would respond to the offer of wages does not occur to people. Yet such was once the prevailing condition of affairs, and is still to a large extent the condition of affairs in many "primitive" and undeveloped parts of the world.[13]

Obviously restrictions on the buying and selling of the capacity to work (labor power) must be lifted if such a labor market is to arise and such persons are to come into existence. These restrictions fall into two main types: the people involved either cannot or do not want to become wage laborers. Those who cannot sell their labor power are unable to do so because they do not possess it, because they live under conditions in which it has not yet become a commodity: slavery or feudalism. Those who do not want to sell their labor power although in a position to do so are historically independent artisans and peasants who own their means of production (land and tools), and are thus in a position to survive in either a self-sufficient economy or by producing for exchange. This second group will "want" to sell its labor power only if compelled to do so. This will happen when its members can no longer support themselves in the traditional manner. Two developments transformed the "do not want to" into "have to." One was the simple expropriation of the land either by violent means or "legally," as happened in England in the transition from feudalism to capitalism. In the other, artisans were driven out of the market through the superior production methods available to the incipient capitalist by combining the skills of many workers under his control.

According to S, the entire market process "is undertaken *without coercion*" (42). His failure to deal with the forms in which production has taken place in various historical eras has led him to identify a single type of coercion as the only one, and this in turn has made it impossible for him to grasp the peculiar type of coercion inherent in capitalism; instead he has characterized it as "volition" (42). Yet upon careful reading we discover that even he gives us an inkling of the type of coercion inherent in capitalist production. He concedes, even though parenthetically, that income distribution—in other words, the quantitative power the various members of society bring to the marketplace—"is highly dependent upon the *initial* distribution of property ownership" (45), an insight quickly buried by mentioning it as merely one of many factors such as genetics, discrimination, education, etc.; he then descends still another step by emphasizing "luck" (68 n. 3).

Before continuing with the explication of S's implicit admission of the existence of another form of coercion, we would like to make some observations on this sort of distribution referred to by S. Clearly he uses the term in a very special sense, since "usually, when an economist is talking about 'distribution,' he means the distribution *of incomes*" (18 n. 1). And in fact S does not return to this "initial" distribution ever again, undoubtedly because a discussion of this type of distribution would involve an analysis of capitalist production as a particular historical mode of production with distinctive social relations—not just technological ones.

S's main reason for raising the subject seems to be quantitative, that is, the way in which property ownership affects the quantitative distribution of income. But the crucial aspect of this "initial" distribution lies in what we might call the qualitative sphere—how the exclusive concentration of the means of production in the hands of one relatively small class determines the form of production and distribution. It is only at this point that one can speak of the means of production as capital, and it is only here that the distribution of products assumes the form of wages and profit. And it is only at this point that a specific social quality can be attributed to distribution relations.[14] It is also essential to understand how this initial or original distribution or expropriation which forms the prehistory of capital reproduces itself in the course of capitalist development, taking the form of the concentration and centralization of capital on the one hand, and the increasing dependency of the mass of the population on wage labor on the other.[15]

Returning to coercion, let us look at an interesting section entitled "A Volunteer Army?" which S used to jazz up the 8th edition. While insisting that "reliance on supply and demand" can be substituted for government controls and their concomitant coercion and arbitrariness, S at the same time graciously concedes that "blacks, and other minority groups who face less lucrative alternative occupations in civilian life, will presumably bulk larger in a volunteer army than in an equitably-run draft" (8th ed., pp. 63f.; although this extra pressure on "non-white" groups should not be underestimated, it might have been more to the point to compare those from working-class backgrounds and those from other classes, regardless of "race"). In other words, S acknowledges in effect that the voluntariness of a "volunteer" army is a sham, that it is merely another form of coercion. He further confirms this when he says that in case of a high casualty rate in a war, the number of "volunteers" should prove inadequate, "supply-and-demand . . . must be supplemented by some *more direct form* of coercion" (8th ed., p. 63; our emphasis). S further emphasizes the advantages of a "volunteer" army by claiming that the additional wage costs are compensated for by the fact that those with more "lucrative" nonmilitary jobs will not have to squander their valuable talents; furthermore, there is a bonus in the form of "greater tolerance for risk (of death) and military discipline" on the part of the above-mentioned "blacks, and other minority groups" (p. 64).

By this time it has become clear that there are very definite *ideological* advantages inherent in this market approach. The roots of the "illusions" of the "market" are to be found in the inability of bourgeois economics to grasp the distinction between labor and labor power, or that between value and use value. But even this formulation is misleading insofar as it gives the impression that we are dealing with a subjective failing, or even with a deliberate falsification on the part of bourgeois economists. The fact is that this "illusion" is generated by the very nature of capitalist production: with the transformation of the means of production into capital and that of the capacity to work into the commodity labor power, the sale of labor power on the labor market conceals the relations which exist when this commodity is consumed outside the market, in the sphere of production. But whereas the market lies on the surface of events, accessible to all, when we reach the threshold to the sphere of production where exploitation takes place, we are told: "No admittance except on business."[16]

This does not mean that no one may inquire as to what goes on within factories, although S has nothing to say about working conditions. Moreover, exploitation is not unique to capitalism. What is unique is the manner in which superficial relations of seeming equality and freedom conceal the exploitation.

To summarize our findings up to this point: on the market, class relations between two antagonistic social classes—capitalists and workers—disappear in favor of buying-and-selling relations indistinguishable from those obtaining between buyers and sellers of any commodity. Furthermore, all production relations are reduced to those of the commodities themselves: on the market the relations which members of capitalist society in their multifaceted interdependence enter into disappear. All that remains are relations of exchange—how many apples bring how many shoes. This masking of relations is the result of the peculiar manner in which producers in capitalist society create their growing objective dependence on one another, for the individual producing units—the individual capitals—remain independent of one another; they remain private producers despite the objective process of socialization. Under these circumstances the individual producing units can express their relations to one another only through the "market." But S simply takes these peculiar relations for granted. Since he cannot explain why they exist he unwittingly becomes involved in tautologies which he mistakes for explanations. But a basic understanding of the conditions that give rise to capitalist market relations would show that S is merely describing what must happen on the surface once he has made his assumptions about the given conditions. Let us illustrate this point as follows: on the one hand, S states quite properly that "there exists a *system of prices*, a concept that is far from obvious" (59), yet on the other hand, the existence of prices has become so obvious in the capitalist mode of production that it is very difficult to think in any other terms. Thus in trying to characterize the determinants of the "price system," S lists these factors: "people's desires and needs," "engineering methods," "supplies of natural resources and other productive factors" (59). Not one of these factors is peculiar to capitalism; the jump from changes in these quantitative determinants to prices is unjustified.[17]

FREEDOM AND THE "MARKET"

At first glance S's position seems quite straightforward: the many references to "dollar votes," etc., give the clear impressions that he is operating with an extended analogy between the marketplace and a certain conception of political democracy, although his is a formal analogy: he does not establish any relationship between the two. One might even say that he pursues the ideological goal of having the reader transfer positive associations based on political democracy to the economic sphere. (The fact that given the unequal "initial" distribution of "dollar votes," the political concept of "one man, one vote" does not obtain in the marketplace does not seem to faze S.)

Quite aside from the deficiency of this conception of political democracy, S's position in fact turns out to be ambiguous, for at the same time he contrasts "the *impersonal* workings of supply and demand" with the presumably arbitrary decision-making of politicians (59).

Given the lack of methodological sophistication that marks S's discussion of this point, perhaps no great significance should be attached to this inconsistency. However, there is a reason for it, namely, with reference to state intervention into "market" processes; for despite the allegedly democratic nature of such intervention, it does interfere with processes endowed with the majesty of extrahuman powers (48f.; thus S speaks of "collective fiats" [8th ed., p. 55], meaning that even if they were democratically and perhaps even universally decided upon, they are decisions which people take upon themselves, in contrast to the laws of the "market," which all must obey and which were not devised in the interest of any one individual or group).

The inability of bourgeois economics—and this is a trait shared by Adam Smith and S—to grasp how interests are shaped by social relations was punctured by Marx's analysis of "mutual dependence" in capitalism. According to Marx, the classical economists formulated the problem in this fashion:

> Everybody pursues his private interest and only his private interest; and serves thereby, without wanting or knowing it, the private interests of all, the general interests. The point is not that, with everyone pursuing his own private interest, the totality of private interests, that is the general interest, is attained. Rather, from the same abstract phrase the conclusion could be drawn that everybody mutually hampers the assertion of the interest of the others, and that instead of a general affirmation a general negation results from this bellum omnium contra omnes. The point is rather that the private interest is already a socially determined interest and can be attained only within the conditions set by society and with the means provided by society; that is to say, the private interest is bound to the reproduction of these conditions and means. It is the interest of private people; but its content, as well as the form and the means of realization, are given by societal conditions independent of all.[18]

The neglect, indeed the denial of, the basic social conditions of capitalism whose reproduction determines the social interests of the antagonistic classes, is inherent in the "market approach." This inability to come to grips with social reproduction is revealed quite strikingly in S's attempt to describe the smooth rhythm of a "free enterprise system"; according to S, its "functioning alone is convincing proof that a competitive system of markets and prices . . . is not a system of chaos and anarchy. There is in it a certain order and orderliness. It works" (42). Even granting the "functioning" of capitalism at any given time, nothing has been said about the forces that interfere with "normal" reproduction of capitalist relations; aside from the ahistorical aspect, we detect an inability to transcend the counterposing of rigid opposites. It is of course true that anarchy in the sense of cessation of the reproduction of social relations cannot for long characterize any society. Yet one can certainly speak of anarchic social reproduction. The point is that science can discern order or regularity in the results of human activity without eliminating the *real* anarchy that characterizes the social aggregate efforts leading to those results. Not order and anarchy, but rather anarchy and planning, are the true opposites. Order and anarchy are not only not opposites in capitalism in S's presumed sense of being mutually exclusive, but, on the contrary, they condition each other. The anarchy on the aggregate level in capitalism must be joined by the despotic authority of the individual capitalist within his sphere of power.

As Marx points out, the processes that transform exploitation into equal exchange between capital labor in the marketplace are the basis for "all notions of law of the worker as well as of the capitalist, all mystifications of the capitalist mode of production, all its illusions of freedom, all the apologetic trash of vulgar economics."[19] S gives us no explanation for the inequalities expressed in the marketplace, although there is the implicit admission that there is something immanent in the "free enterprise system" driving in the direction of a reproduction of inequality. In any event it is instructive that while S avers that the "ethical" questions of income distribution—namely whether the "market" should be replaced by another mechanism—go "beyond the mere mechanics of economics" (47), he is not at all reticent about suggesting that the "relevant choice for policy is not a decision between such extremes" as "laissez faire and totalitarian dictatorship of production . . . but rather the degree to which public policy should do *less* or *more* to modify the operation of particular private economic activities" (43). In less dramatic language, it apparently lies within the purview of economics to say that socialism is not "relevant," although S had in fact promised to leave such " 'value judgments' " to "the citizenry" (7 f.).

III / "SOME FUNDAMENTAL CHARACTERISTICS OF THE PRESENT ECONOMIC ORDER"

An interesting inversion takes place between S's introductory language (41) and his subsequent substantive analysis; for if earlier he considered capital, money, and division of labor in the context of "our mixed economy" (41), later he quietly transforms them into "three further features of modern economic society" (49). S's change in language is not fortuitous (although he may not have been aware of it) since the thrust of his discussion imputes these "features to all societies characterized by superficially similar levels of development of the forces of production, regardless of differing social relations. In fact, one might say that the purpose of this discussion is to blur the distinction between socialism and capitalism by asserting that they have in common some essential economic relations. But at the same time, these relations are deprived of their unique social forms, reduced to allegedly technological relations, so that capitalism itself loses its characteristic social form and is equated with economic activity per se.

The other significant methodological aspect of S's argument here is also revealed by its formulation—his contention that he will look at "some" features related to one another and to the price system. This is typical of his methodological naiveté, or rather his lack of method; phenomena are heaped one on top of the other without explanation of why one follows the other. One gets the impression that these "features" could be presented in any order whatever, before or after the discussion of the price system, without affecting the argument or creating havoc. The absence of any apparent logical or historical structure is doubtless no accident, for S does not seem to see any structure which economic science would have to reflect. This methodological chaos wreaks its revenge: it prevents S from coming to grips with capitalist production.

"CAPITAL"

S admits that mass production would be impossible without a particular division of labor, and that the latter in turn would be impossible without money (52, 55), yet he nevertheless opens his discussion with "capital." He can do this because that which he subsumes under capital did indeed exist before either money or division of labor. And what does he mean by "capital"? Here too we are not given a clear-cut answer. In this major definition—we feel justified in calling it that becaue it is set off in colored ink—capital is said to "represent *produced* goods that can be used as factor inputs for further production. . ." (50). This determination is designed to contrast capital to land and labor, neither of which "is regarded as a result of the economic process," and both of which exist primarily "by virtue of physical and biological rather than economic factors" (50).

There is of course "something" to this distinction, since in past eras the physical existence of land and natural resources and the biological existence of man were in some sense above and independent of human influence. But it is clear that with the increasing socialization of production, the "natural" and the "biological" began to recede into the background in favor of the social formation of natural resources and human labor. Without wishing to minimize the distinction between land and man-made means of production (e.g., land, unlike a machine, if properly treated does not wear out) or between the latter and human beings created by human beings, we must be careful, lest we wind up calling the development of the human hand "capital formation," since the hand would satisfy S's criteria of "capital." And, in fact, bourgeois economics in recent years has brought matters to their logically absurd conclusion with respect to capital and labor by subsuming labor under capital ("human capital").

Thus S's principal definition of capital is hardly unobjectionable with regard to its primary determination—namely, setting it off from the other "factors of production," land and labor. For the time being, at any rate, S has defined "capital" to mean man-made means of production common to almost all societies. So broad indeed is his definition that one is tempted to call man a capital-creating animal, for as Marx noted: "The use and the creation of tools, although embryonically peculiar even to certain animal species, characterize the specifically human process of labor and Franklin therefore defines man as 'a toolmaking animal.'. . ."[20]

But on the other hand, S also offers a definition of capital which is supposed to apply specifically to "modern economic society": "Modern advanced industrial technology rests upon the use of vast amounts of *capital:* elaborate machinery, large-scale factories and plants, stores and stocks of finished and unfinished materials. 'Capitalism' got its name because this capital, or 'wealth,' is primarily the *private* property of somebody—the capitalist" (49 f.). In contrast to the major definition the emphasis here apparently is on the private ownership aspect. Yet on closer examination we find a definite confusion. First S states that contemporary technology depends on "capital," whereby "capital" is described in turn as—contemporary technology! If this seems as though we have not gotten very far, we are pushed back still further when we realize that the definition has not changed at all, for we are still dealing with "capital" in the above sense of "an input which is itself the output of the economy" (50). The question arises how the "modern" form of "capital" came into existence. S does not really pose this question, but we will come back to it later.

All we have learned up to this point is that the "present-day economic system" differs from earlier economies in that it "rests upon the use of" quantitatively more, or perhaps also qualitatively different, capital. Next we are told that other economies may have as much or even more capital than "ours," but that someone other than the "capitalists" owns it, and therefore these economies were given other "names." Or to be exact, we are not told this but rather figured it out ourselves after having been told that capitalism got its "name" from the fact that the "capital" in that society is owned by "capitalists." Strange reasoning indeed, for if capital is strictly defined as the means of production, then it would seem logical to name almost every human economic society "capitalism." Furthermore, in that society "somebody" who owned "capital" would have to be called a "capitalist." But the fact is that capitalism got its name because in that society the means of production were, for the first time, transformed into capital by becoming the private property not of "somebody," but rather the monopoly of a single social class. This process of expropriation of the means of production from the immediate producers, and their accumulation in the hands of nonworkers, gave birth to two new social classes—the working class, which did not own any means of production but only its ability to work, and the capitalist class, which owned all the means of production and did not have to work because it could live off the work of others.

Aside from a basic misconception—S speaks of "capital" in the Soviet Union—his description of the collective ownership of the means of production leads to some interesting conclusions. For it seems that in the society in which "productive property is collectively owned," "the government . . . decides" how to distribute income, what share of production should be devoted to producing means of production and means of consumption, etc., as opposed to the decision-making of "individuals" (52); however, it is S's contention that in the society in which the overwhelming mass of the people is excluded from the ownership of productive wealth, the few owners cannot thwart the aggregate will of "the people." In other words, not only does capitalism exist in all societies, but capitalism is actually more "communist" than communism!

At this point the question must be raised about the relation between means of production and capital. We know that under certain conditions means of production can become capital. But under what conditions? The impression might have been created that capital is synonymous with the means of production when these are used in the exploitation of the labor of those who work with them. According to this interpretation means of production would not become capital in a nonclass society—that is, in a "primitive" society with collective ownership, production, and consumption, in one of small property owners, and under communism. On the other hand, capital would exist in every class society.

But as we have noted, exploitation does not take the same form in all class societies. It is only under capitalism that the immediate producers are "free"; in slave societies, the masters owned slaves like all their means of production. Exploitation in slave societies was obvious, because the entire product went to the slave owner, and he decided how much his slaves needed to live, just as he decided whether or not a hammer had to be replaced. Furthermore, precapitalist class societies were essentially oriented toward fulfilling the consumption "needs" of the ruling class, that is to say, means of production and labor were combined to produce a large but limited and known quantity and set of use values. In capitalism this situation no longer obtains. The exploitation of the immediate producers does not have as its sole end the enhancement of the consumptive powers of the exploiters. In fact, production for consumption is not primary, but rather the creation of the largest possible increment in value over that which existed at the start of any round of production. Under conditions of production in which the coordination of labor efforts is not planned, the expenditure of human labor assumes the form of value. Where independent and private individual producers must exchange their products, direct and transparent relations of cooperation or domination must be replaced by an indirect form of sociality. Under these circumstances—i.e., capitalist exploitation mediated by value relations—the means of production acquire a new function: to extract the largest possible amount of labor from the workers (embodied as value), so that this increment can be accumulated in the form of new capital (including the purchase of additional labor power) toward the end of increasing the increment even more during the next round, etc. In the last analysis, this function can be reduced to decreasing that portion of the labor day which the entire working class must work in order to produce the commodities which its wages must purchase; the smaller this portion of the working day, the more labor can be appropriated by the owners of the means of production. This may not be a conscious goal of the individual capitalist, but in the aggregate the results of this process will impose themselves on him. In any event, the individual capitalist's decision to introduce new machinery does not hinge on increasing productivity per se. New machinery is not introduced in order to save the *worker* labor time, but to reduce that part of the labor day for which the capitalist must pay the worker, and then only if the reduction succeeds the cost of the machinery.[21] It is this peculiar capitalist form of productivity that determines the introduction of new machinery, and it is the cumulative process of the creation of this increment that is decisive. This consideration in itself makes a shambles of S's contention that the reason society does not rush into ever more productive production processes lies in "the initial disadvantage of having *to forgo present consumption goods. . .*" (51). First of all, this view presupposes that these processes are aimed at increasing consumption (and/or diminishing the burden of work); but as we have seen, that is not the case. Ironically, S is able to make this claim only by identifying capital and means of production, thereby imputing to capital the use-value production properties of the means of production, although the large-scale use of the means of production occurs only with their transformation into capital.

Consumption, as we have learned, is not the end of capitalist production, and it is therefore irrelevant to speak of forgone consumption as a motive that works against "capital formation." This claim becomes even more absurd when S speaks of "people" as either "willing" or not to "abstain" and "wait for future consumption," since no conscious decisions are being made here. But even in bourgeois theory the process of "capital formation" is a result of unplanned aggregate "decisions" of "people" who have given no thought to such matters.

The final step in the deconceptualization of "capital" is taken when S speaks of "people" in this context without differentiating as to class. This procedure is consistent with his equation of "capital" with means of production, but it will hardly suffice for capitalist society. The process of "saving," even in the superficial form in which S applies it, cannot be understood without first understanding the empirical class breakdown of "saving." By and large, the working class has no net savings, and hence can be as concerned or "unconcerned about the future" (51) as it will and still not be able to do anything about it. The capitalist class, on the other hand, can save and consume according to its "needs" without having either to "wait" or "abstain." Thus the meaning of "to snatch present pleasures at the expense of the future" (51) becomes considerably less clear, for the one class cannot do so, and the other does not have to.

In general, S's characterization of "economic activity" as "future-oriented" (51) is the expression of a suprahistorical science incapable of coming to grips with any particular society. In this case, precapitalist societies cannot adequately be characterized as future-oriented since they lived from hand to mouth. In fact, only the growth of large-scale industry under capitalism gave meaning to S's term "future-oriented." But this "future" is a short-term affair, restricted to foreseeable effects on the profitability of individual capitals, and necessarily associated with the enormous waste and destruction of human and natural resources, even of the "capital" structure itself, precisely as a result of the "really remarkable" fact that no one "is *consciously* concerned with" the planned coordination of social reproduction (41).

CAPITAL AND MONEY

Carrying forward the reasoning behind our discussion of capital, we can establish a *necessary* historical and logical relation between the development of money and of capital, in sharp contrast to S, who maintains that "along with capital and specialization, money is a third aspect of modern economic life" (55). Apparently, in his view money and capital are not intrinsically related but rather "become related through credit activities of the banking system and through the organized capital markets where securities can be transformed into money by sale or vice versa" (50).

Thus, according to this view, if there were not capital or money "markets," money and capital would not be related. In other words, if capitalist enterprise generated its "funds" internally—that is, if it could finance all investment from its own sales proceeds and hence never had to borrow or issue stocks or bonds—if it were a "neutral" economic unit, the relation between money and capital would be severed.

Bourgeois economics would equate such a society with a hypothetical (or rather historically nonexistent) society of farmers and artisans who owned their means of production and did not employ propertyless "hired hands," one whose relations among themselves were restricted to buying and selling.

But upon closer examination of S's argument, we find that there is nothing surprising in this equation, for even after introducing the relation between money and capital, he persists in seeing capitalism as a nonclass, use-value-oriented mode of production. Just as capital itself has been equated with means of production used to produce more commodities, so money has been reduced to a technical mechanism to facilitate barter, that is, the exchange of the products which "capital" helped to create (55).

Thus, just like "capital," "money is a means, not an end in itself" (55). But even though money is merely an "obscuring layer" spread over barter, "the King Midas fable . . . reminds us that means may themselves become perverted into ends" (55). It is interesting that in the context of this perversion S should invoke Midas in the context of an analysis of the real perversion of their society. The changes then taking place involved the transition from self-sufficient producing units to exchange, and then again the rise, development, and accumulation of money.

Aristotle considers the development of money a mere convention, since its assigned function could not have been carried out "naturally" or in accordance with the internal nature of the exchange, because the things which are being exchanged must be comparable, yet by nature, that is, with reference to their own physical properties or the physical properties of the labor producing them, are not. Money introduces this comparability in a conventional, nonnatural, external fashion.[22]

And finally, using money to make more money was considered the most unnatural way of acquiring wealth. It is significant that Aristotle does not take money in any of its functions for granted. S on the other hand, while not adding anything to Aristotle's explanation of the rise of money, takes a giant step backward, for he is incapable of transcending the society that has created the social basis for this comparability. Whereas the Greeks were amazed at the social changes implicit in the development of money, S is so rooted in capitalist production that he cannot imagine production without these social relations.

It is not the function of money to facilitate barter, for the same forces which bring forth money also transform barter in the exchange of commodities. Unlike barter, the production and exchange of commodities means that goods are produced for sale, in other words, that they have no use value to their producer but only a value expressed in the labor-time they embody. Exchange cannot be reduced "to its barest essentials" and turn out to be barter, because the realization of this value through sale is an essential characteristic of exchange, as opposed to barter. Money itself arises as a form of value.

Let us now proceed to the relation between money and capital. It is supreme irony that in the 9th edition S attempts to press Marx into service in support of his notion of "perversion." In a long passage which purports to paraphrase and even quote from Marx, S describes various phases in the evolution of this perversion. Barter, according to S's version of Marx, represents the sequence "commodity-commodity-commodity. . . !" (57). This is false, for Marx restricts the concept "commodity" to a situation in which products have ceased to be solely use values for their producers and have also gone beyond the stage of being produced occasionally or coincidentally for exchange. (In fact, the German term for barter [*Produktentausch*] literally means "exchange of products.")

The next phase, which S calls "a natural money economy," consists of the "sequence . . . 'commodity-money-commodity- . . . ' " (57). Here money is supposed to serve merely as a medium for acquiring commodities not accessible through barter. Although S does not say so here, this is the "sequence" which he assumes to exist everywhere in capitalism. Now to begin with, Marx nowhere uses the term "natural money economy." In fact, to the best of our knowledge, S is the first one to have done so. Both bourgeois and Marxist economists use the terms "money" and "natural economies" as dialectically nonmediable opposites: natural economy by definition is one in which no money is used.

The surface appearance of money and commodity exchange may be common to societies other than capitalism—for instance, the world market may perhaps mediate exchange between societies not all of which produce commodities; it may mediate the products of slave labor, etc.—but only in capitalism does this process become pervasive. The point, however, is to mediate this surface with the deeper relations of production characteristic of capitalism. S presumably believes he is doing just that when he continues: "But, Marx points out, when capitalism becomes perverted, people want to pile up money for its own sake and not for the commodities it can buy; money's sole purpose then is to use commodities to beget more money in the perverse sequence: 'M-C-M. . .' " (57). The depth of ignorance and distortion revealed in this alleged paraphrase of Marx is breathtaking.

To begin with it is not clear whether money or capitalism has become "perverted." It seems fairly clear that S believes that money has, but now it appears that capitalism has suffered a like fate. At this point suffice it to say that Marx always thought of capitalism as "perverted" because its mode of production did not aim at the satisfaction of needs per se but rather only to the extent that this did not interfere with the production for profit.

S seems to think that there was a time when Marx did not think of capitalism as "perverted." This presumably was the C-M-C "sequence," which as we have seen does not correspond to a previous era of capitalism but rather to the sphere of commodity circulation that marks the entire history of capitalism. At some point this presumably was "perverted" into M-C-M. But M-C-M can also refer to pre-industrial capitalist societies, to a type of hoarding, as well as to early trading capital and usury. S is of course playing with this notion of hoarding when he speaks of piling up money for its own sake; by the time we reach the early trading capitalists, however, it is clear that a new factor has been introduced—namely the search for profits for further expansion.

Yet at the same time this process cannot be a stable, self-reproducing one, for the trading or money capitalists can gain profits only by extracting values or money from others. In other words, the process M-C-M, in contrast to C-M-C, is senseless unless the final M is larger than the first, since the object is to obtain more money than one began with. This whole development, however, takes place within, or rather is, the process of circulation, not of production. In the process of circulation an individual can gain money only if another loses it; it is only in the process of production that new values can be created because only here is new labor added. As representatives of the circulation sphere, trading and money capitalists merely mediate between producers or between producers and consumers.

And they have also mediated between two societies of which only one was commodity-producing ("trade" was often a euphemism for plunder, piracy, etc.); in the long run, the extraction of values from both extremes would have led to their depletion and collapse (which is precisely what happened in various colonies).

The process of money-making can become a stable, self-reproducing one only when it transcends the sphere of circulation and takes direct control over the process of production. That happens when money can buy a commodity which, when used, will create more value than it itself possesses. That commodity is labor power.

But it is not true that "money's sole purpose" is to make more money or that "people want to pile up money for its own sake." Money has several functions, and fulfilling one of them does not necessarily preclude the fulfilling of another. The term "people" distorts the issue, for different people belonging to different social classes acting as economic agents in various roles "want" money for different purposes. Thus consumers of means of consumption (in "our" society, largely workers) do not pile up money for its own sake and do not use commodities to get more money; rather, the sphere of simple commodity circulation in which people exchange money for means of consumption is an attribute of capitalism.

The capitalist enters the "market," as everyone except S seems to know, in order to buy machines, raw materials, and labor power—that is, commodities—so as to produce other commodities which he can sell on the market in order to extract more money from the sphere of circulation than he had put into it. He is able to do so because "his" workers have added value to the commodities he has bought, and so he sells commodities worth more than his original purchase.

Thus the capitalist seems to follow the M-C-M sequence, whereby the second M is greater than the first. The point is that once this process has become self-reproducing through the exploitation in the sphere of production, that is to say, once money functions to introduce and conclude the process of exploitation, it has also become capital. Similarly, the machines the capitalist buys on the "market" are not simply commodities but also capital.

To summarize: money is not just a measure of value and a means of circulation. (S makes this assertion through the 5th edition, Chapter 3; in later editions Chapter 15 lists other functions, but these do not conflict with our argument.) Once money has developed this far in a value-producing society, it develops still further into a general symbol of wealth. This is precisely what Plato and Aristotle, as representatives of a society beset by new value-producing relations were protesting against. But the ability of money to assume an independent existence is given with the exchange process itself and is developed further by exchange. Once this happens, once money becomes a concentrated and mobile social power, it is only a matter of time before it will be in a position to buy the commodity that will enable it to grow and reproduce itself. But that is not a "perversion" of money: the abstract nature of wealth, the result of value and commodity production, already contains the seeds for the subsequent amassing of money for its own sake, for the peculiar qualities of the use values which militate against such accumulation begin to be subordinated to the quantitatively limitless possibilities for the accumulation of values. And inherent in this "hoarding" is the possibility for money to become capital as soon as it can buy labor power; and thus labor, the source of value, can be pressed into service in the limitless production of value beyond and/or without reference to the production of concrete use values.

DIVISION OF LABOR

S's discussion of division of labor is marked by his inability to distill what is peculiar to capitalism, and by a superficial description of what is peculiar to it, which is then attributed to economic development in general. This approach is consistent with S's general inability to understand the social and historical content peculiar to production relations under capitalism. The peculiar development of the division of labor under capitalism simply cannot be explained without considering two basic aspects of this mode of production: the production of value and the exploitation of labor in the form of the production of surplus value. By neglecting this yet at the same time unconsciously presupposing it, S's account cannot fail to be both ahistorical and tautological.

He introduces the subject by stating that "the economies of mass production upon which modern standards of living are based would not be possible if production took place in self-sufficient farm households or regions" (52). Since a self-sufficient economy is a natural economy—that is, one in which there is no exchange since there are no independent producing units—and since the mass production S mentions refers specifically to a capitalist commodity-producing economy, all he has in fact told us is that we cannot expect identical developments in nonclass, non-commodity-producing societies and in class, commodity-producing societies. Furthermore, a non-commodity-producing society is not antithetical to a division of labor, although it is not the same division of labor S is trying to describe.

Starting from this ahistorical approach, S appears to equate "a division of labor" with "specialization of function," that is to say, from the existence of various productive activities he jumps to the conclusion that one person must be welded to each activity. And then he proceeds to the claim that such a specialization allows individuals and "regions" "to use to best advantage any peculiar differences in skill and resources." And although he also admits that specialization can reinforce already existing differences, he also claims that this too will work out for the best (52).

But what exactly is it that becomes "better" or "best" through "division of labor"? He does not specify, but we can gather from his remarks on "improved techniques," on "the simplification of function made possible by specialization [which] lends itself to mechanization and the use of labor-saving capital," and the "efficiency" of automobile assembly lines (53) that he has in mind the "advantages" accruing from a very specific division of labor which developed during the two centuries before Adam Smith published his *Wealth of Nations* (1776), and which is known as capitalist manufacturing before becoming transformed into capitalist large-scale industry. At the beginning of this development stands the process of expropriation of the immediate producers and its consequences alluded to earlier. These producers now become wage workers, "employed" in large workshops by capitalists who have concentrated enough capital to buy the machines, raw materials, and "labor" necessary to carry on large-scale production. At the same time, the very separation of the former immediate producers from their conditions of production, which compelled them to sell their labor power, ensured the growth of a market for the commodities that had previously been acquired through self-sufficient activities. Marx explains this new division of labor as follows:

> *Division of labour* in one sense is nothing but *coexisting labor,* that is, the coexistence of *different* modes of labor which presents itself in the *different kinds* of produce or rather commodities. The *division of labor,* in the capitalist sense, qua analysis of the particular labor, which produces a certain commodity, into a sum of simple concurrent operations distributed among different workers, presupposes the division of labor within the society, outside of the atelier, as *separation of occupation.* It increases it on the other hand. The product can be produced in a more eminent sense as commodity, its exchange value becomes the more independent of its immediate existence as use value . . . the more one-sided it itself is and the greater the manifoldness of the commodities for which it exchanges, the greater the series of use values in which its exchange value expresses itself, the greater the market for it. The more this the case [sic], the more the product can be produced as commodity. . . . The indifference of its use value for the producer expresses itself *quantitatively* in the mass in which it is produced, which stands in no relation whatever to the consumption need of the producer even if he is at the same time consumer of his product. One of the methods for this *production en masse* and therefore for the production of the product is however the *divi-*

sion of labor within the atelier. Thus the division of labor on the inside of the atelier rests on the division of occupations within the society.[23]

As Marx also points out, the political economists who witnessed the rise of this division of labor viewed it realistically for what it was—namely as a

> means to produce more commodity with the same quantity of labor, thus to cheapen the commodities and to accelerate the accumulation of capital. In the strictest opposition to this accentuation of the quantity and exchange value the writers of classical antiquity cling exclusively to quality and use value.[24]

The development of modern industry, the cheapening of commodities, the exploitation of labor, and the subjugation of the worker to the capitalist turned the worker into an appendage of the machine, which, being capital, is not designed to improve the life of the worker but rather to extract as much surplus labor for its owner as possible. The labor saved by "labor-saving capital" is labor for which the capitalist has to pay the worker; conversely, it "saves" the laborer from any labor altogether since it renders his use value as a worker null and void. To be sure, S, who never ceases to applaud the "efficiency" resulting from eliminating the "wasteful duplication" connected with dealing with a group of jacks-of-all-trades, or the time-saving effected by having people do one job instead of their moving about (53), does not deny that this "may" have untoward consequences: "(Specialization may involve some costs, breeding half men-anemic clerks, brutish stokers—and producing social alienation.)" (8th ed., p. 49).

Back in the 3rd edition (1955; p. 46), these were merely "hidden costs," but by the 9th edition the "social alienation" among S's readers had apparently become so great that he thought it necessary to expand this sentence into a whole section and place Karl Marx's seal of approval on it. Apparently the fact that "real incomes rise in modern society" is what breaks the camel's back and leads people to the realization that specialization "may" make work "without purpose" (53; this in itself is unclear, for in the use-value production sense the "purpose" of every part of the division of labor is not hard to find. Perhaps one should look at the social context within which this production takes place to see what is responsible for the lack of purpose, for the only purpose a worker sees for himself is to collect his wages; all other objectives are imposed on him by the capitalist process of production). Marx, we are told, while still a "neo-Hegelian," had already grasped the "alienation" of modern industry "prophetically" and had still not forgotten it when he wrote *Capital* (53f.; this misinterpretation is due in part to the fact that S cannot find anything but metaphysics and mathematics in *Capital*).

Contrary to the impression S tries to convey, Marx does not hold "technology" responsible for the crippled detail-worker. Furthermore, Marx does not say that capitalism does not demand that the worker learn to perform many different tasks. On the contrary, the quest for the highest possible profit makes for unprecedented movements of capital and labor from one branch of production to another and creates new branches. What is at issue, however, is how this "mobility" comes about. Because of the anarchy of capitalist production, workers thrown out of one "employment" do not find another job right away, and unemployment and a highly "inefficient" use of labor power become the order of the day. Secondly, although capitalism makes it necessary for workers to be able to perform many different tasks if they are to find new jobs, this does not mean that workers are given the opportunity to prepare themselves for a variety of productive tasks. That is precisely the point Marx is trying to make: and because sudden changes in the scale of production in various branches and the sudden opening of new branches are unplanned, the result is "inefficiency," and therefore the individual worker is wasted and society as a whole is the loser. Capitalism's inability to create a versatile labor force as the norm is among the factors leading to its decline and the establishment of a society able to create such workers. S's own description of the "loosening up of the elaborate division of labor" makes it clear that whatever changes may come about will be the result of pressure by the workers and fear on the part of the capitalists; in other words, capitalism still struggles against "humanization" and will permit it only insofar as it "may be profitable" (54).

Having thrown a sop to the "socially alienated," S feels free to proceed to "one further serious problem" created by "specialization and division of labor"—*"interdependence"* (54). At first glance "interdependence" might not seem like either a "serious problem" or a "cost"; on the contrary, global cooperation would seem to be a potent productive force. And it is not interdependence per se that is a problem, but rather the form it assumes in world capitalism. To illustrate this "complete mutual dependence," S has recourse to such relevant examples as Fiji "natives"; and his attempt to incorporate examples nearer to home into his schema proves even more revealing: "In the backwash of a strike or war, a breakdown in transportation and the economic fabric of exchange reveals how perilously modern economic life depends upon exchange" (55). It is interesting that S finds it necessary to fall back on what he considers factors extraneous to economics like strikes and war in order to pinpoint the dangers of an economic phenomenon like interdependence. Also, he associates, or rather almost identifies, two phenomena that belong to two qualitatively different spheres: transportation and circulation. Transportation belongs to the sphere of use-value production, although in capitalism its productive nature is "concealed by the circulation form" (138). The physical transportation of products which happen to be commodities must not be confused with the transformation of the value of commodities (and capital) from commodity to money to productive form. It is this aspect that is relevant when speaking of the dangers of "breakdown" growing out of interdependence.

The real economic danger arising from the peculiar form that interdependence assumes under capitalism has been spelled out by a German encyclopedia of the social sciences, namely that "this dependence becomes a particular disadvantage in partial crises which through this more easily become general crises."[25] But all S does is hint at the manifestations of anarchy inherent in capitalism, at the "facts subconsciously familiar to every person" (5th ed., 1961, p. 57).

IV / CONSUMPTION

S's treatment of consumption in these chapters serves a dual purpose: to lay out the basic terms for the demand aspect of the supply-and-demand determination of price, and to establish the far-reaching ideological claim that economic activity under capitalism is subordinated to the needs of consumers as expressed on the market. In this section we will deal largely with the latter point, although we will also touch on the first. Our discussion will be restricted to broad ideological considerations, leaving the more specific theoretical critiques of utility and marginal utility to Chapter 15.

"CONSUMER SOVEREIGNTY"

The notion of " 'consumer sovereignty' " (58) has been the ideological centerpiece of recent bourgeois discussions of consumption, and it has been offered up in two versions, one weak and the other strong. The weak version holds that in order for a "good" to be sold, it must satisfy some human need or want. The strong version further asserts that the psychological makeup ("structure of preferences") of consumers determine the optimal allocation and utilization of productive resources with regard to the satisfaction of consumer needs and wants.

The strong version corresponds to the above-mentioned global ideological claim, but before we look at this thesis more closely let us examine some of the implications of the weak version, for although the strong version presupposes, and would fall with the refutation of, the weak version, the latter can also stand on its own.

In the almost tautological sense that a consumer must want to buy what he buys, the weak version is not peculiar to bourgeois economics. On the very first page of *Capital,* Marx also notes that a commodity must be of use value to its potential buyer if it is to be sold. The exact nature of this need, and the manner in which the commodity satisfies the need, is not, however, of interest to Marx, and he even excludes use values as use values from the sphere of political economy altogether.[26] Insofar as political economy in Marx's time was still characterized by an approximation to objective reality despite objectively caused theoretical inversions of that reality, Marx's approach was adequate as a critique of political economy. And it is still adequate today as an analysis of the fundamental forces operating in capitalism. To the extent, however, that bourgeois economics has degenerated into an openly apologetic ideological system, the critique of bourgeois economics must also take on a new quality: it must analyze aspects of it which make it less than a science of political economy. That is to say, not all categories of bourgeois economics— among them use value as use value or needs and their satisfaction—present an opening for a critical understanding of the essential forces in capitalism. Although Marxist critique will lead to a refutation of the claim that the satisfaction of consumer needs is the goal of capitalism, we will not arrive at this conclusion by examining consumer psychology. Yet since there is a formal similarity between Marx and contemporary bourgeois economics with respect to the weak version of consumer sovereignty, a distinction between them must be made.

Marx reduces the weak version almost to tautology. But even thus he is not talking about use value as use value but rather about its relation to the production and exchange of commodities that also have a value which must be realized. As pointed out repeatedly, "labor" under capitalism becomes "free" in the sense that the immediate producers are released from relations of direct domination as well as from their own means of production. Similarly, we might also say that "consumer sovereignty" originates in this process of transition to capitalist relations of production. This sovereignty also carries with it the very interdependence that worries S. For once production takes place for an "anonymous" market, as it must under capitalism, we are confronted with the likelihood and even the necessity that particular (masses of) commodities may have no use value for anyone and therefore will lose all or part of their value. This, of course, is the surface appearance of all crises—overproduction. And although this surface appearance does not explain the crises, the fact that value and use value, although inherently separable, must exist simultaneously in order for both to be realized lies at the base of capitalist crises. Or to put it differently, the fact that the restoration of the balance of the use-value structure of production with the social relations of value and surplus-value production and realization inevitably involves massive over and underproduction, wasteful and "inefficient" production spurts and cutbacks is not merely a consequence of producers' not producing use values for themselves (i.e., the existence of division of labor within the society): rather, it is due to the fact that use-value production is not immediately coordinated on a social level, but only indirectly through value production.

This emphasis on the internal unity of value and use value which asserts itself in crises through external antagonism must be counterposed to a recent bourgeois attack on the weak version of consumer sovereignty, J. K. Galbraith's conception of managed demand,[27] as well as to the weak bourgeois counterattack. According to Galbraith's thesis the large corporations have been forced to, and have succeeded in, planning and managing wants and needs, thus in fact reversing the notion of consumer sovereignty. In reply, the less extravagant economists such as S point out that not even "the large corporation" is "an absolute monarch," and so not even "all the wizardry of Madison Avenue" can foist a lemon like the Edsel on a resistant public (510). Or more generally: "Firms do not know when consumer tastes will change; therefore they may *overproduce* in one field and *underproduce* in another" (47). For S this represents a "drawback to the picture of the price system" which cannot be eliminated by the lessons firms draw from experience, for once they have adjusted, "the situation may have changed again" (47).

Essentially, S's reply merely insists on the ultimate sovereignty of the consumer: despite possible "imperfections" and "abuses," somewhere deep down the free-enterprise system harbors an irreducible element of sovereignty. In other words, S's response takes as its point of departure the "freedom" that characterizes the "market" relations between consumers and firms. Although this would appear to be diametrically opposed to Galbraith's position, it in fact rests on the same theoretical base—namely, the character of "market" relations. Well, one might ask, how else are we to approach a subject like the consumer?

The trouble with this approach lies in its inability to understand how "the consumer" is mediated with other, more deep-seated forces than the "market." This is demonstrably so, even if we grant some validity to Galbraith's thesis of need-management by the large corporations, which, like S's counterargument, continues to view use values as use values. It is obvious that in some sense "the" consumer must be sovereign in capitalism—namely in the sense that the agents of production (the owners of "land, labor and capital") must formally be able to convert their claims to social-value production into particular use values (within the quantitative limits set by value); in other words, capitalism would not be capitalism if automobile workers were to be paid in cars or tires or fenders rather than money. The products of labor must take on the abstract form of value, i.e., money, and circulate in that form.

Once an agent of production has received his claim to the annual social product in the form of money it is irrelevant how this money is spent and what mechanisms influence the spending. Thus individual large firms may be able to convince masses of workers that they "need" cigarettes or hair tonic or what have you, but this still will not prevent the value aspect of commodities from asserting itself. For as long as there is capital, that is, as long as individual capitals exist in competition with one another, a fundamental anarchy is expressed in value and surplus-value relations which transcends the "micro" problem of which commodities are chosen for consumption, and the "macro" problem of whether current income is spent in its entirety or not. To put it succinctly: given the present social relations of production, not even the most refined techniques of subliminal motivation can prevent economic crises.

In the end we find that the formal freedom that characterizes consumption in capitalism—i.e., production, exchange, and distribution of value—lies at the base of capitalist crises, regardless of the substantive realization of this freedom with regard to use values as use values, that is, with regard to the substantive satisfaction of needs even within the limits of the capitalistically determined quantitative distribution of income ("budget constraint").

We can conclude then that in a certain sense the weak version of "consumer sovereignty" has validity, and if the strong version is to be refuted, it must be attacked for aspects other than those it shares with the weak version. But it must be pointed out that our acceptance of the weak version is restricted to what we called a "formal" aspect, which is abstracted from a substantive examination of use values as use values. More specifically, we have not examined the question of how needs are formed, and to what extent "real" needs as opposed to "false" ones are being satisfied even within the limits of income distribution. Although this question is not an intrinsic part of the political economy of capitalism, still it must be dealt with since it forms a part of contemporary bourgeois economics. In any event, the structure of needs in any society, be it capitalist or postcapitalist, is a highly complex social phenomenon. At this point suffice it to say that the contradictory character of need structure in a value-producing society cannot be adequately reflected through the market, let alone "rationally" dealt with in reality. Although S contends that "consumer votes do not by themselves determine WHAT goods are produced," because "business cost and supply decisions . . . do help to determine WHAT" (45), it is clear that if consumer sovereignty in the strong version is to retain validity, demand must dominate supply. This means that supply must be determined by demand, subject only to limitations imposed by so-called technological conditions ("physical efficiency" [44]). But since "the profit seeker is society's agent to determine HOW" (45), it must be shown that the search for profit ("cost efficiency" [44]) coincides with "physical efficiency" and does not run counter to consumer interests. This theory is erroneous, a fact which will be brought out later. At this point we merely wish to point out that S suggests that it buttresses the strong version of "consumer sovereignty," although even within his theory such a conclusion does not seem warranted.

Before proceeding to an examination of how "consumer sovereignty" operates in capitalism, let us take a brief look at the position of the consumer in socialist societies. Thus a recent symposium on economic reforms in the Soviet Union asserted:

> Since the majority is said to enter socialism and to remain for some time in a state of vestigialness, the power to decide on what kinds of consumer of goods and services to produce must reside with the Party. To the extent, therefore, that the citizenry continues to desire items that are deemed by the Party to be unnecessary, wasteful, or reflective of *bourgeois* decadence, consumer satisfaction is purposefully not met.[28]

The author then goes on to provide his version of Marxist ideology with respect to the consumer during the period of socialist construction:

> Life and work in a socialist economic environment causes a gradual transformation in the attitudes and behavior patterns of the people. *Bourgeois* attitudes and behavior give way to "socialist consciousness." . . . The general living standard is said to rise and every effort is bent to produce that which is most desired by the progressively less vestigial, more socialist-conscious consumers. Consumer freedom, then, is like political or any other freedom. For a person is only truly free, according to Marxist-Leninist doctrine, when he does or wants that which is historically necessary.[29]

Balinky states that "the traditional Soviet approach has been to regard all items of consumption as imbued with either an ideological, practical, or neutral content."[30] And he concludes that "the Soviet consumer may be said to be gaining real freedom of choice if progressively more items of consumption are losing their ideological and practical content."[31]

The comparison with political freedom in fact holds the key to understanding "consumer sovereignty." As Balinky himself points out, "there are significant limits to such freedom even in the most highly market-oriented economies."[32] Thus, for example, there is no "free market" for heroin.

Another question relates to the extent to which the "citizenry" has come to "internalize" socially accepted norms. Balinky's description clearly implies that "the consumer" would rather see resources used for facilities able to turn out a hundred thousand winter coats in a wide variety of colors and styles than for facilities capable of turning out a million coats in one style and color. In other words, there is the assumption that under socialism "the consumer" is an individual without social attitudes, that he cannot participate in determining total producton on the basis of a wide range of considerations that transcend the single criterion of whether he or she "wants" something, regardless of any other social or personal considerations, such as the production conditions of a commodity.

Labor power and means of production are not purchasable under socialism, and therein lies the most significant "deviation" from so-called consumer sovereignty. It is here that we can see how use values enter into the determination of social forms of production, and also of how consumption is connected to production relations. Socialism progressively reverses the process that transformed all products of labor and all natural resources as well as the capacity to work itself into commodities, which represents a formal reduction in "freedom" for all owners of money; in fact, however, only the capitalist class is denied access to the purchase of the commodity form of its capital. Here again we can observe the changing historical and social meaning of freedom: just as it has become a "popular prejudice" in capitalism that the "freedom" to sell oneself (i.e., slavery) is no freedom at all and must be outlawed, so too in socialist societies there is a popular view of wage slavery and capital as a historically obsolete freedom.

Let us now proceed "to see just how this spending of money votes—this system of 'consumer sovereignty'—takes place. . ." (58). This in turn will lead us into a preliminary discussion of supply and demand. S cannot be accused of presenting a theory of consumption as a constituent part of a process of social reproduction; that is to say, the role consumption plays with respect to production, exchange, and distribution in capitalism (or in any society for that matter) is not examined. S fails to do so not only because he attaches no importance to theories of social reproduction but more specifically because of a by now deep-rooted conviction of bourgeois economics that consumption is the sole end of economic activity. Once this assumption has been made the dominant role of consumption within social reproduction in general and within capitalism in particular has been tacitly though wrongly assumed as well; production, distribution, exchange thus become subordinate activities whose roles apparently need not be defined. It is this self-explanatory nature of the role of consumption that frees S from any methodological obligation toward his reader and that ultimately forms the basis of his false theory of "the consumer."

S opens his discussion (which, we repeat, only implicitly deals with consumption) thus: "Let us take an example. You wake up this morning with an urge for a new pair of shoes" (58). Since he eschews any analysis of such "urges," we are thrust into the middle of an extraordinarily complicated set of processes without any guide as to how we got there; moreover, we are not even told that we are in the middle of a process but rather are given the impression that we are starting at the beginning.

The starkness of this example may possibly be even too much for S, and so he attempts a touch of local color: "Or, to take an actual case from history, suppose men begin to get prosperous enough to afford meat every day and do not have to fill up on potatoes. How does their desire to substitute meat for potatoes get translated into action?" (58 f.). In this "actual case" we are led to believe that something happened to raise their incomes, and that this event had certain consequences. Exactly what it was that brought about this change toward greater prosperity apparently is not part of history," and thus we are still left in the middle of a complicated process.

But let us look at this "actual case" not for its concrete merits but as an example of the sort of reasoning that underlies "consumer sovereignty." Since S did not find it worthwhile to let us know which period of U.S. nutritional history he is talking about, it is not easy to pursue the matter.

Trying to pinpoint the "actual case" was not made any easier by the fact that not until around 1960 did U.S. per capita beef consumption rise above the 1830 level. Furthermore, although per capita potato consumption decreased during most of this century (this trend began to reverse itself in the late 1960s), meat consumption did not increase until the 1950s. If we really wanted "to take an actual case from history," we would look at 1973, with its escalating food prices, particularly those of meat. As meat boycotts and declining real spendable earnings have demonstrated, capitalist "consumer sovereignty" offers consumers the freedom of not being coerced into buying meat if they do not have the money for it.

Perhaps the most striking aspect of S's description of the chain of events set in motion by change in consumer tastes relates to the effects on the immediate producers: "Ranch labor finds it can hold out for higher wages, and many a potato digger quits his job for a better-paying job elsewhere" (53). This theme runs throughout the book: the changes wrought by "market forces" lead to ever higher levels of welfare for society as a whole and for the individuals involved in particular—if not immediately, then in the long run. In this context, it may be instructive to look at an "actual case from history" which points up a number of interesting and related aspects of the chain of events allegedly set in motion by consumer tastes:

When evidence began to mount that cigarette smoking was a causative factor in lung cancer and heart disease, the tobacco monopolies began to turn out filter cigarettes which removed some of the cigarette's flavor along with tars and nicotine. To compensate for this, they substituted stronger burley tobacco for the milder flue-cured variety. This switch was accompanied by a massive advertising campaign that implied that cigarettes were safe. In the end, the profits of the tobacco monopolies remained "largely unaffected. The growers of tobacco were not in the same favorable position." While demand for Kentucky and Tennessee burley tobacco rose, "the tobacco growers of Virginia and North Carolina faced a serious depression."[33]

Even on a superficial level this picture is not quite accurate. It speaks of the tobacco growers in an undifferentiated fashion; in reality the effects of such a shift in a raw-materials source will vary according to the economic position of the agents of production. First of all, a distinction must be made between large and small farms; the former will be able to mechanize while the latter, unable to do so, will be driven out. A further distinction must be made between owners and tenants, and between tenants and farm workers, the latter being the most likely victims of mechanization. By and large, these small farmers and agricultural workers not only will not find "a better-paying job elsewhere," but are unlikely to find any job anywhere.

CONSUMPTION AS A CONSTITUENT PART
OF SOCIAL REPRODUCTION

It would seem as though in capitalism the notion of "consumer sovereignty" assumes the primacy of consumption as opposed to production, yet a closer look at the relation between consumption and production will show that no such primacy exists in any society, least of all in capitalism, where consumption is not even the end of economic activity. The reason that primacy of consumption over production is not the simple truth S makes it out to be is connected with the inability of bourgeois economics to see consumption as part of a comprehensive process of social-material reproduction rather than as a "given," outside "the system," somehow always there to furnish "economic activity" with its directional and substantive thrust, whose reproduction is tacitly assumed and never explained. Although superficially this would seem to make consumption a very active force, it ultimately transforms it into a passive agent.

By viewing "production and consumption as activities of one subject or of many individuals,"[34] certain aspects of production and consumption and their relation to each other can be established for all societies, or even without reference to any society. These relations can be useful despite their abstractness because they can be reduced to terms that enable us to avoid repeating the chain of reasoning that led to them; on the one hand, they themselves do not provide an explanation of the peculiar forms these relations assume in various societies, and "the whole wisdom of the modern economists"[35] consists precisely in forgetting this.

Keeping this in mind, we can see how Marx abstractly determines the influence of consumption on production:

> Consumption produces production doubly, 1) inasmuch as only in consumption does the product become real product. E.g. a dress first really becomes a dress through the act of wearing; a house which is not lived in is in fact no real house. . . . Consumption, by dissolving the product, gives it the finishing stroke; for production is product not as objectified activity, but only as object for the active subject; 2) inasmuch as consumption creates the need for *new* production, that is, the ideal, internally driving reason for production which is its prerequisite. . . .[36]

Thus consumption created the purpose of production and reproduced the need that calls forth production. On the other hand, it is possible to find similar influences exerted by production on consumption. It is obvious that production provides the material of consumption and it also determines the method in which consumption takes place. In other words, production, by creating the mode of consumption, also creates the consumer. And finally, production, by helping shape the mode of consumption and the consumers themselves, also produces the specific needs of consumption.

We can thus see that even abstracting from any particular social development, very definite self-reproducing interconnections between production and consumption can be established. On the same level of abstraction, the priority of production can also be established:

> What is important to stress here is only that, whether one views production and consumption as activities of one subject or of many individuals, they in any event appear as moments of one process in which production is the real point of departure and therefore also the overriding moment. Consumption as want, as need is itself an internal moment of productive activity. But the latter is the point of departure of the realization and therefore also its overriding moment. . . . The individual produces an object and returns to itself through its consumption, but as productive and self-reproducing individual. Consumption thus appears as a moment of production.[37]

What then are the basic errors in S's conception of consumption? The first derives from the uncritical fashion in which (marginal) utility theory accepted the needs and wants of individuals as the dominant forces of economic activity, although this approach necessarily neglects the role of production in the creation of the needs and wants of all societies. It is no accident that this theory also views these needs and wants as somehow given, since only by positing their externality (to "the system") can one extract them from the process of self-reproduction and disregard the priority of production. Consumption has thus been artificially severed from this process of self-reproduction and transformed into a point of departure. But precisely because its real relations to social production have been concealed, consumption has been deprived of its real active role and reduced to a pseudo-active one; all we are left with is the image of someone with an "urge" for shoes setting the process in motion by casting his dollar votes into the great economic machine.

This first error can be understood without reference to any particular society. The second one relates to bourgeois economics' convenient way of "forgetting" the level of abstraction that characterizes the relations between consumption and production. This set of relations is bound to elude the bourgeois economists because they define economics not as a science of social relations but rather as a study of the relations between human beings and physical objects (whether natural or man-made). Thus when S sees the ability of "the market" to satisfy the needs as the primacy of consumption, he ignores the mediating relationship between consumption and production which appears in the relationship of exchange and distribution. (This does not imply that specific social relations do not appear in the sphere of production itself; they do, but the identification of production with "technology" has blinded bourgeois economists to them, so that the sphere of distribution becomes the sole possible repository of social features.)

The second basic error rests on the unheralded transition from the weak to the strong version of "consumer sovereignty." For although the effect of consumption on production mentioned by S does exist, it in no way proves the claimed primacy of consumption over production. All it proves is that nothing can be sold unless someone "wants" to buy it. The inconclusiveness of S's assertion is underlined by the fact that he chooses to introduce the process at the point at which the "urge" to consume crops up literally from nowhere. By proceeding thus, he is able to avoid an absolutely crucial aspect of capitalism, one conveniently forgotten when speaking of "the market" and the relationship between consumer and merchant, namely the fact that no need can be satisfied unless it also satisfies capital's "need" for "competitive profit"; everything in the chain S sees as deriving from changes in consumption patterns or tastes is mediated by profit requirements in the sphere of production.

Moreover, not only must the desired use value be produced profitably, but the distribution of income that forms the basis of consumption and changes in consumption is itself determined by the same profit requirements in the sphere of production; thus, for instance, a failure on the part of capital to "earn" its average profit will not only bring production of the "needed" commodities to a stop, but result in the firing of or wage cuts for the workers producing these commodities, so that their "needs," as expressed by their purchasing power, will also diminish.

The notion of "consumer sovereignty" is insolubly linked with that of "demand." This latter notion is not quite so simple as most textbooks would have us believe. The demand for something contains both subjective and objective elements. Subjectively, someone must want that which is being demanded. This in itself, however, is clearly insufficient, because wanting cannot be equated with demanding. This is where the objective aspect comes in: some sort of right or threat or power must back up the wish (although the power may not be strong enough to turn the wish into a command).

S equates demand for a commodity with the quantity in which it is purchased (59). This in turn leads to endless paradoxes, such as: the poor demand low-cost housing, but the demand for it is nonexistent or at most negligible. These paradoxes stem from S's juxtaposition of the connection of demand with wants and rights and its positivistic identification with the quantity of the commodity actually bought. He is unable to confront this paradox because, while equating the quantity bought with demand, he also needs the "wants and needs" connotation of the term—unstated, of course—in order to save demand theory from circularity.

Thus we can see that the paradoxes of demand in capitalism are created by the inability of bourgeois economics to make the transition from the abstract relation between production and consumption to the specific one, for a study of the capitalist mode of production shows that the profit needs of capital necessarily insure that certain other needs will go unsatisfied due to the lack of solvent or effective demand (the result of income distribution)—or of its production-sphere expression (low profitability).

Take housing: in the late 1960s, according to the U.S. Department of Commerce one-half of the 20 million households with annual incomes below $5,800 (average income $4,400), approximately 50 million people, constituted "an urgent market for genuinely acceptable low-cost housing."[38] At about the same time a published estimate pointed to "7.8 million households which are unable, because of their incomes, to afford standard housing. [Projections] show little diminution in the number of these families . . . for 1978."[39] The reason becomes quite obvious when we learn that "it is most difficult to . . . make a reasonable profit" by constructing housing that people with low incomes can afford.[40]

We now understand what S means when he says that "the profit seeker is society's agent to determine HOW" (45)—namely, to determine how not to produce at all when there is no promise of profit.

V / SUPPLY AND DEMAND

The fact that S offers only "the bare elements" of supply and demand and postpones a discussion of the underlying "microeconomic" theory renders a critical analysis very difficult. Similarly, a rigorous Marxist critique of supply-and-demand theory presupposes the development of a series of categories which cannot be treated adequately here. Nonetheless, we shall attempt at least to lay the groundwork for such a critique.

When S tells the instructors that "supply and demand comes as a natural sequel to Chapter 3's more general description of the market process,"[41] he is correct in a sense of which he is doubtless unaware. For the sort of supply-

and-demand theorizing offered here does indeed flow directly from the essential characteristics of the "market" approach discussed earlier, one that endows relations which exist but are superficial in the sense of being subordinate to and derivative of other relations, with conceptual eminence. Worse still, these relations lose even their secondary value by being severed from more fundamental ones, and without them they become mystifications.

Just as money, prices, division of labor, etc., cannot be understood apart from the complicated system of capitalist profit production, so supply and demand also are transformed into meaningless, even distorted categories when their role in profit production is neglected. And this neglect is a logical step in S's concentration on the "market," for the market, as we know, does not show what mode of production created the commodities bought and sold there. But the laws that guide the market are those of the mode of production whose commodities are being exchanged. On the "market" it would appear that commodities are merely bought and sold and that what is taking place is simply an exchange of money and products between buyers and sellers whereby an equivalence (in value) between them is presupposed. But in fact "the commodities are not exchanged simply as *commodities*, but rather as *products of capitals*," "and . . . as far as commodities are products of capital, they presuppose capitalist production processes, that is, relations complicated in a way much different from the mere buying and selling of commodities."[42]

When we talk of demand, we must specify whether we are talking about demand by consumers (largely by workers for means of subsistence) or by capitalists, and within the latter category we must distinguish between demand for "labor" and for machines, raw materials, etc. These distinctions are important because they serve to explain the differential effects of the aggregate process of capitalist production on the various components of demand and supply.

Demand for "consumer goods" largely depends on what share of the "national product" goes toward wages (and in part to the capitalists as consumers; the more complicated redistributional aspects of taxation and government expenditure with respect to "demand" will be gone into in Chapters 6 and 8); this relation, on the other hand, also determines what is left for capital in the form of profit; and this index of profitability in turn determines the demand for machines, raw materials, "labor," etc., as well as the supply. (The forces that determine these basic relations through which supply and demand operate and must be understood are in fact very complicated and comprise the bulk of Marx's *Capital*.) S in his own way is aware of this problem. Unfortunately, after having impressed the reader with the primacy of supply and demand, he relegates a modification for "the alert reader" to a footnote (68 n.3). But even this note loses its potential critical force because he (1) reduces inequalities in the "distribution of money votes" to "luck" and genetics; (2) in the end reestablishes the supremacy of supply and demand by shifting it to the "factor markets." And finally, the note gives us a fascinating glimpse of how "the text is carefully—nay, even cunningly—prepared so that each reader can go as far with it as he cares to go" (vii): namely, the student is motivated to read it because it shows how to avoid getting only "50 per cent credit . . . on a final exam" (68 n.3).

To give the reader some insight into the positional value of supply and demand in Marxist theory, we will offer a violently abbreviated version: the price at which a commodity will "earn" the capitalist producing it an average rate of profit is called the price of production by Marx. This price arises apart from the value of the commodity through competition among the individual capitals. If this price did not exist—that is, if the commodities were sold at their value—then the rates of profit in various branches of production, depending on the ratios of the amount of living and dead labor employed, could not be tendentially equalized, and without this tendency the "market freedom" that characterizes capitalism would disappear. The role of supply and demand must be looked at in connection with the equalization of the rates of profit and the transformation of values into prices of production; then we see that capital withdraws

> from a sphere with lower rate of profit and throws itself into another which yields higher profit. Through this constant out- and inmigration, in a word, through its distribution among the various spheres, depending on whether the rate of profit drops there and rises here, it brings about such a relation of supply to demand that the average profit in the various spheres of production becomes the same. . . .[43]

Thus to understand the function of supply and demand one must understand the process of production of surplus value and its distribution among various capitals. This understanding in turn rests on that of commodity production, for on the aggregate level supply and demand recapitulate the relation between use value and value, between commodity and money, that applies to the individual commodity. This becomes clear when we realize that what is being supplied and demanded are not mere physical products. The demander must supply a value equivalent for the use-value demanded, while the supplier intends to realize (demands) the value of the commodity supplied.

The foregoing process results in two important methodological points. First, supply and demand functions on a concrete level which is not the proper subject matter for a general theoretical text, let alone an introductory one. Concrete in this context is synonymous with "superficial" in the sense of lying on the surface of events; it is a matter of scientific concern, but not a fundamental one. But when, like S, one omits the base and transforms supply and demand into that base, "superficial" also takes on the meaning of shallow and uncomprehended as applied to the theory itself.

Secondly, S's discussion of the equilibrium of supply and demand ("At that equilibrium intersection, and there alone, will everybody be happy" [67]) does not quite explain what it is supposed to —namely, prices and/or the forces at work tending to force the existing price-structure toward some sort of equilibrium. This reasoning in effect boils down to saying that when supply and demand are equal we have an equilibrium price, and when we have an equilibrium price, supply and demand are equal. The trouble with this line of reasoning lies in the fact that when supply and demand are equal they cease to influence concrete prices and hence cannot be used to explain why the price is exactly equal to one sum of money and not to another. Not only does supply and demand fail to explain the underlying forces of capitalism, but they must be presupposed to be "in equilibrium" (as in fact pre-Marxist classical political economy did) so that these basic forces may be studies in their pure form, undistorted by the price oscillations brought about by supply and demand.

What supply and demand, when theoretically mediated, could explain are the price oscillations. These oscillations, as well as the tendency toward their elimination—or, in other words, the elimination of the effect of supply and demand—are explained by other factors. But this "equilibrium," which never exists at any one point but merely as an average for a given period of time, is hardly one that makes "everybody happy." In fact, statements such as these reveal the profoundly apologetic thrust of S's theory. This "equilibrium" is the result of the countervailing rises and falls of supply and demand in the wake of the unceasing search for greater profit on the part of individual capitalists. Both the equilibrium and disequilibrium of supply and demand are superficial expressions of the anarchical nature of capitalism. To say that the effects of this anarchy make "everybody happy" is a prime example of rationalizing demagoguery.

APPENDIX / STOCK MARKET FLUCTUATIONS

This section was first appended to the 6th edition "to provide a motivating example of supply and demand."[44] The "motivation" presumably relates to making a bundle, since the bulk of the material is devoted to practical matters.

Or perhaps S thought this section pedagogically relevant, because "to the public the most dramatic example of a competitive market is in Wall Street. . ." (73). Two major objections to this interpretation may however be raised: first, as S himself points out in a rare critical moment, the numbers involved in stock ownership make a myth of "people's capitalism" (74 f., 113); and secondly, a good deal more "drama" would appear to inhere in "the labor market," where "relations" for 80 million workers (and their capitalist antagonists) "are not always so peaceful. To the family breadwinner his wage is not simply another price; it is the difference between "luxury and comfort, between comfort and privation" (45).

It would thus seem more likely that the real pedagogic relevance of this appendix lies in its consolidation of the image S has been playing with throughout: "the market" as "auction" (cf. 63, 67-69). We do not mean to imply that supply and demand suffice to explain phenomena such as stock prices, etc. We are also dealing here with more deeply rooted phenomena connected with capital accumulation, rate of interest, etc. But these are very concrete factors which can only be explained after the mediating links to a general theory of capitalism have been established.

3 Income Distribution and Poverty
S's Chapters 5, 39, 40

I / INTRODUCTION

The various changes made in the title of this chapter in the various editions reflect the relationship of bourgeois economics to poverty in the post-World War II era. The first edition (1948) contained two chapters which more or less covered the same material presented here. They were entitled "Individual and Family Income," and "Individual and Family Income: Earnings in Different Occupations." In subsequent editions some of the material was dropped and other portions shifted around until one chapter remained: "Individual and Family Income." And there matters rested until the 7th edition (1967), when three words, "Affluence and Poverty," followed by a colon, were inserted in front of the old title. Substantive change was minimal: it consisted in the addition of two relatively vapid and brief sections with the headings "Affluence for Whom?" and "Definition of Poverty." The 8th edition retained "poverty" and "affluence," but not in the title; rather, they were banished to Chapters 39 and 40, where they are treated separately. That is the reason for our decision to lump Chapters 39 and 40 together with Chapter 5.

S, as we know, is not only an ideologist but also an entrepreneur. This felicitous combination finds clear expression in these two "new" chapters that grace the 8th and 9th editions dealing with poverty, racism, and sexism, a transparent gesture with obvious commercial overtones.

The various superficial changes bespeak of an inability and/or disinclination to give serious consideration to the subject of poverty in capitalist society. S's basic position has not changed significantly over the past quarter-century, and the fact that he continues to repeat certain assertions even though they have been refuted empirically—in part unwittingly by S himself—points to the very sort of dogmatism he claims to be fighting: "Obviously, the present approach cannot avoid controversial problems and would not if it could. What it can try to do is avoid indoctrination and propagandizing" (1st ed., p. vi).

II / S's CRITIQUE OF MARX

The "dogma" which S so vigorously castigates is, of course, the alleged Marxist variety, and thus naturally Marx comes in for mention right at the start. (In the first edition the urgency was not quite so great, and so he could wait a few pages before dragging Marx in.) S loses no time in distorting Marx's position, but before we look at this let us examine the real differences he has with Marx.

Repeated throughout nine editions is the introductory presentation of income as the single most relevant "fact" to know about a "man" (79). By income, S means "a steady stream of money," i.e., a quantity flowing to others. On that basis S then proceeds to adduce various figures concerning income levels, distribution, etc. It is doubtless true that in capitalist society the size of one's income tends to color one's personality. However, if political attitudes, education, health, and related factors can be "correlated" with income, this does not really exhaust the possibilities for causal explanation. Income can hardly be the only dimension. It is barely possible that income in turn is related to other basic phenomena of capitalism.

Both the classical economists and Marx found such a causal origin in the qualitative distribution of income among workers, capitalists, and landowners. But before we pursue this point any further, we would like to note that although S ignores this particular aspect, still his "macroeconomic" approach bars him from going beyond the sort of superficial journalistic treatment characteristic of the first nine chapters. On this level it is only possible to compare various quantities without understanding the underlying social qualities. As to Marx, S says that his "assertion that the rich will become richer and the poor will become poorer cannot be sustained by careful historical and statistical research" (80). Instead "there has been a steady secular improvement in minimum standards of living. . ." (80). But contrary to S's assertion, Marx did *not* develop an "iron law of wages." What Marx did was to show how a "moral and historical element" enters into wages, so that the value of the worker's labor power varies over time and place.[1] In addition, Marx explained how wages can in fact rise during a period of intensive accumulation, although "its increase at best means but a quantitative decrease of the unpaid labor, which the worker must perform. This decrease can never proceed to the point at which it would endanger the system itself."[2] As far back as 1849, in *Wage Labor and Capital*, and also in *Value, Price and Profit* (1865), Marx stressed what he called the relative wage—that is the wage as compared to the surplus value appropriated by the capitalist.

Although S is certain that Marx's predictions about the future of capitalism have been refuted, he himself is not able to offer an accurate picture of the reality of present-day capitalism. Thus he conveys the erroneous impression that the putting-out system (homework) and child labor belong to a remote past (80). But according to a report in the *Wall Street Journal* of March 30, 1971, child labor, though a violation of law, is on the increase, and as to the putting-out system, it too lingers on. According to *Der Spiegel* of March 22, 1971, approximately 300,000 people in West Germany, mostly women, children, and the physically handicapped, slave at home for a fraction of the wages paid in industrial plants.

S's misunderstanding of Marx's concept of classes and their relations in capitalism finds expression in another interesting section (one no longer included in the current edition) entitled "The So-called 'Class Struggle.' " As is to be expected, S can give us Marx only in an "oversimplified version," because it is "an oversimplified doctrine" to begin with (1st ed., p. 71). Thus according to the "economic or materialistic determination of history theory . . . the job makes the man, and a man's economic interests determine his political opinions. The well-paid college professor of economics writes textbooks that are apologies for capitalism; the newspaper editor, supported indirectly by advertisers' contributions, inevitably takes on a conservative slant" (1st ed., p. 70).

The irony here lies in the fact that S previously held that income levels determine political opinions. Apparently he did not think that ridiculous. Now he merely changes the content and ascribes the principle, though the wrong content, to Marx and omits all the links between objective economic condition and subjective consciousness.

We do not know who formulated the theory that the job makes the man, but in any event, in the form in which S presents it, this "theory" contradicts Marx. After S's slanted digression on jobs, we are told that Marx like Smith and Ricardo "came to attach importance to the nature of a man's income" (1st ed., p. 70). Thus Marx "was not simply" interested in wealth or poverty but also in its class origin (1st ed., pp. 70 f.). But S is disturbed by this class approach (here it is no longer clear whether he attributes this to Marx or Smith or Ricardo). Marx speaks of the bourgeoisie "(a 2-bit word for the businessman-capitalist)" as " 'the ruling class' " succeeding the feudal landowners. S recounts all this with the apparent condescension of a "modern." He fails to inform the reader that Marx did not originate the concept of class—either for capitalism or any previous society; he fails to explain that Marx did not invent the term "bourgeoisie" (it had also been used by John Stuart Mill). All S can say is that "the old-fashioned economist liked to work with the classifications land, labor, and capital. Consequently, he divided property incomes into land and capital, or into rent and interest" (1st ed., p. 73). This constitutes a perfect example of "the modern approach . . . that insists on the irreducibly subjective element of our perception of facts depending upon the theoretive system *through* which we look at those facts" (7th ed., p. vi).

Now if S wishes to be one of those "moderns" who commit themselves to this methodology that is his business, but this in no way gives him the privilege to ascribe this approach to the "old-fashioned economists." They certainly did not proceed as they did because they "liked to"; their concepts were not arbitrary "classifications" devised by them. They were the scientific observers of objective changes taking place in Europe. The bourgeois class itself proudly and self-importantly spoke of its rise and its differences with the class above (landowners, aristocracy, feudal nobility) and the class below (proletariat and peasantry); and neither did the outgoing ruling class mince its words.

But ironically S himself again provides the refutation of his argument. Thus immediately after his remark about the old fashioned economists he continues: "But it does not seem crucially important to us today that the Astor fortune is invested in New York real estate while the Marshall Field fortune comes from capital holdings" (1st ed., p. 73). It does not seem crucial because it no longer is; with the development of capitalism, the remnants of feudal society are progressively eliminated by being transformed. Initially the land monopoly of the noncapitalist classes, a social phenomenon inherited by capitalism, was a carry-over from another society, another mode of production which capital had to adopt and adapt to. (The monopoly itself was needed to prevent the peasants from staying on the land and out of the factories.) With time, however, capital itself invaded landownership, and income from land became "fruits" of "investment" like any other (although it is determined by different laws than those governing profit formation).

Again S furnishes support for the opposing view when he admits that the incomes of a clerk at Woolworth's and of the owner "differ in character": "The clerk is paid for her *personal effort or labor:* for standing on her feet all day, for desisting from robbing the cash register, and for waiting on infallible customers. Miss Hutton receives her income from *property*" (1st ed., p. 72).

This would seem to be more in line with the class analysis attributed to Marx and Co. (aside from the fact that S has determined wages according to labor and effort as opposed to the value of labor power, that is to the value of the commodities necessary to sustain the worker and produce the next generation); and such an analysis would also seem to make sense in connection with the shaping of "political opinions." If he alleges that this is the sense in which Marx meant that the job makes the man, then the clerk might well form views that differ from those of the occupant of the "job" property-income-recipient.

But this promising approach is dropped. Subsequently we are only given information about income differences within the working class or the decline of the pensioner.

III / THE DISTRIBUTION OF "WEALTH"

The discussion on the distribution of "wealth" appears as an interesting aside, to be included after one has disposed of income distribution. Unfortunately, however, this approach stands causality on its head, and in his own backhanded fashion S admits this in a most significant parenthetical statement: "(Of course, the character of the resulting distribution of income is highly dependent upon the *initial* distribution of property ownership. . .)" (45). S assumes the initial distribution of property as given, yet this is precisely what needs to be explained here. Instead of trying to find out why wage income leads to relatively little wealth, S makes the totally irrelevant suggestion that "if labor could be ignored, the distribution of incomes would tend to be that determined by the distribution of wealth. . ." (88). At this point S drops the whole matter and diverts the reader by saying that income from capital is more unequally distributed than income from labor. This is of no interest here. The question is why wealth should be associated with one form of income and not with the other, why capitalist income is greater and increasing considering the diminishing proportion of the population making up this class. But instead of comparing the two classes S divides them in order to investigate the secondary problem of distribution within labor and capital.

Although bourgeois economists on occasion like to indulge in "chicken or the egg" debate, when it comes to reality of income redistribution they are very quick to leave the realm of fantasy. It is generally recognized that income redistribution is simply an indirect method of confronting inequality: the expropriation of capital at its productive source would be a much more direct assault. If we accept that laissez faire capitalism will continue to produce income inequalities on an ever increasing scale, then it is clear that any attempt to compensate for this which does not intervene in the production of capital itself is bound to be a Sysiphean labor: income would have to be redistributed on an ever wider scale simply to maintain a fairly constant relative level between rich and poor.

This is "inefficient." Why then don't bourgeois economists suggest direct intervention into the sphere of production and ownership? Oddly enough for reasons of "efficiency"! S claims that regardless of the social ownership of the means of production, laws regulating production remain unchanged. Implicit in this theory is a disclaimer of any scientific determination of the relative merits of socialism and capitalism, because basically they are the same and questions of who should own the means of production belong in the sphere of ethics, not economics. Yet he nevertheless rules out any discussion of state or popular ownership of the means of production as a serious alternative to the so-called welfare state. Thus in a section entitled "Ethical Aspects of Income Distribution" he says:

> The questions are discussed repeatedly in Congress. Whether incomes should be completely determined by a competitive struggle . . . is an ethical question that goes beyond the mere mechanics of economics. In the modern mixed economy, the electorate insists on providing minimum standards when the

market fails to do so. Economics teaches how interventions can be accomplished at least costs in terms of efficiency [47].

In the seventh edition the last two sentences instead centered on the price system and how it works "to cause resources to flow toward goods which people with money and ability to earn wages will pay for" (45). The "and" ought to read "or."

Efficiency here means that given the Sisyphean method I have chosen with the help of a value judgment not known to you, my theory will tell you the most efficient way of pretending that effect is cause. It is interesting to learn that a competitive struggle takes place in the economic sphere, but outside of it there are only discussions and questions. Since S fails to present any data on the distribution of wealth we feel it incumbent upon us to refer the reader to helpful statistical sources.[3]

In view of the extremely vague and indistinct conceptual approach that characterizes this section, an explanation of the phenomenon under study becomes very difficult. Nowhere is wealth defined. Wealth can be divided into two categories: consumptive and income-yielding. In the first we would find houses, TV sets, yachts, etc. In the second, capital (both tangible, like factories, or paper, like shares or bonds,) as well as land and other rentable properties like houses). The first is a dead end as far as further amassing of wealth is concerned: watching television or sailing a boat will not make anyone richer. Thus in discussing the origin and development of such wealth, causality runs in one direction: to find out which population groups had large enough incomes to permit them to "indulge" in so-called consumer and more highfalutin forms of conspicuous consumption, one apparently must look at the size of income. But at the same time—at least according to Samuelsonian ledger causality—one would have to consider assets and liabilities or savings and debts to determine the influence of income on both kinds of wealth. According to a Federal Reserve Board study for 1950 on the percentage of total savings for certain income groups and the percentage of spending units accounted for by each income bracket, the lowest 73.3 percent of the spending units accounted for minus 0.4 per cent of savings, or, in other words, about three-quarters of the population had no savings whatsoever, for their debts balanced assets.[4]

Statistical groupings say nothing about social classes, but in all likelihood the working class is well represented in the bottom three quarters and the capitalist class at the top. S, who of course knows all this, finds it difficult to admit it because it does not accord with the Keynesian psychological "laws" which allegedly determine saving "propensities." The most S manages to concede is this parenthetical remark: "(Workers, however, have generally seemed to save less than the self-employed)" (211). Yet even this is not an explicit reference to classes, since the self-employed encompass doctors, lawyers, small businessmen, farmers, etc.

We know that the higher one's income the more likely one is to accumulate wealth of any kind, and that basically it is the capitalists who have high incomes. Thus from the vantage point of income it should be obvious that capitalist incomes rather than workers' wages favor the accumulation of wealth. But what are the links between wealth and income? We already know that consumption-wealth and income are not linked. On the other hand, only capitalists (or landowners) possess income-yielding property (we will not consider stocks, etc., owned by noncapitalists which in the aggregate are negligible). Evidently, here possession will lead to still greater possession—and this within one social class. It thus is obvious that the possession of productive wealth—capital—leads to the creation of greater wealth both in the form of income directed toward consumption and of additional capital which will lead to another round . . . etc. If we look at this process from the point of view of capitalism as an aggregate functioning system rather than from the point of view of an individual with savings, primary causality must be attributed to productive wealth in the production process itself, for it is here that all income is created prior to any subsequent distribution. Money income in itself will not lead to wealth in the absence of a system of capitalist production in which this money can function as capital. In this respect a would-be individual capitalist is merely re-enacting the historical origins of capitalism, whereby an individual with money becomes a capitalist by hiring workers and providing them with machines and raw materials.

IV / EMPIRICAL MATERIAL CONCERNING INCOME DISTRIBUTION IN THE U.S.

The balance of this chapter is devoted largely to an attempt to prove Marx wrong and to show that equality is on the rise. Yet notwithstanding all this, S gives a rather realistic notion of the relative level of poverty in the U.S. Thus he points out that 90 percent of the population cannot afford a Mercedes (in previous editions it was a Buick) "and all the other good things that go to make up comfortable living" (82). This realistic appraisal is in answer to those who would promise Americans pie in the sky under capitalism, and to this extent S is critical. Of course, the potential impact of this is lost since it is embedded in a theory that denies the possibility that capitalism can be superseded. What he is saying in effect is that in the world's richest nation 90 percent of the population is condemned to second-rate economic citizenship in perpetuity.

In any event, S's emphasis serves apologetic ends insofar as he tries to convince the reader that poverty, if not the fault of the individual, is a permanent feature of any society, since there will always be a lowest 20 percent. This view corresponds to that enlightened modern position according to which "fault" is to be found in the mechanics of human society rather than in individual psyches. Thus in the first edition, before human capital qua education had become a fashionable concept and before it met empirical refutation, S focused on the eternal nature of the human division of labor:

This does not mean that everyone should aspire to or achieve a high-paid job at the top or that everyone ought to go on to take the highest college degree possible. Somebody must perform the humble tasks of hewing wood and drawing water [op. cit., p. 87].

Granted, so long as the performance of certain tasks demanded by some people of wealth are not automated they will be performed by human beings. But that one person should spend his life operating an elevator or cleaning somebody's toilet while another does nothing except "supervise" the micro or macro projects he owns can only be asserted by someone who believes in the static theory of comparative costs according to which bankers should bank and not clean their own toilets even if they can do a better job than the "natural" toilet cleaners.

Let us now look at S's empirical findings on income distribution. The method he follows is the logical outgrowth of his undifferentiated quantitative approach. Earlier we mentioned the failure of statistics to spell out the class distribution of income. Still these statistics are not without interest, for from them we can deduce which class is safely ensconced on top and which hovers at the bottom. S is primarily interested in the very poor at the lowest end of the distribution who through nine editions "have drawn a blank in life" (85). How have these unfortunates fared over the years?

One way of looking at S's empirical material on income distribution would involve the comparison of the data he himself has presented throughout the various editions to see whether they bear out his contention that "inequality is definitely less in America than it was back in 1929, but little different today from 1945" (86).

In the 1948 edition S gave the following figures for the years 1935-36:

Percent of people	0	10	25	50	75	100
Percent of income (op. cit., p. 66)	0	1.7	6.8	20.5	43.1	100

Unfortunately he does not reveal his source and so we cannot check on it. Since the population percentages here do not conform to the deciles or quintiles now published, we were able to find comparable figures only for the 10 and 50 percent categories. For 1966, we find that the corresponding income percentages are 1.2 and 21.4 respectively.[5] This would indicate that the poorest 10 percent of the population received an even smaller share of the national income thirty years after the Keynesian revolution, while the bottom half received a slightly higher share.[6] Taking another comparison, we can see the development of the percentage of the population "earning" a certain sum of money. Thus in the 7th edition (p. 109) the data for 1964 indicate that 11 percent of all families had an annual income of less than $2,000, and these families accounted for 2 percent of all income. By the 8th edition (p. 109), with figures for 1967, 13 percent of all families had incomes of less than $2,000, and they still accounted for a mere 2 percent of all income. Now these figures are not very meaningful for an overview of a number of years since with inflation the number of people below a certain income level will shrink regardless of real wages. Yet nonetheless the percentage in the lowest group, those with less than $2,000 per year, increased, and still accounted for the same total share of income, a clear indication of rising poverty.

Another way of presenting distribution statistics is to concentrate on the relative shares of equal percentages of the population. Since S admits that nothing much has changed since World War II, there is no need to go into this except to say that he does not seem to realize that this refutes the entire theory of the mixed economy as a "modern" institution, and it also refutes his views on the progressive attrition of concentrated wealth and power.

S's discussion of income distribution is ambiguous. Thus in the text he contends that inequality is "definitely less" today than in 1929 (85), but in the summary at the end of the chapter this is modified to "the modern distribution of American income appears to be less unequal than in 1929" (98). In a footnote he asserts that the past seventy-five years, have seen the refutation of Pareto's law on the universal and inevitable distribution of income along a constant pattern (86 n. 5). However, the "experts" are no longer quite so certain about that.[7]

S maintains that "within the affluent society the public war against poverty goes unceasingly on. As each rampart is slowly conquered, higher standards of performance must be by *society* for *itself*. The vicious circle by which poverty is environmentally inherited has to be broken if the antipoverty war is to claim victories" (98; our emphasis).

Apparently society is not at war with itself but with its environment. And what is that environment? According to bourgeois economics it is the structure of "market incomes" which by its own admission cannot be permanently changed, at least not without decreasing the size of the whole pie, but can only be continuously rearranged via taxation.

But the question of whether or not Pareto's "law" has a rational kernel remains. To begin with, is it really true that "society itself" is on the warpath? If pressed, S himself would probably agree that by and large those whose incomes are to be reduced in order to supplement those of others will not fight for income redistribution. But let us not jump to the conclusion that what we have in mind are the large capitalists, for it is by no means certain that it is they who will bear the burden of redistribution, or even that they nurse such fears. In fact, it is largely the middle-income brackets—workers and small capitalists—who are called upon to subsidize the working poor and the jobless.

Two aspects here must be kept apart. On the one hand, a political struggle is taking place, and within certain limits it is possible for the working class to increase its share of the national income either by direct attacks on profits through wage settlements or indirectly through taxation. Yet on the other hand, there are certain limits beyond which capital could not function profitably, and if this did not manifest itself immediately on the domestic scene it would rather quickly on the world market.

Thus there is "something to" Pareto's so-called law in

the sense that immanent laws of capital formation exist which class struggle override *within* capitalism. That is to say, although the political overthrow of capitalism is possible at some point, economic demands become incompatible with profitable production and will be resolved through political means—strikes, factory takeovers, the smashing of trade unions, the use of the army, civil war, etc.

V / INTERNATIONAL COMPARISONS OF INCOME DISTRIBUTION

S's treatment of income distribution in other societies is important for two reasons: first, because it underlines his sovereign disregard of the prerequisites for *any* scientific undertaking (in this instance, reference to statistical sources), and secondly, because it sheds light on his neglect of the essential differences between modes of production (precapitalist, capitalist, postcapitalist).

A / "UNDERDEVELOPED" COUNTRIES

To begin with, S claims that a Lorenz curve "will show greater inequality" for "a country like Ceylon" than for the U.S., U.K., and Holland (87). The only proof for this assertion is a graph (87) with no source given showing concentric curves for Sweden, the U.S., and Ceylon. We are not told how they were constructed in the absence of data on income distribution for Sweden and Ceylon.

We will attempt to supply the missing data (with sources), but before doing so we should point out that the social content of statistics differs in different societies. The income-distribution statistics on which the Lorenz curve is based are most widely used in the U.S.; most other capitalist countries do not use it. The Lorenz curve distribution is a very superficial category, dealing as it does with "statistical groupings" of the population without any class content. This emphasis on so-called personal as opposed to functional distribution (labor versus capital) is characteristic of a society in which conscious class struggle has not played the same role as in Western Europe.

To get back to Ceylon: S presumably chose it because some years ago, in a debate on income distribution, bourgeois economists used Ceylon as an example of an "underdeveloped" country.[8] The graph reproduced here[9] shows two combined income-distribution Lorenz curves, one for the U.S. and U.K. and one for Ceylon and India. It is of interest here that the curves are not concentric; at some point they intersect. This in concrete term means that the poorest 30 percent or so of the Ceylonese population receives a larger share of the income than the correspond-

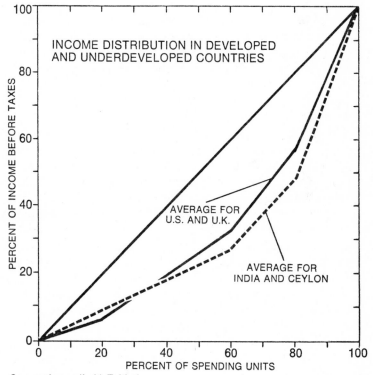

INCOME DISTRIBUTION IN DEVELOPED AND UNDERDEVELOPED COUNTRIES

AVERAGE FOR U.S. AND U.K.

AVERAGE FOR INDIA AND CEYLON

PERCENT OF INCOME BEFORE TAXES

PERCENT OF SPENDING UNITS

Source: Appendix 14, Table 1.

ing 30 percent in the United States. Without attaching too much important to these figures we nonetheless believe that the *relative* position of the poorest and most exploited classes takes on significance in any political-economic study of a class society.

B / SOCIALIST COUNTRIES

Bringing his analytical powers to bear upon the issue of income distribution in socialist societies, S denies their comparability with capitalist countries: "No one knows how to compare the inequality in the Soviet Union with that in mixed economies" (86). The reason for this assertion remains unclear until we note the qualitative incommensurability mentioned by S in the 1st edition—namely that "the inequalities and dispersions" of the wage structure in the Soviet Union "were not accompanied by further inequality resulting from unequal property incomes" (pp. 81 f.). This being so, any comparison of the distribution of wage income alone becomes invalid, since wage income in capitalist countries is distributed more equally than is total or capital income.

S, again without giving his source, claims that a 1965 study showed employment incomes to be more equally distributed in Australia and Sweden than in Poland (86 n.6). But this comparison is not very meaningful since even S's own data puts Poland into the category of "intermediate" development, and Australia and Sweden are "highly developed" (767). If, instead, we consider two "highly developed" countries both historically and socially more comparable than Australia and Poland—i.e., the Federal Republic of Germany and the German Democratic Republic—we find that even on the basis of the factor most favorable to capitalism, namely the distribution of wages and salaries, income distribution in the socialist country is considerably more equal. The following table and Lorenz curves (based on official West German sources) show the distribution of after-tax net income accruing to statistical groupings of wage and salary recipients in 1967 (the curves also show the development from 1960 to 1967):

Households		Federal Republic	GDR
poorest	20%	8.7%	10.5%
next	20%	13.0%	15.8%
next	20%	17.1%	19.7%
next	20%	23.0%	23.6%
richest	20%	38.2%	30.4%
		100.0%	100.0%[10]

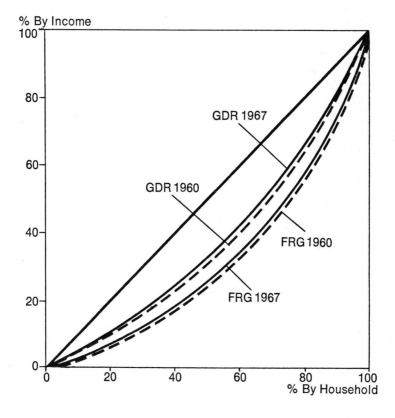

The greater equality in the GDR can be seen especially in the higher shares of the "poorest" groups and the lower shares of the "richest."

C / "MIXED ECONOMIES"

S singles out Israel and Sweden as mixed economies with low inequality of income. Let us therefore look at some of the available statistical data (which S once again has failed to provide). Israel's pattern of income distribution in the past two decades resembles that of the U.S. Thus between 1950-51 and 1968-69, the share of the "lowest" 20 percent of the population declined from 12.4 to 4.7 percent, while that of the "highest" 20 percent rose from 31 to 42.7 percent.[11]

With respect to the other of these two "welfare states" (804), we find that according to U.N. statistics Sweden does not head the list of West European capitalist countries. The following table shows the Gini coefficient for selected West European countries in the 1960s:

Norway	.36
Denmark	.39
UK	.40
Sweden	.40
Netherlands	.44
Finland	.47
W. Germany	.47
France	.62[12]

Thus we can see that not only is Sweden out-"equaled" by Denmark and Norway, but that it rests on an even level with the U.K. with its "peers and tycoons" who "own tremendous concentrations of land and other property" (87 f.).

S attaches great importance to the alleged redistributional effects of Swedish "socialism" (872), but there, as in most other countries, it is not the very rich who bear the greatest burden with respect to the income that does get redistributed. Rather, it is the average-income groups who defray the cost of distribution,[14] a development strengthened by the imposition of a value-added tax in 1969 (in fact, a continuation in another form of the former general sales tax), which accounts for 19 percent of national tax revenues. It is not our intention to deny the obvious advances made by

the Swedish working class in comparison to the U.S.
worker, but rather to document S's uncritical approach.

VI / "HUMAN CAPITAL":
SLAVES AND WAGE SLAVES

The failure of human-capital theory to take into account the
relations specific to certain classes and societies is made
painfully obvious by S when he states that "modern
economists have analyzed the problem of putting capital
into people through education and training, in much the
same way that one puts money capital into plant or equipment" (807). Who is "one"? A capitalist could put capital
into people the same way he "puts" it into machines only
if he owned slaves, which of course would make him a
slave owner rather than a capitalist. A wage worker in
capitalist society does own his labor power and thus could
conceivably be seen as "investing" in himself when he
spends money to refurbish it. Unfortunately, however, he
does not control the exercise of that labor power—its translation into labor—and thus he does not gain control over
the value he produces above and beyond the "compensation" of the costs that go to make up his labor power. For
him, then, "investment" in his education is merely an
example of equivalent exchange within the sphere of circulation.[15]

A / SLAVERY
In his very first paragraph on the slave trade S reveals his
ahistoricity: "We do know how the profit motive led to the
slave trade: pursuing maximum profit—equating maximum
revenues and costs, so to speak—merchants used bribery
and force to abduct Africans in order to export and sell
them in the New World" (788). Apparently the profit motive and marginal analysis—"so to speak"—are valid also
for societies in which plunder and robbery prevail, where
"the market society" does not even exist. Presumably the

same psychological "laws" governing consumption and investment "propensities" that Keynes "discovered" are also valid for pirates.

Equally enlightening is a passage that apparently is meant to be critical of the working conditions in capitalist wage-slavery: "So long as a plentiful supply of replacement imports could be counted on, each slave was regarded as an exhaustive resource: just as a vein of copper can be worked to depletion, a slave could be worked to death without regard for natural reproduction or old-age incapacity" (788).

S does not specify which New World societies he has in mind (South America, Caribbean, U.S., etc.) nor the era, and therefore it is difficult to be specific in answering him, yet one would think that U.S. slaveholders, for instance, would have had some interest in treating their slaves as well as they did their tools (to the extent that they were under some competitive pressure on the world cotton market): He does not tell us how that treatment differs from that of "free" workers for the simple reason that S does not touch upon that area of capitalist life. After his ahistorical review of the development of slavery, S treats us to a masterpiece of childish nonsense: "When conscience led to legal abolition of slave importation, around 1800, the economics rapidly adjusted" (788). Does he really think that anyone still believes that the struggle between the ruling classes of the North and the South was a matter of conscience? Wouldn't it seem more appropriate to look for the reason in the expansionist needs of two systems in a limited

At this juncture S turns to a subject that allows him to unfold his special brand of scientific method. Contemptuously critical of (nameless) historians who ignorantly propagate the "myth" that antebellum slavery was becoming unprofitable and would have "collapsed under its own weight" even had there been no Civil War, S mentions two men who allegedly "convincingly utilized econometric analysis to show how unfounded this idea was" (789). The work referred to by him is probably *The Economics of Slavery in the Antebellum South*.[16] The two issues at stake are profitability and vitality, in other words, whether or not slavery would and could have survived. Whether or not slavery was profitable in the accounting sense (that is, whether revenues exceeded outlay) is still a matter of controversy. Even on this level the evidence is by no means as convincing as S would have us believe. Many authors have argued that slavery was a moribund mode of production despite its profitability. But in order to understand this paradox, one must first see slavery as a mode of production; S lacks this insight. Thus he wonders how "anyone but an economic illiterate" could believe in the economic decline of slavery at a time when labor productivity was increasing (789). Neither S nor his authorities seem to understand that by its very nature slavery stood opposed to and resisted the sort of "productivity increases" characteristic of capitalism: namely, the increase of the amount of means of production (constant capital) a worker could operate (or rather, in capitalism, be operated by). Slaves worked poorly and could be made to work "well" only under prohibitively expensive supervision. Unable to handle tools properly, they were given the crudest possible implements, which in turn lowered their productivity. Not only did they work below capacity, their capacity itself was below the level they might possibly have attained under different conditions. Their nutrition was poor, not necessarily because their owners were trying to starve them but because the slave system itself ruled out essential crop diversification.

In their desire to use universally valid concepts like the profit motive, marginal productivity, etc., authors like S and his authorities seem to forget that slavery was not subject to the same laws of motion as is capitalist production. Thus to the extent that the world cotton market did exert competitive pressure on the slave-owning producers, their mode of production placed severe restrictions on their ability to respond. For instance, increased production demanded more slaves and more land, yet the amount of available land was limited, as was the number of slaves who could be properly supervised without undue cost. Consequently, although the slaveowners did definitely "accumulate," they did not do so in typical capitalist fashion, i.e., by increasing the organic composition of their productive "inputs" (or, for that matter, the technical composition).

If a slaveowner did accumulate in the characteristic capitalist manner, certain contradictory processes developed which S and others seem to be unaware of. S contends that with the depletion of the soil in the upper South, and the higher marginal productivity of land in the lower South, the "Invisible Hand of competition" brought about a specialization of slave production in the former and slave labor in the latter (788 f.). This is demonstrably false. Virginia and Maryland (upper South) saw an antebellum movement toward "reform" or diversification which presupposed the better utilization of means of production to make the slaves more productive; this in turn would have obviated the necessity for more slaves. The production and export of slaves to the lower South seemed to solve a dual problem: it financed the purchase of needed means of production and got rid of surplus slaves.

However, all this was contingent on slaves being purchased in the lower South. But by the 1850s the same pressures that had brought on the "reform" in the upper South began to make themselves felt there.

The point here is that once the slaveowners were beginning to accumulate, slavery was already on the way out: the increased productivity made the old system irrational in comparison with Northern competition.

This does not mean to say that all slaveowners wanted to become industrial capitalists. On the contrary: this stood in direct contradiction to their whole mode of production. It is of course possible that the slaveowners would have been willing to carry on even if they "earned" less than the prevailing rate of interest. But if they wanted to compete with the Northern capitalists they would have to accept certain processes that spelled the demise of slavery. The fact that the slaveowners as the protagonists of a dying order put up a fight does not mean that slavery was a thriving mode of production.

B / "HUMAN CAPITAL"

In order to understand the alleged connection between education and income, we must examine the thesis underlying the notion of "human capital," according to which the *cost* of education is a value-creating factor (quasi independent of the total process of capital accumulation). The commercial advantages of education were extolled at a time when the U.S. economy demanded more literate workers in a variety of positions. The basic error of S's presentation lies in his failure to see the connection between capitalism's need for a certain degree of literacy and the subjective desire of people to go to school and improve their earning potential. As Galbraith put it quite succinctly: "Had the economic system need only for millions of unlettered proletarians, these, very plausibly, are what would be provided."[17]

S's enthusiastic endorsement of education qua socialism grows out of his inability to understand either the origin or development of the phenomenon he is describing. The concept of the "meritocracy" or social mobility he speaks of (807) refers to one of the mechanisms of capitalist society to find the best minds, as it were, of the exploited class and channel them into jobs that seem less baldly exploitative. It is by no means coincidental that the first flood of studies correlating income rewards of education appeared at approximately the same time that this mechanism was being introduced:

> Educators and social reformers at the turn of the century were not insensible to the accumulation of a large, heavily immigrant industrial proletariat in the cities; they feared the prospect of class warfare, and found in educational opportunity a ready formula for the remedy. The academic meritocracy was thought to promise a remedy for poverty and inequality. Schools would provide a mechanism whereby those who were qualified could rise on the basis of merit.[18]

Aside from all the factors blocking the realization of such an equalizer, it should be borne in mind that even if the program were to succeed, it would inevitably lead to an intensification of the relative educational impoverishment of the non-"elite." S voices a common view when he says "There has long been social mobility in America: all the cream rose to the top some time ago, leaving naturally less-gifted people at the bottom" (93). "Society" obviously has not compensated for the gifts nature failed to bestow; that is to say, although a larger share of the population have completed four years of college than in the past, this education has not been "wasted" on so-called blue-collar workers. Thus, while in the 25-29 year age group the percentage of those attending four or more years of college rose from 5.6 in 1947 to 16.9 in 1971, the average factory worker had completed or almost completed high school, as compared to junior high school in the immediate post-World War II period: the median years of school completed by "operatives" rose from 9.1 in 1948 to 11.4 in 1971; for nonfarm laborers and foremen, 7.8 and 8.8 respectively.[19]

"This country," according to the *Manpower Report of the President* of March, 1972, "has a heavy investment in the education of its professional workers, and any underutilization of their talents and training represents a national loss." It is interesting that the Federal Government should be the one to issue this warning, for the "burden" of the "investment" did not originally fall on the individual capitals. That is to say, the large expansion in college and graduate education took place mainly in public institutions and was therefore financed by "general" taxation. And although corporations obviously have to pay higher salaries to those with superior training, this obligation ceases once they fire these people: the amortization of "human capital" becomes the problem of the individual and/or state in the form of unemployment "benefits," and some may begin to wonder whether all that education was worthwhile. The capitalist class is not, of course, totally uninterested in the problem, for if "every instance of joblessness or underutilization of doctoral training . . . represents the waste of a social investment which has been estimated at about $50,000 per individual with the Ph.D.,"[20] then this in part means a loss of surplus value. But perhaps more importantly, especially for those individual capitals and branches which have become increasingly dependent on more highly trained scientific workers, a two-fold political-economic "problem" arises. The "recession" that began in 1969 marked the first deep penetration of the industrial cycle into the hitherto relatively protected sphere of nonproduction workers. As thousands of college graduates are beginning to find out, human capital is at a slight disadvantage vis-à-vis the ordinary run-of-the-mill capital: it cannot be divorced from the "human" and banked to "grow interest" when the "human" is "idle"; in other words, unemployed human capital gathers no interest. S's foresight was no better than that of many of his colleagues when he uncritically praised public education as a "socialism" that subverts privilege (807). A recent feature article in *Business Week* puts an end to this myth:

> Ironically, the supply-demand gap has opened just when the nation has come to embrace the idea that everyone is entitled to a degree: rich or poor, black or white, male or female, clever or dull. Now, most educators and economists, as well as corporate executives concerned with the problem, agree that this premise will have to be rethought. . . .
> Yet the balancing of jobs and job candidates may be more than any government can bring off. So there may be a rude awakening from the Great American Dream: that thanks to education, successive generations will advance from blue-collar to white-collar to executive pin-stripe.[21]

Business Week sees the origin of this change in the end of the "explosive growth" of the 1950s and 1960s. "Ironically," it finds the only hope in the reality of Marx's concept of abstract labor, for although theoretically bourgeois economists deny the existence of that phenomenon in practice they are confronted with it daily. Thus later on in his chapter on wages S asserts that "There is no single factor of production called labor; there are thousands of quite different kinds of labor" (581). But as Marx explained, in capitalist society a given portion of human labor is shifted from one branch of production to another in accordance with the changing direction of demand for labor. The demand for nonproduction jobs fell off, and students got the message in the form of news reports, fewer visits from corporation recruiters, fewer job openings, etc., and so they turned to driving cabs, planting marijuana, etc. However, this market savvy is not appreciated by the powers that be:

> The welfare of the Nation, the quality of its life, and its protection within and without rest more heavily on the relatively small numbers of professional personnel than on any other occupational grouping. . . . Freshmen enrollments in engineering, for example, dropped sharply between 1970 and 1971. If the shift away from engineering education should continue—under the influence of the current job-market situation—the numbers of new graduates entering the profession could fall below those required to meet expected long-run needs for engineers, thus hampering future efforts to solve the country's urgent problems and speed economic growth. [22]

The government reports calls the fact that people are leaving a field which may expand in the future an "anomalous" situation. But there is nothing anomalous about it. As a matter of fact, it is not a departure from the normal workings of capitalism but a return, or rather an introduction, to it after an atypical period. Nor can the reason for the great to-do that is being made lie in the crucial dependence of U.S. capitalism on these workers, for it holds equally true for manufacturing workers, soldiers, etc.

This brings us to the second aspect of the "problem," part of which has to do with the fact that these people have undergone comparatively long training and therefore represent a proportionately larger share of total social variable capital (i.e., that part of the total value of labor power of the whole working class paid for not by the individual capitalist but by "society" in the form of taxation) than do other "occupational groupings." The other side of this relates to the time needed to train such laborers. Since it takes longer to train a highly specialized worker like a nuclear physicist than an assembly-line operator, there is need for a certain level of "labor market" stability or predictability for these jobs to allow aggregate planning over a period of years.

With respect to "ordinary" production workers, this need has not been nearly so pronounced in the U.S. because of the vast reserve army of unemployed "eager" to lend a helping hand to spur "recovery." Although it is impossible to train highly skilled workers in a short time, it is theoretically possible to allow a reserve army of them to accumulate who could then be "encouraged" to re-emerge at a moment's notice.

Business Week, commenting on the prospect of a surplus 1.5 million college graduates by 1980, agonizes:

> It is hard to guess what sort of impact on society that would have—hard to measure the psychic damage to a generation that grew up amid the dislocation of the most controversial war in history and then was cast into a job market that could not use all its abilities.[23]

Such considerations lead to conjuring up the horrible image of an academic proletariat on the rampage:

> Unemployed scholars, either because they consider nonuniversity work beneath them or because they could not adapt to it, might turn into an alienated intellectual proletariat, ready to turn in anger on the society that does not use them in the style they have come to expect.[24]

4 The Capitalist Firm
S's Chapter 6

This chapter offers S's idea-type, fairy-tale version of the rise of monopoly-capitalist corporations. He takes us through a trinitarian development: from single proprietorship to partnership to corporation. And although he admits that "one should not infer that all corporations go through three stages" (111), still he insists on offering this fiction as "an extensive case study" (100). It is his contention that "we gain insight into the principal forms of business organization . . . by following the history of a particular business venture as it grows from a small beginning into a good-sized corporation" (101).

Now even if there were some merit in studying business organization before economic structure (and there is not), an ideal type can be set up only if it synthesizes the essential aspects of a phenomenon. However, S's glamorized version bears no relation to reality. Furthermore, it seems senseless to describe the formal, legal structure of economic units before analyzing their content. Why go into detail about stock issues before we know what profit is or where it comes from?

It is significant that S, who tends toward a radical positivist approach to existing capitalist reality, leaving history to others, here finds it necessary to go into the seemingly historical derivation of modern monopoly capital. As we shall find out, this pseudo-historical description serves to conceal the actual historical process and ultimately serves to legitimate the existence of monopoly capital.

The analyses of the "single proprietorship" and "partnership" in particular are essentially meaningless: "At the end of the month whatever is left over as profits—after all costs have been met[!] is yours to do with as you like" (102). But what is profit? And what is cost? He leaves his reader to work with whatever misinformation he has picked up here and there, and since it all sounds somehow familiar, the reader will go along with S's story. The transition to "partnership" is the result mainly of greed: you want to make more money because "the business is prospering tremendously . . . but you find yourself harder pressed for cash than ever before" (102). Why? Because you are not *paid in advance* for your sales, whereas you must pay your workers and suppliers promptly on receipt of their services (102). Really! The worker's "services" are the use of his labor power. One might get the impression that a worker, after being hired on Monday and signing a contract offering his "services," gets paid for the week he has *not* yet worked, while the poor capitalist whom nobody pays in advance has to lay out the wages. But in reality it is the worker who "lays out" his labor power for the week, trusting that he will not starve or be evicted from his home in the interim.

S also introduces other difficulties for this "single proprietor" having to do with credit and interest; these relations have even less meaning at this point than does profit. And so it goes with the partnership as well: it, too, in some mysterious way keeps making profits and outrunning its supply of capital (?), thus necessitating a new form of ownership. The main difference here is that S insists that the "drawbacks" of the legal forms ("unlimited liability," etc.) bring about fundamental economic changes (105 f.), whereas most realistic people assume that legal forms evolve in response to economic change.

In any event, "we" decide to incorporate. At this point, in an effort to lend some historical validity to all this nonsense, S explains how in days gone by the sovereign conferred the privilege of corporation charters, but that "within the past century, this procedure began to seem unfair [?!]"

and so now almost anybody can form a corporation (106). S obviously does not see that these early monopolies may possibly have been connected with the rise of capitalism, with the need to protect a nascent system against competition, to support merchant capital, and that once capitalism became self-supporting it no longer had need for such props.

On closer examination it becomes obvious that S has not given us a historical view (in all fairness he has never claimed to have done so but merely gives that impression) but rather a description of three types of "business" structure that happen to exist side by side. In point of fact, it is a rare capitalist monopoly that would develop along these lines; by setting up the hypothesis of such a triadic development, however, S implies that this course is the standard; yet very few "single proprietorships" make the jump to "partnerships," just as very few partnerships make it to corporations.

As for the corporations themselves, their origins are a good deal different from the pastoral scene painted by S. A truly historical analysis of the rise of capitalism would have to deal with "so-called original accumulation"—i.e., the historical process of the brutal, extra-economic expropriation of the land and tools of the European peasants and artisans (and in the U.S., of the Indians, small farms, slavery, etc.); it would have to deal with the immanent problems of capital accumulation, the increased exploitation of relative and absolute surplus value, and above all with the class struggles growing out of this enormous exploitation. According to S, the only problems involved in acquiring capital are technical ones which easily can be resolved by technical and/or legal means. The working class, through whose labor and over whose broken bodies the "giant corporation" made it into the "honor roll of American business" (111), is not mentioned even once. S is held spellbound by the magic powers of capital, by its ability to "grow" all on its own.

Marx's analysis of the development of corporations follows a very different course. In Chapter 27 of the third volume of *Capital* he derives them from the role of credit in capitalism. The existence of money as means of payment made for the abstract possibility of credit (thereby establishing a creditor-debtor relationship), a possibility that became more concrete through the release of money capital, the result of the different time intervals between the labor and circulation periods within the turnover of capital. Credit thus becomes necessary to mediate the equalization of the rate of profit; simultaneously it makes possible a vast expansion of the scale of production that individual capitals cannot match. At the same time the rise of corporations symbolizes the transformation of the functioning capitalist into a mere director, an administrator of other people's capital, and that of the owner-capitalist into a money-capitalist. Thus what Berle and Means[1] et al. were thought to have discovered—namely the separation of ownership and management—had been analyzed by Marx three-quarters of a century earlier. But Marx, more analytical, did not restrict himself to the enumeration of surface phenomena; he pointed out that this process represented the final step in exploitation, for at this point the right to parasitic income (i.e., dividends) ceases to be contingent on any productive activity but turns into the naked appropriation of surplus labor.

The contradictory nature of the corporation finds expression in the renewed state intervention and the creation of a new parasitic financial aristocracy brought on by the rise of monopolies, as well as in the unprecedented overproduction made possible by the availability of other people's capital. S, on the other hand, merely spells out the "advantages and disadvantages of the corporate form": "The corporation has solved most of the problems that bothered [!] you about the partnership. It is an almost perfect device for the raising of large sums of capital" (108).

In his description of the process of incorporation S sees it as a purely legal formality and/or arbitrary procedure. "You" (the use of the personal pronoun is designed to turn the reader into the self-interested capitalist) merely decide how much capital you want, how many shares, at what price, etc., and the investment bank does the rest, whereby the latter's profit, "as with any merchant," "comes from the difference between their [the securities'] buying and selling prices." If you had been powerful, you could have "held out" for more from the bank, thus cutting its profit margin (107). All the figures seem to be arbitrary. Marx, however, explained that with the rise of corporations capital appeared to double; that is, the capital paid in by the shareholders becomes industrial capital, whereas the shares themselves continue to circulate at a given price; the money needed to circulate these shares has nothing to do with the capital of the corporation, just as the price of the share is not part of the corporate capital. The share is not a title to the capital of the corporation but a revenue title, a title to a part of the profit. Its price depends on the profit made by the corporation and on the prevailing interest rate. The yield is capitalized, and this determines the price of the share. The yield thus appears as a second capital, but that is merely fictitious. Thus the sum of the "share capital"— i.e., the sum of the price of the titles to the capitalized yields—may diverge from the sum of the capital originally transformed from money into industrial capital. For example, a business capitalized at $1 million decides to "go public"; its rate of profit is 15 percent and the prevailing interest rate is 5 percent; its profit is $150,000. The yield, $150,000, is capitalized as an annual revenue at 5 percent interest; this means that at 5 percent interest it would take $3 million to get a "yield" of $150,000. On that basis the corporation can sell shares totaling $3 million because it is sufficiently profitable to offer investors 5 percent on their money. The Marxist economist Rudolf Hilferding called the difference between the $1 million and $3 million *Gründungsgewinn* (founding profit), derived from the transformation of profit-"bearing" capital into interest-"bearing" capital.

S for his part sees this as the usual merchant's profit (selling price minus purchase price) and the haggling over the difference as a mere technicality. Hilferding sees a conflict among fellow capitalists:

> The stronger the power of the banks, the more fully will it succeed in reducing the dividends to interest, the more fully will the promoter's profit accrue to the bank. Inversely, strong and stable enterprises will succeed, when increasing its capital, in

securing for the enterprise itself a part of the promoter's profit. There ensues a sort of struggle for the distribution of the promoter's profit between the corporation and the bank.[2]

S's reply to all this is that "you need not concern yourself with the people to whom he [the investment banker] has sold the shares or with the fact that they may resell their shares. The names of the owners of the shares are registered. . ." (107). He then launches into a paean to corporate democracy, and here we finally discover where dollar-vote democracy resides, for here we have one dollar, one vote. After trying to persuade us that the capitalists are actually trying to maintain real democracy, S comes to the infamous problem of capitalism: the divorce of ownership and and control. First we are told the story of "people's capitalism" (though S does not want to associate himself too closely with it), and then we are given to understand that management owns only 3 percent of the common stock. (Of course, we are not told that about 150 of the country's 500 biggest industrial corporations are owned or controlled by a single individual or family.)

The purpose of this whole account is to convince the reader that managers are less profit-motivated than owners, and that consequently we will have a capitalism with a growing concern for the interests of the people.

On the one hand, so the story goes, ownership is dispersed and therefore separated from control (but S admits that a 20 percent minority ownership is sufficient to maintain working control [113]), and then in a footnote (113 n. 10) S shows how through pyramiding, this working control can lead to control over billions of dollars. Never mind that the one assertion contradicts the other. The phenomenon that is really being described is how small sums of money (even small savings) can be mobilized and centralized—not by the autonomous managers but by the monopoly capitalists themselves, who by gaining minority control are not only able to exploit labor but even do so with the worker's own money (as well as with that of other capitalists).

S admits that "generally speaking, there will be no clash

of goals between the management and the stockholders. Both will be interested in maximizing the profits of the firm" (114), yet he still attributes autonomy to management insofar as it seeks to make the organization "grow and perpetuate itself" (115); also, whereas the old-time capitalist had a "public-be-damned" attitude, the new managers are more "adept" at "handling of people" (114). But as C. Wright Mills has pointed out:

> . . . the top man in the bureaucracy *is* a powerful member of the propertied class. He derives his right to act from the institution of property; he does act in so far as he possibly can in a manner he believes is to the interests of the private-property system; he does feel in unity, politically and status-wise as well as economically, with his class and its source of wealth. . . . They are managers *of* private properties, and if private property were "abolished," their power, if any, would rest upon some other basis, and they would have to look to other sources of authority.[3]

In sum, the big capitalists do not have to beat the managers into submission: "External authority is not necessary when the agent has internalized it."[4] With respect to the quantitative growth of monopolies, S states that "recent economic research shows the falsity of the widespread view that the giants are gulping up more and more of modern industry. Statistics suggest that, relatively, the giants have probably lost a little ground since 70 years ago" (7th ed., p. 88; similarly in the 9th ed. [112]). The only possible sense in this statement is that if 100 corporations increased their control over industry from 10 percent to 50 percent by 1920, then even if they had gained 100 percent control by 1970, their relative increase would have dropped from 400 percent to 100 percent.

The following table shows the development of the percentage of value added by the largest U.S. manufacturing corporations from 1947 to 1966:

No. Largest Corps.	1947	1958	1966
50	17%	23%	25%
100	23%	30%	33%
200	30%	38%	42%[5]

Thus we see that in 1966, for instance, the 100 largest manufacturing corporations had attained greater specific weight in this area than the largest 200 twenty years earlier. Moreover, since many of these corporations are controlled by the same finance-capital groups (Rockefeller, Morgan, etc.), the degree of concentration is in fact much greater than these figures indicate.

S's discussion of monopoly is similarly superficial:

> In view of all the above facts, it is not suprising to find the most important American industries are characterized by a few large corporations whose share of the output of that particular industry is vastly greater than their numerical importance would warrant [?!; 116].

This is either wrong or tautological. S has not bothered to explain how monopolies came into being; he has merely categorized them as "corporations" and informed us that "their power did not grow overnight"; "Large size breeds success and success breeds further success" (112). He is being tautological in that he adduces statistics indicating concentration, but without any explanation. In fact he considers explanations irrelevant: "From an economic point of view it does not much [?!] matter which of the following monopolistic devices cause price to be too high. . ." (116), and then he runs through mergers, cartels, etc. He fails to distinguish between concentration of capital as a result of accumulation (as a matter of fact, he does not discuss accumulation at all here) and the centralization of capital, i.e., the concentration of scattered capitals in one hand, the expropriation of one capitalist by another.

In his documentation of the "worst" aspect of monopoly pricing, S manages to come up with the example of "too many barbers standing around, doing too little—and because of the entry of other imperfectly competitive barbers, the consumer may pay too high a price *without* the monopolist barbers' ending up making any more money than they would under perfect competition!" (8th ed., p. 92.) As if this were a typical problem confronting giant corporations, and as if the corporate bosses sat around all day "under-utilized." S's description of monopoly as of all other phenonema is limited to the sphere of circulation without touching upon production.

APPENDIX / ELEMENTS OF ACCOUNTING

A / PROFIT

It is S's contention that "without some comprehension of accounting, there can be no deep understanding of the economics of the enterprise" (100). Let us see how his accounting explains profit—certainly the proof of the pudding for any enterprise. First we are introduced to the "fundamental identity of the Income Statement": "Total Profit=Total Revenue minus Total Costs" (122). On methodological grounds such an equation is impermissible since profit, revenue, or cost have never been defined. In fact, earlier in the chapter he stated that a merchant's profit stemmed from the difference between purchase and selling price (104). This would seem to imply that there exists another type of profit (industrial?) based on some other factors, but we are never told what that might be. In this section he goes back to merchant's profit, elevating it to the rank of the sole type of profit and thereby establishing a permanent niche for it in the "fundamental identity."

How does capitalist commodity production itself result in such theoretical inversions of reality? In the first chapter of the third volume of *Capital*, Marx supplies the key to this with his introduction of the cost-price category: cost-price, he said, equals c plus v, that is, that part of the commodity value which replaces the price of the means of production and the price of labor power; therefore it replaces what the commodity "cost" the capitalist. However, "What the commodity costs the capitalist and what the production of the commodity itself costs, are to be sure two very different magnitudes,"[6] and that because the surplus value created by the worker "costs" the capitalist nothing. Thus the specifically capitalist cost of a commodity is measured by the expenditure of capital, whereas its real cost is measured by the expenditure of labor.

But, Marx adds, this cost-price category is not confined to capitalist bookkeeping: the autonomization of this part of value is real in the production process itself inasmuch as it must be transformed from its value form through the circulation process back into the form of productive capital (means of production and labor). On the other hand, this cost-price has no bearing on the formation of value or the self-expansion of capital. The point here is that it subsumes two heterogeneous elements—constant capital and variable capital—under one rubric. The value of the constant capital is merely transferred to the new commodity and is preserved; the value of the variable capital, on the other hand, does not enter into the creation of new value, for in the process of production, living labor, the *creator* of new value, takes the place of labor power as value. The value of labor power merely determines how much of the total newly created value goes to the worker. By combining two functionally heterogeneous elements, cost-price eradicates the distinction between constant and variable capital, thus hiding the origin of surplus value: the profit appears to stem from the total outlay of capital (hence the talk about the productivity of capital).

It is these superficial aspects which capitalist bookkeeping perpetuates. What is interesting here is that S, before even theoretically developing the economic relations represented by mathematical formulas, foists contentless mathematics on the student. Having thus buttressed his unscientific method with pseudo-scientific mathematics, he has prepared the student to accept all kinds of nonsense about the productivity of capital and the origins of profit.

B / DEPRECIATION

It is a revelation to see how S manages to inject a heavy dose of apologetics into a seemingly neutral appendix on accounting, i.e., how he seeks to pass off the rapid early depreciation system as one in which "mistakes . . . will ultimately 'come out in the wash' anyway": "Suppose that the truck lasts 15 years rather than the predicted 10. We have then been overstating our depreciation expenses during the first 10 years. But in the eleventh and later years there will be *no* depreciation charged. . . . After 15 years, everything is pretty much the same. . . . That is, except for taxes" (124). He then launches into a discussion about how capitalists like this method because they fear taxes and "hope" that later on corporate tax rates will decrease when the profits are overstated by comparison with the earlier years, when the abnormally high write-offs reduced stated profits.

Here S falls victim to the very same "fallacy of composition" he is forever warning others about (e.g., 14); what is true for the part is not necessarily true for the whole. His assertions are true only with respect to an isolated object of fixed capital: if too much is written off at the beginning, correspondingly less can be written off later. Since it is the function of amortization to insure the simple reproduction of the fixed capital, write-offs that exceed the objective measure of real depreciation encompass a part of the profit accumulation, its transformation into additional capital—investment. This also becomes clear when we look at the entire reproduction process of the fixed capital of a corporation, its total amortization fund, rather than at an isolated machine.

Now if the amortization fund is increased at the expense of profits—that is, if profits are used to expand the business—then the write-offs not only cannot decrease but must increase; this results in a spiral, since additional profit leads to bigger write-offs, ad infinitum.

There are two important aspects to this phenomenon.[7] First, since World War II, increasing concentration and centralization of capital have intensified competition among the dominant monopoly capitals, an intensification demanding increasingly larger investments, which in turn depend on ever higher profits. At the same time the increasing concentration of capital impedes capital flow from one investment sphere to another. Thus self-financing, i.e., internal accumulation, is essential if the competitive edge is to be maintained. This is where abnormally high write-offs, facilitated by the development of monopoly prices and profits, come in. The more powerful monopolies are able to siphon off (i.e., redistribute) the surplus value of the smaller capitals by raising their prices while forcing the others down proportionally. Under these conditions the monopolists can continue to gain higher profits through higher write-offs and, consequently, stimulate internal accumulation.

The other side of the coin is taxes. Since profits (i.e., that portion concealed in higher write-offs) go untaxed, and since the capitalist state needs a good deal of money to tend to the national and international "business" of the ruling class, additional taxes must be levied against—guess whom?

5 The Working Class and Trade Unions
S's Chapter 7
(A draft of this chapter was written by Clay Newlin, Philadelphia.)

This chapter is devoted to the second of the "chief institutions of an economy" (100). S does not explain what he means by "institution," but it is clear from his juxtaposition of (Big) "business, labor and government" that he has in mind here "labor" as a *political* force; in the popular mind it stands opposed to "business," and both are regulated by "government." It would appear that on the basis of this symmetry, "labor" would be accorded the same formal treatment as is "business" in Chapter 6. However, as we shall see, there are significant differences.

"Business" is treated in a businesslike manner, that is to say, it is viewed primarily in its economic functions, and, more specifically, in the nonsocial function of production in general. Leaving aside such "aberrant" manifestations as monopolies, etc., "business" as a synonym for production becomes a higher category to which "labor" can then be subordinated (as in fact it is to capital). Seen in this fashion it becomes easy to hold "business" innocent of pursuing direct political goals, for although individual businesses may try to transform specific interests into political advantages, "business" as a whole, if equated with the "economy," cannot be accused of political motives.

Not so "labor." From the very start it is seen as a political foreign body in the "economy." (Interestingly enough, this chapter in the first edition was entitled "Labor Organization and Problems"; "business" in this sense poses no "problems.") This political aspect can assume a variety of forms, the most blatant of course being a labor movement dedicated to the eradication of the distinction between "business" and "labor"—namely, a movement of producers to win control over social production. This would also mean the end of "business" in the bourgeois sense of "rational economizing." Secondly, labor may seek to win special concessions at the expense of "business." And finally, where an economic content is imputed to the demands of labor, it is usually outside the context of normally functioning "business"—chiefly as the response to "abuses" that can be corrected.

S seems to view labor unions as a necessary political evil so long as they keep their place, a realistic approach insofar as the economic structure is after all characterized by political relations. Implicit in this is the admission that heterogeneous interests do in fact exist. On the other hand, the emphasis on, or rather the view of, organized labor as a political force ignores the real economic roots of labor unions in the capitalist mode of production. By drawing a dividing line between the political and the economic, they can be made into a relatively superficial phenomenon. Since economists like S are aware of the "danger" inherent in labor unions, or rather in "labor" dedicated to to the overthrow of capitalism, it is fair to say that these theoretical exponents of capitalism are ideologically motivated in their denial of the immanent economic base of unions. The antilabor bias of the "labor" theories of bourgeois economics is a logical product of its general position. In this respect economic theory is a fair representation of capitalist reality, for it reproduces the real or objective antilabor "bias" of capitalism. In sum, then, this chapter is a particuarly good example of the politics of bourgeois economics because it not only points to the very clear " 'value judgments' " (8) which it disclaims, but also because it shows that this lack of "value freedom" is not a subjective human failing but is grounded in the capitalist mode of production itself.

Let us begin our analysis with an examination of the economic content and origin of labor unions, after which we will look briefly at the historical development of unions and their function, and finally at the political role of unions with reference to the state.

I / THE ECONOMIC CONTENT AND ORIGIN OF LABOR UNIONS

According to S, the origin of unions is related to a dysfunction of capitalism. He sees them as the product of the subjective "urge" of individual workers faced with rapacious individual capitalists or with a historical epoch of (past) capitalist brutality. Under the heading "the urge to unionize" (apparently analogous to the "urge for a new pair of shoes" [58]), S offers us the following analysis of the "historical" rise of trade unions:

> Why were men tempted to join such organizations? . . . In past centuries wages were low everywhere. Productivity was then low, so that no way of dividing the social pie could have given the average man an adequate slice. But workers often *felt* that they were at the mercy of the boss; they *felt* poor, uninformed, and helpless to hold out economically against the employer, with his greater staying power in any conflict. Shops were organized on dictatorial principles, and orders were passed down from on high; the worker was but a cog in the machine, a dehumanized robot. Such was the worker's image of the situation as revealed in historical records [134f.; our emphasis. Cf. 45].

Because this passage seems to hold the key to S's view of the origin of unions, let us examine it carefully. His vague chronology takes on crucial significance: "in past centuries" conveys the impression that everything that follows refers to some indeterminate past; at the same time the reader is given the impression that the modern mixed economy has done away with all these very unpleasant phenomena. Yet on closer examination we find that some of these phenemona are of relatively recent origin and have not been affected by unionization.

Apparently the prime reason workers were "tempted" to organize was the low standard of living way back then. But it seems that S considers this an irrational response, since productivity was allegedly so low that nothing could have been done to alleviate the problem. This somehow leaves us with the impression that the workers back then were not asking for a bigger piece of the "social pie," but rather for an impossible, pie-in-the-sky, utopian standard of living. It is apparently impossible that workers might have been cognizant of their miserable exploitation and their impoverishment, of the expropriation of the former immediate producers. In any event, S makes it clear that their demands were objectively nonsensical at that vague time (and by implication still today), but now because the mixed economy has given us the welfare state.

The key word here is "but," indicating that workers began to make organized demands *despite* the objective impossibility of their fulfillment. Then comes the repetition of "felt," which serves to underline the utter subjectivity of the workers' views. Curiously enough, though, it is difficult to figure out where S stands, since he has already admitted the extreme poverty of the workers. The workers "felt" poor because they *were* poor; they "felt" at the mercy of the capitalists because they *were,* etc. (In a summary of this chapter in the 2nd edition [1951], S dissociates himself from unions which "insist" that the individual "worker . . . is inferior" to the capitalist who "is supposed" to have greater staying power, etc. [p. 207], thus, even under present conditions S wants to have such views clearly identified as the subjective feelings of workers.) So much for S's analysis for the time being.

It is no secret even to bourgeois authors that trade unions are not the product of individual discontent but of fundamental forces of capitalism.[1] As long as social relations that encompass the sale of labor power by one class and the ownership of the means of production by another are accepted as given, unions will remain as defense organizations. But the reasons that some national labor organizations fail to enter the political arena against capitalism while others do does not lie in the unions themselves. Some capitalist societies have brought forth "revolutionary" labor organizations while others have not. It is not the form of the trade union per se but rather the social and historical conditions peculiar to a particular society that determine this question. On the other hand, since labor unions arise in response to objective class antagonisms, they contain the possibility of formulating demands which can no longer be met in capitalism. In other words, the dividing line between political and economic demands is an illusory one.

The next step in the genesis of unions was man's gradual discovery "that in numbers there is strength. One hundred men acting in concert seemed to have more bargaining power than all had by acting separately" (135). This again puts emphasis on subjective factors and ignores the objective basis. No reference is made to the fact that the developing capitalist economy was spawning a working class concentrated more and more in factories, a class subject to increasing exploitation by ever larger concentrations of capital. Capitalism itself produced the physical and social aggregation of large numbers of workers as well as their specific common interests. And at the same time capitalist exploitation compelled the organization of the workers. American unions date back to the Revolutionary era. The rise of merchant capitalism merely accelerated a process that began when workers fell under the control of a producing capitalist class, the "masters."

S interrupts his story of the "urge to unionize" with a comment on the parallel urge to fight unions: "Naturally, employers fought back. They, too, learned that strength came from formal cooperation. . . . Not unexpectedly, employers invoked the powers of the law against labor conspiracies and group actions" (135). Although S saw nothing self-evident in the "urge to unionize" (after all, it contained so many irrational elements), the capitalist struggle against unions is "natural." Disregarding the fundamental implicit difference between the banding together of workers and owners, S inverts the picture by drawing an analogy between the two processes. Finally, in passing he mentions the organized capitalist repression of and terror against unions. Up to the sixth edition he devoted two pages to these capitalist practices. But beginning with the sixth edition (1964), he "abbreviates earlier discussions of the bad employer practices of an earlier era."[2] True, the massive organized violence of the 1930s may be a thing of the past, but to omit mention of these struggles merely enhances the image of the subjective reasons leading to unionization.

II / THE HISTORY OF THE U.S. LABOR MOVEMENT: THE QUESTION OF A "POLITICAL" LABOR MOVEMENT

S's discussion of the history of U.S. labor is predicated on the distinction between an economic and political movement, presumably because this implies a future of harmonious labor-capital relations now that we enjoy the blessings of the "mixed" economy.

S does not provide us with a conceptual apparatus for his distinction, but we can infer it from his vague imagery. His most general statement reads: "In contrast to the labor movements in many foreign countries that have politically waged the class struggle for major reform, American unions exist primarily for *economic* betterment: to try to get higher wages, shorter hours. . ." (135). This conjures up a picture of a labor movement taking control of the government versus unionized workers content with improving their station under capitalism. This may not be entirely wrong. The labor movement of Western Europe is more explicitly anticapitalist than that of the United States. However, S is right for the wrong reasons. He wrongly equates "political" struggle with demands on the state or struggle for control of the government. Even a cursory glance at the victorious labor or social democratic parties of Scandinavia,

Great Britain, and West Germany shows that these explicitly political labor movements cannot be equated with anticapitalist movements.

In order to break through this obviously faulty distinction we must find the *raison d'être* for unions within the capitalist mode of production. The day-to-day existence of workers as wage workers led to the formation of trade unions. In concrete terms this means that workers organized themselves as sellers of the commodity labor power. The value of this commodity like that of any other hinges on the labor-time necessary to reproduce it. The price of labor power (i.e., wages) may deviate from this value at any given time. It is the conscious intention of the worker to maintain this price at the highest possible level, and it is the conscious intention of the buyer of labor power (i.e., the capitalist), to drive this price down to the lowest possible level. Thus, although the value of labor power is determined largely by unconscious factors, the forces of supply and demand that determine the deviations of price from value can be influenced by "market power." In this respect, trade unions grow out of the attempt on the part of wage laborers to secure conditions most favorable to the sale of their commodity. By concentrating labor power in a single organization workers seek to counter the advantages accruing to the capitalists through their ownership of the means of production in concentrated form. However, the "interference" of trade unions in capitalist production is not restricted to jockeying for the best position on the labor market. The capitalist's "consumption" of the commodity he is purchasing does not take place in the "marketplace"; his use of the commodity labor power is synonymous with the actual labor of the worker, and this takes place in the process of production. And because the worker sells his commodity for only a specified length of time and under specific conditions, the union is compelled to follow the worker from the market into the factory, and that is where the day-to-day struggles of the unions take place.

It is thus the function of the union to enforce the terms of sale and to protect the worker from the tendency of capital to profit at the expense of the worker. With this in mind let us look at the alleged distinction between economic and political struggle. In this context we should like to cite an illuminating passage from a letter by Friedrich Bolte, a German-American socialist, to Marx, dated November 23, 1871:

> The political movement of the working class naturally has as its end goal the conquest of political power for it, and to this end naturally a previous organization of the working class to a certain point is necessary, one growing out of their economic struggles. On the other hand, however, every movement in which the working class as a *class* confronts the ruling classes and seeks to force them through pressure from without is a political movement. E.g, the attempt to win from the individual capitalists a limitation of the labor time through strikes etc. in a single factory or even in a single trade is a purely economic movement; on the other hand, the movement to compel an eight-hour etc. *law* is a *political* movement.[3]

For Marx, a political movement was "a movement of the *class* to assert its interest in general form, in a form which possesses general, societally coercive force."[4] He draws a distinction between the achievement of political power as the end goal and the political movement of the workers as a class making certain "economic" demands. These demands may or may not be directed at the state ("laws"), according to historical phase of capitalism. Marx specifically had in mind the movement for and the ultimate passage of laws to shorten the working day in nineteenth-century England, legislation to curtail a form of exploitation that Marx called absolute surplus value.

In summing up the distinction between political and economic trade unions we can say that seemingly economic demands may become political by becoming *class-wide*, as for instance the agitation for universal limitation of the working day.

The example of the short work day may not seem particularly relevant today, so let us look at a more immediate issue—so-called productivity restraints (145). As far as S is concerned, these are "artificial" (584), yet even some bourgeois labor economists recognize that what is in fact "artificial" is the neglect of the underlying class structure of production relations:

> An analysis of the working rules of unions which employers classify under the term "restriction of output," shows that these seek to curb the *dictatorship of the employer* and to assert the workers' right to participate in determining "working conditions."[5]

S advances a variety of reasons for this behavior: one is the worker's notion that he has a right to or owns his job; another, the defensive reaction against threats to job security in the broad sense (loss of job, demotion, reduction in work time, etc.). Thus one is ideological and the other material. As to the worker's odd notion that he has a right to his job, the capitalists and bourgeois economists should put the blame on the capitalist mode of production which is responsible for the idea that what the worker is selling is his *labor* rather than his labor *power*. Marginal-productivity theory requires this assumption to prove that the "factor of production labor" is not being exploited, and thus it should not come as a surprise that the worker agrees. If this assumption does not appeal to the bourgeoisie, it is free to accept the validity of Marx's (and capitalism's) distinction between labor and labor power.

In capitalist reality, of course, the job and the objective conditions of the work place are inseparable, and as long as both job and work place remain the property of the capitalists—that is, as long as labor remains at the level of a mere coordinate "factor of production" without control over the labor conditions—the right to a job will be thwarted by the laws of capital accumulation and the "management decisions" mediated by those laws.

Despite the theoretically unfounded and ideological nature of job rights under capitalism, the protection of already existing jobs derives from the struggle for survival of the workers involved, and the history of U.S. trade unions in part reflects this process. With the shift to relative surplus-value production—that is, to the increasing productivity needed to reduce the share of value going to labor by reducing the value of the commodities bought with its wages—the older skills and crafts gave way to capitalist industry. As workers began to lose their skills to machines, the basis of craft unions began to disintegrate, to be replaced by industrial unions based on the development of industrial capitalism.

The fights waged by the unions may or may not be political, but the criterion does not lie in the militancy or even the success of the movement. In illustration of this point let us take the example of the building-trades unions where the workers have retained control over their labor conditions to an unrivaled degree. The reason for this phenomenon, according to the AFL-CIO, is that the contruction worker's "autonomy is firmly footed in ownership of his tools, through which he symbolically owns his job and controls his destiny. . . ."[6]

This situation is of course dependent on the present condition of the construction industry: its capital concentration, the technical composition of capital, firm size, etc. If, as may well come to pass, the industry will be "revolutionized," the "autonomy" of its workers will shrivel, and then we would see whether the demands of the unions would be economic or political.

To return to the problem of class-wide demands as they relate to so-called productivity restraints: these demands or defensive holding actions remain economic insofar as the workers or unions see themselves and act as what they are—owners of the commodity labor power, the production-labor factor concerned with the preservation of the source of and the greatest possible increase in the income it considers its "due." Although obvious antagonisms in the sphere of *distribution* exist between this factor and capital in the same branch, still in this conception labor sees itself as a "partner" with capital in that branch as opposed to all others, as well as with that particular firm as opposed to all others. This "partnership" seeks to create conditions in the particular producing unit most likely to produce the highest possible income for all "cooperating" factors of production.

To the extent that unions accept these premises and their conclusions, that is to say, to the extent that they fall victim to the false consciousness created by capitalist production, they have limited themselves to economic demands and also laid themselves open to the charge of playing the role of a particular or special interest group trying to gain an "unfair" advantage at the expense of their "partners" as well as of society as a whole.

Economic demands can improve the day-to-day situation of the working class even though they have their clearly defined limits based on their acceptance of the "ground rules" laid down by capitalism. This dogma has been revived in the form of the wage-price spiral. S in the 9th edition puts his stamp of approval on it by the simple insertion of the single word "vain": "Organized labor tries to improve its money wage rates, in the vain hope that this will not induce a commensurate rise in prices . . . " (144).

At the end of the discussion of political versus economic demands we see that there is no unilinear progression from the latter "up" to the former, just as there are no rigid boundaries between them. The factors responsible for the formation of a political labor movement do not lie in the unions themselves but rather in the development of capitalism in a particular country. More specifically, one would have to determine what prevents or helps the working class of a country to be aware of its objective condition.

S's discussion of the Knights of Labor and the AFL simply underscores his inability to understand the nature of a political labor movement. He ascribes the decline of the Knights of Labor to the fact that "America did not seem susceptible to such a political labor movement" (136), while the " 'business unionism' " of the AFL was far better suited to this country. But in point of fact the Knights began to decline when its leadership was captured by non-working-class elements such as farmers, shopkeepers, and businessmen who deflected the organization from class struggle, strikes, etc., and substituted utopian schemes for the brotherhood of man and cooperatives in their stead. And what really finished the organization was its negative attitude toward the movement for the eight hour day. Contrary to S's contention, the difference between the Knights and the AFL was not one of political versus nonpolitical approach but rather the *right* versus the wrong political approach.

In closing our discussion of the political aspects of the labor movement let us look at S's treatment of the role played by "communism," for that little section affords insight into the basically anticommunist orientation of modern economics.

The very title of the section—"Communism and Corruption in Unions"—tells us all we need to know about S's eschewal of value judgments. Back in the days of the Korean War and McCarthy, in the 2nd edition (1951), S made his point with unmistakable clarity: "Fortunately it is becoming increasingly easy to identify those who follow the Communist line and take their cue from the foreign policy of the Soviet Union" (p. 195).

Why "fortunately"? No doubt because S associates the rise of Marxist-oriented trade unions with the crisis of the 1930s, which "had soured the American public on many of the slogans of the 1920s and had excited class antagonisms" (137). And this doubtless is also what he means when he says that the Communists gained influence by "using Machiavellian tactics" such as "identifying themselves with popular labor causes" (138 f.). Rather strange reasoning, for in the last analysis S is reproaching them with having implemented their theoretical views which happened to coincide with the "class antagonisms" that capitalism itself had "excited" among the working people. In other words, what "excites" S is not so much the Communists' "cleverness in strategy" (139) as the objective situation created by capitalism itself.

6 The Capitalist State
S's Chapters 8-9

The Welfare State is often compared to Santa Claus, and that comparison is usually drawn by those who object to presents for poor people. But in fact the Welfare State resembles Santa Claus because he gives more to rich children than to poor ones.
—J. Pen, *Income Distribution*, p. 370

METHODOLOGICAL INTRODUCTION

Inasmuch as these two chapters deal with the state in capitalism in a more explicit fashion than other parts of the book we believe that they should be treated together. It is obvious from the structure of these two chapters, if not from any programmatic remarks, that these two chapters form the final link in the so-called macroeconomic discussion of Big Business, Big Labor, and Big Government.

Unlike other chapters, including those on Business and Labor, these two offer a relatively large amount of information which could conceivably form the starting point for an introduction to the topic if it were presented within a theoretical framework conducive to an understanding of the historical development of the contemporary capitalist state. Instead, we are offered emphasis on "the facts" within an ideological context. More specifically, these two chapters are meant to bridge the gap between "the citizen's" general knowledge of the state and the Keynesian theory of state intervention of Chapters 11 through 14. To the extent that S is unable to transcend superficial common sense he is violating his promise to "avoid indoctrination and prop-agandizing" (1st ed., p. vi), for these chapters are preoc-cupied with the preservation of an economic system which S's science concedes cannot be justified in scientific terms but only via so-called value judgments. But more impor-tantly, because he gives an ahistorical account of the evolu-tion of the capitalist state and its functions, S fails to make clear that it is his intent to preserve a specific social system at a specific time in history. What we get instead is a highly abstract explanation that could apply to any society, plant, or animal:

> Unyielding conservatism defeats its own purpose. Iron without "give" will break suddenly under strain; flexible steel will bend. Brittle economic systems without the flexibility to ac-commodate themselves in an evolutionary manner to ac-cumulating tensions and social changes . . . are in the greatest peril of extinction. . . . If a system is to continue to function well, social institutions and beliefs must be able to adjust themselves to these changes [150].

Not only has S failed to offer any scientific reason for this salvaging operation but his analysis of why this overhaul-ing has become necessary—assuming that certain powerful social interests will support such an undertaking—is also very weak. In order to focus on the chaotic methodology of S's science and to bring order into the chaos we have de-cided to rearrange the sequences within the two chapters.

We will begin with S's derivation of the general need for a state as a component part of "economic life," which he has put at the end of Chapter 8. From there we will go to his analysis of the growth of government activity as well as of the specific functions attributed to the state in the so-called mixed economy. S's conception of democracy and how he uses it within this theory will form an important aspect of both discussions. The remainder of our analysis will center on the distribution of income, allegedly the major characteristic of the welfare state, as well as on the types of taxation used to achieve that redistribution.

We consider our restructured outline deficient in one

major respect—namely in our failure to incorporate the discussion of national income that forms part of Chapter 10. By putting these chapters on the state before that on national income, and by placing the state in the same series with Business and Labor, S is able to prejudge the question of whether the state contributes to national income or whether it merely is a channel for income produced elsewhere. This is not merely a procedural point but touches on the very ability of the Keynesian programs to salvage capitalism. We have elected to treat Chapter 10 separately, and to refer to it here only as necessary.

I / DERIVATION OF THE STATE

After ten pages of descriptive prose, S finally gets around to posing the important question of *"Why is governmental use of goods and services ever required at all?"* (158). His answer to this rhetorical question consists of a rather confused mixture of traditional bourgeois political-philosophical derivative material on the state (e.g., Hobbes, Locke, Rousseau) and his own ahistorical concept of the development of capitalism and its state.

He opens his argument by setting up the hypothetical, or perhaps not so hypothetical conditions (the text is ambiguous) under which "zero government" might prevail, when "all commodities could be produced efficiently by perfectly competitive enterprise at any scale of operations"; no "indivisible" commodities; neither altruism nor envy; "equal initial access to human and natural resources"; "activities" could be carried on "independently" by each producer (158).

S goes on to explain that if all these "idealized" conditions actually existed there would be no "need" for a mixed economy, or a government or society for that matter, "since the world could then be regarded as an array of independent atoms with absolutely no organic connection among them" (158). He then proposes some modification to bring the model closer to reality, such as division of labor and the pricing system, which, he concludes, would lead to a laissez-faire government protecting private property within and without its borders (158). And finally he brings us back to "real life" by pointing out that "each and every one of the idealized conditions . . . is lacking in some degree in real life as man has always known it" (159). Therefore we will have to rethink "the important compromises that a free society must make" (159). The first part of this exposition is an attempt at an *ad absurdum* argument to demonstrate the internal contradiction of an assertion—in this case, that the conditions for zero government could not exist since they, if realizable, would be tantamount to societyless atoms and hence to "governmentlessness."

The fundamental error of S's argumentation lies in his unwitting identification of "government" with the capitalist state. If he were merely trying to postulate the reasons for the existence of the capitalist state, his argument would be tautological (since capitalism is characterized by such and such conditions, it cannot not have a state—a situation derivative of other conditions). S, however, is concerned with the reason for "governmental use . . . *at all*" (our emphasis).

For the time being let us confine our discussion to the differences between the capitalist state and other pre-capitalist *class* societies. In these societies the possession of the objective conditions of labor (human and natural resources) did not appear as private property but rather as property of a directly social nature. This means that all the activities which are necessary for the collective existence of the society (e.g., irrigation, roads, acquisition of new territory through war, reparation of reserves, etc.) are in essence a component part of the social reproduction of life through labor. Thus instead of being tasks which come to light after the work of private capitals has been completed and has proved unable to perform them they are, in pre-capitalist societies, the direct social activities of all members. (In this context it is irrelevant that in feudal and slave class societies the performance of these tasks may have been involuntary.)

The privatization of what in precapitalist societies were social activities led to the necessity of a state which then became the only political sphere and the only social organization with the power to compel the individual producers to contribute to the general social task. Whereas in previous societies this "contribution" took the form of direct labor, here it assumed the form of deductions from the primary appropriations of the national product—wages, profit, rent—transferred to the state as taxes.

This is the type of "government" S has presupposed in his argument. To prove his point he has simply selected certain characteristics of capitalism, turned them into what he sees as their opposite or negation, and then announced that such a society could indeed exist without a state—if at all.

The features he has selected for his nonexistent society represent a peculiar mishmash. The first, concerning perfectly competitive enterprises, accords with the common bourgeois conception of premonopoly capitalism; the "indivisibilities," or rather in this case their absence, relate, at least in the form presented here, to no society except perhaps a very primitive one in which nothing was done except to pluck fruit off trees and eat and sleep. But this fantastic image is either a tautology or a false identification of different phenomena. That is to say, either S has defined indivisibility in the specific capitalist sense of use value which cannot for various reasons be produced according to indvidual capitalist "principles," and which therefore must be produced or run by the only social organization not subject to the constraints of profitability and equal exchange (i.e., power of taxation)—namely the state—or he means any use value in any society which is consumed collectively. If he means the latter, then we would have to go to the Garden of Eden for an example of a society without indivisibilities. But then we would also have erased the essential distinction between capitalism and other societies. For in that case S is deriving the necessity of indivisibilities from the use-value aspect, from the technology of producing or consuming them; this in turn means that he will characterize all societies possessing this particular use value as having a state. This view eradicates the distinction between the state in capitalist society as a necessity external to the basic social relation of private capital production and the direct social performance of these tasks in precapitalist societies. In other words, by concentrating on the use-value aspect, S is able to equate all societies producing so-called indivisibilities and ascribing to them all the specific social content associated with indivisibilities in capitalism. Thus it would be possible to have a society producing collectively consumed use values without a state in the sense in which S understands this.

To continue with the mixed bag of conditions for the absence of a state: "neither altruism nor envy" is yet another example of S's inability to see the differences between modes of production. S, whose horizon does not extend beyond competitive capitalist egotism, apparently cannot understand that altruism is the obverse side of egotism, whereas societal solidarity, the product of the objective conditions of a society lacking the heterogeneity of class interests, has nothing to do with altruism. What he probably means is that altruism and envy would, for different reasons, lead to a "social contract."

The last two conditions, equality of resources and independence, presumably refer to the early bourgeois myths of a simple commodity-producing society in which all men are property owners and none is a wage laborer. Why should S stress "initial" equality if the destruction of the initial equality allegedly brought on state intervention? In any event, we are offered a potpourri of several features from several societies. It is not clear what S is driving at since he has thrown in contradictory conditions: he speaks of perfectly competitive enterprises and of independence "much as in frontier days." Does he have in mind independent producers (farmers who also met their own nonagricultural needs)? But this is obviously incompatible with any sort of competition.

The transition to laissez-faire capitalism is even more manipulative. Here he says "yet even in this case . . ." and then adds the "if" clause with the introduction of division of labor and a pricing system. "Even" in this case can only refer to the retention of all the features just mentioned, plus some; yet division of labor plus "a pricing system such as that described in Chapters 3 and 4 in Part Three" must include capital and wage labor, which would destroy equal opportunity and independence. There then follows the traditional description of the state as the protector of private property.

In saying all this, S is merely repeating the 300-year-old myths of bourgeois political philosphers on the founding of the capitalist state by free and equal property holders. But if the state is a specific social development relating to the deficient sociality of capital, it is also subject to the same vicissitudes of capitalist society, not in the sense that it can only act like an individual capital but rather in the sense that as the ideal aggregate capitalist, as the social organization taking care of the general needs of capital, it must operate to preserve the contradictory system of capitalism. As Marx explains: "What then is the power of the political state over private property? *Private property's own power,* its essence brought into being. What is left to this political state in contrast to this essence? The *illusion* that it determines where it is determined."[1]

In other words, there are limits to the "activities" of the state. It is not, as it were, a compensation for the contradictions of the individual capitals but merely a further expression of them.

The transition from laissez-faire capitalism to the mixed economy takes place as mysteriously as that from the regime of small commodity producers to capitalism. The only difference we can see among the conditions enumerated between the two periods of capitalism relates to the rise of monopolies and the decline of "perfect competition." Although we do not agree with this distinction in the form it is presented by S, this might be an important point of departure for understanding the transition if there were one. But S does not pursue this point; he is just as interested in "biological" disparities with respect to abilities, shaky ground indeed for the derivation of the mixed economy. In fact, he ends up discussing two points—military spending and external economies. We fail to understand how these two factors define the specific differences of the mixed economy.

"National defense" is of course also put under the heading of external economy or indivisibility. The entire discussion is marked by a continuation of the bourgeois myths of the social contract. The traditional grouping of man into bourgeois and *citoyen* runs throughout this section. Thus the capitalist in his role as *citoyen* must put up with things he does not want—i.e., expenses that reduce this surplus value without contributing to the creation of more—as long as he wants to remain a capitalist; that is, as political man, as citizen, he must pay taxes to provide internal and external defense of his private property even though it will also aid his competitor. This myth of the social contract also assumes that everyone is a productive private property owner and will thus benefit from the state expenditure to protect private property. Perhaps there were objective reasons for this belief 200 years ago, but they certainly do not obtain today.

At this point S confuses us completely by telling us that "laissez faire" could not provide national defense against a minority as long as there was no "political voting and coercion" (159). Does he mean to say that capitalism before the mixed economy could not support wars, etc.? Are coercion and political voting the distinguishing characteristics of the mixed economy? Or is laissez faire a myth?

But perhaps a look at previous statements will provide enlightenment. Back in Chapter 3, S said that in "the past few centuries" the "twentieth-century industrial nations" showed a "trend . . . toward less and less direct governmental control of economic activity," leading to the demise of feudalism and the rise of "what is loosely called 'free private enterprise,' or 'competitive private-property capitalism.' " (41). But: "Long before this trend had approached a condition of full laissez faire (i.e., of complete governmental noninterference with business), the tide began to turn the other way. Since late in the nineteenth century," governmental economic activity has increased (41). At this point through the seventh edition there followed this abdication of theoretical responsibility: "We must leave to historians the task of delineating the important factors underlying this significant and all-pervasive development. Suffice it to say here" (7th ed., p. 39), and then in bold brown letters: "Ours is a 'mixed' economy in which both public and private institutions exercise economic control" (41).

We take this to mean that "full" laissez faire had not existed before; apparently late in the nineteenth century the trend toward defeudalization was reversed in the sense that government activity took an upward turn. The reasons for this are not known to economists. All we know is that we now have a mixed economy, although what distinguishes it from not a full laissez faire is beyond our powers of explanation. If there had been a trend toward less government activity is it not possible that at some time prior to the late nineteenth century that activity was greater than it is now? S's vagueness on this point is highlighted by a footnote in the second chapter: "There has never been a 100 per cent purely automatic enterprise system. Even in our capitalistic system, the government has an important role in modifying the workings of the price system. This is what is meant by saying that we live in a 'mixed economy' " (7th ed., p. 16 n.2; the fact that in the 9th edition [18, n.2] "even" is replaced by "certainly" does not speak for consistency).

S has given us only the skimpiest quantitative and absolutely no qualitative criteria for judging the differences while at the same time renouncing all competence for explaining the why of the matter. None of this is particularly propitious as far as "modern economics" and its attempt to explain the workings of the modern mixed economy are concerned.

II / THE GROWTH OF GOVERNMENT ACTIVITY

In this section S presents his most important information,

that dealing with the quantitative growth of government expenditure in capitalist countries in our century. Let us take a look at how he deals with this material.

A / QUANTITATIVE ASPECTS

He starts off by pointing out that government expenditures rose from one-twelfth to one-half of national income between pre-World War I days and the height of World War II, for during the latter war "it became necessary for the government to consume about half of the nation's greatly expanded total output" (147). It would, of course, be more accurate to say that to fight the war the nation had to produce more. And if we look at the table in Chapter 10 (203), we see that although the Government's part of GNP almost doubled during the Depression of the 1930s (rising from 8.2 percent in 1929 to a high of 15.3 percent in 1938), by 1940 GNP still fell short of its 1929 level.

When we consider that military spending as well as social-security contributions were minimal during the 1930s, we find that the share of GNP devoted to nonwar governmental expenditure is not much larger today than it was forty years ago.[7] In any event, the impetus toward greater government revenues and expenditures lies in the war economy the U.S. has enjoyed uninterruptedly since World War II. Although S provides the information needed to arrive at this conclusion, he does not hit upon the explanation.

In a now-deleted passage that appeared in the first edition (in a section entitled "Efficiency and Waste in Government"), to explain the changes then taking place thus:

> The trouble, if there is a trouble, goes much deeper. It lies within ourselves as citizens. We want government economy, and at the same time we want the government services that cost money!
>
> To put the matter in a more sophisticated way: Government expenditure is a way of utilizing national output so as to meet human wants and needs. When national income rises, people want more and better schooling and other forms of government expenditure. . . . Our social conscience and humanitarian stan-

dards have completely changed, so that today we insist upon providing certain minimum standards of existence for those who are unable to provide for themselves [p. 158].

First we should note S's recognition of the bourgeois-*citoyen* dichotomy in the form of "trouble . . . within ourselves as citizens." What this really means is "we" want external economies without having to reduce our profit to pay for them, and to the extent that those not burdened by the worry about profits because they have none are also compelled to pay, this "trouble" can be considerably reduced.

But moving on to the more important "sophisticated" view of government "services," the capitalist state by its very nature is rooted precisely in the absence of the unity of interests and will implied in the "we's" and "our"s that dot the passage. Going beyond this fundamental point, we note that the description of the empirical development of state intervention just does not accord with the reality described. Thus war and not "human wants and needs" was responsible for the greatest increase in government expenditures. Despite S's claims about a rising tendency of government expenditure as correlated with rising income, his own figures show that at the time of the first edition (1948), government expenditure as a percentage of GNP had dropped to precisely the same level it had attained in 1931 (12.2), at a time when GNP was little more than a quarter of the 1948 level (203). This of course was related to the demobilization; and again S's own figures show that the G share of GNP did not take off, as it were, until the Korean War, and it remained at that level until the additional boost provided by the Vietnam War.

S does not limit the growth to the U.S. alone: "for more than a century . . . in almost all countries and cultures, the trend of government expenditure has been rising even faster" than national income and production. "Each period of emergency—each war, each depression, each epoch of enhanced concern over poverty and equality—expands the activity of government. After each emergency is over, expenditures never seem to go back to previous levels" (147). This would indicate that rather than a rational intervention of social conscience and humanitarianism we find the state having to intervene in times of crisis. As far as war is concerned, if military expenditures do not go down even after the emergency is over, we would question S's acquiescence in the statement that "nothing is more vital to a threatened society than its security" (159). And similarly with respect to depressions, if in fact the emergency is over—that is, if employment and incomes attain a high enough level to eliminate the need for extra-market redistribution—then these expenditures also would disappear. If in fact they remain constant (as a percentage of GNP) or increase, then one would have to question whether the "emergency" is really over and whether "we" want increased welfare spending or whether merely some of "us" are fighting for it. S does not distinguish between countries and "cultures." Thus he does not consider whether the rise of societies in which the national production is controlled by a state might have forced additional centralization on the capitalist states. Having specifically excluded this phenomenon from "our attention" (41), he can at best see both developments as a common convergent trend. In some respects this is, of course, true, inasmuch as both systems can be viewed as responses to the historically increased level of productivity; but one of the systems represents an attempt to bind these productive forces within an outmoded set of social relations.

Just as S is vague with respect to the transition from laissez faire (or feudalism for that matter) to the mixed economy, he is vague with respect to the allegedly universal and apparently irresistible, irreversible, and interminable trend toward ever greater government intervention ("nor is the end in sight"—147). He can of course avoid the central issue here by sticking to absolute levels, but aside from their patent irrelevance in a time of rising GNP, his own table on international comparisons of relative GNP shares indicates that absolute figures do not mean much.

By his undue emphasis on the U.S., S presents a skewed picture of the historical development of the mixed economy, first because military expenditures by the U.S.

prior to World War II were absolutely low as well as low relative to Europe. This is one of the reasons for the relatively low share of government expenditures in GNP through the 1920s. The second reason relates to the U.S.'s belated adaptation of social-security programs which make up an increasingly larger share of the GNP attributed to the state by bourgeois economists and statisticians. Many other capitalist countries had a twenty-five- to forty-five-year head-start on this point. With social-security contributions amounting to approximately $50 billion annually, and war expenditures to approximately $113 billion,[8] these two items account for about four-fifths of the U.S. budget. In view of their nonexistence or minimal levels before World War II, it is not appropriate to take the U.S of those years as a point of reference. If we look at Germany, we see that by 1929 the state already received 23.1 percent of GNP.[9] By the mid-1950s the figure had risen to between 32 and 34 percent; and according to S, it reached 35 percent in 1970.[10] Thus while it is true that in the U.S. the G's share increased about 150-175 percent during this forty-year period, in Germany (and West Germany) it rose only about 66 percent. Moreover, in most capitalist countries the increase is slowing down considerably.

Nor is the rise quite so unilinear and irresistible as S would have it. Thus in the U.K. taxation as a percentage of GNP dropped from 32.5 percent in 1950 to 29 percent in 1955 to 27.6 percent in 1960, which one author explains by saying that "the objective of tax reduction took priority over schemes for the extension of social welfare."[11]

And finally with respect to the U.S., S's own table (203) indiates that the upward climb has been neither steady nor relentless. To begin with, the government's share of GNP during the five years before World War II and during the same time span before the Korean War was approximately the same (14-15 percent); and with the exception of the Korean and Vietnam wars, that share has fluctuated about 20 percent. Thus there has been remarkably little movement beyond the level of twenty years ago.

The problem with S's approach is that it fails to delineate

the limits of an increasing share of the state in the capitalist economy; and this despite his emphatic assertion that "If a good can be subdivided so that each part can be *competitively* sold separately to a different consumer with no external effects on others in the group, it is not likely candidate for governmental activity" (16o). This means that the welfare state will always remain an appendage of a relatively profitable capitalist economy. The precise quantitative limits cannot be predicted, but given the fact that in most West European countries it hovered in the 33 percent vicinity since the 1950s, one wonders whether further increases of the G's share are imminent.

S's attempt to establish some correlation between G's share of GNP and growth rates is utterly gratuitous. First of all, the figures are based on a table (149) whose sources are not cited in anything remotely resembling accepted scholarly practice. As for the figures themselves, their accuracy is questionable. We are not told which items are and which are not included in these statistics, and so we may wind up comparing noncomparable data. For instance, do the data include revenues from all levels of government, social-security contributions, revenues from government production, etc.? We assume that the table does include all levels of government, else the percentage for the U.S. would not be so high. Since he has not specified how he arrived at his percentages it is pointless to refer to other data giving different figures. We will confine ourselves to the following table:

Total taxation to GNP at market prices average 1968-70

(a) Excluding Social Security		(b) Including Social Security	
1/Denmark	35.6	1/Sweden	43.0
2/Sweden	34.8	2/Netherlands	39.7
3/United Kingdom	31.6	3/Denmark	38.7
4/Norway	29.3	4/Norway	38.4
5/Finland	28.5	5/United Kingdom	36.6
6/Canada	27.8	6/France	36.3

7/Ireland	27.4	7/Austria	35.8
8/Iceland(2)	26.7	8/Germany	34.0
9/Austria	26.6	9/Belgium	33.8
10/Netherlands	25.5	10/Finland	32.8
11/Australia	24.4	11/Luxembourg(1)	32.4
12/Belgium	24.0	12/Canada	30.2
13/Germany	23.2	13/Italy	30.1
14/Luxembourg (1)	22.9	14/Ireland	29.8
15/United States	22.7	15/Iceland(2)	28.6
16/France	21.8	16/United States	27.9
17/Greece(1)	20.1	17/Greece(1)	26.3
18/Italy	19.2	18/Australia	24.4
19/Switzerland	18.3	19/Switzerland	21.5
20/Turkey	17.4	20/Portugal	21.1
21/Portugal	16.5	21/Turkey	20.4
22/Japan	15.8	22/Japan	19.4
23/Spain	11.8	23/Spain	19.2

(1) Average of 1968 and 1969 only.
(2) 1969 only.
Source: OECD, Revenue Statistics of OECD Member Countries 1968-1970, p. 14.

Let us examine these figures in conjunction with S's statement that "mixed economies, such as Sweden, France and (supposedly laissez faire) Germany spend relatively most on government. And these happen to be the kinds of nations which have shown the greatest growth and progress in recent decades" (148). What are these "kinds"? First of all, this sort of correlation directly contradicts another of S's statements, in Chapter 41 on Problems of Growth: "When one considers how different France and Germany have been in many of their governmental institutions, the similarity of their development is striking. The similar growth patterns of socialistic Sweden and individualistic Switzerland present the same paradox" (8th ed., p. 796). Only someone who asserts the correlation to begin with can even ask whether this is or is not a "paradox." But even empirically it is not true that the three countries S put at the top of the list "happened" to have the highest GNP growth rates in the 1950s and 1960s. Switzerland's was greater than Sweden's, West Germany's was greater than France's, Japan, at the bottom of S's list, showed the greatest growth rates of all capitalist countries, the U.K., with a very high share of G showed very low growth rates, Norway, not shown, also combined a high share with below-average growth rates.[12]

To round out the correlation, S in a blurb to his Table 8-1 asserts that "governments of poor, underdeveloped countries show a tendency to tax and spend less, relative to national product, than advanced countries" (149). What about this tendency? We, too, have "selected" some countries from this category and calculated the following shares of central government revenues alone in GNP for 1970 unless otherwise indicated: Zambia (1969: 34 percent); Algeria (1969: 29 percent); Guyana (1967: 25 percent); Chile (22 percent); Ceylon (22 percent); Venezuela (21 percent). (Source: *International Financial Statistics,* October, 1972.) Although we do not put much stock in such statistical games, we mention them to show how slipshod is S's scientific method.

B / STATE "REGULATORY" ACTIVITIES

Not being satisfied with a mere quantitative rundown of G's share in GNP, S proceeds to a discussion of various aspects of laws, regulations, and executive fiats. First he informs us that as a "result" of nineteenth-century America's close approximation of laissez fare, it "was a century of rapid material progress and an environment of individual freedom" (148). But it "also" knew business cycles, waste of natural resources, extremes of poverty and wealth, government corruption by "vested interests," and monopoly. One might assume that since "modern man" apparently opts for more government, the mixed economy, in contrast to laissez faire, would have seen a reduction in all these phenomena. But instead, monopolization has increased, the extremes of poverty and wealth persist, corruption most definitely is still with us, the waste of natural resources goes on unabated. And although the unemployment rate has not climbed to the levels of the Great Depression, business cycles are still with us.

The trouble with S's approach is that it looks at the state as an autonomous factor: its absence brought prosperity in the nineteenth century, and its presence is bringing prosperity in the twentieth. Seeing the state as an artificial creation of man which "he" can "use" or not in accordance with the "beliefs of an era" blinds S to the essential unity of a capitalism which, in the course of its development, anarchically generated the need for a state which it fought so strenuously in its infancy, when it sought to assert itself against a dying feudalism. The fact that the historical forces of production which in large part were developed by laissez faire capitalism were breaking through the confines of the individual capitals—in other words, that the social character of capitalism was coming into conflict with its own achievements—and that this process took place over a long period and was unplanned in no way contradicts the fact that when this objective tendency was finally realized, sentient human beings "planned" various details.

Let us examine some of the specific acts of government intervention mentioned by S, such as the "regulation" of the railroads by the ICC. As Galbraith has said of the so-called regulatory agencies in general, they "become, with some exceptions, either an arm of the industry they are regulating or servile."[2] The ICC came into being during the political struggle of the farmers against the monopoly prices charged by the railroads, a protest that must be seen in the context of the general populist movement of the post-Civil War era, when "the trend in the economic world was strongly toward the consolidation of smaller units into larger ones, the elimination of competition, and the concentration of control in relatively few hands."[3] But competition and monopoly are not understood here as mutually exclusive forces, for "the formation of great rail arteries, while reducing the number of competing roads, intensified competition."[4] As was to be the case so often in the future, this "regulatory" measure, a response to popular pressure, "proved a disappointment in many respects. . . . The railways, for the most part, continued their evil ways though with greater regard for external appearances than before."[5]

As for monopoly and the Sherman Act, S himself concedes that this law was increasingly turned against labor unions, supposedly not what it was intended for. (142). As was the case with the ICC, the façade erected here served the same purpose of co-opting the burgeoning antimonopoly movement. According to Arthur M. Schlesinger, the ten-year period ushered in by the Sherman Act "saw the formation of more industrial combinations than in the entire preceding period."[6]

C / THE STATE AND LABOR AND CAPITAL

S's account of the history of certain labor legislation has some basis in fact, even though he may not always be aware of its significance. There are two important aspects to this development: class struggle and disunity within each class. With respect to class struggle, there is no "solution" that conforms to the "principles" of economic theory or rational democracy. It is a political struggle that transcends market "rationality" and "equity," although the economic limits are established by the capitalist mode of production. Disunity within each class must also find a mandated solution. As Marx points out, the working class must force the passage of a law that would prevent workers from voluntarily signing a suicide pact with capital.[13]

"Unity" is also essential to the capitalist class; eventually the state will pass laws forcing "recalcitrant" capitalists to comply with the laws of competition.

"Progress" with respect to so-called social legislation is thus not simply a matter of "humanitarian legislation" (1st ed., p. 153), the product of the minds and hearts of increasingly civilized people acting through the instrumentality of their neutral, human state. The impetus for such legislation has always come from the oppressed classes, against the powerful and often violent opposition of the ruling class. That the state has had to exercise and even broaden its "authority" in order to enforce the victories won is not an expression of the increasing subordination of the market to man's political will, but rather the expression of a social order in which the fundamental processes of the reproduction of life have brought about the evolution of special social institutions able (1) to take responsibility for those aspects of social reproduction which the basic form of economic activity, individual capital, could not involve itself with, and (2) provide an ideological shield, as it were, for the relations of direct exploitation in the "sphere" of production as opposed to the democratic process in the political "sphere." Broader governmental "authority" does not mean broader control over the "economy"; what it does mean is that capital has so increased the forces of production that more and more economic activities have outgrown the sociality capital can cope with. This refers both to such general production conditions as transportation systems, atomic energy, pollution control, etc., and such "social arrangements" as hospitals, schools, and various social-security programs. The "core" of capitalism, private property production, has remained unchanged qualitatively and expanded quantitatively. What has also increased is the sphere of activities this "core" can cope with only by setting up a social institution not subject to the same fundamental constraints of surplus-value production, yet one which can attend to the activities without damaging the core.

In this sense, the theory of the mixed economy is correct; there is an objective trend in this direction. But what that theory cannot understand is that the development, like all processes in capitalism, is twofold. Its proponents can see only one of the aspects: greater objective "socialization." As far as the "subjective" human forces arrayed on both sides are concerned, and which in any concrete instance determine the outcome of the struggle, the theory of the mixed economy does not address itself to it. Its neutral stance on "nontechnical" issues leaves value judgments to ethics. Thus the usual "explanation" refers to "society" as having decided on this or that value and having implemented it via government.

This explanation falls down in several ways. First of all, it fails to recognize that the state cannot be neutral between capitalists and workers, for its very existence is rooted in and functions as an integral part of capitalism. Secondly, it fails to recognize that the so-called value judgments society processes in the courts and legislatures are narrowly defined and "biased" in the sense that they represent defensive moves on the part of the working class for equal treatment of its "factor of production." It denies that alongside its ideological neutral functions, the state must be given "expanded authority" to put down, by force if necessary, "demands" that transcend the co-optive capabilities of capitalism.

The rise of fascism is perhaps the most blatant example of the "setbacks" on the road to a more and more mixed society. Although S himself toward the end of the book concedes that fascism is "against free and militant trade-unionism" and hence supported by the capitalists (87), he is essentially unable to fit this into the theory of the mixed economy.

D / STATE EXPENDITURES AND DEMOCRACY

S begins this section, in which he outlines Federal expenditures and five aspects of changing governmental functions, with a reference to the paramount and growing specific weight of war expenditures in the welfare state. One-half of all Federal expenditures, among which S includes GI benefits, debt servicing, space research and technology, and international affairs, is devoted to war production. Surprisingly, S concedes that expenditures on international affairs and finance represent the costs of "future wars" (151); however, the reader will doubtless be relieved to find that in Chapters 36 and 38 he does not pursue this potentially fruitful approach to foreign "aid."

The great weight of war in the budget appears so important to S that he repeats it: "It needs emphasizing that the bulk of Federal expenditure and debt is the consequence of hot and cold war, not of welfare and development programs" (8th ed., p. 143), an emphasis so out of character that it no longer appears in the 9th edition. The first edition contains a similar, though in content somewhat different point: "It is to be emphasized that the bulk of postwar Federal expenditure and debt are the consequences of war and not the depression" (p. 157). The irony here is that by reiterating this general point for a quarter-century, he gives the lie to the notion of a welfare state originating during this period. In fact, as he himself notes, the ratios between war and "purely civilian expenditure for domestic peacetime purposes" have been reversed since the pre-World War II period.

This merely serves to underscore the unrealistic character of S's intermittent comments on the democratic process insofar as it relates to taxes and spending. Thus at various times he claims that *"legislative decision"* determines the share of GNP going to the state (156); that "in deciding how to tax themselves . . . the people are really deciding" how to make this division (163). This notion of popular control is open to attack on two levels. It is improper to attribute primary causal force to the state, for as we know it is reacting to the general profitability of private production within a very circumscribed sphere. And it is wrong to convey the impression that "society" arbitrarily devises the division of the GNP pie annually, for although within minor upward and downward limits those who actually control the decisions enjoy some subjective leeway, the objective tendency toward greater state expenditures is dictated by the development of capitalism itself. If the state portion of the GNP were to rise substantially it could do so only by invading the sphere of profitable private production—a contingency that presupposes that the working class has taken control of the state.

Although the state has to be invested with compulsory powers to assert the interests of capital in general against recalcitrant capitalists and labor, S's contention that decision-making takes place in the legislatures is somewhat naive. The fact that he has once again indulged in apologetics would not be particularly noteworthy if the particular subject were not crucial to his assertion that in contrast to communist countries, in the mixed economy "the people" are in charge.

Let us now concentrate on the aspect he labels "social consumption of public goods." This supposedly means that "as a nation we are consuming more of our national product *socially* rather than individually," as for example paying for roads via taxation rather than buying railroad tickets (152). Well, that does indeed sound sociable. But when we recall the share of government expenditures allotted to war spending it is far more likely that instead of consuming commodities individually "we" are compelled to part with wages to pay for nonconsumable B-52s or submarines. To use the term "consumption" here is pure ideology, for consumption as an integral part of the process of social reproduction can have nothing to do with the production and use of products of labor which are by their very nature designed to leave the system of reproduction without having been productively consumed.

And in fact if we look at the development of the various components of GNP, we see that between 1929 and 1970, consumption dropped from 75.5 to 63.5 percent, while G rose from 8.5 to 22.5 percent; and similarly, if we examine the components of industrial production, we find that between 1939 and 1969 means of consumption dropped from 39 to 28 per cent, while the production of military equipment rose from almost zero to 7 percent.[14] These figures clearly demonstrate the tendency of the mixed economy to replace individual consumption with no consumption at all.

True, lesser amounts are expended on "social consumption," more conventional types of "external economies" such as roads, schools, etc. But once S has admitted that these are *largely produced by private enterprise* (152), and that the government "pays" for them, one wonders what qualitative change has been wrought, since governments have been buying cannons if not typewriters for quite some time now. We are not necessarily refuting S, all we are saying is that he has failed to prove that an essentially new development has been set in motion.

The same holds true for "government production"—at

least with respect to the example of the U.S. used by S, for he himself admits that "there has been little expansion . . . in recent decades" (153). Despite certain apparently historical reasons, S contends that "economically" the reasons for nationalization of some branches and not others are not "completely arbitrary." The reason then seems to get lost in the shuffle as S brings us before "the courts" and their decisions on public utilities, but it has something to do with lack of "effective competition"; soap and perfume, on the other hand, are obviously not a "natural candidate for governmental operation" (153). This passage does not make quite clear the connection, if any, between economics and nature and soap and electricity. The point S is trying to make relates to the possibilities of profitable production; if it is possible for an individual capital to produce commodities for sale to individual consumers at a profit the state will not "interfere" with nature or whatever and go into production itself. If individual capitals cannot produce certain use values, the state may or may not tax "the people" in order to produce them, depending on the use values and their role in the development of capitalism at any particular point in history.

Because certain branches of public utilities are vital to all capitalists, they have an interest in not monopolizing them; since the huge capital costs involved in duplicating them competitively are more obvious to the bourgeoisie than is milk, for instance.

That S has failed to understand the significance of nationalizations within the capitalist mode of production is borne out by his using Sweden, which he calls socialist, as an example (871). One of his major problems lies in his equating nationalization with socialization. As Engels pointed out almost a hundred years ago, "if the nationalization of tobacco were socialistic, then Napoleon and Metternich would be counted in among the founders of socialism."[15]

How far did these nationalizations go, and why were they undertaken altogether? It may come as a surprise to learn that the state-owned Swedish plants account for 3 percent of Sweden's industrial production,[16] or that about 5 percent of the entire economy is state-owned (as compared to 25 percent in Austria and 40 percent in Italy) and that at least 4 percent had belonged to the state even before the Social Democrats came to power.

Nationalizations take place in response to the following needs: (1) state financing; (2) "defense"; (3) subsidizing private enterprise. This of course does not mean that all nationalizations are somehow reactionary and ought to be opposed. They do not necessarily serve the exclusive interests of the capitalist class; under certain conditions, especially when they serve to foster production—as was the case in Sweden's atomic energy corporation and some of its iron works—nationalization may raise the workers' standard of living. But as long as the capitalist class remains in control these nationalizations are of a dual character.

The final aspect S touches on is "welfare expenditures"; he categorizes these as the transfer of the purchasing power "to the needy or worthy," such as veterans, the aged, handicapped, pensioners, and unemployed. This leads him to the remarkable assertion that owing to this "our system is sometimes called the 'welfare state' " (154).

What follows then is a more income-theoretical discussion of transfer payments which we will take up in Chapter 7. Suffice it to say here that S does not bother to distinguish between transfers of income from the present to the future within the same class and transfers in the present possibly but not necessarily between classes. Or more concretely, it is wrong to say that social-security "benefits," unemployment insurance, etc., are transfers of purchasing power between classes; they are merely deferred wage payments, and although the individual worker may not get back exactly what he or she contributed, the transfers are effected between generations of workers or within a generation.

S ignores this aspect and instead concentrates on such factors as aid to the blind, which does in fact represent transfer payments in the sense that the recipients have not made contributions which are now being repaid to them.

But in 1971, for example, social-security expenditures totaled $66 billion while aid to the blind amounted to $101 million.[17]

Why, we wonder, does S distort the picture by emphasizing the atypical and by failing to distinguish among the various types of expenditures? Is it that such an approach becomes necessary for ideological reasons once he has sought to pass off the mixed economy as a welfare state? For if one strips away these so-called welfare programs, one is left with military spending and redistribution within and to the capitalist class.

But although S very definitely pursues the course outlined here he does not push it to its extreme. More explicitly, he asserts that "an increasing part of the national income is being 'transferred' by taxation and government *welfare* from the relatively rich to the relatively poor" (161), but he offers neither theoretical proof nor empirical evidence for his assertion. True, he contends that he will demonstrate how taxation leads to redistribution, but as we shall see, this is not quite accurate. In addition to his flawed theories on redistribution he asserts that even disregarding so-called transfer payments, the "progressive" taxation system itself would tend to accomplish redistribution: "suppose the government made the very rich pay all the taxes for national defense and most of the taxes for civilian programs. Is it not evident, then, that it would be altering the inequality in the distribution of the after-tax disposable incomes that different classes have to spend. . ." (155). The key word here is "suppose"; for in Chapter 9, S is singing a different tune: "Eighty-five per cent of all income taxes came from the low-bracket rates of 20 percent or less: it is not the rich who pay for the bulk of government; they are too few. It is the median-income group, who, by their numbers, predominate" (171).

It is important to note that S says this within the context of a discussion of loopholes; we take this to mean that even if loopholes were closed, it would be unrealistic to expect the rich to pay for everything. Yet in Chapter 8 he is "supposing" precisely what he later asserts to be impossible.

S presumably introduces this supposition as a safeguard in case the redistributive results of the transfer programs turn out to be negligible. Thus he says that "within reasonable limits" (155) most people will see nothing "improper" in having "the more fortunate citizens" subsidize the consumption of "the less fortunate." At first glance "reasonable" appears to be a vacuous term used to explain any particular outcome. And in fact in his more esoteric arguments S does lean heavily on this vacuity, for instance when he speaks of "the general principle . . . that taxation should be arranged to accomplish whatever the good society regards as the proper *redistribution* of market-determined incomes" (164). The next step, then, according to S's pet notion of revealed preference, is to say that society wishes to do whatever it in fact does.

But we are also faced with a hidden strain of reasoning in which S points to the relatively limited nature of redistribution, a line which can only be traced by juxtaposing many separate and perhaps even unintended remarks. But to return to one last point—namely that of the "supposed" referral of war taxes to the "very rich"; this is a very strange notion of "altering the inequality in the distribution" of after-tax income. It assumes first of all as the point of departure the very situation which the mixed economy brought about; namely, that beginning with World War II the bulk of the population was compelled to pay for the war; and as S himself notes, the tax system never returned to the prior situation, when "life was simple" (150). Thus even though he charges that "one must maintain a sense of historical perspective" in order to understand the development of government spending (149), he "supposes" as a typical welfare-state situation one which directly contradicts the entire thrust of the mixed economy.

Secondly, disregarding all this, S merely asserts that we could return to the prior situation—that is, when the "rich" paid most of the taxes; so aside from the unreal nature of that supposition, all the "less fortunate" are getting is what they had before the humane mixed economy took over.

Lastly, this supposition also testifies to the farcical nature of the "general principle" that "equals should be taxed equally" (164). For the shunting of the "national defense" tax "burden" on to the "rich" would be tantamount to admitting that these "public services . . . are peculiarly for the benefit of recognizable groups" (165).

III / SOCIAL SECURITY IN THE WELFARE STATE

A / THE HISTORY OF "WELFARE"

Before launching into an analysis of the various social-security programs, let us examine S's view of the development of social institutions designed to deal with "poverty." In the chapters under review here, S restricts himself to vague and meaningless pronouncements on "society's" increasingly civilized standards. But some of his comments in Chapter 40 are indicative of his peculiar relationship to history. Interestingly enough, he stresses the persistence of poverty and of palliative measures. Thus, for example, he says that "Governments have always had some responsibility for the poor," or sees private charity as "the conscience money that the lucky paid to the unlucky," or that "each working generation took care of its parents in retirement," or finally, that "private charity was never adequate" (809).

Each of these contains a kernel of truth also for the modern mixed economy; but the irony here is that S is basically unaware of the essential historical differences as well as the similarities growing out of certain general characteristics common to all class socieites.

His attribution of an on-going concern on the part of the state for the poor is rooted in the inability of bourgeois science to grasp the peculiarities of the capitalist state. As to "private charity," S ignores the specific historical conditions in which it developed. In the religious literature of the Middle Ages, poverty is seen as a manifestation of the will of God, not as something despicable; charity served to assuage the most extreme expressions of poverty. To call such charity inadequate testifies to a faulty understanding of the past. Adequate to what or whom? This view of adequacy fails to understand the objective function of such charity, which was simply to keep the lid on revolt, a general need of all class societies past and present. The charity of the Middle Ages was adequate as long as the feudal mode of production was "adequate"; once that began to prove itself inadequate, as the estates and guilds grew less stable—that is to say, as the primitive accumulation of capital began to separate the agricultural and artisan producers from their means of production and, by extension, means of subsistence—this charity proved inadequate to the magnitude and intensity of the poverty that sprang up. Now poverty ceased to be the will of God and turned into the fault of the individual.

The following list of expenditures of "public assistance" (in billions of dollars) for 1970 will give the reader an overview of the range of welfare programs in the narrow sense (public assistance) and also of their contribution to total societal income redistribution:

Aged, disabled, blind	3.3
Aid to Families with dependent children (AFDC)	6.7
Medicaid	7.1
Food stamps	2.0
Other nutrition	1.5
Housing subsidies	1.3
General Assistance	0.9
Total	22.8[18]

In order to understand the redistributive effect of such expenditures we must first understand the historical context within which such programs arose and developed:

"Federal grants to share in the costs of state welfare programs were part of the original social security legislation of the 1930s. They were viewed as interim programs to aid those unable to work, during the transition period, until everyone had earned protection under the social security programs against loss of income."[19]

The key word here is "earned," because it implies that elimination of welfare payments and incorporation into social security depends on the ability of capitalism to create jobs, so that those formerly on welfare can "earn" enough in wages to pay enough for later social security "benefits." It is precisely this failure on the part of the mixed economy that leads to the continuation and growth of the welfare rolls.

The inability to recognize that it is the failure of the mixed economy to provide jobs for those that were prevented from obtaining vital skills seems particularly suspicious in the light of an analysis prepared by the First National City Bank of the Federal Government's billion dollar Public Employment Program. After noting that it had cut unemployment by 0.2 percent, the bank commented that if the program were to be expanded, it would draw workers out of the "market for private-sector jobs at a time when the unemployment rate is beginning to slip downward. It would reduce the supply of labor on the market, by artificially forcing up wages, would discourage employers from creating new marginal jobs in private enterprise."[20]

Thus the only "problem" seen by the bourgeoisie is that of redistributing enough income to this enormous reserve army to keep the lid on social "unrest." This is the crux of the problem: to keep those separated involuntarily from the process of production below the poverty level without destroying the "independence" of the working poor by giving them anti-incentive payments that might "artificially" interfere with the supply and demand on the labor market rooted in the process of capital accumulation.

Just how little such programs have contributed to a greater equalization of income distribution is attested to by two basic facts: namely that the "poor" themselves in part finance these programs, and, secondly, that "benefits" as a percentage of average national income or average wages have not risen. As to the first, we already know that state-local taxes are, by S's own admission, regressive, and account for about 37 percent of public-assistance revenues; as for the second point, average payments under these programs as a percentage of the median income of employed males has actually dropped from 19.9 percent in 1950 to 16.7 percent in 1960 to 15.9 percent in 1968.

B / SOCIAL SECURITY

1/ *Methodological observations*   In his own way S, with his vague statement that "in an earlier time, the extended family system meant that each working generation took care of its parents in retirement" (809), has provided us with an approach to the problem of social-security programs. Elaborating on this we might say that under capitalism the national working class as a whole becomes the extended family insofar as it provides for the older generation.

As we mentioned earlier, not all aspects of state revenues and expenditures dealing with the various components of social security can be looked on as a redistribution between "the owners of tangible resources such as land and property" and "the owners of labor power" (164), because the social-security contributions of the workers as well as of the capitalists represent a component of the value of labor power; whether the subsequent "benefits" serve to support the worker in old age, to repair his health so that his labor power may be preserved, keep him alive when unemployed, all this can be reduced to the heading of deferred wages. The fight for these programs represents a victory for the working class as compared to the nineteenth century when no such programs existed in the sense that a closer approximation of the value of labor power may now be reproduced in the form of total wages. Prior to such programs the wages workers received did not cover the full value of their labor power since they made no provisions for sickness, unemployment, "retirement," etc. In this sense the struggle for social security has been basically a defensive action on the part of the working class to have the "laws of equal exchange" apply to the commodity labor power.

In large part social-security contributions and taxes represent state administration of total variable capital, some of which is not paid directly from the individual capitalists to the individual workers in the form of wages but is centrally collected and disbursed for the reproduction of aggregate labor power. Once we see this we understand that the state is merely "registering" the results of the class struggle insofar as it surrounds the issue of preserving the value of labor power. We are here dealing with two related points—the payments by the workers and those by the capitalists. As far as the workers are concerned, it would seem that we are dealing with a fairly straightforward operation involving insurance, not redistribution. But many economists have confused the issue by failing to distinguish between the individual workers and the class. Thus S in the first edition maintained that he "would question the social wisdom of linking a particular tax to a particular expenditure benefiting those taxed. So long as social-security legislation had to be (somewhat dishonestly) sold to the public as an extension of private insurance, this may have been tactically necessary, but surely that day is long past" (p. 170, n. 1).

Two points are to be made here: (1) insurance and (2) alternative taxing methods. The introduction of the individual insurance approach is inappropriate precisely because we are dealing here with an institution that had to develop on the aggregate class level because individually workers were not strong enough to win these demands. The state had to intercede to force equal competitive conditions for all capitalists. As to alternative taxing proposals, usually made in the context of taxing out of general revenues, the objection here is the same as that to all such plans for substituting one "progressive" income tax for all other existing tax structures: it is all very well, but sheer demagoguery in view of the fact that the trend of taxation in capitalist societies is toward increasingly complicated systems which tend to obscure the real burdens and benefits.

There is widespread agreement even among non-Marxist economists that social security does not make for any significant income redistribution as between labor and capital. This is clear as regards employee contributions; but even employer contributions are ultimately borne by the worker either in the form of lower wages or higher taxes. Since the inception of the U.S. system forty years ago, the benefit rates have been raised periodically, so that there is a built-in progression: the older workers will receive more than they paid in because the level and scale of benefits have been raised. But this has nothing to do with redistribution between classes. Even *Business Week* (July 15, 1972) concedes that social security "is essentially a pact between generations, through which today's workers finance the pensions of yesterday's workers. . . ."

2/ *Empirical material on social security contributions*   Let us look at some of the aspects of regressivity for which S obviously has no patience. The above-cited issue of *Business Week* points out that 20 million workers deemed too poor to pay income tax paid $1.5 billion in payroll taxes, which the article calls highly regressive. (The figures given are for 1971.) It points out that since workers ultimately pay the employers' share as well, a worker making $9,000 per year pays a $1,000 payroll tax, or 11 per cent. And it quotes Milton Friedman, who counters traditional claims that the tax regressivity is compensated for by the poor getting more benefits per dollar contributed, with the argument that the better-paid workers start working later in life and thus work and contribute for fewer years while living longer and thus receiving benefits for more years.

Equally significant, and similarly neglected by S, is the fact that this highly regressive tax constitutes an increasingly higher proportion of all Federal taxes. Even according to bourgeois standards of regressivity and progressivity, there is a definite trend toward reduction of the share of progressive taxes (estate, corporate, income), and a growing trend toward payroll and excise taxes. With income taxes remaining more or less stable, the crucial shift has taken place between corporate income and payroll taxes. Whereas in 1960 the former were 50 percent greater than the latter, by 1968 payroll taxes had overtaken corporate taxes, and by 1973 they accounted for almost twice as large a share—31 percent versus 16 percent.[21]

3/ *Social-security benefits*   In view of the fact that S likes to speak of the "welfare state" without offering any information on the scope of existing social security, some data on this subject might prove useful.

To begin with let us focus on the core of all social-security systems—old-age pensions. According to a Brookings Institution study of the social-security system, 30 percent of all persons over the age of 65 can officially be classed as poor. Thus the major problem of the aged is poverty, not affluence, and despite a series of increases, the average benefits are still low.[22] The minimum benefit for a single retired worker amounts to 50 percent of the official poverty threshold.[23] Furthermore, old-age benefits as a percentage of average weekly manufacturing wages have fallen from 17 percent in 1960 to 15.3 percent in 1967.[24] This shrinkage is also evident in other programs. S does not bother to talk about what goes on inside factories, but an official government document notes that workmen's-compensation coverage as a percentage of the work force has not risen since 1953.[25] Even Nixon's National Commission on State Workmen's Compensation Laws found that in thirty-one states benefits fell below the official poverty figure of $4,137.[26] A similar situation exists with regard to unemployment benefits: in the late 1960s weekly benefits had leveled at about 35 percent of average weekly wages, the same as in the early fifties, and considerably below the slightly more than 40 percent of 1939.

Even this brief view shows that the welfare state has barely touched the great extremes of poverty which capitalism, as with all class societies, uses to "discipline" the direct producers. The declining percentages of average weekly wages, and the fact that at least in one of the programs the percentages were higher before World War II, would indicate that fears the welfare state might weaken work incentives are totally unfounded.

IV / THE CLASS NATURE OF THE TAX SYSTEM

In this section we will analyze the various types of taxation on the Federal and state-local levels discussed by S. We will do so with a view toward providing the basis for qualitative judgments on income redistribution in the mixed economy. The incorporation of similar studies for the capitalist countries of Western Europe as well as a brief comparison with the socialist countries of Eastern Europe will complete this review.

A / PROGRESSIVE AND REGRESSIVE TAXATION: DIRECT AND INDIRECT TAXES

Preparatory to his discussion of taxes in the concrete, S offers the reader some semantic distinctions—as between progressive and regressive taxation and direct and indirect taxes—in a subsection entitled "Pragmatic Compromises in Taxation"; presumably this part was meant to acquaint us with the connection between these two types of taxes and the "philosophical questions" of sacrifices, benefits, recognizable groups, etc. However, all we are offered are "technical terms" (165) dealing with numerical proportions of the classification of taxes according to whether they are levied against goods or persons.

After all this we are told that "modern tax systems are, to repeat, a compromise" (166). If that is so, we must assume that these "technical" distinctions are in some sense expressions of that compromise, the legal or formal vehicles by which "society" implements its value judgments, and in that case S should say so by appraising the development and trend of these various modes of taxation with respect to that compromise. But he does not do that. One could, perhaps, claim that later passages fulfill this function. However, S falls down very badly on this score; not only does he not provide any trend material whatsoever, but by separating Federal and state-local taxes, he avoids any aggregate evaluation of the tax system.

Thus he states that "we generally associate direct and progressive taxes together; indirect and regressive (or proportional) taxes together" (166). But he fails to make clear whether "we" refers to the pre-Samuelsonian man in the street who is forever being berated for falling victim to the fallacy of composition and a myriad other myths, or whether he himself accepts this; he adds to the confusion by tacking on the "many exceptions to such a rule" (166).

This section does not prepare the reader for an analysis of taxation; on the contrary, in part it reinforces the view that on the whole taxation is progressive. Thus S contends that "extensive reliance has been placed on *graduated income taxes*" (7th ed., p. 165; in the 9th, "extensive" has been replaced by "considerable"). Similarly, later on in the text S first emphasizes the progressive nature of the tax and only toward the end does he admit that much of this remains on paper.

If one were to take seriously the suggestion that "modern" tax systems are a compromise, one might do better to concentrate first on the social classes which are doing the "compromising" and then on the "technical" modes of taxation that formalize the result of these social struggles rather than merely to present the "technical" side with the vague references to groups, benefits, etc. The most important "distinction" here of course would be that between labor and capital, between wages and profits, as sources of taxation and receivers of redistributed income. But then of course we would run into the "technical" objection that data collection with respect to these "classifications" is not conducive to precise analyses.

Before proceeding to an examination of the individual taxes, let us look at S's two classificatory distinctions more closely. The two are not on the same level, since the progressive-regressive distinction in itself involves the clear assertion of income redistribution, whereas the direct-indirect distinction does not in itself necessarily imply any income redistribution whatever. In this sense, the latter would have to be called technical, whereas the former even in their formal sense necessarily imply income redistribution.

Let us then look briefly at how "society" understands the direct-indirect distinction. First of all, it should be noted that indirect taxes have undergone a social change. More than a century ago, Ferdinand Lassalle, a German socialist leader, pointed out that indirect taxes were not invented by the bourgeoisie, but that the bourgeoisie were the first to develop them into a system.[27] Even then there was popular opposition to this type of taxation, and it found clear expression in a document prepared by Marx in 1866 for the First International:

> 7. Direct and Indirect Taxation
> (a) No modification of the form of taxation can produce any important change in the relations of labour and capital.
> (b) Nevertheless, having to choose between two systems of taxation, we recommend the *total abolition of indirect taxes,* and the *general substitution of direct taxes.* Because direct [sic; must read indirect—ML] taxes enhance the prices of commodities, the tradesmen adding to those prices not only the amount of the indirect taxes, but the interest and profit upon the capital advanced in their payment;
> Because indirect taxes conceal from an individual what he is paying to the state, whereas a direct tax is undisguised, and not to be misunderstood by the meanest capacity. Direct taxation prompts therefore every individual to control the governing powers while indirect taxation destroys all tendency to self-government.[28]

The passage of a hundred years has not diminished the validity of this appraisal. Two major aspects of this deserve closer examination: economic burden and democracy. Let us begin with the first, which at the same time will serve as an introductoin to the content the mixed economy has given to the indirect-direct distinction.

The following table shows taxes on goods and services as a percentage of total tax revenues for OECD countries on the average for the years 1965-71:[29]

Ireland	52.1%	Denmark	39.6%
Turkey	49.4%	Italy	38.5%
Greece	42.6%	Austria	37.1%
Finland	42.3%	Belgium	36.8%
Portugal	41.2%	Spain	36.4%
Norway	40.0%	France	36.3%

Canada	35.6%	Switzerland	28.0%
Australia	33.1%	Netherlands	27.2%
Sweden	31.1%	Japan	24.6%
W.Germany	30.8%	Luxemburg	22.7%
UK	30.0%	US	19.5%

Thus we can see that the majority of the countries of Western Europe derived more than 30 percent of their tax revenues from taxes on goods and services, regressive taxes which flow from the Samuelsonian dictum that the rich unfortunately are not numerous enough to pay for everything. As a U.N. report put it:

> If the yield of indirect taxes is to be—as it generally is—15 per cent or more of the gross national product, then the taxes must be very widely spread. To find items for selectively high taxation, to balance the regressive effects of the large revenues received from taxing commodities largely consumed by the bulk of the households, is becoming increasingly difficult.[30]

It is for these social reasons that indirect taxes have long been seen as regressive in nature.

As to the second of the aspects touched on by Marx, namely the undemocratic concealment of tax "burdens" inherent in indirect taxes, S fails to mention this altogether, presumably because it is not "technical" enough to warrant attention. More importantly, however, it would seem that this is one of those rare occasions when bourgeois science is correct in asserting that the development of capitalism has overtaken Marx's prescience, though this particular development by no means redounds to the honor of that science.

More specifically, it would appear that Marx's distinction between direct and indirect taxes with respect to their powers of concealment has disappeared in practice, not because indirect taxes have become less disguised, but rather because direct taxes have become more disguised, due to the established fact that with the rise of the mixed economy the direct taxes on the wages of workers rose precipitously.

Once the bulk of the population became subject to the direct income tax, the most undisguised aspect of direct taxes disappeared; capitalists gained the possibility for massive circumvention of tax payments, and created the "technical" distinction between nominal and effective tax rates.

In this context it can be said that in contrast to the "laissez faire" of Marx's day, concealment is the hallmark of the tax programs of the contemporary mixed economy.

B / SPECIFIC TAXES
Let us now go on to some of the specific taxes. In this connection it would be well to look at the composition of the Federal tax system. According to S, two of the major taxes are progressive, one "intermediate," and two regressive, but he fails to describe the trend of these various components, as for example the definite tendency of the payroll tax to displace the corporate income tax. (Even if one were to read nothing but S, this could be established by comparing the corresponding figures from the first edition [pp. 168f.] with those of the ninth.) Since S himself admits that "inheritance or death taxes do little these days to redistribute wealth and income" (8th ed., p. 158), there is in effect nothing left but the personal income tax to counterbalance an otherwise regressive system. Having already dealt with the payroll taxes (and S himself admits the regressive nature of tobacco, alcohol, and gasoline taxes), we will concentrate on the other three taxes.

1/ *Corporate taxes*   S ranks the corporation tax as an "intermediate" tax (166) because it is progressive in its redistributive effect insofar as it is shifted on to the stockholders, and regressive insofar as it is shifted on to the consumers. He then proceeds to adduce arguments in support of and in opposition to increased corporate taxes. The opponents maintain among other things that such taxes are tantamount to double taxation since shareholders also pay income taxes on dividends received. Others, presumably working on the hypothesis that taxes are not shifted on to consumers, support higher corporate taxes on the basis that the retained earnings are not distributed to the shareholders. In the 7th edition, S closes this debate while straddling a fence: "This problem is too complex for a final evaluation here" (p. 158). The 8th and 9th editions do not even go this far, they simply leave the matter hanging.

S does not give us any "evaluation" whatsoever! If we understand his various arguments correctly, they focus on the pros and cons of progressive taxation; for what they refer to is the taxation of high capitalist incomes and/or direct profits without the possibility of passing them on to the consumer. If that is the issue, then it is obvious why he cannot offer a final evaluation. In a later section he concedes that "economic science" cannot "resolve these various crosscurrents of progressive taxation. In the end, therefore, a voter must try to judge the costs and decide on ethical grounds whether he favors a more or less egalitarian society. . ." (8th ed., p. 162). But what, after all, is the use of a "science," especially one with pretensions of educating the voter (8th ed., p. V11), that leaves its disciples in the lurch at the critical moment, abandoning them to "ethics"?

Secondly and more importantly, S is fudging here, because earlier in this chapter he had pointed "to the economic fact of life that increasing certain taxes, however favorable it might look to an ardent redistributionist, would at the same time be expected to do great harm to people's incentives and to the efficiency of society's use of resources" (7th ed., p. 157). And further fudging has taken place by substituting "some harm" (166) for "great harm." However, the important point here is that S is right: a true profits tax beyond a certain point would threaten the capitalist mode of production with respect to international competition and its continued profitable existence.

But that is nothing new: most bourgeois economists like to talk about the "equity-efficiency" contradiction (or rather "problem"), namely, that too much income redistribution leads to smaller profits and thus to a drop in investment and production, whereas too much efficiency leads to too much concentration, too great a portion of national income going to capital, and "resistance" on the part of the rest of society. These are correct descriptions of the surface expressions of the basic contradictions of capitalism that periodically make themselves felt in the form of industrial cycles. All this then merely points up the limits of the mixed economy as welfare state: even if the subjective goal of "society" were the redistribution of income in some essential way, this could not be done within the capitalist mode of production since it would interfere with its central regulator—the rate of profit. In this sense the common notion of the welfare state is a myth, and the mixed economy, if it is supposed to be identical with it, becomes a contradiction in terms.

Why, then, do corporations oppose corporate taxes if they can pass them on anyway? Although S is careful to say that corporations with net incomes above $25,000 "must pay 48 cents of each extra dollar of earnings" in taxes, and although he has a footnote referring to 82 percent excess-profits taxes in wartime periods (167 and n.2), he never mentions that just as there are large gaps between nominal and effective personal-income-tax rates, so there are in the corporate tax as well. Thus despite his categorical assertion, a recent Congressional study (corporate tax data are not open to public inspection) indicated that in 1969 the effective tax rate on corporations amounted to 37 percent, while the top one hundred corporations "managed to reduce the toll to 26.9 per cent."[31]

In view of the fact that the largest capitals pay the lowest taxes, the effective tax rates make this a regressive tax. This can affect the competitive position of a firm. During those phases of the business cycle when, or in those branches where, conditions permit the passing on of the tax to consumers, corporations able to avoid the paying of taxes will obviously accumulate more; on the other hand, when conditions do not allow the passing on of taxes, the corporations that are forced to pay the tax themselves are clearly at a competitive disadvantage vis-à-vis those able to escape payment.

Given the secrecy and concealment that surround the matter of corporate taxes, a precise determination of who pays what cannot be made. But the important point here is that within certain quantitative limits it is possible to tax corporations without causing capitalism to collapse, as "business" propagandists like to prognosticate.

2/ *Inheritance taxes* Although S calls them one of the two Federal taxes with a progressive effect, he relegates them to the section on state and local taxes. The reason for this is not clear, since the Federal tax system receives three to four times more revenue from them than the state-local system.[32] As S himself points out, these "progressive" taxes have little effect, a view shared by most economists. Thus *Business Week* (August 12, 1972) concedes that "most wealth can be passed from generation to generation untouched by Uncle Sam." And Pechman offers this incisive comment. "One can only guess why the estate and gift taxes have not been more successful. A possible explanation is that equalization of the distribution of wealth by taxation is not yet accepted in the United States."[33] He presumably means that the people, dreaming of upward mobility, oppose such laws for fear of what they might have to pay should they become rich. But this is blatant nonsense. It is not the mass of the people who draw up these laws or set up foundations to protect their accumulated wealth.

Contrary to S's assertion that things have changed since the time of Louis XIV, when peasants were taxed while the ruling nobility got off "scot-free" (164), the paltry use made of inheritance taxes is just another example of how "down through history the dominant classes, groups, factions, clans, interests or political elites have always been scrupulously prudent in avoiding taxes at the expense of the lower orders."[34]

3/ *Income tax* The personal income tax is the crucial tax with respect to income redistribution. Payroll and sales taxes are regressive, the corporate tax probably also, and the inheritance tax, though progressive, is almost nonexistent. So if any progressivism is to come out of the system, this is the last hope. And S does everything he can to give the reader the impression that the income tax makes all the difference. Hence the big table (169) on the progressive nature of the rate structure. But after everything is said and done, his material indicates that in fact the whole business looks better on paper than in fact. And he closes the section with the statement that the rich are too few in number to "pay for the bulk of government" (171).

In the end, S has told us absolutely nothing, which is reinforced by his summary: "The personal income tax, except for loopholes and erosion of the tax base, is progressive, tending to redistribute from rich to poor" (177). This is

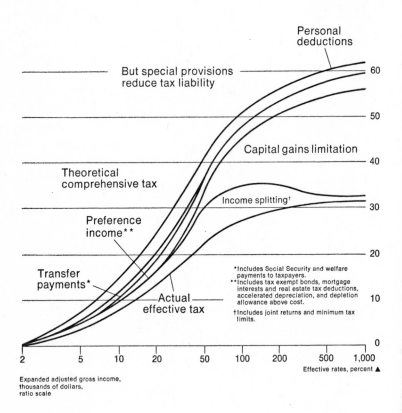

about as useful as saying that the weather was dry except for a few thunderstorms. S makes no effort to sort out the effects quantitatively and arrive at a considered conclusion. Worse still, this approach avoids the issue of the purposeful use of the high nominal rates to make people think the system is progressive. By taking the nominal rates seriously, and then talking about loopholes, etc., in the attempt to get around the basically regressive nature of the tax, S distorts the ideological function of the rates. Furthermore he provides no proof whatsoever for his claim that redistribution is the end result. He paints a multicolored figure to "show" this, but admits that this is "hypothetical" to begin with and moreover "exaggerated for emphasis" (169 f.). Talk about the perversion of science for propaganda purposes! Incapable of proving the main contention of these two chapters as well as of Chapters 5, 39, and 40—namely the ability of the mixed economy to redistribute income to alleviate the inequality of the system criticized by Marx—S resorts to outright falsification. As the accompanying graph from *Business Week* shows, the actual effective tax rates for the highest income brackets are approximately one half of the nominal rates S devotes so much space to, and considerably lower than the sample effective rates he mentions without documentation. And although S mentions so-called erosion and loopholes, he does not make clear that it is chiefly the rich who benefit from them.

To see just how progressive the personal income tax really is, let us look at some recent material from a Census Bureau study by Roger Herriot and Herman Miller showing the tax rate for various income groups, including income received from social security and public assistance, i.e., the tax rate calculated here is based on total income. Farm subsidies, paid largely to the richest farmers, apparently are not included, nor are the numerous subsidies paid to government contractors, which go to the owners in the form of salaries, dividends, etc. The inclusion of such subsidies would narrow the gap between high and low tax rates even more.

Income Groups	Taxes Paid
Under $ 2,000	25.6%
$ 2,000-4,000	24.7%
$ 4,000-6,000	27.9%
$ 6,000-8,000	30.1%
$ 8,000-10,000	29.9%
$ 10,000-15,000	30.9%
$ 15,000-25,000	31.1%
$ 25,000-50,000	33.6%
$ 50,000 Up	46.6%
Total	31.6%[35]

The same Herriot-Miller study offers the following data concerning the development of the proportion of total taxes paid by each income group during the 1960s:

Income Group	Income Range	1962	1968	Change
Lowest Fifth	Under $ 3,800	3.7%	3.7%	—
Second Fifth	$ 3,800-8,200	8.9%	9.4%	+ 5.6%
Middle Fifth	$ 8,200-12,100	14.4%	15.2%	+ 5.6%
Fourth Fifth	$ 12,100-17,500	21.3%	22.1%	+ 3.8%
Highest Fifth	Over $ 17,500	51.7%	49.6%	− 4.1%
Top 5%	Over $ 29,700	28.1%	24.8%	− 8.5%[36]

The reporter again comments that "This indicates that during the prosperous mid-1960s the situation of the middle 60 per cent of income recipients was worsening. Their burden was growing, not because the poor paid a smaller share of the taxes, but because the top 20 per cent paid proportionately less."[37] In fact, on closer inspection we see that the second and third fifths, which doubtless encompass the bulk of the working class, bore the brunt of the increase.

4/ *State and local taxes* We do not intend to devote much attention to these since S himself concedes that "the principal taxes . . . are 'regressive taxes' " (172; though he makes this observation, S fails to inform the reader that state-local taxes have been increasing more rapidly than Federal taxes).

To begin with the property tax, S very generously concedes that it may be regressive relative to income" (172). Even the *Wall Street Journal* said that "Perhaps worst of all, since housing accounts for a very high percentage of low-income budgets, the property tax, by increasing the cost of bought or rented housing, falls disproportionately hard on low-income families, including many elderly retirees."

That sales taxes are regressive is self-evident; suffice it to say that the *Wall Street Journal* of May 9, 1972, reported that those with incomes below $6,000 accounted for 12 percent of all income, but paid 16 percent of all sales taxes and 17 percent of all property taxes.

The last tax we will look at, the state corporate tax, is a particularly good example of the differential effects of taxation since the rates vary from state to state. We will therefore restrict ourselves to the following report from the *Wall Street Journal* (June 5, 1972) stressing precisely this point:

> Interviews with the tax managers of some of the nation's largest corporations turn up little of the passion that individuals vent about higher taxes these days. Taxes are going up, but apparently the corporate people don't feel squeezed. . . . Many businessmen seem satisfied that, eventually at least, tax increases are passed along to consumers in the form of higher prices. "The biggest problem," says Robert Boehike, tax manager at Swift & Co., "is being able to determine in advance what our tax ability is going to be so we can price our products accordingly."
>
> In fact, business men seem more concerned that state and local taxes are uneven than they are high. Businessmen don't like to pay taxes that don't fall on their competitors too. They also get perturbed when short-run market conditions don't permit a price increase to pass along a higher tax.[38]

V / AGGREGATE REDISTRIBUTION EFFECT

To return to the matter of the total effect of the mixed economy on income distribution, all the evidence we have marshaled, based on data and analyses of bourgeois

economists and the media, indicate that no progress whatsoever has been made by the mixed economy toward the
alleged social value of income redistribution. In fact, *Business Week* claimed that the fact the gap between the rich
and the poor "was widening rather than narrowing" in the
period between 1947 and 1970 deals "a body blow to the notion that the U.S. is moving to a more egalitarian society."[39] That S, despite this impressive array of evidence
from his own camp, can blithely draw before- and after-tax
Lorenz curves—based on data not revealed to the

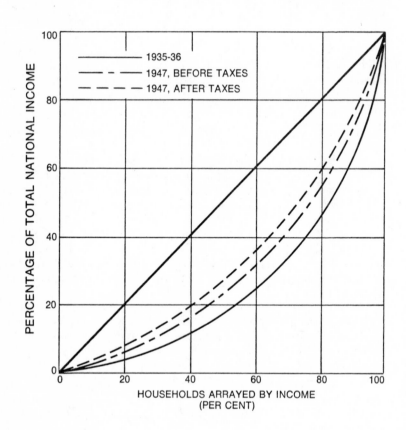

reader—which "for emphasis" indicate exactly what is not happening, is merely the final consequence of apologetics parading under the name of science. For comparison we offer the following before- and after-tax Lorenz curves for the U.S. for the year 1947—when the tax structure was in no way less "progressive" than today—which shows how miniscule the change is.[40]

To demonstrate further how little has been changed by our mixed economy let us cite some relevant statistics. Thus in 1966, the bottom 50 percent of the tax units (families and/or individuals) accounted for 21.42 percent of income before taxes and wound up with a whopping 23.22 percent after taxes. The following table shows the percent of income (1) before and (2) after taxes by population deciles:

Tax Units		(1)	(2)
lowest	10%	1.20%	1.36%
next	10%	2.94%	3.24%
next	10%	4.39%	4.79%
next	10%	5.80%	6.24%
next	10%	7.09%	7.59%
next	10%	8.31%	8.86%
next	10%	9.67%	10.20%
next	10%	11.44%	11.94%
next	10%	14.23%	14.58%
highest	10%	34.93%	31.20%
		100.0%	100.0%[41]

The accompanying Lorenz curve shows how minimal has been the shift of income. The authors attempt to calculate a percentage of inequality reduction. This is a comparison of the Gini coefficients for both Lorenz curves. With O equal to "perfect equality" and 1, maximum inequality, the before-tax coefficient equals .446 and the after-tax coefficient .409, or a reduction of inequality of 8.3 percent.

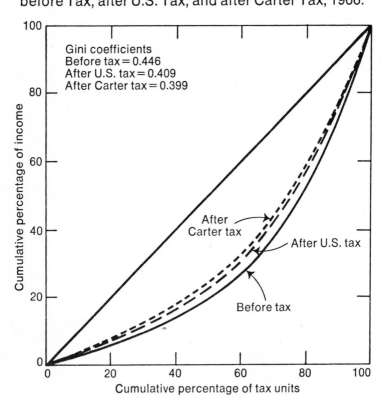

Graph V

Comparison of Distribution of Individual Income
before Tax, after U.S. Tax, and after Carter Tax, 1966.

Gini coefficients
Before tax = 0.446
After U.S. tax = 0.409
After Carter tax = 0.399

After
Carter tax

After U.S. tax

Before tax

Cumulative percentage of income

Cumulative percentage of tax units

APPENDIX

A / INCOME DISTRIBUTION AND REDISTRIBUTION IN WESTERN EUROPE

The failure of the mixed economy to redistribute income is not restricted to the relatively backward United States. According to a report of the U.N., in France, Finland, and Sweden

> the share of total income received by persons in higher income groups rose while the share of those in lower income groups declined. In Sweden the watershed falls between the sixth and the seventh, while in France it is in the seventh decile. Finland shows the most marked widening in income dispersion. All three countries show a notable fall in the relative incomes of the poorest groups.[42]

For another group of countries—the Netherlands, United Kingdom, and Denmark, the report speaks of a "very modest" reduction in income dispersion; in the U.K., though, the lowest 30 percent actually lost ground. The report contends that "a clear tendency towards a reduction in income inequality, displayed at both ends of the scale, appears only in Norway." Yet in the very next paragraph it concedes that "there was no significant change" at the lower end. And it summarizes thus:

> Though not much can be read into small changes over a relatively short period, the impression remains that the income gap between people in low income groups . . . and people in middle income groups has increased in several countries; *the poor have become poorer* in relation to the middle groups, whether the rich have become, by the same measure, richer or not [our emphasis].[43]

The section of the report dealing with the social redistribution of income seems to point to a stationary situation:

> The degree and the pattern of income redistribution varies between countries; but, broadly speaking, the reduction in income dispersion appears to be very modest among the bulk of

the households deriving their income from employment, self-employment and property. The redistribution which has occurred is largely in favour of non-active persons (principally pensioners) and has been *largely financed by their own payments in the past,* either by social insurance contributions or by general taxes.

On the whole, therefore, it seems legitimate to conclude that for the bulk of the population the pattern of primary income distribution is only slightly modified by government action [our emphasis].[44]

In fact, the report says, "perhaps the major individual force leading to a reduction in income inequality during the 1950s and the first part of the 1960s has been the shift from self-employment (a high dispersion group) to wage- and salary-earners." Thus "structural changes," that is to say, the accumulation of capital leading to ever greater centralization of capital and the proletarianization of the petty bourgeoisie, rather than "governmental policies" continue to play the central role in income distribution. As far as the mixed economies of Western Europe are concerned, either income distribution and redistribution have not undergone any change or there has been a continued tendency toward greater income inequality, or the working class wielding some political power has been able to maintain the status quo through redistribution. In either case, the mixed economy has hardly lived up to the myths S has clothed it in.

B / COMPARISON WITH THE SOCIALIST COUNTRIES OF EASTERN EUROPE

Although the U.N. report does not make any explicit comparisons, it does present some comparative data for Eastern and Western Europe. The only country for which the report offers a Gini coefficient ratio (ratio of the area between the 45-degree line and the Lorenz curve to the whole area underneath the 45-degree line; 0 is maximum equality, 1, maximum inequality) is Hungary (1962). This ratio is 0.27, and thus 25 percent lower than the lowest Gini coefficient for Western Europe, i.e., Norway, at 0.36.[45] And Hungary apparently is not an exception among the socialist countries.

A more complete comparison is possible on the basis of the so-called quartile ratio, which measures inequality with respect to fourths of the population. Although the data for the socialist countries refer to wage and salary workers, a comparison of the same statistics for Western Europe indicates that the capitalist country with the lowest level of inequality still outranks the socialist country with the highest level.[46]

Crises and Keynesianism

7 The Theory of National Income
S's Chapter 10

> In the notion of a "national income" most difficulties of
> economics culminate. The "Wealth of Nations" has been
> the prime concern of economists as long as there has
> been any systematic writing in economics, and so it will
> be for the future. Neither the conceptual nor the statisti-
> cal problems in this field have been resolved to anyone's
> satisfaction. . . .
> —Oscar Morgenstern, *On the Accuracy of Economic Obser-*
> *vations,* pp. 243 f.

INTRODUCTION

In evaluating the role of this chapter within S's book we
must consider the twofold plan its author had in mind:
"the unifying summary of Part One's introduction to the
basic economic processes and institutions of modern mixed
societies" and "the introduction to the treatment of macroeconomics of Part Two" (179). Thus by S's own admission, this is a crucial chapter.

However, let us not simply accept his claim at face value,
but rather examine to what extent he carries out his plan
and also determine precisely what the key role of the chapter is. For it appears that S is vague on this point. With respect to its retrospective function as a synthesis of the preceding material, this chapter wraps up the discussion of Big
Business, Big Labor, and Big Government. The national-
income account presumably represents the statistical sum-

mary of the economic activities of these three sectors as they express themselves in their peculiar forms of income. The "statistical-technical" treatment accorded them here reinforces the impression of harmonious and equal coexistence; for the mere ability to establish a quantitative relationship among these elements—whether it be in the form of adding apples and oranges or wages and profits—presupposes qualitative sameness. This means that if all these incomes or products could not be reduced to a "common denominator," the very possibility of the cohesive existence of "society" would be called into question. As we know by now, this common denominator turns out to be money; and since S has already told us that money is common to many different societies, the specific characteristics of the mixed economy—as well as those of the classes constituting that society—are eradicated. (As we shall see, the view of money as a mere technical expedient will involve S's theory of national income in internal contradictions.)

In summary, then, Chapter 10 serves to consolidate the theory of the mixed economy as that of a society without either classes or history, the former insofar as classes are turned into recipients of incomes with only quantitative distinctions, and the latter insofar as consumption subject to quantification by means of an external "measuring rod" is seen as the "goal" of all societies. As to Chapter 10's role as an introduction to Chapters 11-19, we must direct our attention to the construction of a framework within which the Keynesian theories and the intervention of the state can become plausible. We shall seek to direct the reader to what is to come so that this chapter can be read more critically with regard to the author's design.

The basic feature in this respect is the emphasis on the sphere of circulation, a fact essentially connected to the absence of a theory of reproduction, of a theory of value (at least at this juncture), of a theory of productive labor, and finally, to the stress on subjective explanatory criteria. We say circulation sphere because in this chapter S is not concerned with production; the major aspect of the theory of income presented here relates to consumption (and/or expenditure) and revenue. True, bourgeois theory sees receipt of income as synonymous with production of value, and we shall deal with this at the appropriate time. But since the reader has not yet been made aware of this in any systematic way, the connection to production is blocked. The lack of reference to production precludes a theory of reproduction. What we wind up with is a constant flow of expenditures and incomes without any understanding of how the boxes labeled "business" and "public" (Fig. 10-1) generate commodities and incomes. Similarly, a theory of productive labor—i.e., the question of what labor produces value—becomes irrelevant once the sphere of production has been relegated to a later chapter. A theory of value of sorts, in the form of utility, will be presented later, but this does not help the reader at this point.

This seemingly chaotic organization is no mere accident, nor do we believe the only reason to be the commonly voiced contention that there is no criterion for putting the macro course before the micro course, or vice versa. We say this because Keynesian theory itself is characterized by all of these features. In fact, it may be said that it could hardly be otherwise, for all practical efforts to ward off the demise of capitalism must, if they are to avoid the concerted resistance of the capitalist class, proceed through the sphere of circulation. This instinctive shying away from direct control over production coincides with the whole thrust of development of bourgeois economic theory since the post-Ricardian era (ca. 1830); increasingly, this theory has sought refuge in the indvidual and subjective, where the objective crises of capitalism could best be ignored.

The sphere of circulation knows neither capitalists nor workers, only consumers. Though the contradictions stemming from the sphere of immediate production have not disappeared, the connection may conveniently be neglected. It is the matrix for all bourgeois ideas about preserving capitalism through various methods of redistribution. The latest variant is Keynes; but as we shall see, his neglect of the fundamental features of capitalism, the severing of the sphere of distribution and redistribution (state) from the sphere of production, the absence of a theory of reproduction and productive labor, all these make for such a weak theoretical foundation that practical application becomes much more limited than its proponents realize.

THE CHAPTER STRUCTURE

With this general outline in mind, let us proceed to an analysis of the chapter itself. Its structure—i.e., its tripartite arrangement of "simple" economy "with no government and no accumulation of capital or net saving going on" (180); introduction of capital accumulation (186-88); and introduction of the state (188-91)—could lend itself to a fruitful methodological approach to the problem of national income. The abstraction from capital accumulation and the state finds justification in the bourgeois notions of model-building: "all analysis involves abstraction. It is always necessary to *idealize*, to omit detail, to set up simple hypotheses and patterns by which the facts can be related. . ." (9). Although Marx would not accept this reasoning, he, too, comes to a similar conclusion concerning the exposition of what he calls simple reproduction before that of expanded reproduction (which encompasses accumulation):

> Simple reproduction, reproduction on the same scale, appears as an abstraction, inasmuch as on the one hand the absence of all accumulation or reproduction on an extended scale is a strange assumption in capitalist conditions, and on the other hand conditions of production do not remain exactly the same in different years (and this is assumed). . . . However, as far as accumulation does take place, simple reproduction is always a part of it, and can therefore be studied by itself, and is an actual factor of accumulation.[1]

However, two basic differences mark Marx's and S's approach. Marx states explicitly that a "simple" economy is a contradiction in terms, and he wants it understood that simple reproduction does in fact exist *within* expanded reproduction. S, on the other hand, does not heed any such methodological caveats, perhaps because "no mind can comprehend a bundle of unrelated facts" (9). There is nothing real in the abstraction, it is merely a pedagogic device. Looking at S's content, we can see why the methodology conforms to it; but it is precisely the function of this chapter to blur distinctions between modes of production, so-called factors of production, and between the state and the private sector. The manner in which capital accumulation is introduced derives from a subjective view which must necessarily blind the reader to the objective differences between modes of production and classes within capitalism; similarly, the introduction of the state as a coequal partner along with land, labor, and capital blurs the essential distinction between capital production and the secondary redistribution effected by the state.

Thus the model is well suited to S's purpose here: that is to say, the methodology behind the model is as removed from reality as is the content. The development of both these aspects has its origin in the failure of post-Ricardian bourgeois economics to adhere to an objective value- and class-oriented analysis, and this in turn led to models devoid of reality-oriented content.

In our discussion we will follow S's implicit tripartite arrangement. Since the first section on the "simple" economy contains fundamental methodological principles that guide his entire analysis, this will be the place to examine them in detail, although the critique applies to the entire chapter. In the course of this first section it will become obvious that what is at stake here is a basic feature of bourgeois science in general, and of economics in particular.

I / THE "SIMPLE" ECONOMY

The most striking aspect of this section is the author's emphasis on "definitions"; instead of developing a theoretical concept of national income, S repeatedly asserts that national income "is the loose name we give"; "the final figure you arrive at"; "is definable"; "also definable, from a second viewpoint"; is "measurable" or "convenient" to measure in this way or that, etc. (179-81).

These extracts are not evidence of nit-picking on our part, nor of simple sloppiness on S's, as we can see from his codification of this procedure as "an important rule of approximate measurement in economics. *Often it does not matter which definition of measurement you use, so long as you stick to one definition consistently*" (199).

Presumably the reasoning here is connected with analogies to physical measurement where the absolute magnitude of the standard is irrelevant, since the objective there is to set an arbitrary comparative standard. Assuming this to be a technical necessity, one must still demonstrate a property common to the things to be measured (length, volume, etc.), with no regard to qualitative differences and concentrating on a single relevant quantifiable aspect.

This "measuring rod" is, of course, money. Unfortunately, however, the matter is not quite that simple, for one still has to find the characteristic shared by the "goods and services" being measured. Bourgeois theory does have such a common characteristic—utility—but this is not without its problems. But S has not touched on this theory, although it is basic to any discussion of the problem of "measurement."

The problem of national income is, as the quotation from Morgenstern hints at, not a new one; nor are the methods for dealing with it. Eclecticism is the basic feature of this chapter: that is to say, S has picked and chosen that which appears correct or plausible from various theories, and based on this has tried to develop a unified, coherent new theory of national income. The fundamental problem of S's eclecticism lies in his uncanny knack of picking elements from conflicting systems of economics, so that the new creation turns out to be full of contradictions. More specifically, the attempt to fit the subjective theory of value into the older national-income theory based on a theory of classes and objective value leads to the "arbitrary rules" and "paradoxes" that permeate this chapter. S's failure to offer even the vaguest reference to the development of the theory erects an almost insurmountable barrier to understanding.

A / METHODOLOGY AND HISTORY OF THE THEORY OF NATIONAL INCOME

From its very beginnings, bourgeois political economy saw a connection between the wealth of nations, or in this case the concept of national income, and productive labor. However, unlike contemporary discussions of arbitrary "rules," this view was rooted in clearly observable historical changes in the mode of production. The attention paid to wealth which arose with capitalism differed essentially from that of the slave societies of ancient Greece or of the feudal period. The old authors concentrated on the use-value aspect and quality of that which was produced; although money and the concept of money wealth originated with the incipient development of commodity production— i.e., development beyond mere production by slaves or freemen for themselves, but also for a market—these authors were not interested in what we would call exchange value. Nor is this surprising since commodity production, and thus exchange value, had not yet become the motive forces of the economic system. The interest in national wealth evinced by the early bourgeois authors is not an expression of a coarse materialism but rather of a new quality that wealth had assumed in the new mode of production. The members of this new society, keenly aware of the differences between them and their feudal predecessors, were not at all reticent about formulating them, particularly since they were convinced that they were witnessing a turning point in the history of civilization.

The first important bourgeois economists, the mercantilists (from about the sixteenth to the eighteenth century) measured productivity in terms of export value—i.e., if the exported goods yielded more money than they cost, in other words, if the producing country could accumulate gold and silver. As Marx points out, these early prophets correctly formulated money-making as the end of bourgeois society by referring to gold and silver as the only form of wealth.

The next important advance in this context is attributed to the French eighteenth-century physiocrats (Quesnay, Turget, et al.); in contrast to the mercantilists, they recognized the creation of surplus value within a country. That is to say, profit was no longer restricted to transactions with other countries. The physiocrats saw the origin of surplus value in the work of the agricultural producers, in the sense that these workers produce a net product in excess of their wage, and this net product was then appropriated by the second major social class—the landowners. The third class, the sterile class, comprised all others, including industrial workers and capitalists. In view of the fact that capitalism in France was then still emerging out of feudalism, it is not surprising that the physiocratic system appears as a strange combination of feudal and capitalist elements. Since exchange-value production had not yet gained a hold on all branches of production, the physiocrats did not have a concept of abstract labor and, therefore, no real theory of value. They saw the production of a surplus product in the immediate use-value form in agriculture, where one can easily determine that a producer produces more than he eats and productively consumes in the form of raw materials. In this theory the landowner appears as the real capitalist, as well he might have at a time when a fundamental prerequisite of capitalism was taking shape, namely the expropriation of the immediate producers.

Unfortunately we cannot go into these interesting contradictions in the physiocratic system. We merely wish to point to the rise of a new concept of productive labor in the context of an objective change in the development of capitalism finding expression in new class relations.

Adam Smith (1723-1790) took an important step in the development of bourgeois political economy when he extended the notion of productive labor to all surplus-value producing labor:

There is one sort of labour which adds to the value of the subject upon which it is bestowed: there is another which has no such effect. The former, as it produces a value, may be called productive; the latter, unproductive labor. Thus the labour of a manufacturer [i.e., worker] adds, generally, to the value of the materials which he works upon, that of his own maintenance and of his master's profit. The labour of a menial servant, on the contrary, adds to the value of nothing. Though the manufacturer has his wages advanced to him by his master, he, in reality, costs him no expence, the value of those wages being generally restored, together with a profit, in the improved value of the subject upon which his labour is bestowed. But the maintenance of a menial servant never is restored. A man grows rich by employing a multitude of manufacturers: he grows poor, by maintaining a multitude of menial servants.[2]

With that, Smith formulated the basis of the capitalist mode of production—the production of capital by workers who produce a greater value than they consume for a capitalist who is not interested in the use value of the products or of the useful character of the labor he "employs," but only in the excess of value of what "his" workers produce above what he pays them.

Productive labor then is labor which exchanges immediately with capital for the purpose of increasing the capitalist's capital; consequently all labor which is exchanged against revenue—that is, against profit, interest, rent, or even wages, without the objective function of creating profit—thus becomes unproductive labor.

This makes clear that productive labor is determined not by a concrete activity or the product of that activity, but rather by its social relationship. Smith explicitly formulated the essence of capitalism within the framework of the ideological struggle against the dying feudal mode of production; and in this respect he emphasized the distinction between personal services and capital-producing wage labor.

Parallel to this deeper insight, Smith also developed a determination of productive labor oriented at the criterion of physical-material embodiment:

> The labour of some of the most respectable orders in the society is, like that of menial servants, unproductive of any value, and does not fix or realize itself in any permanent subject, or vendible commodity, which endures after that labour is past, and for which an equal quantity of labour could afterwards be procured.[3]

Insofar as it formulates the elementary form of production in capitalism to be that of commodities, this in a certain respect is a more elementary definition of productive labor. Moreover, Smith was obeying a sound instinct, since in his time the production of nonmaterial commodities—services—was more or less associated with unproductive labor in the first sense—namely personal services outside the capitalist-wage laborer relationship. Smith felt that disregard for the second determination would open the gate to all sorts of unproductive labor in the first sense.

But as Marx points out, Smith descended to a more elementary yet less fundamental form of determination, for in the last analysis he returned to the material form of the product or the concrete form of the labor rather than the social realtionship.

For political (class) reasons, the bourgeoisie has been forced to alter much of its originally critical stance, gradually dropping the concept of productive labor altogether—which means the first Smithian determination on the distinguishing characteristic of capitalism as well as the second, insofar as the earlier bourgeois understanding of commodity production as a qualitatively new form of social reproduction is gradually eliminated—and of social classes as potentially or even inherently antagonistic social forces. Once this cornerstone of political economy was removed, the whole structure threatened to collapse unless a new foundation was laid. While this was under construction, an eclectic substitute was being assembled.

In summary then we may say that as far as the classical political economists like Smith and Ricardo are concerned, national income is created in the sphere of production which embraces all production taking place in the form of immediate exchange of labor and capital; the redistribution of the income originally appropriated in the form of wages, profits, and rent—whether it be to the state or for personal services—is a secondary problem which should not interfere with a theoretical understanding of the primary question.

B / S'S APPROACH

Let us now return to S's presentation and the contradictions brought on by his eclecticism. The first point S makes relates to the "equivalent" approach or method of calculating national income or product—namely from the vantage point of market prices of consumed goods or of factor earnings (181). The first approach is based on utility theory, the second on the production factor or marginal productivity theory. This is no coincidence since it is these two theories that gradually began to replace the classical theories of value and surplus value. Because of S's chaotic organization, our analysis of the theory of national income as based on these two theories must remain incomplete. There is simply no justification for presenting a theory of national income before discussing the underlying theories of value. This structure—and more significantly S's apparent lack of awareness that such a procedure requires theoretical justification—doubtless stems from the inherent incoherence of the "neoclassical synthesis." Rather than presenting a harmonious union of classical or neoclassical microeconomics and modern Keynesian macroeconomics, S has concocted a mixture of objective and subjective theories which can coexist only at the expense of content and methodological focus.

The theory of national income is stamped by its classical provenance. It has been revitalized in the hope of developing a policy to master the crises stemming from the contradictions in the sphere of production, but the price of this revitalization is an internally contradictory theory. Consequently, we will confine ourselves to a study of the theories of utility and production factors insofar as they touch on the matter of national income and show up the necessarily contradictory nature of that eclectic creation.

Let us begin with S's "flow-of-product" approach. Without explaining how money can be the magic wand that strips "the diverse apples, oranges, and machines that any society produces" (18) of their inherent difference and converts them into ledger entries with only quantitative distinctions—that is, without explaining how the price *form* arose altogether—S answers his own questions as to why market prices are used "as weights in evaluating and summing diverse physical commodities and services" with a reference to the thesis in Part Three, according to which "market prices are reflectors of the relative desirability of diverse goods and services" (181).

Yet we all know or can imagine socieites in which "relative desirability"—whatever that may mean—is not reflected in money and hence in market prices .What then happens to "the yardstick of an economy's performance" in such a society? The very notion of a yardstick, that is to say, a quantitative reduction and measurement, is a relatively recent one, and it has blossomed forth in only one mode of production—capitalism.

In line with the analysis in Chapter 3 of money as a technical expedient for facilitating barter, "in measuring NNP we are not interested in consumption and investment goods merely for their money value: *money is the measuring rod used to give some approximate figure to the underlying 'satisfactions' or 'benefits' or 'psychic income' that comes from goods"* (201).

What is the underlying aspect S refers to by various names, all of them in quotation marks? (We shall, for simplicity's sake, call it "good vibes," without quotation marks, to show our associating ourselves with it. S's Chapter 22 does not offer any discussion of utility going beyond the sketchy remarks made here.) Now S does not minimize the formidable difficulties involved in establishing a good vibes NNP; on the contrary, he concedes that "strictly speaking" or "in principle" each act of consumption should enter NNP at "its fair market value" (201). Such a procedure, unfortunately, turns out to be impossible; for although "enjoyment of a physical pleasure does tend to get into NNP," it does so only "indirectly" and as a "rough measure." By this S means the replacement of a worn-out commodity. Despite this seeming pessimism, he backtracks and asserts that "this all works out well enough, except in one case," so-called consumer durables, which allegedly last and thus spread out their good vibes over a long period, in contrast to their one-shot purchase and thus incorporation into NNP.

However, even a fairly cursory investigation would show that this does not all work out well enough. Using the example of a phonograph record S cites, we can well imagine that of two people buying the same record, one gets very good vibes but unfortunately does not have the money to replace the new but worn-out record, whereas the other listens to it indifferently but replaces it anyway since he found no better use for his money. All we are trying to say by this is that if S wants to see replacement as an indirect expression of good vibes had by all, he is on extremely shaky ground.

Behind all this palaver is the very significant attempt by S to determine value through use value. Whereas the classical authors understood that use value was a more or less permanent relation between the individual and/or society and the object involved, that therefore no explanatory elements for any particular society inhered in this relationship since it belonged to the realm of production and consumption in general (or in the abstract), and that therefore the relationship of use value remained an implicit prerequisite of the capitalist mode of production, "modern" economists try to construct a theory of capitalism based on this relationship which is not specific to capitalism. Whereas the classical economists recognized value production or exchange value as the essential new social relationship produced by capitalism, "moderns" try to blot out what is specific by attributing this new quality to all other societies (in the last analysis by reducing commodity exchange to barter). And finally, whereas the critical element in classical political economy was the discovery of the laws that determined the specific way in which the general or abstract aspects of production and consumption (including use value) found their expression in the new *form* of social existence (capitalist commodity production), eclectic contemporary bourgeois economists attribute prime explanatory value to utility without being able to sever all ties to the tradition of objective value still hovering about in the form of market price or money. Although the attempt to rely solely on utility must fail, the attempt to combine utility with, or even reintegrate it into, the older tradition of objective value must necessarily lead to an inherently contradictory mishmash, since the classical theory denies the possibility of determining value by use value. It is this impossibility which gives rise to the many "paradoxes" and "brain teasers" S tosses about as evidence of the "arbitrariness of some current practices."[4] He apparently does not understand that these are not mere technical quirks but fundamental expressions of his own contradictory eclecticism, the result of trying to impose one schema onto its negation.

Now let us turn to the second approach—that of factor earnings. Here NNP is equal to the sum of the incomes going to the productive factors land, labor, capital (plus the "residual" profit). S characterizes these as "costs of production" (181). This approach, like the first one, is rooted in the sphere of circulation. Its starting point is not what is produced but rather what meets the eye on the market, whether in the form of commodity prices or factor incomes. Unlike the former approach, however, this one links up to a much older part of classical theory; for although Adam Smith at times adhered to the labor theory of value in the sense that labor creates all value, at other times, and predominantly, he held to the view that the value of a commodity resolves itself into the various revenues (now called "factor incomes").[5] At this point we will refrain from going into the reason for this development; we merely want to point out that the theory of production factors dates back to the beginnings of bourgeois economics. At that time, a tension still existed between the deeper understanding and the more superficial theory; that is to say, within the system of economic theory a struggle went on between the two elements. But in modern theory we are left with only the dogma of the factor incomes, without any tie to production of value. Yet the contradictory element remains. An example of this may be found in the notion of value added, by which is meant the factor incomes paid out at each stage of production. S views "value added" as a statistical means of separating out the "intermediate products" bought from other capitalists.

Now one might think that in order to understand value added one must first understand value. In principle, it is an expression of the classical discussion of a value being created in the process of production which is added to the value of the already existing product—namely the capital, the value of which does not increase but merely has its value carried on.

The problem with the notion of value added as presented by S is that it does not really refer to the process of value-creation in the process of production, but rather to the distribution of that which has already been produced. Economists and statisticians break their heads trying to determine what ought to be included in factor incomes. The basic problem here relates to the fact that the theory attributes productivity a posteriori to all "factors" receiving an income. Once this imputation from outside the process of production has taken place, all further exclusions must appear arbitrary. Thus, on the one hand, rent is included for those who own their homes, on the basis of so-called opportunity costs. (S claims that this "makes sense if we really want to measure the housing services the American people are enjoying" [193].) On the other hand, the "services of a housewife do not get counted in the NNP. . . . This item is not omitted for logical reasons, but rather because it would be hard to get accurate estimates of the money value of a wife's services" (199). Yet there are "logical" reasons of sorts at work here. Obviously it would be just as easy to calculate the "opportunity cost" of a housewife as of a fictitious rent; all one would have to do is add up the going rate for a cleaning woman, cook, sex partner, babysitter. The reason for the omission lies in the fact that the woman does not sell her labor power to her husband *as a commodity*, and since national-income accounts take the flow of commodities as their starting point, these "services" fall by the wayside. The failure to include them in national accounts is subtle acknowledgment of the qualitative distinction between what S would call barter and the exchange economy.

The final ambiguity refers to S's exclusion of second-hand sales from NNP, because "nothing has been produced" (201). Of course nothing has been produced, because by definition nothing is produced in the sphere of circulation, only in the sphere of production. Neither is anything produced when a fresh loaf of bread is bought and sold; the bread had been produced earlier. In the sphere of circulation the only change taking place is in the form of the already existing value. This means that the bread capitalist who at the end of the process of production holds a certain amount of value in the form of commodities now receives the same amount of value—this time in the form of money.

As S himself notes, "the total dollar volume of all intermediate transactions greatly exceeds the volume of the final transactions that we call national income or product" (201). But these are not examples of intermediate products in S's sense of raw material and machinery bought by capitalists who will use them to produce consumer commodities; for second-hand sales are final consumer sales—or, alternatively, the original sale of a car, etc., should not have been considered "final." The point is that the examination of the sphere of circulation alone cannot provide any criteria for determining whether "items" ought to be included in NNP or not; for as S himself points out, mere buying and selling does not make for inclusion. The reason S suddenly calls to mind the priority of production lies in the obviousness of the case—if a country somehow were to develop a great propensity for reselling, its national product could tendentially rise to infinity without any new production. Not only is there no "logic" for the exclusion of such deals, it in fact contradicts the "logic" upon which all other calculations are based. The fact that the buyer and reseller have "just *exchanged assets,*" money for second-hand goods (201), in no way distinguishes it from any other "transaction," for as we have just seen, the sphere of circulation is one in which value is not "added" but merely changes form—money for commodity and commodity for money.

The reference to production is, then irrelevant: It has never served as a criterion before, so why now? Production is simply dragged in to ward off an avalanche of non-production-generated NNP. (Interestingly enough, S in the footnote to this passage asserts that brokers' fees in such second-hand deals are included in NNP because brokers and salesmen "produce satisfactions in the form of bringing transactors together" [201 n.1]). But production is a red herring here for another reason: because it insists upon the physical aspect of production, presumably the criterion of whether some new material good has been brought forth. (We say "presumably" because S does not say what he means by "nothing has been produced"; exchange obviously does not produce anything material—at best it "produces" good vibes, which is not what S means, for that would upset his whole national-accounting procedure.)

Obviously the mere material production of new objects cannot be the defining characteristic of national product, for then all the "do-it-yourself" activities that culminate in new material products would also have to be included. In order to avoid this stumbling block the money aspect is brought in—hence the exclusion of housewifely activities. But then money becomes something more than the covering it usually passes for in bourgeois economics; for if it were merely the technical means for facilitating barter, then there would be no distinction between activities included in NNP and those not encompassed.

Money then brings with it a new type of social relation. What exactly is this relation? It is not determinate because the circulation of money between buyer and seller takes place in many different economies (although in a massive and predominant form only in capitalism). Thus the use of money as a form of human relationships does distinguish some economies from others and, within a certain economy, some relations from others. But it itself is too vague to allow a precise determination of whether it is an expression of a socially productive act (i.e., one which deserves honorable mention in NNP). We know that neither physical production nor the passing of money alone is a sufficient criterion for determining what "items" can enter national accounting. One could plausibly add that what we need are both these criteria plus that of demand, that is, the underlying satisfaction which is expressed in the act of buying.

This determination, however, is of no help, because it could just as well apply to do-it-yourself activities directed at producing some tangible object of "satisfaction" apart from the activity itself. But there is "something" to this thesis insofar as it hints at a social situation in which producers must subject themselves to forces not directly geared to their interests. By this we mean that workers work not to produce what they as individuals or as members of society need, but to acquire the social power (money) to satisfy these needs elsewhere. This is not to be confused with the bourgeois conception of *the* division of labor where "we" must all satisfy our wants indirectly by producing for others. Whereas many different societies are characterized by a division of labor within the process of production, and thus interdependence exists objectively in all these societies, it is only in capitalism that interdependence remains confined to the objective plane.

We are not concerned here with whether land and capital are "productive," and we are not saying that only labor is productive and that all incomes other than wages are derivative. This is irrelevant here, for what interests us is that the production-factor theory is unable to determine where income is produced.

Just as it is true that "the total dollar volume of all intermediate transactions greatly exceeds the volume of final transactions" entering NNP as far as the "flow-of-product approach" is concerned, it is also true that, to use S's terminology, the total dollar volume of all redistributed incomes may exceed "value added," or the income originally created.

When dealing with the practical problem of inflation, bourgeois economists are forced to admit that no matter how much income is floating about, no more can be consumed than has previously been produced. But the problem is that the factor-of-production theory does not provide any criteria for establishing what is original income and what is merely being redistributed to others and counted twice or even three or four times. To succeed in formulating such criteria a theory must be able to show first where value is produced, and only then how it is distributed and redistributed into primary and secondary incomes. But value is a social relation and presupposes an understanding of (capitalist) society as a definite and objective totality of relations. The start that was made by classical political economy in formulating such a fundamental understanding of the definite economic formation it was examining—and which culminated in Marx—underwent a retrograde development in the post-Ricardian era, but it was not wholly obliterated; and it is precisely the eclecticism of the "moderns" that leads them into their basic contradictions, which are expressions of the inablity of modern economics to formulate a consistent concept of what "the economic" is— that is, what constitutes the subject matter of economic science.

EXCURSUS ON ECONOMIC THEORY

We have deferred a detailed discussion of S's programmatic statements on methodology on the grounds that since it cannot be discussed meaningfully apart from content, S's methodology could not be criticized in isolation from its concrete application. We feel that this point in the book offers the appropriate context for such a methodological discussion.

S's opening chapter features a small section entitled "What Economics Is," in which he offers several definitions because, as he puts it, "beginners often want a short definition" (3). Although he avers that it is "hard to compress into a few lines an exact description of a subject," he manages to incorporate most of the points mentioned in the various definitions into one he contends "economists today agree on":

> Economics is the study of how men and society end up *choosing*, with or without the use of money, to employ *scarce* productive resources that could have alternative uses, to produce various commodities and distribute them for consumption, now or in the future, among various people and groups in society [3].

Since S fails to develop this definition, we shall try to determine to what extent it hinders or advances his theory.

With respect to the definition itself, we suspect that despite the apparent attempt to come up with an all-encompassing concept, S is not asserting its universal validity—or rather he is not asserting that economics has universal applicability. And he makes this revealing comment: "On our way to the state of affluence where material well-being will fall to the second level of significance, we do need a summary measure of aggregate economic performance" (179, 195-7; cf. 8th ed., pp. 776-78).

Let us look at the definition of economics more closely. The key terms there appear to be "choice," "individuals and society," "scarcity," "consumption," and "distribution." It is a definition composed of various layers (implicit or explicit) derived from different economists writing at different stages in the development of capitalism.

Since the fifth factor relates to the study of wealth the name that comes most readily to mind is that of Adam Smith, the author of *An Inquiry into the Nature and Causes of the Wealth of Nations*. And this approach indeed continues to exert a major influence on many who write on the subject of economic science. According to one influential work of the 1930s: "The definition of Economics which would probably command most adherents, at any rate in Anglo-

Saxon countries, is that which relates it to the study of the causes of material welfare."[6] And it goes on to say:

> The causes which have led to the persistence of this definition are mainly historical in character. It is the last vestige of Physiocratic influence. English economists are not usually interested in questions of scope and method. In nine cases out of ten where this definition occurs, it has probably been taken over quite uncritically from some earlier work.[7]

Robbins has hit upon a fundamental inconsistency in the neoclassical economics of his day, for once subjective-value theory replaced the classical objective-value theory as the basis of economics, its claim of being a theory of society, a social science, lost its validity.

When Smith wrote his famous work, capitalism had just established itself as the dominant mode of production in England. For him to have arrived at a consistent view of capitalism would have presupposed an understanding of capitalism as a historical mode of production not only in the sense of growing out of a previous mode, but also in the sense of being a historically limited one which would in turn be supplanted by another. And this was impossible at a time when society had not yet proved capable of solving the problems it itself poses. In fact, even later classical political economy never adequately recognized the historically limited nature of capitalist production. The more critical economists like Ricardo and John Stuart Mill implicitly conceded the historically limited nature of capitalism only from the viewpoint of distribution.

In the original preface to his *Principles,* Ricardo has this to say on the subject of political economy:

> The produce of the earth—all that is derived from its surface by the united application of labour, machinery, and capital, is divided among three classes of the community, namely the proprietor of the land, the owner of the stock or capital necessary for its cultivation, and the labourers by whose industry it is cultivated. But in different stages of society, the proportions of the whole produce which will be allotted to each of these classes,

under the names of rent, profits, and wages, will be essentially different; depending mainly on the actual fertility of the soil, on the accumulation of capital and population, and on the skill, ingenuity, and instruments employed in agriculture.

To determine the laws which regulate this distribution is the principal problem in Political Economy. . . .[8]

The crucial difference between S's and Ricardo's definition of distribution is Ricardo's emphasis of factors specific to each society; S sees distribution as flowing directly from the physical nature of production itself.

The legacy of the major classical authors, Smith and Ricardo, is by no means unambiguous. Despite critical awareness, they were unable to develop consistently critical theories. But their inconsistencies are genuine, in the sense that they correspond to the original working-out of a theory during the formative stages of an ascendant society. And they are also genuine in the sense that they are not concealed, the inherent contradictions they lead to in the theory stand there for all to see. It is only the successors who made conscious attempts to "touch up" the contradictions. After 1825 it became increasingly clear that the laws of capitalism were not identical with the laws of nature, and this awareness inevitably led to apologetics. Smith and Ricardo did not live to see the first unmistakable indications of the barriers to "human progress" being erected by capitalism, but their followers could ignore these signs only by developing theories that were out of touch with reality.

Thus John McCulloch (1789-1864), a Ricardian who vulgarized Ricardo's theory in a number of essential ways, opens his major work with this definition:

Political Economy may be defined to be the science of the laws which regulate the production, accumulation, distribution, and consumption of those articles or products that are necessary, useful, or agreeable to man, and which at the same time possess exchangeable value.[9]

This is a fine example of the eclectic approach which was to characterize political economy in years to come. On the one hand, we have the classical emphasis on specific societal considerations, and on the other, the concessions McCulloch finds it necessary to make to the more superficial aspects of the classical strain are made obvious by his statement, "products that are necessary, useful, or agreeable to man." At first sight this might appear to be nothing more than a reference to use value as the underlying prerequisite of all production, but further reflection leads to the conclusion that in reality this opens the way to discarding the societal theory and reverting to the use-value concept. And finally McCulloch arrives at the suprahistorical formulation which has become the hallmark of the "modern" definition of economic activity: "The end of all human exertion is the same—that is, to increase the sum of necessaries, comforts, and enjoyments."[10]

In this respect McCulloch is the forerunner of those who define economics as being concerned with some aspect of human welfare, and by using this subjective, ahistorical "end" as a point of departure, flounder in confusion about the "definition" of productivity and income.

The next important turning point came with Alfred Marshall (1842-1924), a decisive figure in the transition from classicial political economy to the subjectivist tradition. Marshall's eclecticism brought him to his key position, an adherence to utility theory as well as to a cost-of-production theory. Thus on the opening page of his *Principles* he offers this definition:

> Political Economy or Economics is a study of mankind in the ordinary business of life; it examines that part of individual and social action which is most closely connected with the attainment and with the use of the material requisites of wellbeing.[11]

But this proved to be too broad for him, and so he zeroes in with this shift from the older suprahistorical approach to this distinctly "modern" one:

> Economics is a study of men as they live and move and think in the ordinary business of life. But it concerns itself chiefly with those motives which affect, most powerfully and most

steadily, man's conduct in the business part of his life. . . . The steadiest motive to ordinary business work is the desire for the pay which is the material reward of work. . . . The motive is supplied by a definite amount of money; and it is this definite and exact money measurement of the steadiest motives in business life, which has enabled economics to outrun every other branch of the study of man. . . . It concerns itself chiefly with those desires, aspirations and other affections of human nature, the outward manifestations of which appear as incentives to action in such a form that the force or quantity of the incentives can be estimated or measured with some approach to accuracy; and which therefore are in some degree amenable to treatment by scientific machinery.[12]

What makes this approach eclectic is the intention to retain the superficial result of the objective-value theory (i.e., money) within the new theory which junks the base upon which money and prices arose as "measures."

Political economy is not supposed to postulate the existence of money and then to use it to "measure motivations" that exist in all societies, but rather to explain how in certain societies the natural human processes involved in living taking on peculiar forms; why, for instance, does labor in capitalism appear as value (money), products of labor as commodities, labor as wage labor, etc.? To take the development leading to these forms for granted is tantamount to abandoning the function of science, which is to mediate content and form, to explain why the content *must* assume the peculiar social forms it does. The specific neoclassical eclecticism of Marshall and others becomes weighed down with the internal inconsistencies of trying to hold on to threads of the older objective tradition while developing another theory which negates the thrust of that tradition.

A similar eclectic role, but one which shifted the emphasis toward the subjective, was played by A. C. Pigou (1877-1959), the "father" of welfare economics. Although he, too, adheres to the now familiar suprahistorical definition of economics as dealing with well-being, Pigou contends that the "elements of welfare are states of consciousness."[13] He, like Marshall, is aware of how "rough" a measure of good vibes money is. Moreover, he explicitly points to the interdependence of the definition of the subject matter of economics and that of national income.[14] It is his contention that both concepts are subject to "elasticity," so that "it is only possible to define this concept by introducing an arbitrary line into the continuum presented by nature."[15] Here Pigou touches on the core of his problem. The "arbitrary line" he imagines to be "introducing" as an active scientific subject is nothing more than a hazy and uncomprehended expression of the "arbitrariness" the capitalist mode of production has "introduced" into the continuum or heterogeneity "presented by nature." The essence of the struggle carried on by bourgeois economics around the concept of income and the subject matter of economic theory relates precisely to its drawing the criteria for judging a specific socioeconomic formation from nature, or alternatively, to its drawing the criteria for judging the eternal aspects of production from capitalism. Both these approaches are rooted in the fundamental inability of bourgeois economics to grasp the historical nature of capitalism.

Thus although the economists involved in the development of the theory of income were in varying degrees aware of the inconsistencies outlined by us, as long as they tried to integrate utility theory with the older objective tradition, these inconsistencies remained firmly fixed.

With the rise of the ordinal- as opposed to the cardinal-utility theory, the development of income theory took a decisive turn. For once the attempt to "measure" utility was abandoned, the final link to the classical theory was broken. Thus John Hicks, a recent Nobel laureate and one of the more influential formulators of the ordinal-utility concept, comes to a "very upsetting conclusion." After defining income as that which a person "can consume during the week and still expect to be as well off at the end of the week as he was at the beginning," Hicks concedes that "social income" remains a "subjective concept."[16]

Robbins, who wrote his work on economics at about the time Hicks was formulating his ordinal theory of utility, and who supported the Hicksean position, elaborates the consequences of the ordinalist approach for income theory; according to him, the "term 'economic *quantity*' is really very misleading":

> A price, it is true, expresses the quantity of money which it is necessary to give in exchange for a given commodity. But its significance is the relationship between this quantity of money and other similar quantities. And the valuations which the price system expresses are not quantities at all. They are arrangements in a certain order. . . . Value is a relation, not a measurement. But, if this is so, it follows that the addition of prices or individual incomes to form social aggregates is an operation with a very limited meaning. As quantities of money expended, particular prices and particular incomes are capable of addition, and the total arrived at has a definite monetary significance. But as expressions of an order of preferences, a relative scale, they are incapable of addition. Their aggregate has no meaning. . . . Estimates of the social income may have a quite definite meaning for monetary theory. But beyond this they have only *conventional* significance.[17]

The above statement represents the final dissolution of the ties to the classical tradition of objectivity. It allows Robbins to eliminate the inconsistencies that had plagued the eclectic approach, and it opened the way for a redefinition of economics that would mark a radical departure from previous efforts to retain some semblance of a social theory. Given the key role of scarcity in utility theory, it is no surprise that it also plays a crucial role in defining economics.

According to Robbins, then, we must understand that once "we have been turned out of Paradise, behaviour necessarily assumes the form of choice."[18] Form apparently is very important for this conception: "here, then, is the unity of the subject of Economic Science, the forms assumed by human behaviour in disposing of scarce means."[19]

It should be clear from some of the above-cited material that the shift from welfare to scarcity does not eliminate the "paradoxes" of income theory insofar as that theory is still supposed to lead to practical applicability; statistical method is still necessary. What the shift does do is to cut the theory of income loose from the "definition" of economics. Thus where income assumes a theoretical significance of its own, as in Keynes, recourse is had to the "compromises" of Marshall and Pigou.

Thus cleansed of any social taint, the "definition" of economics can now serve as the internally consistent basis of what passes for a theory of value. But unlike the older connection between value theory and "definition" of political economy rooted in a theory of history, a theory of society, and hence of reproduction, the present connection between the "law" of scarcity and utility is devoid of social and historical content and therefore cannot include a theory of reproduction. The connection is formal and, especially in S's case, ornamental. Whereas previous theories fought over the differences between capitalism and all other societies, as well as between capitalism and an alleged state of nature, the scarcity concept represents the conscious capitulation of the "social" in favor of the "natural."

The most important feature of the new conception relates to the notion of "choice." For Robbins it becomes synonymous with economics. The issue cannot be ducked by saying that all results must have been a matter of choice, for this would knock down the essential identity Robbins is trying to establish. If it is to be established, then it must be proved that just as Robinson Crusoe decided or chose to divide his time into picking berries, sleeping, eating, and building defenses, so individual Americans have the choice of how much time they will spend on production, consumption, "leisure," and "common defense." For our purpose here it is irrelevant whether the time is spent on "defense" directly, or indirectly via taxation. What matters is that a conscious choice has been made. That is the reason S places such emphasis on the notion of democracy in Chapters 8 and 9, for if it could not be shown that the American people want military spending, without proof that they are in fact "taxing themselves," the underlying essential identity of all societies collapses. But S's version of ordinal utility, namely revealed preference, argues backward, from objective result to imputed motivation, and in doing so S forgoes the rigorous proof of choice necessary to the argument of essential identity. But it is not only on the issue of "defense" that the theory breaks down, for in capitalism the length of the working day (i.e., its division into production and leisure), the magnitude and variety of production and consumption, its distribution, its increase and decrease (capital accumulation, industrial cycles), etc., are not "chosen" in any sense consciously decided on. True, individuals do make choices, as did Robinson Crusoe, but in "our complex, interconnected modern industrial society" the interactions of all these individual decisions may lead to unintended results. (Cf. "The Paradox of Thrift," 237-39.)

But this does not refute the theory because at this point S can bring in the society part of "how men and society end up *choosing*"; in other words, to offer an example of social choice. Of course, this distorts the meaning of choice, and furthermore, instead of preserving the essential identity of all societies it singles out capitalism as a special case.

By introducing the notion of society's choosing, S has avoided some of the more obvious absurdities of Robbins' conception, but he has done so at the expense of an originally consistent and rigorous "definition." In the *Instructor's Manual* to the 6th edition, which marked a change in this subsection, S presents his relation to the Robbins' conception:

> The major revision has been in the direction of spelling out clearly various definitions of what economics is. The one finally given here tries to capture what it is that is good about the Lionel Robbins abstract definition of "economics as the study of choices among alternative means to accomplish prescribed ends;" but it at the same time tries to be less narrow and restrictive and also less abstract.[20]

This is a good example of S's lax attitude toward methodological questions; it shows us that S believes that one can pick and choose, that one can pick out one part of one conception and leave out another, combine it with some other "definition" and wind up with yet another one. But the fact of the matter is that one cannot simply add this or subtract that and arrive at a "more or less" abstract "definition." To be sure, levels of abstraction do exist, but they are not formed at will by the agents of scientific research. The only justification for the changes S has introduced into the Robbins definition would be found in the realm of ideology; by drawing a subtle distinction between "men" and "society," S seeks to prepare the reader for a definition of national income that includes the governmental sector, and particularly military production, an inclusion essential to the theory and practice of Keynesian macroeconomics.

COMPARISON WITH MORE RECENT DISCUSSION ON INCOME THEORY

S uses Robbins' conception to the extent that utility theory demands this, but he also makes it "less abstract" in connection with the application of income theory within Keynesian macroeconomics. How do the economists who do make the explicit connection between "definitions" operate?

Simon Kuznets, another Nobel laureate, knows that the concept of income depends on the formulation of a "goal" for the society in question; for, he says,

> if no ultimate goal is set to economic activity—except mere increase in the supply of goods—all consumption becomes part of the production process. . . . But if we assume that the primary objective of economic activity is to provide goods to satisfy wants of the members of the nation; that national income is for man and not man for the increase of the country's capacity and national income, then ultimate consumption can be defined as the use of goods in direct fulfillment of this primary objective. . . .[21]

And how does Kuznets "justify" the "basic assumption" underlying this "widely accepted definition of national income"—namely "that to provide goods to consumers is the primary purpose of economic activity"?[22] He adduces "two grounds":

> The first is the unique relevance of satisfying men's wants to national income as an *appraisal* notion. National income is not a measure of activity, of how much effort, toil, and trouble economic activity represents; but of its contribution, of its success in attaining its goal. Viewed in this light, there is no longer-standing purpose except to provide the material means with which wants of the members of society, present and future, can be satisfied.
>
> Second, the entire pattern of economic organization in modern society seems to have the provision of goods to consumers as its primary goal. The concern various social institutions manifest for maintaining and increasing the flow of goods to its members, and the subordination of other goals to that end cannot be demonstrated statistically, but is an impression conveyed by measures taken to ensure this primary goal and to overcome any serious obstacles to his attainment. At any rate, it is difficult to formulate a different goal of economic activity of equally primary importance for most nations in the last century and a half.[23]

The most striking aspect of these passages is the subjective and formal conception of the "goal" of any particular mode of production. Kuznets appears to be surprised, or at least disappointed, that no "statistical" proof can be adduced for consumption's being the goal of capitalism. How statistics could be used to supplant a theory of history and a theory of social reproduction remains Kuznets' secret. And the apologetic note in his reasoning is quite obvious.

The formal element of the system emerges with particular clarity when Kuznets plays the role of statistician working with received categories. In the absence of a theory of social reproduction the concept of national income itself becomes interchangeable: its constitutent elements can be shifted around at will like building blocks.

Since national income exists for man and not vice versa, national income "defines the production process to exclude the goods consumed in maintaining the inhabitants and enabling them to grow and multiply."[24] Or as Pigou phrases it, the maintenance of the working class (food, clothing, etc.) may not be deducted from gross income like the maintenance of capital, because the wear and tear of human beings does not result "from their being used or held ready for use as production agents."[25]

Thus although for the individual firm wages are a cost which the capitalist seeks to minimize, on the aggregate social level they are transformed into an element of net income. This in turn grows out of the equating of "costs of production" and "factor earnings"; but precisely this identification should give pause, since it points to the existence of a social struggle within capitalism that would exclude the rather naive definitions of income based on a conception of capitalist society as a unified, subjective whole. For when we consider that what is a cost for the capitalist (variable capital) is for the worker revenue, and hence purchasing power on the commodity market, we see that the form of wages itself involves a conflict between capitalist and worker, which makes impermissible the inclusion of wages in that part of the social product that capitalist society seeks to maximize.

Marx, summarizing the views of the classical economists and their predecessors, the physiocrats, notes that by distinguishing between gross and net income, they conceptualized surplus value as net revenue, or that part of the annual total profuct in excess of the replacement of the capital advanced by the capitalist in the form of machines and raw materials (constant capital) and/or wages (variable capital). According to him, neither the individual capitalist nor capitalist society as a whole see production of use values or the material and living means of production as their objective "goal"; and without adequate profit, the worker as producer and consumer very soon is made to realize the actual objective of capitalist production. It is of little value to him that the Department of Commerce, Kuznets, Pigou, or even Samuelson all think of him as the end of production if the capitalist mode of production does not.

II / CAPITAL ACCUMULATION

In this section, S introduces more realistic elements into his model of national-income accounting, even though his methodology is not exactly a model of realism.

> In real life . . . *People often want* to devote part of their income to saving and investment. Instead of eating more bread *now*, they will want to build new machines to make it possible to produce more bread for *future* consumption. . . . In short, we must recognize that the final goals of *people* do include net investment or capital formation, not simply current consumption [186 f.].

Just how real is this "real life"? And what society is S referring to? People in "our modern mixed economy" do not save or invest because they want to consume more bread in the future. That society is composed of two relevant classes—workers and capitalists. Workers by and large can neither save nor invest. Capitalists, on the other hand, can and do, but not because they want to have more bread in the future. They are interested in accumulation and profit, and if this should demand the curtailment of the production of consumer goods then production will be curtailed. S's argument that "the final goals of people do include net investment or capital formation" is inconsistent, for net investment is merely an "intermediate goal" within his conception. If it were really a final goal, then he would be admitting that it served some purpose other than the ultimate increase in the flow of goods.

The reason S has to call net investment/saving a "final goal" is related to the necessity of distinguishing between the production of additional (net) capital "goods" and that of so-called intermediate goods, which "we don't want . . . to be double-counted along with final product" (184). Lacking a theory of reproduction that would allow him to establish immanent criteria for distinguishing between the replacement of old capital "goods" and the production of new ones, S is forced to seek refuge in irrelevant subjective-psychological criteria.

THE DISTINCTION BETWEEN GNP AND NNP

Let us now examine S's attempt to differentiate between the replacement of used-up capital and the production of new capital (goods). According to him, GNP equals NNP plus depreciation, just as gross investment equals net investment plus depreciation. S considers this a basically technical distinction of statisticians; the difference refers to the using-up of capital in the production process. Since measuring the net figures involves more difficulties, emphasis is placed on the GNP statistics (186-88).

What in fact underlies these technical-statistical distinctions? Depreciation is the total sum value of the means of production used up in one year; it is at the same time equal to the sum value of the investments made in one year to replace the machinery used up. In other words, NNP does not include these "costs." The machinery used and replaced is no different from the machinery that is part of net investment as far as its value is concerned. If we view capitalism merely as the production of use values for consumption, that is, merely from its "technical" aspect divorced from all social relations, as in fact S does, then it is impossible to draw a distinction between the replacements and the additional machines.

Why then, we may ask, does S exclude replacement of used-up capital from net national product? Why is it that the productive factors land, labor, and capital are not credited with their contribution to this part of GNP as they are with respect to all other components? Let us try to unravel this mystery. To do so, we must find out how value is created in the process of production:

> The worker adds new value to the object of labor through the addition of a certain quantity of labor abstracting from the determinate content, purpose, and technical character of his labor. . . . The value of the means of the production is thus preserved through its transfer to the product. This transfer happens during the transformation of the means of production into the product, in the labor process. It is mediated by labor. But how?
> The worker does not work double in the same time, not once

in order to add a value to the cotton through his labor, and another time in order to preserve its old value, or what is the same, in order to transfer the value of the cotton which he is working and of the spindles with which he is working to the product, the thread. Rather through mere addition of new value he preserves the old value. Since however the addition of new value to the object of labor and the preservation of the old values in the product are two completely different results, which the worker brings forth in the same time although he works only once in the same time, this twosidedness of the result can manifestly be explained only from the twosidedness of his labor itself. At the same point in time it must in one capacity create value and in another capacity preserve or transfer value.[26]

Explaining this "twosidedness" of labor, Marx says that the value of labor is created through the expenditure of human labor power, that it takes place in abstraction from the specific character of the labor. This property is unique to commodity-producing societies which do not plan the social content of labor by determining what is to be produced, and thus how society's total labor is to be distributed among the various branches of production. In commodity-producing societies labor turns out to have been expended socially if a product is sold, and in capitalist societies if sold at a profit. In these, the sociality of labor finds indirect expression in the value it produces as reflected in commodities. Thus, value here is created by labor in abstraction from its concrete use-value-producing aspect. The only relevant point is its specific social character of being abstract human labor.

What matters here is the facility that enables the worker to produce a certain use value by utilizing means of production (machines and raw materials); in this process the old form of the use value of these means disappears and reappears in the new product. The value created by the labor that produced these machines and raw materials is thus transferred from them to the new commodity, a transfer effected by the labor of the worker producing the new commodity. For it is only by virtue of the worker's purposeful utilization of these particular instruments that the use value, and hence also the value, can be "transferred" to the new commodity. Marx calls the ability of labor to preserve value while adding value "a gift of nature,"[27] because it refers to the production of use values as a suprahistorical process. But the property of labor to maintain or preserve value can take place only in a society in which value exists; hence more than a gift of nature is needed—nature alone does not suffice. Later Marx adds that:

> This natural power of labor appears as the power of self-preservation of the capital into which it has been incorporated, just as labor's social productive powers appear as capital's properties, and as the constant appropriation of surplus labor by the capitalist appears as the constant self-expansion of capital. All powers of labor project themselves as powers of capital. . . .[28]

What is the reason for this inversion of reality? Bourgeois economics treats labor and capital as two equal productive factors—one cannot function in the absence of the other. This of course is true as far as use-value production is concerned. But it assumes a peculiar significance when we talk about the production of commodities in capitalism in view of the circulation-sphere approach, according to which every factor that receives an income is productive. But as S himself observes: "(Of course, the character of the resulting distribution of income is highly dependent upon the initial distribution of property ownership. . .)" (45). S never returns to this line of reasoning; Marx makes it the basis of his: ("But before distribution is distribution of products, it is (1) distribution of the instruments of production. . ."[29]). Now in capitalism this distribution of the instruments of production is highly selective—God did not endow all his children with capital. This means that those not so endowed are forced to sell that which God did give them in abundance—their labor power.

Because the capitalists own the means of production while the workers have nothing but their labor power, the capitalists can appropriate part of the annual product (surplus value and its more concrete forms—profit, interest, and rent). But once they have appropriated part of the newly created value, the rest of it must go to the workers for their "productive services." Thus as a result, labor, the sole creator of value, is transformed into "factor of production," together with capital and land. This is how it appears on the surface on the basis of the peculiar class distribution of the means of production; and this is the way bougeois economics, unable to delve beneath the surface, theorizes.

Thus from the point of view of value creation, the natural power of labor in the process of production appears as the power of self-preservation of capital. How does this seem from the point of view of income distribution? The answer should be evident; for since NNP excludes depreciation or replacement of the used-up capital, bourgeois economics maintains that this value is not to be imputed to the productive factors land, labor, and capital. With the alleged technical-statistical distinction between GNP and NNP, bourgeois national-income/product theory expresses the ability of labor to transfer the value of the means of production as a quasi-natural property of capital to preserve itself. Implicit in this "natural" conception of the transfer/preservation of the captal value is the idea that capital has a right to reproduce itself, to be replenished, to be kept "intact," a natural right which takes precedence over the social distribution of income.

Now we know that old value is not transferred/preserved before the new value is added; the two processes take place simultaneously. Bourgeois economics is unable to grasp the twofold nature of labor insofar as it is relevant to this question, and this inability has significant implications. The first of these is the recognition of the priority of keeping capital intact. This means that if within the sphere of production the natural power of labor to transfer/maintain value is attributed to capital, then in the sphere of income distribution the "rewarding" of the productive factors must take second place to the reproduction of capital.

Secondly, there is an irony here in the treatment of this

question by subjective contemporary economics. Whereas the classical economists considered surplus value or profit to be society's net income and tended to view wages as a "cost of production," "modern" economists, determined to deny that profit is the end of capitalism, shifted wages into the net-income category of "society."

This ideological consideration, no doubt a conscious motivation on the part of some apologists, is not simply manipulative; it is rooted in the reality of capitalism. Bourgeois economics must fail to understand the twofold nature of labor as use-value- and value-producing, for if it did it would lead to insight into surplus value and the mechanism of exploitation; and once this were to happen, the difference between capitalism and all previous class societies would disappear—namely, that the exploitation of the direct producers is obscured by the superficial appearance of equal exchange between capital and labor. This potentially "subversive" chain of reasoning led from Ricardo to Marx, and then away from Ricardo when Marx developed an actually "subversive" theory.

It is ironic that although the conscious objective was to assert that "man" was not a mere part of the process of production but rather its end, and that for this reason the reproduction of labor was not to be considered a mere cost of production, this would logically lead to a surprising conclusion, namely, that the process of production called production of capital takes priority over "man." For capital's natural right to reproduce itself is taken care of first; "man's" right to reproduce, that is the payment of wages, is not a natural right but rather a part of the secondary process of social distribution. Thus, although apologetic bourgeois economics seeks to assert the priority of "man" over production, it in fact winds up asserting the priority of capital's reproduction over "man's."[30]

ACKNOWLEDGMENT OF THE SOCIAL CONTENT OF THE GNP-NNP DISTINCTION IN BUSINESS-CYCLE THEORY

Although bourgeois economics, in its programmatic discussion of national income, insists that the difference between

GNP and NNP is merely a technical-statistical one, in analyzing the so-called business cycle, it reintroduces the distinction in a decidedly social context. The connection, however, remains closed to it. Thus Keynes himself, in discussing Pigou's attempts to determine the meaning of "keeping capital intact" a question inextricably linked to differentiating between GNP and NNP (namely, between gross and net investment), states that

> these difficulties are rightly regarded as "conundrums." They are "purely theoretical" in the sense that they never perplex, or indeed enter in any way into, business decisions and have no relevance to the causal sequence of economic events, which are clear-cut and determinate in spite of the quantitative indeterminacy of these concepts.[31]

Later, however, he points out that

> consumption is, *cet. par.*, a function of *net* income, *i.e.*, of *net* investment (net income being equal to consumption *plus* net investment). In other words, the larger the financial provision which it is thought necessary to make before reckoning net income, the less favourable to consumption . . . will a given level of investment prove to be.[32]

In other words, since Keynes assigns an important role to consumption, it turns out that the "withdrawal" of a large part of the national product from national income spendable by consumers (namely the prior "replenishment" of capital) can have serious consequences.

Keynes had in mind particularly the boom, crisis, and depression phases of the industrial cycle of the 1920s and '30s; following the overaccumulation of capital in the 1920s, individual capitalists did not reinvest large parts of the value preserved by "their" workers, because they did not expect "effective demand" to keep up with the greater output available on the basis of the increased investments. Thus in times of crisis, the size of the depreciations becomes critical, for it is here that capital asserts itself as the dominant relation in capitalism. The individual capitalist will hold on to the amortization funds during a crisis regardless of the effect on aggregate effective demand, just as he will continue to reinvest during a boom regardless of effective demand.

As further evidence of the bourgeois economist's inability to understand these connections, Keynes in the same chapter asserts that "Consumption—to repeat the obvious—is the sole end and object of all economic activity."[33] And despite his implicit demonstration to the contrary, Keynes continues to speak "of the fact that capital is not a self-subsistent entity existing apart from consumption."[34]

S, on the other hand, has not reached even the level of implicit, unintentional understanding. He continues to insist on the technical/statistical nature of the distinction between NNP and GNP:

> Even if the economist . . . likes to talk about NNP, he is content to work with GNP data, knowing that the two concepts do move together during any period that is not too long. For most general purposes, GNP and NNP can be used interchangeably [8th ed., p. 177].

It seems doubtful whether examining the critical elements of the industrial cycle is seen as a "general purpose" by S. (According to his own data, depreciation as a percentage of GNP rose from 7.65 percent in 1929 to 12.6 percent in 1933, an increase of about 65 percent [203]).

CAPITAL FORMATION AND THE WORKING CLASS

Before leaving this subject and turning to the state sector, we would like to touch on one more point—namely the effect of "gross or net investment" on the workers using the machinery. Bourgeois economics excludes consideration of the effects of working from national-income considerations. In a sense this is of course justified, for this aspect has no direct bearing on value-creation and distribution. However, from the point of view of bourgeois economics itself, there is a contradiction here insofar as national income theory does recognize, and indeed ultimately tries to measure indirectly, the " 'psychic income' " (201) of consumers. Presumably the justification for ignoring the psychic income of producers results from the exclusive concentration on consumption as the sole end of economic activity. But the characterization of productive activity, as distinct from play, as not an end in itself is itself an admission that capitalist production generates no measurable "psychic income." And in fact, bourgeois economics explicitly introduces the notion of "disutility" in connection with labor.[35] But even when discussing such "disutility," bourgeois economists only see it as some sort of deduction from the utility of the consumer.

Kuznets, for example, speaks of "what some may consider the gravest omission" from national income,

> the deliberate exclusion of the human cost of turning out the net product; i.e., such disadvantages as are concomitants of acquiring an income and *cramp the recipients' style* (and others') as a consumer. One example would be long working hours. If to turn out a net product of a given size requires a work week that leaves little time for leisure, the producers cannot derive much satisfaction as consumers, i.e., as individuals who have certain wants and preferences. Another example would be the strain some jobs impose. If by and large a task is disagreeable, exhausting, dull, monotonous, or nerve wracking, the cost to the producer as a consumer is higher than when the task is light, instructive, diversified, or amusing.[36]

Kuznets is unable to see the producer independent of his role as consumer. This reflects the demotion of actual labor to "factor-of-production" labor on the surface of capitalist society; having been transformed into the commodity labor power, labor loses its all-encompassing meaning of productive activity and becomes something that can be bought and sold like land and "capital." And not only *can* it be sold, it *must* be sold by those who have no other recourse. At this point, labor ceases to be a productive function and turns into a mere instrument of earning one's daily bread. Production in capitalism is determined within the factory by the capitalist (or his agent); with the exception of rela-

tively minor defensive inroads into "management preroga-
tives" achieved by unions, capital decides under what conditions both the mute and the vocal means of production
will toil. In this respect Kuznets is correct in calling consumers "individuals who have certain wants and preferences" without attributing these characteristics to producers
"as individuals." For, in fact, producers as individuals have
almost no "wants and preferences" that capitalist society
recognizes. And it is for this reason that "turning out the
net product" must take place with "human cost," namely
the entire gamut of phenomena of alienation at the point of
production developed by Marx whose connection to
capitalism is not recognized.

But not only the net, the gross product also has to be
turned out. Capital in the form of machinery is an essential
element in this labor process. But what end does the
machinery serve? It is not introduced at the behest of individuals as producers in conjunction with their "wants and
preferences." The individual capitalist introduces machinery to increase profits, more specifically, to reduce his
"labor costs." He is not interested in whether this change
results in the reduction of the total labor-time embodied in
production, only in the labor-time he pays. Thus his only
concern is whether the machine costs more than the wages
of the laborers it replaces. If the criterion were increased
productivity, that is, whether the same amount of use values can be produced with less total labor-time, then individual capitalists would make decisions that contradicted
their "financial prudence" as profit seekers. Whether the
capitalist introduces machinery depends then in large part
on the value of labor power. As Marx points out, depending on the rate of surplus value (that is, the proportion in
which the working day is divided up between the value
going to wages and surplus value), the use of machinery
will vary from time to time, country to country, and branch
to branch. A further "advantage" accruing to the capitalist
from supplanting human beings by machines is that
machines do not rebel and do not go on strike. Hence the
introduction of "labor-saving" machinery is determined by

forces other than the "wants and preferences" of individual producers. (S says that rising wages may "induce" employers to introduce such machinery [749].)

In recent years we have heard about workers revolting against assembly-line production, particularly in the automobile industry. We have also heard about the introduction of new "team" type production in Italy, Sweden, Great Britain, etc., which is supposed to meet worker demands for less "alienating" working conditions. Obviously, "capital formation" in the shape of assembly lines was not taking place in order to lighten the burden of labor, and it must also be obvious that to the extent that workers succeed in forcing "management" to modify their working conditions this in no way can be likened to the so-called anonymous and impartial response of the market through the price system to the wants and preferences of consumers. For the alleged rationality of the capitalist circulation sphere stops at the factory gate: here power rules. Whether workers or capitalists gain the upper hand in a particular struggle depends in large part on the concrete economic situation. To the extent that workers through strikes, sabotage, slowdowns, etc., can force rollbacks it is a political struggle transcending the bounds of capitalist rationality. Within the sphere of production "wants and preferences" get expressed not in dollar votes but in political struggle between two social classes that do not shy away from the use of violence. And such struggles point to the inherent contradiction between the "wants and preferences" of the workers and those of "capital formation" and capitalist productivity.

III / THE STATE SECTOR

The most striking aspect of S's discussion of the government component of national product is its arbitrariness: "Somehow NNP and GNP must take into account the billions of dollars of product that a nation collectively consumes" (7th ed., p. 178). The solution to his problem as of all other social problems S so "conveniently" transformed into technical-statistical ones lies of course in scholarly ratiocination: "After some debate, the income statisticians of the United States and United Nations decided on using the simplest method of all. To the flow of (1) consumption product and (2) investment product, they simply add (3) *all* of government expenditure on goods and services" (189). S stressed the arbitrary nature of national-income accounting with respect to G even more clearly in the 1st edition:

> Often we speak loosely of government expenditure in the abstract, as if it were simply a subtraction from national production. Actually, the statistical definition of national product is drawn up so that government expenditure on goods and services becomes a way of using and producing economic output. It is not always an ideal way. . . . But it is a way which we could not do without. . . [p. 158].

Let us examine S's reasoning more closely. The presumable justification for including "G" in national-income accounts is related to the product which "a nation collectively consumes." What exactly constitutes this collective consumption?

> Here are examples. Along with bread consumption and net investment in NNP, we include in it government expenditures on roads (i.e., cement and road-builders), and jet bombers. We include government expenditure on the *services* of jet pilots, judges, policemen, national-income statisticians, firemen and agricultural chemists [189; our emphasis].

Why does S believe it proper to include these items in national-income reckoning?

> Because they do cover services rendered, they do use up resources and production, and they do provide collective direct or indirect consumption to the citizens of the United States. . . . Such dollars are as much a part of national income as the dollars used by a railroad company to provide transportation services to its customers [154f.].

Thus the criteria appear to be the rendering of services which the citizens of the U.S. consume collectively and consume while rendering. We will ignore the analogy to railways, for it is merely a repetition of the circulation-sphere approach dealt with earlier. If we concentrate simply on the circulation of "dollars" we can establish no criteria for determining the components of national income. So let us stick to the other criteria mentioned. That one should have to "use up resources and production" in order to render a service fit for inclusion in national income is somewhat mysterious; how the mere act of consumption can become the source of national product remains S's secret.

The reader might object that Marxists also say that capital consumption—i.e., the labor involved in transfering/ preserving the value of the means of production—is productive, so that even if it does not produce new value and hence income, at least it preserves value by productively consuming it. And the reader might well have a point here were it not for the minor circumstance that the services rendered by jet pilots, etc., do not preserve anything. And therefore we cannot understand how such consumption can be seen as a source of national product. Furthermore, it is also unclear why resources have to be used up in the process. S might suggest that we, instead of concentrating on the sphere of military-services production, should focus on the crystal-clear sphere of circulation, for after all what counts is that these people are being paid, ergo they are rendering a service.

Fair enough. But then the criterion of using up resources is superfluous, unless by that is meant consuming the goods which the service-renderers buy with their incomes. If that is the case, then all consumption becomes production as long as it is mediated by "payment for services rendered," in which case we are back at the tautologies of the factor-income and flow-of-product approaches.

We do not want to labor this point, although it is interesting insofar as this distinction reflects the national limits of capitalism. On the other hand, a consistent application of the principle would lead to the conclusion that a worldwide nuclear war in which every country used up resources in using up (i.e., destroying) the resources of other countries would make a vast contribution to the NNP of every country as long as there was no world government to outlaw this.

It appears then that the criterion of last resort for S's inclusion of "G" in national-product accounts relates to whether collective consumption is actually taking place as a result of this expenditure. His discussion of democracy in the chapters on the state serves to justify the inclusion of military expenditures. In principle, the way to such an approach was opened when subjectivist theories of value began to supplant the last vestiges of a theory of capitalist society as a specifically historical and class phenomenon as embodied in classical political economy. From this point on the "decision as to whether government expenditures—particularly war expenditures—were to be included in national income revolved about the adequacy of the analogy of consumer preferences in the "private sphere" to the "public sector."

Although definite social changes influenced this discussion, given the general framework of utility and production-factor theory, the development of the necessary criteria gave much subjective leeway to economists and statisticians. And it is for this reason that S concedes in a footnote that "how to treat government items in NNP is still somewhat controversial" (190 n.9).

Once subjectivist theory had gained preeminence, all theoretical barriers to the inclusion of state expenditures in national income were in principle removed. This, to repeat that important point, stems from the undifferentiated circulation-sphere approach, which identifies every expenditure with the creation of income.

In illustration of our point we would like once again to refer to Kuznets who seems to be more aware of some of the underlying social questions than many of his colleagues. He maintains that the "thorny problems" associated with national-income theory "arise largely from the conflict between the aim of the investigator and the recalcitrant nature of reality."[37] In other words, in spite of the most high-powered and sophisticated mathematical apparatus, there remains an unshakable piece of societal objectivity which even "modern" economists are constrained to acknowledge.

What is this underlying social reality? In part Kuznets takes up this point in conjunction with his debate with Hicks, who had maintained that in a laissez-faire economy one might well exclude the state sector because of its negligible relative magnitude. Once this relative size increases, however, one is confronted with certain "qualms" about whether one opts for inclusion or exclusion: qualms with regard to inclusion because "everyone must have felt how peculiar it is to reckon a large production of armaments as a contribution to current economic welfare"; and qualms with regard to exclusion because "if we accept the actual choices of the individual consumer as reflected in his preferences . . . then I do not see that we have any choice but to accept the actual choices of the government, even if they are expressed through a Nero or a Robespierre, as representing the actual wants of society." Hicks sees the problem as an all-or-nothing affair, since he thinks it impossible to separate the final from the intermediate "government product," which would lead to exclusion altogether, or so-called double counting.[38]

Changes within capitalism, the transition from laissez faire to mixed economy, are responsible for the new ratiocinative gyrations of "modern" economists. Kuznets, in his response to Hicks's agnosticism on the issue of sorting out intermediate and final product in the governmental sector, defines final government product as "services to individuals as ultimate consumers and government capital formation"; the remainder of government product he defines as intermediate "whether it represents a specific service to business firms or is used for defense, maintenance, or expansion of the social system as a whole."[39] Kuznets places particular emphasis on this distinction between intermediate and final product because Hicks's all-or-nothing approach can then be avoided.

Now let us take a closer look at these so-called intermediate government products. Here is how S depicts the issue: "Some experts say . . . that part of G is really 'intermediate' rather than 'final' product—much like dough rather than bread—in that it merely contributes to final private product already counted in (e.g., weather information for farmers who help give us our daily bread)" (190 n.9). The choice of so unrepresentative an example is typical of S's "scientific approach" in general, and of his strong desire to distract from the central role of war in the mixed economy in particular.

The difference between the classical and modern economists is not that the former were "pure" theoreticians trying to conceptualize a flowering capitalist mode of production while contemporary bourgeois economists are "pure" practitioners interested solely in devising policies to manage recurrent crises. Although the classical political economists did have a notion of a total social theory obviously lacking in contemporary economics, they were also eminently practical men. The difference, rather, lies in the form which the two very different objective situations gave to the theory-practice relation. In Ricardo's time the need for "practical policy," currently understood as state intervention, was different in the sense that the crises of capitalism, that is, those political-economic crises which threaten the very existence of capitalism, had not yet cropped up. They date back more or less to the immediate post-Ricardian era. Until that time, state activity was limited also largely by the fact that class struggle was still mired in the conflict between individual capitalists and workers. And only when the concentration of, and hence increased exploitation by, capital brought on the organization of the workers as a class and the subsequent struggle against the capitalists as a class did the state feel compelled to "intervene." Therein lies the rational kernel of the notion of laissez faire: as long as the crises of capitalist production had not brought forth a proletariat that had to be suppressed or pacified as the occasion warranted, the type of state intervention characteristic of the mixed economy had not become necessary.

What is the connection between these general remarks on the relation of theory and practice and the subject of national income? As implied earlier, S's inclusion of all of G in national income is dictated by the practical application of Keynesian theory. Whereas Ricardo saw profit production as the sole objective of the capitalist mode of production and treated the level of employment just as capitalism treated it, namely as subordinate to the production of profit, in the Keynesian era the working class had made clear that it was not willing to be treated as subordinate to the needs of capital. Keynes was looking for a political solution; for a "cure" to unemployment as potent as fascism and communism that would not destroy capitalism. He was interested solely in overcoming a specific crisis, the mass unemployment of the 1930s which had assumed critical political dimensions. He introduced a new subjective "goal": full employment, the basic concern of "the modern analysis of income determination" (7th ed., p. 352). But like all other subjectively oriented theories of national income, this too remained rooted in the sphere of circulation.

The important point with respect to our subject is Keynes's prescription of government spending. With full employment elevated to a "goal" of the mixed economy, all spending leading to it is thus subsumed in the national product. Keynes's main interest lay in the results of spending, however it was effected, in systematizing those efforts which in other societies may have provided employment only coincidentally.

Whether "the real national dividend of useful goods and services"[40] is increased by government expenditures on jet bombers and pilots, judges, policemen, etc., is something S does not delve into. He is merely using "the simplest method of all"—namely adding "G." But since such spending has become the mainstay of the mixed economy, S cannot readily exclude it from national accounts, that is, he cannot admit that it "subtracts" from national production.

We might thus say that all "civil servants," including soldiers, are unproductive workers; they do not create value and therefore contribute nothing to national income;

they do not create the value from which their income stems. In this sense they are like any other "servant": they stand outside the capitalist mode of production in the sphere of consumption. Whereas a private servant's income derives from the component part of surplus which the "master" has title to, the income of civil servants derives from state revenues, which in turn derive from surplus value or wages. In this context S is correct when he says that

In using the flow-of-product approach to compute NNP as C+I+G, we would not have to worry about taxes or how government finances itself. Whether the government taxes, issues interest-bearing IOUs, or prints new noninterest IOU greenbacks, the statistician would compute G as the value of government expenditures on goods and services (evaluating items at their cost, *wherever the money came from*). . ." [190; our emphasis].

Since income originates in production, it *is* irrelevant "where the money comes from" that "pays" that income by exchange for the produced commodities in the sphere of circulation. But in our example it is not irrelevant, since we are dealing with those cases in which no income is produced. Here we do "worry" about where the money came from because no equivalent exchange has taken place. The value of the commodities produced by state "servants" is not being realized when transformed into the money form of value in the sphere of circulation, for here nothing is being bought and sold. Thus the wages of state employees itemized in national-income accounts represent double counting because they have already been counted in the before-tax-factor incomes. And this turns out to be no small sum. Thus with a national income of $851.1 billion in 1971, wages and salaries of military and civilian government employees totaled $18.6 billion and $105.2 billion respectively.[41] In other words, about 14.5 percent of national income "flowing" to state workers would have to be subtracted from the stated total to arrive at an accurate income concept.

SO-CALLED TRANSFER PAYMENTS

The last point we will touch upon in this context is S's "treatment" of so-called transfer payments. In Chapter 8 S tried to draw a distinction "economically" between the income of government employees and that of pensioners. Government employees were seen as producing their income, that is, their income is included in NNP because they render services, use up resources and production, and provide collective consumption to the people of the United States. Pensions, however, are an entirely different matter:

> Socially, it may be one of our most desirable expenditures, but nevertheless it is not a part of GNP or national income. Why? Because the widow does not render any concurrent services to the government or its citizens in exchange for the pension. She does not provide any labor, land, or capital. . . . These goods and services *that she buys* . . . are *attributable* to the people and private factories that have produced them, not to her [155].

Let us clarify one point S fails to state clearly enough, namely that there is a difference between so-called welfare transfer and social-security pensions. The latter cannot be counted in NNP because they are counted when paid in. To figure them also when they are paid out would constitute double counting. And in this sense social-security payments are different: they are not deferred wages. But are they as different from the salaries of jet pilots as S would have us believe? Of the three criteria mentioned by S, we can eliminate the using up of resources and production, having already discussed it above. This leaves services rendered and collective consumption provided. In our opinion these two criteria coincide, and we can thus treat them jointly. Again we find ourselves back at the problem of whether "services" are in fact being rendered.

S offers no criterion that by some stretch of our marginal-utilitarian imagination would not just as well apply to blind widows as to jet pilots. Both provide collective consumption. If the pilot provides labor, then so does the widow, as demonstrated by her skill to survive on her skimpy allowance. The rest of S's reasoning falls down completely. Thus the goods and services that no one buys are "attributable" to the buyers: by definition they are simply exchanging the money form of value for the same magnitude of value in commodity form. This in no way determines how the pilot and the widow got their incomes in the first place. And finally, is it any less true of jet pilots' salaries than of widows' pensions that "unless these expenditures are financed by new money creation or by bond borrowing, larger taxes will have to be levied on the public, and it is for this reason tha they are usually called 'transfer expenditures' "? (155). Do jet pilots any more than blind widows produce the fund from which they are paid?

NNP AND GNP / DISPOSABLE, PERSONAL, AND NATIONAL INCOMES

In this last section we will examine S's analysis of the statistical relations among the various "items" in the national accounts.

S opens these subsections by stating that since we are already "armed with an understanding of the concepts involved," we can now look at the data (191). Of course, S has not developed any concepts up to this point; he has merely given us arbitrary definitions. And although he characterizes them as statistical-technical in nature, they conceal important social relations he is unaware of. And here, too, so-called statistical relations conceal relations of capitalist reproduction. Consumption is highlighed: NNP, for example, is called "the harvest we have been working for: the money measure of the American economy's over-all performance. . . : (193). Then, too, disposable income is accorded much space; defined as NNP minus taxes and undistributed corporate profits plus transfers, "the result is, so to speak, *what actually gets into the public's hands, to dispose of as we please*" (194; in the 7th edition [p. 183] it was getting into "our hands").

Other "items" appear almost as afterthoughts. Thus depreciation, which bourgeois economics itself admits must be taken care of before any distribution can take place, turns out to be an "item" "we add . . . back into the figures" in order to obtain GNP (8th ed., p. 180). And profit "should come last because it is the residual *determined* as what is left over after all other items have been taken into account" (193; our emphasis).

To regard profit as a "residual" may be seen as a vestige of the classical view of profit as the only component of net income: with depreciation and wages depicted as production expenses, what remains is a surplus, part of which will be claimed as income by various agents of production (rent, interest, and entrepreneurial wages), with the balance available for accumulation. But contemporary bourgeois theory offers no rationale for this view, since all "factors of production" are treated as equal. The only "problem here arises from the fact that S and his colleagues are perplexed about what to do with profit. The economist, taking his cue from the statistician, also regards profit as a residual. There it is justified by looking at the individual firm where materials, wages, interest, and rent are subtracted from sales revenues to arrive at the residual profit. But to assume that that which holds true for the individual capitalist also holds true for capitalism as a whole merely means falling victim to that "fallacy of composition" S is always inveighing against. Moreover, this sort of reasoning contradicts other aspects of income theory; for if we were to take the individual firm as our guideline, we would have to consider wages as a cost; we would also have to say that depreciation is not an afterthought but a prior deduction.

In any event, income "accounting" is not identical from the point of view of the individual capitalist and the aggregate economy. And this factor, implicit in the "complexities" of national-income theory, reflects essential characteristics of the capitalist mode of production.

S tells us that we are interested in disposable income because "it is this sum . . . that people divide between (a) consumption spending and (b) net personal saving" (194). Whereas "we," "the public," can "dispose as we please" of this part of national product, there is also that other "item," undistributed corporate profits or "net corporate saving," "that part of corporate incomes which *they* fail to distribute as dividends" (204; our emphasis).

What then is the relation between the individual firm and the capitalist economy as a whole? S contends that a "businessman" or a "policy-maker" would be interested in disposable income because the manner in which that income is broken down into consumption and saving, namely the propensity to consume, is an essential aspect of effective demand. And a capitalist is of course vitally interested in the distribution of income insofar as it affects the profitability of his capital. However, the "financial prudence" of the individual capitalist in "writing off" larger sums than he intends to reinvest will not be very prudent as far as capitalist society as a whole is concerned, since he is thereby reducing the amount of income "left there for us to dispose of as we please." Thus although the individual capitalist sees the distribution of NNP as prerequisite for the profitability of his capital, the very nature of competition precludes his taking into consideration income distribution insofar as the results of his own actions are concerned. This would be imprudent.

Similarly with the division of NNP into wages and profits. It is "prudent" for a capitalist to keep wages as low as possible since, all other things being equal, this determines his profit and rate of profit. If every capitalist were to do this, then "effective demand" would suffer. But in capitalist reality, as opposed to ledgers, wages are not deducted from NNP to arrive at the residual profit. Rather both wages and profit are determined by the laws of capital accumulation from which all the contradictions between consumption and investment so faintly reflected in Keynesian theory must derive.

In this sense, the "formalities" of the accounting schema are not equipped to identify these faint reflections. This is not surprising since Keynes arrives at these "paradoxes" through subjective reasoning, whereas the national accounts are willy-nilly useful objective surface information despite their conceptual distortion at the hands of subjective value theory.

8 Keynesianism
S's Chapters 11-13

Keynes' General Theory made use of concepts quite con-
genial to the framework of the national income accounts,
thus giving the latter the status of essential raw materials
for the purpose of testing the theory and prescribing national policies based upon Keynes' system of thought.

—Barry N. Siegel, *Aggregate Economics and Public Policy*, p. 23.

In an important sense, these three chapters represent the
central element of "modern" bourgeois economic theory:
Not only do they form the most significant modification of
bourgeois economics vis-à-vis the so-called neoclassical
tradition, but they also provide the basis for much of the
practical "policy" carried out by the state in the leading
capitalist countries.

This part of "modern" theory is also the one its adherents find most difficult to clothe in "purely" theoretical
terms, since it arose in response to the eminently practical
political problems of the worldwide capitalist crisis of the
1930s. Not only did the practical crisis turn into a theoretical one, but the capitalist reality and theory that developed
out of the 1930s assumed a new quality. A leading so-called
left-wing Keynesian, Joan Robinson, describes the change
thus:

> By making it impossible to believe any longer in an automatic
> reconciliation of conflicting interests into a harmonious whole,
> the *General Theory* brought out into the open the problem of
> choice and judgment that the neo-classicals had managed to

243

smother. The ideology to end ideologies had broken down. Economics once more became Political Economy.[1]

This description is itself "ideological" insofar as it attempts to draw an ahistorical parallel between Keynes and the classical bourgeois political economists (Smith and Ricardo); for the reality of capitalism changed qualitatively between about 1800 and 1930 in the sense that a rising capitalism turned into a dying one.

Keynes made the attempt to conceptualize the practical policy measures undertaken to keep alive a bankrupt socioeconomic formation. Whereas the classical political economists were conscious of the class structure of capitalism at a time when the proletariat had not yet become a revolutionary force, Keynesianism seeks to protect capitalism from the revolutionary political forces capitalism has given rise to. Thus in the political aspect of political economy there exists a crucial difference between the classical authors and Keynes in that the former could "afford" to be rather open and almost cynical about class relations, whereas the Keynesians have quite clearly not "overcome" that aspect of neoclassical economics which tends to deny the existence and/or importance of social classes.

Although the political and theoretical background against which Keynesianism arose is not secret, S makes very short shrift of these origins (cf. e.g. 344 f., 348); and the later editions in particular, saturated as they are with the spirit of optimism which S doubtless deems justified in light of the "performance" of the post-World War II mixed economies, have tended to present the reader with a fixed scheme of "modern" economic thought completely divorced from its historical origins. For this reason we will review the practical and theoretical origins of Keynesianism before proceeding to a critique of Keynesian theory as presented in these chapters.

I / POLITICAL-HISTORICAL BACKGROUND
OF THE RISE OF KEYNESIANISM

A / THE GREAT CRISIS OF THE 1930S

Although capitalism had gone through many periods of depression or stagnation before the 1930s, none was so severe as that which began in 1929 and lasted until the near beginning of World War II. Of the phenomena that mark periods such as this, unemployment is doubtless the most important.[2] Not only does the proletariat suffer, but the the middle classes (the petty bourgeoisie, small capitalists, and "professionals") are also subjected to severe social and economic losses. Aside from the immediate material hardship, the potential effect of the ideological blow to the myth of unlimited "upward mobility" is not to be underestimated.

Although unemployment was not a twentieth-century invention, it had never before reached similar proportions. Thus Keynes, in speaking of the pre-1914 period, says: "The average level of employment was, of course, substantially below full employment, but not so intolerably below it as to provoke revolutionary changes."[3] But with the mass unemployment of the 1930s, revolutionary changes became imminent.

B / KEYNES AS THE CONCEPTUALIZER OF AN ALREADY EXISTING PRACTICE

Amidst the widespread acclamation accorded the "Keynesian revolution" one tends to lose sight of the fact that Keynes merely rendered a theoretical account of an anti mass-unemployment policy in effect in a number of countries. Neoclassical theory was largely unable to offer "policy recommendations" that could lead out of the crisis. This does not mean, however, that no fairly successful measures were taken even if they were not based on any well-developed theory. Increased public works, greater money supply, lower interest rates, and budget deficits were not invented by Keynes. The so-called multiplier theory, for example, gave theoretical shape to already existing efforts to deal with unemployment by means of public works. Two of the responses to the problem of mass unemployment of the 1930s which may be regarded as anticipations of Keynesianism, or rather Keynesianism may be regarded as their later theoretical justification, were the New Deal in the United States and fascism.

1/ The New Deal   The New Deal was a much weaker version of Keynesianism than was fascism. The reasons for this are not of major interest for us here, yet we would like to mention a few. Because U.S. social legislation was relatively backward, its workers did not enjoy the same measure of "security" as did their European counterparts. Consequently this period saw the rise of social-security legislation (unemployment insurance and old-age pensions) in the U.S. Trade-union organization also was much more backward, and this tended to weaken the cohesion of the working class and prevent it from pressing radical demands. This also meant, however, that as a whole capitalism needed unionization, although the individual capitalists fought it with all their might. Although these various measures were not necessarily diversionary, they did serve to deflect the potential drive for more revolutionary demands.

Aside from the Keynes-type "experiments," three other "approaches" were under discussion during the 1930s: the cartelization of the economy with government backing; national economic planning, and incisive antitrust measures. None of these proved feasible. The first, put forward by "business groups," would have met too much popular resistance at a time when the reputation of capitalism was at a low ebb. The antitrust approach was a sham from the very beginning as far as its official state supporters were concerned. With respect to the efficacy of antitrust measures during the 1930s, Ellis W. Hawley notes that such a policy was "likely to be deflationary, at least for a long initial period.":

> To be really effective, it would involve putting the economy through the wringer, subjecting it to a round of debt repudiation, wholesale bankruptcies, corporate reorganization, and major price and wage readjustments. Such a process, to be

sure, might eventually bring recovery, provided it did not produce a revolution first. From a practical standpoint, it was never a realistic alternative.[4]

And as to national planning, even its proponents eventually recognized that it was "politically impossible," and so they as well as many antitrusters began to look at Keynesianism as an "attractive alternative."[5] By contemporary standards, the extent of Keynesianism in the U.S. during the 1930s was limited. Nevertheless, both before and after the publication of the *General Theory* a definite program was being put into effect. With respect to budget deficits as a means of combating unemployment, these were the deficits during the 1931-39 period (in billions of dollars):

1931	−0.5	1934	−3.6	1937	−2.8
1932	−2.7	1935	−2.8	1938	−1.2
1933	−2.6	1936	−4.4	1939	−3.9[6]

As a result of this $24.5 billion increase, the national debt rose by about 150 percent during this nine-year period. Interest rates dropped to levels believed to foster increased investment; thus four-to-six months prime commercial paper, which stood at 5.85 percent in 1929 sank considerably below 1 percent after 1935. Corporate profits rose from $1.1 billion in 1934 to $2.9 billion in 1935, and to $5 billion in 1936, but wage and salary disbursements increased much more slowly: from $33.7 billion to $36.7 billion to $41.9 billion respectively.[7]

It seems doubtful that this improved profitability was a result of government spending alone. That profits rose more rapidly than wages or national income was in no small part the result of the "self-healing" powers of the stagnation—among other factors, of the enormous destruction of capital and increased productivity as well as of wage levels lowered by mass unemployment. Because the pre-depression magnitude of capital was reduced, the rate of profit was based on a smaller invested capital. Similarly, rising productivity contributed to higher "profit margins," not least because it cheapened the elements of constant capital and devalued existing capital.

The results of the combination of the workings of the crisis and government spending become apparent when one compares the data for 1929 and 1941; between these two years, the last prestagnation and the last prewar year respectively, national income rose 19.3 percent, wages and salaries 22.2 percent, industrial production 33.2 percent, and corporate profits 43.6 percent; yet unemployment still remained at 9.9 percent, or considerably more than double that of 1929.[8]

Thus when Galbraith says that "The Great Depression of the thirties never came to an end. It merely disappeared in the great mobilization of the forties,"[9] this is only partly true. To the extent that conditions of profitability improved through the crisis, it is strictly speaking not true that the period of stagnation had not been overcome. On the other hand, profitability had not been improved to the extent that it permitted a new period of accumulation strong enough to absorb the 8 million still unemployed in 1940.

On the one hand, the capitalist class welcomes unemployment, for without it there would be no sudden pulsations of accumulation. Beyond a certain limit and duration, however, unemployment becomes a "social problem" endangering the stability without which capitalism cannot exist.

This, then, was the problem facing American capitalism before the United States entered World War II; but in fact the "problem" turned out to be a political-economic crisis of international capitalism, and Keynesianism turned out to be the theoretical-ideological program that best synthesized the practical requirements of capitalism. Since the beneficial aspects of government spending did not fully reveal themselves in the United States until World War II, let us look at the country that proved to be the future model for other capitalist countries in crisis.

C / GERMAN FASCISM

At first glance it might appear sacrilegious to posit a similarity between fascism and Keynesianism. Not only do bourgeois economists deny the more general connection between the welfare and the warfare state, but more particularly, many repudiate any similarity between Keynesian theory and practice and German fascist economic policy. Before the appearance of the 8th edition it might have been necessary to demonstrate the Keynesian "affinities" of German fascism; but in the 8th and 9th editions S concedes—even though tucked away in Chapter 36 rather than in those on Keynesian theories and practice—that Hitler's "preparations for war 'solved' Germany's mass-unemployment problem and proved—in a tragically unnecessary way—the potency of Keynes-like fiscal and monetary policies" (707).

To be sure, S does not really concede very much, to judge by the quotation marks he puts around "solved," thereby clearly implying that the fascist method of dealing with unemployment was a sham compared with the real article of today's modern mixed economies. Given the fact that the scope of U.S. government spending has never been large enough to stave off large-scale unemployment except for the same type of war production as the Nazis', S's reference to the fascist policies as "tragically unnecessary" seems uncalled for, particularly in light of the fact that Germany was the only capitalist country at the time to have eliminated unemployment.

It is frequently alleged that whereas Keynesian policies are aimed at producing economic welfare, fascist policies produced full employment only as a by-product of rearmament. This is wrong for two reasons. First, with respect to so-called welfare, we have seen how little welfare has been produced by Keynesian or any other policies in recent years. And secondly, to view the elimination of unemployment as a mere by-product of German rearmament reveals a lack of understanding of the social and historical functions of German fascism. It is extremely unlikely that the Nazis would have been able to count on the acquiescence of the masses of workers had there been no jobs. In this sense, the New Deal had precisely the same objective. The fact that military production was the vehicle can hardly be used as the *differentia specifica* of fascism, given the economic development in the United States since World War II.

One of the main tactics in the Keynesian attack on stagnation is allegedly the stimulation of consumption (by increasing the aggregate propensity to consume, the problem of effective demand is supposedly dealt with at least in part). But neither in Nazi Germany nor in democratic America was or does personal consumption form a substantial part of national production; rather it becomes that category which S and others euphemistically refer to as "collective consumption." Looking at the breakdown of GNP in Germany between 1928 and 1936, we find the following shifts.

	1928	1932	1936
private investment	9.8%	3.7%	10.1%
state expenditure	18.7%	13.4%	25.7%
consumption	71.5%	82.9%	64.2%
	100.0%	100.0%	100.0%[10]

Not only did personal consumption drop from the relatively high level at the depth of the crisis when there was relatively little investment, but it also declined as compared with the pre-1929 level. The slack, as it were, was taken up by state expenditures; during the 1934-36 period, military expenditures accounted for 11.1 percent of national income.[11] The relative growth of the production of means of consumption and means of production during the 1930s in Germany is still another expression of the same trend. Taking 1928 as the base year (= 100), we note the following:

	Means of Production	Means of Consumption
1932	46	78
1933	54	83
1934	77	85
1935	99	91

1936	113	98
1937	126	103
1938	136	107[12]

This development is significant insofar as it shows certain constraints in the practical application of Keynesian theories that will also assert themselves in later attempts to apply them in the U.S.—namely those connected with raising the aggregate propensity to consume by increasing the consumption of the masses directly.[13]

This reliance on military production is connected to the commonly heard charge that since deficit spending played a relatively minor role in Germany in the thirties as compared to the U.S., Keynesian policies were not that relevant. Thus Schweitzer states that:

> Having little confidence in the output-creating effect of deficit financing, the business groups pressured the government into placing orders with their own plants, even though this had the potential effect of significantly increasing the volume of public investments.[14]

However, it appears doubtful whether deficit financing is really the key to understanding these policies, and when interest rates on government bonds are extremely low anyway, the distinction between government borrowing and taxing does not appear to be crucial.

The fact that "business groups" had little "confidence" in the multiplier effect of deficit financing does not in retrospect appear to have been bad judgment on their part when one compares the results with those of the New Deal. Essentially the same phenomenon can be observed today in the U.S., when the largest "defense" contractors also "pressure the government into placing orders with their own plants." Such an arrangement involves no risk, since the "market" is guaranteed and one need not wait to see whether the multiplier effect of government public-works spending or whatever will raise effective demand enough so that these commodities—namely means of production—will become necessary for the producers of means of consumption to meet the increased demand. In view of the fact that Keynesian policies originate in political necessities, it would be naive to believe that the distribution of the profits resulting from such policies is determined by some immutable unknown laws.

Although the specific intraclass struggles of the capitalist class will of course differ from one "mixed economy" to the next, the fact that such struggles do exist does not mean that Keynesian policies are not under way. Keynes does not mention such struggles either because of conscious demagoguery or possible naivete, for the extrication from so deep a crisis as that of the 1930s was connected with a vast shake-up of the capital structure involving enormous losses and gains—in short, capital centralization. On the other hand, this neglect also indicates that Keynes had not really resurrected "macroeconomics" and political economy, as has been suggested. Thus, in speculating on the consequences of implementing his proposals, Keynes says that:

> if effective demand is deficient, not only is the public scandal of wasted resources intolerable, but the individual enterpriser who seeks to bring these resources into action is operating with the odds loaded against him. The game of hazard which he plays is furnished with many zeros, so that the players *as a whole* will lose if they have the energy and hope to deal all the cards.[15]

True, in such a period of stagnation total profits do drop, but despite the enormous physical and value destruction of capital, the largest capitals emerge strengthened. We do not mean to imply that they desire such periods of crisis and stagnation, but still there is some understanding of the "self-healing" powers of capitalism on the part of some capitalists and economists. Since the main thrust of Keynesian policies is to restore conditions that will eliminate the necessity for "revolutionary change," the immediate purpose at any rate was not to raise profits (although this of course will become necessary, and these policies are *also* designed to raise profits). In this sense, the largest capitals have the least to lose from such periods and will be willing to let the crisis run its "natural" course as long as it stops short of revolution.

Thus the differential effects of the Nazi economic policies for different sectors of the capitalist class, far from being a refutation of Keynesian programs, are a logical result of such politically inspired anticrisis programs.

The last similarity between fascist and Keynesian programs we will touch on deals with their platform against nonindustrial capital. Although Keynes' anti-"finance" capitalism differs from that of the Nazis in the sense that his avowed goal was to save capitalism while the Nazis demagogically proclaimed an anticapitalist program they had no intention of carrying out, it bears great similarity to that which the Nazis actually promulgated. (Keynes in his own fashion was something of a demagogue in that he asserted that some sort of new capitalism would grow out of his policies.)

In Keynes' conception, a minimal rate of interest would be crucial to increasing investment, and at the same time

> it would mean the euthanasia of the rentier, and consequently the euthanasia of the cumulative oppressive power of the capitalist to exploit the scarcity-value of capital. Interest to-day rewards no genuine sacrifice, any more than the rent of land. . . . But whilst there may be intrinsic reasons for the scarcity of land, there are no intrinsic reasons for the scarcity of capital.[16]

To the extent that large concentrations of capital—whether in industrial enterprises or combined in capital groups controlling banks—enable capitalist industry to provide for its accumulation on the basis of its own profits—in other words makes it largely independent of the capital markets—the development of capitalism itself provides for "the euthanasia of the cumulative oppressive power" of the banks over industrial capital.

The Nazi battlecry against breaking the power of finance capital was an important propaganda tool to win over the petty bourgeoisie and the working class. But the laws passed by the Nazis served to foster accumulation—

especially among the largest capitals. Thus the Dividend Limitation Act of 1934 limited dividend payments to 6 percent of profits, thereby "restricting the distribution of dividends among the shareholders, who, in the view of German economists and lawyers, are a mere nuisance."[17]

This section does not purport to be an analysis of capitalism under German fascism, nor does it suggest that German fascism is to be equated with contemporary U.S. capitalism, let alone the mixed economy as a whole. Rather, it had the much more modest aim of showing up Keynesian economics as a crude sort of "political" economy whose primary end is the preservation of capitalism as a political-economic bastion against the possible alternative of socialism. It also gives new meaning to S's assertion that Keynesian income analysis "is itself neutral" (8th ed., p. 293); for despite S's contention that the theory can be used to "defend" or "limit" private enterprise, we see that its real flexibility lies in its adaptability to formally democratic as well as formally dictatorial capitalist societies depending on the political circumstance and the imminence of "revolutionary changes."

D / THE TRIUMPH OF KEYNESIANISM

Inasmuch as Keynes merely synthesized a process already under way, it can be fairly said that the turning point for this new economic policy came in the period of its first major application—World War II. The rapid absorption of unemployment and the skyrocketing profits set in motion by enormous deficit spending helped to convince capitalists and economists that such a program offered the only way out of the long stagnation. And, of course, this was always coupled with assertions that the effect of war production was only coincidential and that any other type of "peaceful, civilian" spending would have the same beneficial results.

The enormous destruction of capital brought on by World War II as well as large-scale unemployment and the consequent low wages set off another round of relatively high rates of accumulation in Europe, without recourse to Keynesian policies. Thus the political-ideological struggle for the new economic policy did not assume sharp forms in Europe. The U.S., however, not subject to a like level of destruction, found itself in urgent need of continued anti-stagnation policies.

1/ *Full employment* The debates on full employment continued even in World War II; with unemployment substantially reduced, the capitalist class began to worry about the potential effects of permanent full employment. During the height of the war, as the following table shows, the U.S., U.K., and Canada had relatively low rates of unemployment (the same of course is undoubtedly true of Germany), while Sweden did not reduce unemployment to similar levels until after the war. But the United States and Canada failed to maintain their low levels in the postwar period, whereas the U.K., "since the trauma of high interwar unemployment . . . placed heavy emphasis on full employment as a central objective of national economic policy."[18] Given the unstable political conditions of postwar Germany, its high unemploynent rates are not surprising, particularly in view of the large number of immigrants from the Soviet-occupied zone and from the former German territories to the east.

UNEMPLOYMENT (%)

Year	Canada	Germany	Holland	Sweden	UK	US
1940	9.3		19.8	11.8	5.0	14.6
1941	4.5			11.3	1.5	9.9
1942	2.2			7.5	1.0	4.7
1943	0.8			5.7	0.5	1.9
1944	0.5			4.9	0.5	1.2
1945	1.4			4.5	1.0	1.9
1946	1.4	7.5		3.2	2.5	3.9
1947	1.3	5.0		2.8	2.0	3.6
1948	2.2	4.2		2.8	1.6	3.4
1949	3.0	8.3		2.7	1.6	5.5
1950	3.8	10.2		2.2	1.6	5.0[19]

The debate on full employment is marked by a basic tension between the political necessity of avoiding the massive unemployment that could trigger anticapitalist feelings and the political-economic necessity of not interfering with the "natural" laws of capitalism that make unemployment an essential aspect of the process of capital accumulation. The level of "employement" created for the above political reasons at the possible expense of profitability in the short run was determined by a variety of factors, chief among them the degree of existing unemployment, the strength of the working class, the cohesion of the capitalist class, as well as the power of the larger, monopoly capitalists vis-à-vis the smaller capitalists, and the general profitability of capital at any given time. The outcome—which changes with shifts among these factors in one direction or the other—is determined by complex political-economic class factors and cannot be reduced to a "policy decision" or "the will of society." On the other hand, the familiar theses about "trade-offs" between unemployment and some other "variable" are simply superficial reflections of this much more complicated process.

In the postwar period the British ruling class was compelled to support policies fostering relatively low rates of unemployment—and the Tory government in 1951 continued them—partly because of the deteriorating situation of British capital, the result of the setbacks British imperialism sustained after the war. And so the ruling class was not in a strong enough position to subdue its working class at home. However, the fundamental contradictions of capitalism have a way of reasserting themselves regardless of Keynesian state intervention; they can be "bottled up" for just so long before bursting through and making their appearance in originally unanticipated forms.

The definitions of full employment tend to underscore its function as a political response to a political threat. Thus one early postwar British discussion defined full employment as "avoiding that level of unemployment, whatever it may happen to be, which there is good reason to fear may provoke an inconvenient restlessness among the electorate."[20] And a committee of the American Economic Association defined it quite simply: "Full employment is the absence of mass unemployment."[21] The difference between these two definitions reflects objective differences between British and U.S. national capital and between the degree of class consciousness of the British and American working class. But it also points to the objective situation in both countries, for full employment or, rather, low levels of unemployment, are in large measure based on the factors determining the creation of a reserve army of unemployed. To mention an important one: whereas industry in the postwar period the United States—and to an even greater extent is continental Western Europe—provided for a greater supply of industrial workers from among the ranks of those displaced from farms and "independent" trades, Great Britain, in this sense the most developed of all capitalist countries, had already "transferred" an extremely high percentage of its work force into the sphere of industrial surplus-value production. This meant that the "latent surplus population" (Marx) had already been largely absorbed, so that this important factor in the creation of a reserve army of unemployed was lacking. This complex of factors provided an objective basis which considerably facilitated a policy of low employment.

Before taking a brief look at the so-called Full Employment legislation enacted in the U.S. after World War II, we should like to comment on the framework within which full employment is conceived by bourgeois authors, one which very definitely presupposes the capitalist mode of production as its social base. In capitalism, even under conditions of zero unemployment, there will still be a significant number of people who do not work, because in capitalism "people" have the right not to work, whereas in a socialist society they have the right and the obligation or responsibility to work. This "right" in capitalism of course means different things to different social classes: for those with titles to the constituent parts of surplus value it means the right to be idle, whereas for all others it means the right to starve to death, or its "modern" equivalent.

This is an important point inasmuch as it indicates that later discussions of GNP-gaps, etc., do not relate to some sort of technical facts but rather presuppose very specific social and historical conditions in which "labor supply" excludes many who in another society could contribute to the production of social wealth.

In closing, we will attempt to show the headway made by Keynesianism in the early postwar period in the U.S. S offers almost no information on this, and that which he does offer is largely misleading. Thus in Chapter 19 he states that "the historic Employment Act of 1946 brought the United States up to the other mixed economies" by creating "agreement that we must continue to succeed in laying to rest the ghost of instability, chronic slump, and snowballing inflation" (354). In view of the mass destruction of Europe and the relative prosperity of the U.S. one can only wonder what this is supposed to mean. The "mixed economy" as a permanent feature of capitalism as opposed to an ad hoc reaction to various "emergencies" had not yet evolved, nor had a well-developed theory of that economy. That "everyone" is in agreement on such policies is refuted by S himself in the first edition of his textbook, in which he referred to a "fundamental difficulty with full employment"—namely "the fact that wages and prices may begin to soar while there is still considerable unemployment and excess capacity." For in discussing this "biggest unsolved economic problem of our time," S reported this discordant view:

> Some pessimists have argued that there is nothing to do but to hope for a large enough "army of the unemployed" to keep laborers from making unreasonable wage demands; thus, a reserve army of 10 million jobless hanging around factory gates might keep wages from rising and labor from becoming obstreperous [p. 435f].

Fortunately for the "pessimists," forces stronger than "hope" were in play; for capitalism has its own laws that cause unemployment.

Although the motto to Chapter 19 speaks only of promoting "maximum employment," S erroneously asserts in the text that the Employment Act of of 1946 set up bodies "to help ensure full employment" (354). This confuses the Employment Act of 1946 with the Full Employment Bill of 1945, which involved "the notion of the right to employment."[22] This latter bill, against which "the most powerful business groups, led by the National Association of Manufacturers and the Chamber of Commerce, mounted a militant campaign," was severely emasculated so that "what finally emerged was a very different animal from the depression-eater of 1945."[23] And another author has commented that "by its rejection of the Full Employment Act of 1945 the American Congress had indicated that it did not want to bind itself in advance to 'Keynesian' methods of attaining full employment."[24] In point of fact, U.S. capital had decided not to commit itself to the attainment of full employment. As long as there was no united working class to press the demand, the state was not about to make it a present of full employment. This, however, does not mean that Keynesianism had been dealt a mortal blow, but rather that the record wartime profits had made capitalists very skeptical about the need for massive "peacetime" government spending. Thus so-called Keynesian programs were held in abeyance.

2/ *The ideological function of Keynesianism*   Perhaps the greatest virtue of Keynesianism is its ability to serve as a unifying ideology for big capital and left-wing reform movements. Certain sectors of the capitalist class had weakened Keynesian policies in the 1930s because Keynes offered theoretical justification for a process already underway. But he also offered benefits that transcended mere recapitulation; and it is in this ideological sphere that we must look for the qualities of Keynesian economics which have elevated it to its present-day eminence.

The crisis of the 1930s also marked a crisis for bourgeois economic theory. Not only was it incapable of explaining that crisis, but it was part of a century-old tradition that denied the possibility of so extended and deep a crisis. Under these circumstances theoretical straws were literally being grasped at, and an alternative was much sought after, but, of course, not just any alternative, for after all, there already existed a theory—Marxism—that sought to explain crises and other attributes of capitalism and that stood in clear opposition to the discredited bourgeois theory. The search was for a theory that could devise an overall strategy to save capitalism.

It is revealing to look at the almost identical descriptions of the atmosphere which Keynes created, at least in academic circles, by two economists whose course was later to diverge but who in the 1930s were considered rising stars at Harvard. Thus S in his obituary of Keynes confided that:

> It is quite impossible for modern students to realize the full effect of what has been advisably called "The Keynesian Revolution" upon those of us brought up in the orthodox tradition. . . .
>
> The economists' belief in the orthodox synthesis was not overthrown, but had simply atrophied: it was not as though one's soul had faced a showdown as to the existence of the Deity and that faith was unthroned, or even that one had awakened in the morning to find that belief had flown away in the night; rather it was realized with a sense of belated recognition that one no longer had faith, that one had been living without faith for a long time, and that what, after all, was the difference?[25]

Paul M. Sweezy, doubtless the most famous Marxist economist in the U.S. today, told how Keynes restored "faith" in this way:

> Probably only those who (like the present writer) were trained in the academic tradition of economic thinking in the period before 1936 can fully appreciate the sense of liberation and the intellectual stimulus which the *General Theory* immediately produced among younger teachers and students in all the leading British and American Universities.[26]

In the case of Sweezy—and he is merely the most prominent example—the Keynesian influence proved to be lasting, despite his later leftward development. Thus during the 1930s he coauthored a volume with six other Harvard and Tufts economists which proposed a Keynesian method for "recovery" that, allegedly for reasons of political acceptability, stopped far short of revolutionary changes.[27]

But even after Sweezy had become a Marxist, he apparently still considered Keynesian theories unassailable on theoretical grounds. Thus in an important book written in 1942 he contends:

> Generally speaking their (Keynes' writings') logical consistency cannot be challenged, either on their own ground or on the basis of the Marxian analysis of the reproduction process. The critique of Keynesian theories of liberal capitalist reform starts, therefore, not from their economic logic but rather from their faulty (usually implicit) assumptions about the relationship, or perhaps one should say lack of relationship, between economics and political action. The Keynesians tear the economic system out of its social context and treat it as though it were a machine to be sent to the repair shop there to be overhauled by an engineer state.[28]

Thus Sweezy announced programmatically that the Keynesian theory is true in the abstract but that the conditions under which it can develop its real powers cannot be realized in capitalism as a result of political factors which the theory does not understand. And almost a quarter century later Sweezy collaborated with the Marxist economist Paul Baran on an important study of contemporary capitalism which largely operates with a Keynesian analysis supplemented by an anticapitalist class analysis.[29]

S welcomed this development, saying: "Even Marxist economists, who at first resented Keynesian economics as a 'mere palliative' to the ills of captalism, have come to recognize its explanatory powers" (206). By this he does not necessarily mean Sweezy but rather Soviet economists, for in the third edition (1955) he still gave low marks to those unbelievers:

> Perhaps we should be thankful that the Russian economists have not mastered modern elementary economics; they do not

yet understand the "neo-classical" synthesis which . . . clearly demonstrates the ability of resolute free societies to dissipate the ancient fear of mass unemployment [p. 709].

This is clearly a misunderstanding. First of all, the "fear" of mass unemployment—that is the political struggle surrounding it—dates back only to the 1920s and '30s. Secondly, by and large, Soviet economists have maintained a fairly realistic attitude toward the possibilities of political intervention to stem revolution. But thirdly, this has never been accompanied by an acknowledgment of the correctness of the Keynesian analysis of capitalism, which is still considered vulgar economics.[30]

More significant than the influence on such individual theoreticians as Sweezy has been the penetration of Keynesianism into the trade unions and social-democratic parties of many capitalist nations, and this process is an important factor in the ideological struggle to integrate these movements into various state programs designed to thwart revolutionary change.

Since victorious Keynesianism combined a pro-ruling-class ideology with an appeal to the "disaffected" left, it was inevitable that those who opposed increased state spending would accuse the Keynesians of supporting creeping socialism. In locating the root of the crisis of the 1930s in psychological factors, Keynes could appear critical of capitalism while at the same time excusing it on the basis of factors beyond its control. A central element in Keynes' so-called revolution of economic theory involves his refutation of Say's Law, which in turn rests on the proposition that consumption does not rise as rapidly as income, and that the reasons for investment and saving diverge. Keynes' own propensity to ascribe suprahistorical validity to theories with but a rational kernel in certain societies is admirably summarized in this statement:

> There has been a chronic tendency throughout human history for the propensity to save to be stronger than the inducement to invest. The weakness of the inducement to invest has been

at all times the key to the economic problem. To-day the explanation of the weakness of this inducement may chiefly lie in the extent of existing accumulations; whereas, formerly, risks and hazards of all kinds may have played a larger part. But the result is the same. The desire of the individual to augment his personal wealth by abstaining from consumption has usually been stronger than the inducement to the entrepreneur to augment the national wealth by employing labour on the construction of durable assets.[31]

As is true of many other examples of suprahistorical thinking, attention is diverted from the specific characteristics of each economic formation to alleged characteristics of individuals in a given society. Thus for instance "the desire of the individual to augment his personal wealth by abstaining from consumption" has rarely been an important motor of development—or retardation—in any society; although at certain stages in certain societies the miser has served an important function with respect to accumulation, this has never been so universal as to justify Keynes' reference to *the* individual. Those who save to augment their wealth—as opposed to those who put something by for a rainy day— have always known where to look for profit: in capitalist production. If they do not choose to invest there, that reluctance is based on the likelihood of low profitability. It has nothing to do with personal desires and inducements.

But by concentrating on individual psychological defects, Keynes can deflect attention from the objective workings of the specific mode of production to the alleged shortcomings of individual members of capitalist society. Thus he can avoid condemning capitalism while coming down very hard on individual scapegoats. At the same time this permits Keynes to postulate the mastering of the crisis by bringing in the state as deus ex machina, charging it with overcoming the unwelcome psychological propensities of savers and entrepreneurs by means of its taxing and spending powers as well as of its control of the money supply.

In this way Keynes can assert that the most "objectionable" features of capitalism can be eliminated while democratizing capitalism, since "the common will, embodied in the policy of the state,"[32] will assume responsibility for "supplementing the inducement to invest." Formally, this seemed to indicate that the state was merely a tool which could be used to gain control *over* capitalism, to limit its "abuses." And this is also what S is getting at indirectly when he says that Keynesian income analysis can be used to defend or limit private enterprise (8th ed., pp. 193 f.). But this is ideology, for Keynes' theories were not intended to limit capitalism.

Even a "well-intentioned" left-winger would have trouble "limiting" capitalism with the help of Keynes, since Keynes did not develop any theory dealing with the fundamental contradictions of that society. There is of course Keynes' "utopian" strain, which envisions eliminating capital scarcity and thus lowering the marginal efficiency of capital to zero.[33] But in fact Keynes' utopia does not project the disappearance of capitalism but only of its "objectionable features."

Another important Keynesian postulate that has served to make Keynesianism "attractive" to the "disaffected" lies in the removal of "one of the chief social justifications of great inequality of wealth," which Keynes considers one of "the outstanding faults of the economic society in which we live."[34] Key to Keynes' argument is the point that saving on the part of the rich is what impedes the growth of wealth. And even though he recognizes that "saving by institutions and through sinking funds is more than adequate,"[35] Keynes does not seem to understand the significance of this fact for his theory, for it destroys the basis for his refutation of Say's Law—namely that saving and investment are undertaken by different individuals for different reasons. And if it is investment—or rather the profitability of the previous round of investment, the degree to which capital self-expanded—that determines what will happen with savings, then it is basically irrelevant whether profits are retained by corporations or are distributed to shareholders and then reinvested through the return flow of these "funds" through the capital markets. If large incomes were taxed, it would not prove difficult to retain a greater share of the profits within the corporation, necessitating the taxing of profits instead of the taxing of so-called inequitable incomes.

This brings us to our second point, one related to another expression of contradictions in capitalism (sometimes called dilemmas, and more recently, in line with "modern" developments, trade-offs) as they are perceived on the surface of events, especially in conjunction with the "ability" of Keynes' state intervention to shift the phenomenal forms of basic contradictions without understanding what is happening.

We will return to various proposals for income redistribution as a means of increasing the marginal propensity to consume. For the time being we will confine ourselves to the comment that despite the fanfare surrounding this issue in Keynesian literature, as a practical measure it has remained a dead letter.

One final aspect of Keynes that might recommend him both to the capitalist class and left-wing reformists is his attitude toward wage reductions during a depression. Although Keynes disagreed with his neoclassical colleagues on theoretical principle that a reduction of wages could by itself stimulate a recovery (because of effective demand), more than theoretical principle was at stake here. For Keynes was much taken up with "ordinary experience" which "tells us, beyond doubt," that

> Whilst workers will usually resist a reduction of money-wages, it is not their practice to withdraw their labour whenever there is a rise in the price of wage-goods.[36]

For Keynes the practical problem was not whether lower wages would reduce unemployment but how to reduce wages. Ultimately he opted for "more subtle ways of wage-cutting than those traditionally employed"[37] namely "a flexible money policy": in other words, inflation. First of all, the difficulty involved in effecting uniform wage reductions and the comparative ease of raising prices to achieve the same end was no discovery of Keynes'; it was merely an established practice conceptualized and generalized by Keynes.

3/ *The Role of Samuelson's Textbook in the Spread of Keynesianism* In discussing the triumphal entry of Keynesianism into the American scene the key role played by its academic propagators should not be underestimated. Even though Keynes merely conceptualized already existing phenomena, people had to be won over to this conceptualization. The enormous expansion of university-level economics as well as the intensified emphasis on social studies in general was an expression of an ideological need for greater general understanding of the mixed economy. Keynes' followers found themselves faced with three basic tasks: to develop the theory, to propagate it, and to "bring Keynesian ideas to the center of effective policy-making":

> The second task was to bring the message to a wider public. This task fell, as it happened, primarily to one man. In this way, the first edition of Samuelson's *Economics: An Introductory Analysis* (1948) created a stir comparable to that of the *General Theory*. It represented as drastic and refreshing a departure from the textbook of the previous generations as did the work of Keynes, the exposition of whose work forms its heart. It was in addition brash, irreverent, lively, and contemporary. It has now gone through seven editions . . . and continues to dominate the textbook market in introductory courses in economics. Virtually every college graduate who has taken a course in economics in the past twenty years has come under the influence of this book and its imitators.[38]

In other words, Samuelson wrote the first Keynesian bourgeois economics textbook. Since according to S himself his "book is written primarily as a textbook for those who will never take more than one or two semesters of economics (1st ed. p. v), we will concentrate mainly on the purpose he seeks to serve. At that time (1948), S was concerned with the fate of the "intelligent citizen" with a "critical" approach to the sources reporting on the "economic institutions and problems of American civilization in the middle of the twentieth century." Yet this "intelligent layman" was expected to accomplish this with apparently outmoded texts which, "built on foundations laid down at about the time of World War I" and thus without "national income" as "the central unifying theme," could no longer "help" with the "important civic duty" just mentioned (pp. v-vi). S set himself two main tasks: to convince the student of the seriousness of the situation confronting U.S. capitalism, and to impress upon him or her the need for Keynesian policies able to preserve our "own concepts of democracy and freedom"—"a different commodity" from the " 'industrial democracy' " the "Russians claim to have" (p. 588)." The first of these tasks S tends to rather admirably in the following passage.

> Either we learn to control depressions and inflationary booms better than we did before World War II, or the political structure of our society will hang in jeopardy. For the ups and downs in business do not cancel out. At the top of the boom— if we are lucky!—there may be relatively favorable job opportunities for all who wish to work. Throughout the rest of the business cycle, men's lives are being wasted, and the progress of our economic society falls short of our true economic possibilities. If, as before the war, America marks time for another decade, the *collectivized nations* of the world, who *need have no fear of the business cycle as we know it,* will forge that much nearer or beyond it. Worse than that, peace-loving people who do not pretend to know very much advanced economics, will begin to wonder why it is that during two World Wars individuals were freed for the first time from the insecurity of losing their jobs and livelihoods [*ibid.*, pp. 393f.; our emphasis. This is still repeated in the 2nd and 3rd eds.].

When one compares this statement with the euphoria that permeates subsequent editions one begins to appreciate the ideological changes which have since taken place. Of particular interest is S's admission that insecurity is the normal condition of a worker in capitalism. Connected with this acknowledgment is his fear that the victim of insecurity might turn to that system which even according to S can eliminate those threatening factors the mixed economy has not been able to: unemployment and business cycles. This respectful bow to socialism stands in stark contrast to the pedestrian anticommunism of his later editions.

This chronological discrepancy might indicate that what S really was interested in was to prevent the recrudescence of such movements. But how was this to be accomplished, since his potential audience was composed of students rather than workers? The question arises why he is directing his message toward those posing a lesser danger to "the system." The answer would seem to be that it is crucially important to persuade these members of society of the miraculous properties of the mixed economy because they make up the core of the literate electorate, since from the bourgeois point of view they are likely to be in a position to use their abilities and training to discover the aggregate social connections hidden to those of more limited experience. Without the political support of this "segment of the population," the capitalist class, after all a very small minority, would find it difficult to stay in power. And this group is also important because of its influence on the working class. For among the functions of these purveyors of ideology is to divert attention from the basic contradictions of capitalism.

S's book of course is only a part of this process. But if the "head workers" had not been persuaded that the system they are serving was superior to any other, the state would find it impossible to recruit a sufficient number of them to carry out its tasks. This point is one of paramount significance for the students who are subjected to the bourgeois precepts propounded by S and others like him. The uncritical acceptance of the material in their books plays no small part in defining the objective content of the students' future activities as workers; and for this reason, they ought to give careful attention to the objectives pursued in their education.

E / THE FAILURE OF KEYNESIANISM

1/ *Introduction*   The recent crisis in the U.S. (1969-?) characterized by the simultaneity of high levels of unemployment and inflation, has brought consternation to the usually glib Keynesians. Although most recent developments have highlighted the gap between the promise and the reality of postwar Keynesianism, this should not blind us to the fact that the overall record of the mixed economy has left something to be desired. This fact finds superficial expression in the bourgeois notion of the GNP gap, which, according to S, is "the gap between what we actually produced . . . and what our economic system was capable of producing at reasonably high employment and capacity utilization" (235). The key words here are "our economic system" and "reasonably," for they tightly circumscribe the assumed potential. Not only does this definition take for granted a certain amount of unemployment and underutilization of capacity in excess of technological requirements, it also presupposes the existing class relations of ownership which determine how and for what purposes human labor will be used. The absurdity of this limited approach is made crystal-clear by the negative gap during a number of years of the Vietnam War when, as the result of "overfull employment" (under 4 percent officially), national product apparently exceeded what could "reasonably" be produced.

In other words, Keynesian economics is concerned merely with the very tightly defined sphere of the possible and the actual; and if U.S. workers knew, for example, that the U.S. economy was producing more than was "reasonable" in the years 1966-69, they would doubtless find this odd, particularly in light of the fact that their real wages declined during this period.

S says that from 1953 to the early 1960s unemployment and effective demand were troubling for the economy, but that with the advent of Kennedy "the full-employment growth path" once again was taken (234). As the following data on manufacturing output and capacity during these years, based on indices of physical production and capacity, indicate, there was a much wider "gap" than S admits to:

	1953-61	1961-69	1969-71	1953-71
output	+ 18%	+ 70%	− 4.7%	+ 90%
capacity	+ 37%	+ 50%	+ 9.9%	+ 141%[39]

Thus, between the end of the Korean War and 1961 (the "Eisenhower years"), manufacturing capacity rose more than twice as much as output; during the 1960s both production and output increased substantially, with production leading; and during the recent "recession," physical production actually decreased while capacity continued to mount. During the period as a whole, capacity outstripped production by more than one half. In one of the rare passages in later editions which still warn of the possibility of depressions, S points out that the costs of forgone output during the 1930s "were of the same general magnitude as the *costs of all the economic resources which had to be used up in World War II itself*' 234). Perhaps so, but this stands in contradiction to his view of state military production which he considers as productive as any other type of *spending*. In this sense, World War II was no more a "cost" than the production of automobiles today. And in any event, S ought to be careful about calling such spending a cost in view of the fact that it brought unemployment down to less than 4 percent (Korea, Vietnam), which no other spending has managed to do since World War II.

With respect to the powers of Keynesianism, S lists three types of poverty: "ancient poverty due to . . . inadequate production potential"; "unnecessary poverty in the midst of plenty, poverty due only to bad purchasing power behavior of the system"; "poverty due to uneven and bad distribution of an affluent total GNP" (235). The first type was solved by "the triumphs of technology"; the third, "which still does remain a challenge," is relegated to the anomalies in the last part of the book. Keynesianism comes to the rescue on Number Two: "But only with the development of modern income analysis has 'poverty midst plenty'—like that of 1929-1939—been rendered obsolete" (235).

There is "something" to the distinction between Numbers 1 and 2 and 3; capitalism has developed the forces of production sufficiently to eradicate hunger and to create the material conditions of a new type of society. But despite the "obsolescence" of this type of poverty, it continues to exist in the "advanced Western world" not to speak of the "underdeveloped" countries. Secondly, S does not appear to be aware of the fact that not only did Keynesianism have to come to grips with "poverty midst plenty," but that this phenomenon—the polarization of wealth—was the creation of capitalism. And thirdly, there is no recognition of the relation between "bad purchasing-power behavior" and "bad distribution" of income; yet there is no solution of one without the other, and there is no solution of either within capitalism.

2/ *Unemployment* Since the origins of Keynesianism lay in the political need to avert "revolutionary changes" let us examine its "record" on unemployment.

Charles L. Schultze of the Brookings Institution, whose view of the accomplishments of Keynesianism closely resembles that of S, has defended the Keynesians against various attacks of "irrelevancy" and "obsoleteness" leveled at them from within and without the fold:

> The current disenchantment, particularly among the young, with the optimistic, problem-solving approach to social issues that characterized the 1960s not surprisingly has rubbed off on economics. . . . Many members of the economics profession now question the relevance and meaning of the fundamental assumptions underlying the economics that is currently taught and practiced. . . .
>
> One of the major counts in the indictment is that Keynesian economics is incapable of handling the central policy issue of the era: how to make full employment compatible with reasonable price stability. Yet, in the twenty-five years since the Second World War . . . unemployment in no year averaged more than 7 per cent, compared with the 1930s, during which unemployment never fell below 14 per cent. . . .
>
> What we now label a failure of theory and policy has been a roaring success by pre-Keynesian standards.[40]

Yes, Schultze says, maybe we do have too much unemployment today, but 7 percent is better than 14, so what are you complaining about? And this reasoning is not without its logic, for in an important sense the mere fact that capitalism continues to exist at all indicates "success." But success for whom? Obviously for those who profit from it. And at what cost has this success been achieved? True, the Keynesian policies have proved that the dimensions of the stagnation of the 1930s can be avoided, but they have merely delayed and/or altered the phenomenal forms of the basic contradictions of capitalism. It is one of our major theses that the success of Keynesian policies is based on this ability to delay and alter the form in which crises appear. Bourgeois economics itself, of course, implicitly admits this when it speaks of the impossibility, under "modern" conditions, of maintaining full employment, price stability, and growth simultaneously. But one can see these same shifts and delays in the emergence of many so-called structural problems relating to unemployment and production. Bourgeois economists speak of structural unemployment with respect to people with the "wrong" skills living in "wrong" areas. Entire areas and industrial branches also suffer from these structural problems. Instead of long-term depressions we now enjoy chronic underutilization of capacity, etc.; end effects on international competitiveness are also to be seen.

There seems to be no "theoretical" reason for taking the 1930s as an absolute standard for judging "progress." The basis for this is purely pragmatic—i.e., at earlier, lower levels of unemployment the threat of "revolutionary" changes did not appear so overwhelming.

Thus what Keynesianism has accomplished is to restore pre-1930 rates of unemployment (while of course removing much of the "flexibility" associated with the self-healing powers of the industrial cycle). In fact, the neoclassical synthesis has merely set out to reconstruct certain aspects of pre-1930s capitalism. Keynesianism may be a political response to a perceived threat, but coherent anticapitalist movements antedate the 1930s, so that even the partial restoration of pre-1930s capitalism hardly makes the modern mixed economy immune to revolutionary change.

Not all economists, of course, share Schultze's optimism; particulalry in the wake of the 1969-72 recession and the high level of unemployment, many economists began to express serious doubts about the effectiveness of the traditional Keynesian antiunemployment techniques. Thus a recent U.S. Labor Department publication has come to the following realistic-pessimistic conclusions.

> Our postwar track record *during peacetime* is certainly not encouraging in this regard—namely, an average unemployment rate of 5.1 percent, with unemployment at or below 4.5 percent in only 22 our of 64 quarters. . . . Thus we face a very real danger that the 1970's may turn out to be a decade of considerable economic slack, with only occasional periods of full employment. (T. Aldrich Finegan, "Labor Force Growth and the Return to Full Employment," in *Monthly Labor Review*, XCV/2 [February, 1972], 37.)

The 1972 *Annual Report of the Council of Economic Advisers* which, on the basis of structural changes of the labor force, strongly implies the junking of the old 4-percent level as a target, describes the search for a full-employment level in rather unorthodox terms, which clearly derive from a policy decision in the Nixon Administration to attempt to get away from the lower level of unemployment:

> Efforts were made when the 1946 Act was passed and shortly thereafter to estimate the normal size of the transitional group. This was difficult because the country had not been at anything like peacetime full employment since 1929 and relevant data were spotty. However, estimates converged on 4 percent as the proportion of the labor force that would be unemployed at "full" employment. This highly uncertain estimate became solidified over the ensuing years as a result of repetition, even though the 4 percent rate was seldom achieved.[41]

The Kennedy Administration, while setting 4 percent as a target,[42] saw this as an intermediate goal on the way to an even lower level. Thus in an interview in 1966, Arthur

Ross, Bureau of Labor Statistics Commissioner under Johnson, became involved in the following discussion:

> Q. When the unemployment rate was hoving around 6% a few years back, most economists felt that a four percent rate was an achievable target to strive for. Now that the rate has dropped below the hallowed 4 percent goal, what would you say is a Utopian unemployment rate since there will always be some people in transit from one job to another? A. . . . I would guess that there is an irreducible unemployment minimum somewhere between two and three percent.[43]

The war in Vietnam did bring the unemployment rate to below 4 percent for several years, but realistic economists understood at the time that no lasting solution had been found:

> The weapons of destruction in the war call on the very skills and industries which faced structural decline, namely production workers in durable goods industries. It is no accident that in the third quarter of 1965 fabricated metals, electrical equipment, machinery and chemicals showed significant employment increases, while transportation equipment began to revive. The use of expanded draft calls rather than reliance on the Reserves . . . worked to lower youth unemployment. . . . Thus the Vietnam War merely postpones the disquieting question of whether the US will be able to face up to the problems of structural change and adequate demand in the context of a peaceful world.[44]

This is the question Keynesians, apparently undaunted by the constant rebuffs reality has dealt them, have been asking for thirty years.

With the winding down of U.S. military involvement in Vietnam, unemployment promptly rose to about 5 million in 1971, the highest figure since 1941, and brought a measure of realism even to Administration politicians. Thus then Treasury Secretary Connally stated: "We talk in terms of a norm of unemployment being 4 per cent. This is a myth. . . . 4 per cent is not the norm. We have never achieved it except in wartime."[45]

With the prospect of a permanent unemployment rate of more than 4 percent, sophisticated Keynesians were beginning to advocate a return to plain old government make-work programs. But obviously the problem goes beyond merely adding some hundreds of thousands of jobs. A Congressional subcommittee on unemployment, using an index prepared by former Secretary of Labor Wirtz in 1966, calculated a subemployment rate of 31 percent for sixty urban-poverty areas in 1970; this rate measures the officially unemployed plus part-time workers who want to work full time—so-called discouraged workers who have given up looking for a job, and full-time workers receiving wages below the poverty level.[46] But the threat of unemployment is not limited to a small group; even at so-called 4 percent full employment, one out of every five male workers between the ages of 25 and 44 will be unemployed; with unemployment at 6 percent, as it was in 1971, three out of ten will have no work. For those between the ages of 16 and 19, a general unemployment rate of 5-6 percent means two "spells" of unemployment a year per worker. Rates for women between the ages of 25 and 44 are approximately twice as high as for their male counterparts. To date no specific response to the social destructiveness brought on by mass unemployment among certain groups has been found.

Several West European capitalist countries have in fact managed to reduce unemployment to pre-1929 levels. However, their "success" was due not so much to Keynesian policies as to the enormous capital destruction of World War II, which created the conditions for rapid capital accumulation. To the extent that direct state intervention rather than the spontaneous workings of rapid capital accumulation fostered the absorption of the industrial reserve army, this has frequently happened under the pressure of the working class, and has been accompanied by explicit reminders of the dire consequences of widespread unemployment. Thus a 1964 West German official document spoke of "Germany's fate of 1933" as causally related to the "inability of the Weimar Republic to master unemployment," and warned that " 'in the light of the East-West conflict' public policy must ensure that there is no risk of any similar failure."[47] And finally it must be noted that the "free movement of labor" within the Common Market has enabled some countries "literally to export their unemployment":

> When Germany had a recession in 1967, for example, its unemployment went up to an adjusted 260,000 from only 70,000 the year before. But the total would have been much greater if it hadn't been for 395,000 workers returning to homes in other countries in 1967. . . . The outflow consisted of 198,000 to Italy, 75,000 to Spain, 70,000 to Greece and 52,000 to Turkey.[48]

In the absence of widespread solidarity between the domestic and foreign workers, this development can have favorable short-run effects on the political situation of the domestic bourgeoisie.

In North America, unemployment rates have been considerably and consistently higher than in Western Europe. Canada's unemployment level has surpassed that of the years between World War I and the onset of the Great Depression. In view of the overwhelming "investment presence of U.S. capital in Canada,"[49] these trends are to some degree linked to those in the U.S. At the same time Canada sports capitalistically underdeveloped areas in Quebec and the Atlantic provinces which often experience unemployment rates in excess of 10 percent.[50] And since the main burden of unemployment is borne by the French-Canadian minority, this also has the effect of transforming the contradictions of capitalism into a "nationalities" problem.

As for the United States, a comparison of unemployment rates during this period with those of the first three decades of this century shows that the situation has not improved. Despite unparalleled "peacetime" military expenditures and an enormous permanent standing army, only Korea and Vietnam managed to bring the unemployment rate to below 4 percent. Thus Keynesian policies have barely brought us back to the not-so-golden days of the first three decades of our century. A glance at the rates of capacity utilization also indicates that the "success" has left something to be desired; in fact, with one quarter of U.S. manufacturing capacity "idle" in 1971, postwar American capitalism reached a low point.[51]

In sum then we can say that although a depression of the magnitude of the 1930s has obviously been avoided in the U.S. and Canada, the "paradox of poverty midst plenty" has hardly been resolved.

3/ *"Incomes policies" as the heavy hand of the Keynesian state* The periodic manifestations of the contradictions which Keynesian policies have managed to delay or shift have at times occasioned the need for more decisive action on the part of the state. Such impatience was expressed by *Business Week* early in 1972 after unprecedented postwar government deficits had failed to bring about a "robust upswing":

> If the traditional weapon of deficit spending cannot give business a lift, the government may not be able to deliver on the commitment of the Employment Act of 1946 to promote maximum employment and production. Indeed, some observers are already saying that the nation is back where it was when the state of business, like the weather, was considered beyond human influence.[52]

In the summer of 1971, Arthur Burns hinted at the same fear when, among other things, he mentioned the following factors involved in the high rates of unemployment and inflation:

> The increased militancy of workers, whether union or nonunion and whether in private or public service, has probably led to a wider diffusion of excessive wage rate increases through the economy. I cannot help but wonder, also, whether our recent experience with wage settlements in unionized industries may not reflect a gradual shift in the balance of power at the bargaining table.
> Labor seems to have become more insistent, more vigorous, and more confident in pursuing its demands, while resistance

of businessmen to these demands appears to have weakened. . . . More recently, the balance of power—so important to the outcome of wage bargaining—may have been influenced by expansion in the public welfare programs which can be called upon to help sustain a striking employee, valid though these programs may be on social grounds. . . . In my judgment . . . the present inflation in the midst of substantial unemployment poses a problem that traditional monetary and fiscal remedies cannot solve *as quickly as the national interest demands.* That is what has led me, on various occasions, to urge additional governmental actions involving wages and prices. . . .[53]

These developments led to the introduction of a so-called wage-price freeze in August, 1971, policies that resemble those earlier tried in West European countries, particularly Britain, which unlike Italy and West Germany, did not have a large reserve army of unemployed to depress wages and exert a "disciplinary" influence on the workers. Under these conditions direct state intervention to compensate for the absence of a reserve army becomes necessary. The relationship between these direct measures and traditional Keynesian policy has been described as follows:

Postwar commitments to a national full employment policy have strengthened the employee side in wage bargaining, and businesses feel freer to pass on increased costs in the form of price increases because the government is committed to maintain the necessary demand . . . to avoid greater unemployment of economic resources. An incomes policy may thus be viewed as a means to offset this change by strengthening the employer's side in wage decisions and the consumer's side in price decisions. . . . If the policy works through channels that curb money wage rates in relation to prices, and the resulting lower real wage rate per unit of labor makes it attractive to hire more labor, a higher level of employment would occur at a given price level. . . . Central to Keynes' argument for reducing high unemployment levels was a reduction in the real wage rate which could be accomplished by an increase in prices in relation to money wage rates or a fall of money wage rates in relation to prices. This argument can be used in support of an incomes policy.[54]

If for no other reason, the unimpeded continuation of such an inflationary course would find limits in the profitability constraints of the world market, which in turn find expression in the inability to harmonize the "goals" of full employment, economic growth, price stability, and external payments equilibrium. But apart from reasons of world-market competitiveness, domestic considerations also militate against the continuation of Keynesian profit-inflation beyond a certain period of time:

> But once consumers wake up to what is happening and offset the rise in prices through increased wages, the process of profit inflation is at an end. And in modern conditions, with strong labour bargaining power through trade unions, and an increased awareness of the inflationary process, it is much harder to be sure of achieving the constructive benefits of inflation. . . . And once the different sections of the community can contract out of inflation, inflation loses its point—which is precisely to shift income from one section of the community to another.
>
> A modern community is too aware of these things to allow the monetary sleight of hand to continue for long.[55]

The transition from the traditional Keynesian policies to such measures as "incomes policies," especially in the 1960s, marks the transition from the period of "stormy" accumulation in the 1950s and 1960s to that of harvesting the contradictory results in the form of overproduction and overaccumulation of capital; while the individual capital can react to this process within the factory by increasing the intensity of labor, etc., on the total social level, the state intervenes by centralizing the downwards pressure on wages. That recourse to such policies on a long-term basis threatens the smooth workings of the mixed economy is implicitly admitted by S when he says that "they cannot themselves take the place of *stabilizing policies of aggregate demand*" (8th ed., p. 815) during a period in which the neoclassical synthesis has proved inadequate. The shift to more open state intervention in the process of capital accumulation is characterized by a fundamental contradiction—namely that it presupposes class cooperation at a time when workers' living and working conditions are being undermined. Although at different times in different countries it may prove possible for the state to maneuver central trade unions into various degrees of acceptance of "income policies" by offering to "compromise" in other areas, this is a risky move, for it can lead to significant "labor unrest," as recent developments in Britain have shown.

A Brookings Institution study states that "a freeze that continues for any significant time does place a burden on labor since the increased productivity of labor leads to higher profits rather than higher wages."[56] But the Federal Government, appalled by a poll indicating that "nearly 85 per cent of all union members think stockholders rather than employees are the major beneficiaries of productivity gains" plans "a major educational effort, including multimedia advertisements to be supported by $10 million of space and time contributed by the Advertising Council . . . to overcome this kind of misunderstanding."[57]

II / THE THEORETICAL BACKGROUND OF KEYNESIANISM

Having gained an overview of the practical origins of Keynesianism, let us proceed to an examination of the theoretical context in which the "Keynes Revolution" originated. Toward this end, we will touch upon the controversies among the major bourgeois economists at the beginning of the nineteenth century. Since the dominant theories also formed the basis upon which practical policies were based in the 1930s, such a review of the historical development of economic theory cannot remain purely academic. S's conscious failure to place the rise of Keynesianism in any historical and theoretical context weakens his presentation (ix, 845).

A / SAY'S LAW AND RICARDO
Most discussions of Keynes' theoretical "revolution" em-

phasize his opposition to that tradition of bourgeois political economy which denied the possibility of general crises of overproduction. First formulated during the first decade of the nineteenth century and known as Say's Law, it, along with many other dogmas of bourgeois political economy, enjoyed the luxury of being impervious to empirical refutation.

Although the persistent industrial cycle gave food for thought,[58] the sort of practical answer to the problem of overproduction crises furnished in the 1930s and which Keynes tried to conceptualize were not a political necessity prior to that time. That is to say, since the self-healing powers of the crisis phase of the industrial cycle were recognized, and since during the nineteenth century the "social dangers" released by the crisis had not yet reached critical proportions, the practical demands for dealing with the crisis had also not yet created the conditions favorable to the construction of a theory to explain the crisis.

Keynes himself was quite conscious of his position vis-à-vis the classical tradition:

> From the time of Say and Ricardo the classical economists have taught that supply creates its own demand. . . . Thus Say's law . . . is equivalent to the proposition that there is no obstacle to full employment. If, however, this is not the true law relating the aggregate demand and supply functions, there is a vitally important chapter of economic theory which remains to be written and without which all discussions concerning the volume of aggregate employment are futile.[59]

But his understanding of the essential differences among the authors within this tradition is wrong. In point of fact by treating Say and Ricardo under one rubric—that is, by ignoring the fact that Ricardo's adoption of Say's Law stood in crass contradiction to his otherwise critical theory, whereas Say was a superficial apologist for capitalism—Keynes is able to obscure the fact that *despite* his attempt to deal theoretically with crises which could no longer be ignored, he has taken a theoretical step backward vis-à-vis Ricardo.

The manner in which Keynes seeks to build up his own critical credibility is revealed in this passage on Ricardian economics:

> That it could explain much social injustice and apparent cruelty as an inevitable incident in the scheme of progress, and the attempt to change such things as likely on the whole to do more harm than good, commended it to authority. That it afforded a measure of justification to the free activities of the individual capitalist, attracted to it the support of the dominant social force behind authority.[60]

In this way Ricardo is transformed into the reactionary defender of capitalism and Keynes by implication into a man of progress. Yet what Keynes here ridicules is precisely Ricardo's greatest achievement—namely, the awareness that the progress of capitalism is accompanied by enormous misery for the working class; and further that—in Ricardo's time at least—production for the sake of production was a historically progressive process. (S [842] misses this point.) What Keynes succeeded in doing was to lend support to the notion of the survival of a capitalism rid of its blemishes at a time when it could no longer be a progressive society even without the inevitable periodic crises.

Let us keep in mind that in Ricardo's time, capitalist crises originating in the process of production had not yet arisen, so that he was able to explain actual crises on the basis of other, nonfundamental causes.[61] Secondly, despite his inability to grasp the meaning of the overproduction crises in which the contradictions of capitalism explode periodically, Ricardo's understanding of the historical tendency of capitalism was superior to that of his contemporaries, who saw the distribution of income or underconsumption as the cause.

Before taking a closer look at the meaning of Say's Law and its Keynesian refutation, let us continue with our review of Keynes' self-image within the bourgeois political economic tradition. If he misrepresented Say's and Ricardo's positions, we find that with respect to Marx he was simply confused. On the one hand, he ranks Marx with the monetary crank Silvio Gesell and others in whose "under-worlds" Malthus' notion of effective demand "could . . . live on furtively."[62] And on the other, he ascribes "an acceptance of the classical hypotheses" to Marx;[63] in a letter to George Bernard Shaw written before the publication of the *General Theory* (January 1, 1935), he speaks of the "final upshot" of his book in these terms: "There will be a great change, and, in particular, the Ricardian foundations of Marxism will be knocked away."[64]

If it was Keynes' concern to find "the answer to Marxism,"[65] he should at least have determined where Marx agreed and disagreed with Ricardo before going about knocking away Marx's Ricardian foundations, for Marx criticized Ricardo's acceptance of Say's Law in great detail. And since Marx had offered this critique two decades before Keynes' birth, Keynes in fact neither "revolutionized economic theory" nor knocked away the foundations of Marxism.

Ricardo had asserted that since supply creates its own demand, general overproduction was not possible; that money was merely a means, with no independent force, acting on the exchange; that partial overproduction or overproduction in some goods was possible, but that this would lead to price changes and shifting of capital in and out of branches, so that equilibrium would reappear.[66]

Although Say and Ricardo clearly presuppose a condition of barter, adherents of Say's Law occasionally ignored this supposition, and since this aspect of the controversy becomes a crucial and often misunderstood part of the Marxist critique, it should be pointed out that the bourgeois critics of the barter supposition have little in common with Marx. Marx offered a detailed critique of Ricardo's assumption of barter. He considered economists like John Stuart Mill, who sought to explain crises on the basis of the possibility of crises in the abstract, to be no better than Say and Ricardo. He felt that reference to the separation of sale and purchase does not explain *why* crises actually take place, but only that they *can* take place, and that the reliance on the most abstract or elementary form of crises for explanatory purposes was a tautology, tantamount to explaining crises through crises.[67]

Keynes' approach to Say's Law is essentially superficial, since his doctrine of effective demand (whether in the form of consumption or of the dichotomy between savings and investment) is rooted in the withholding of purchasing power from the market: "Contemporary thought is still deeply steeped in the notion that if people do not spend their money in one way they will spend it in another."[68] This notion that in fact "people" do not spend all their money rests upon certain psychological moments to which Keynes ascribes universal validity in recorded economic history. Lack of effective demand as an explanation of capitalist crises is either a tautology or no explanation whatsoever insofar as crises can be explained even under the conditions of Say's Law.

In addition to the three aspects of Say's Law mentioned above another point is perhaps the most important in our context of Keynesianism. This relates to Ricardo's assertion of unlimited possibilities for the accumulation of capital:

> There cannot . . . be accumulated in a country any amount of capital which cannot be employed productively until wages rise so high in consequence of the rise of necessaries, and so little consequently remains for the profits of stock, that the motive for accumulation ceases. While the profits of stock are high, men will have a motive to accumulate. Whilst a man has any wished-for gratification unsupplied, he will have a demand for more commodities; and it will be an effectual demand while he has any new value to offer in exchange for them. . . .
>
> It follows then . . . that there is no limit to demand—no limit to the employment of capital while it yields any profit, and that, however abundant capital may become, there is no other adequate reason for a fall of profit but a rise of wages. . . .[69]

Or as John Stuart Mill phrased it: "So long as there remain any persons not possessed, we do not say of subsistence, but of the most refined luxuries, and who would work to possess them, there is employment for capital. . . ."[70] Here we are dealing with two important though separate issues:

that of "full employment"—at least tendentially—of capital and labor, and that of the cause of a possible impediment to that uninterrupted progress. With respect to the latter, Ricardo believed that only rising wages could halt the accumulation of capital by cutting into profits. Although his explanation is merely of historical interest as far as the theory Keynes was attacking is concerned, the need to reduce wages as the basic solution to the overcoming of stagnation was at the crux of the theoretical and practical debate into which Keynes interjected himself.

The first of the two issues mentioned earlier deals with stagnation and unemployment. One of Keynes' chief charges against Ricardo is related to Ricardo's lack of concern with "the volume of the *available* resources, in the sense of the size of the employable population, the extent of natural wealth and the accumulated capital equipment. . . ."[71] Further, he chides Ricardo for being exclusively concerned with "the distribution of a *given* volume of employed resources."[72] This charge can be met in two ways. First, the virtue of Ricardo's emphasis on distribution consists precisely in its insistence on concentrating attention on the specific features of capitalism. Secondly, inasmuch as Ricardo's interest in capital accumulation (which he saw as identical with increased production) was paramount, it is hardly justified to criticize him for a lack of interest in the quantity of wealth.

The rational kernel of Keynes' charges, however, lies in the practical realm; for what is really bothering him is Ricardo's disdain for discussions of gross income and what Keynes believed to be its connection to total employment. Ricardo's emphasis on profits or net income (equaling rent plus interest plus profits) rather than gross (or national) income stemmed from his proper understanding of profit as the central category of capitalist production; whether the other component of national income, namely wages, increased in the process of rising net income was irrelevant, and from Ricardo's theoretical vantage point—which mistakenly equated every wage increase with a diminution of profits—even harmful. As far as Ricardo's lack of interest in total employment is concerned, this had not yet become the explosive political issue that confronted Keynes in the 1930s.

When we say that Keynes concentrated on national income because "it is the quantity which is causally significant for employment,"[73] we do not mean to imply that he was unaware of the fundamental role of profit-production in capitalism. The crucial point here relates to his understanding of the social nature of profit, of how it is produced in capitalism. Keynes' view of profits as being determined by effective demand within the sphere of circulation plays a key role in the formulation of his policies.

The "paradoxes" growing out of the "modern" attempt to regulate employment within an economy in which labor continues to be the hidden regulator, that is to say in which human activity—labor—reveals itself only indirectly through the value categories of capitalism (commodity, value, price, money, capital, profit, interest, wages, etc.) are unintentionally reflected in the following passage:

> The unemployment rate . . . is one of the most widely watched economic indicators. And yet, although employment draws constant attention in the formulation of economic policy, monetary and fiscal policy tools are designed basically to speed or slow the rate of change in business activity overall—usually by influencing private spending decisions. Outside of direct Government intervention in the labor market, such as special manpower programs, economic policy cannot directly affect the level of unemployment.[74]

In fact, to the extent that Keynesian policies are successful in contributing to more rapid capital accumulation, they merely tend to exacerbate the problem.

Allegedly one of the most important aspects of the Keynesian "revolution" is its reuniting of value and price theory, of the individual and the aggregate view, of the private and social "viewpoint"; in our context here this means overcoming "the divergence between the principles of social and private accounting" which supposedly "holds the clue to the inconsistencies of so-called 'sound' finance."[75] But if there are any inconsistencies here, they are to be found in the attempt to foist "accounting principles" upon the capitalist mode of production fundamentally alien to it. Although the Keynesians may be able to stave off political rebellion by delaying and shifting the forms of appearance of contradictions, Ricardo was correct in denying the subordination of profit to national income, and the Keynesians have misunderstood the laws of motion of capitalism if they believe that subordination can be reversed by governmental decree.

In the third edition of his *Principles,* Ricardo held "that an increase of the net produce of a country is compatible with a diminution of the gross produce."[76] In the abstract one might say that his reason for recognizing the rightness of this view lay in his understanding of capital as the dominant force in capitalist society: state intervention to increase national income without any immediate concern for profits seemed senseless to him. This is not to say that Ricardo would necessarily reject methods to keep the unemployed "quiet" at a minimum of cost. The empirical problem had not yet arisen, although Ricardo admitted the possibility and even desirability of state intervention under certain conditions. But the point here is that the practical aspect of Keynesianism is hardly revolutionary, whereas its theory is rooted in a false conception of value creation and the functioning of the components of national income.[77]

In completing this discussion we must mention that Ricardo entertained the possibility of diminishing productive employment. He voiced this view in connection with a chapter on machinery added to the third edition of his *Principles,*[78] and arrives at the conclusion "that the opinion entertained by the labouring class, that the employment of machinery is frequently detrimental to their interests . . . is conformable to the correct principles of political economy."[79] The statement that "by investing part of a capital in improved machinery there will be a diminution in the progressive demand for labor,"[80] or that an increase in capital will be followed by an increased demand for labor that "will be in a diminishing ratio"[81] expresses the crux of his reasoning. Ricardo does not, however, despair, for although the demand for labor has diminished, and the value of labor power (wages) has been cheapened by machine-produced commodities, the now increased surplus value (capitalist profits) can be used to create new capitals (accumulation) or to increase the "demand for menial servants."[82]

This point illustrates both the similarities and differences between Ricardo and Malthus.[83] Whereas Ricardo commits himself to the continued use of "labor-saving" machinery despite its effects,[84] Malthus indicates that he would join Sismondi and Owen in "deprecating it as a great misfortune" if the effects were those predicted by Ricardo.[85] On the other hand, although Ricardo demonstrates that the process of capital accumulation is accompanied by, or rather itself creates, increasing poverty and degradation, he is as little aware as Malthus that this is a peculiar societal mode of wealth creation—that is to say, that this process is not a "technological" fact but rather the peculiar capitalist expression of increasing the productiveness of labor.

Marx, alive to the possibilities of "revolutionary change" growing out of unemployment which Keynes so feared, analyzed this process thus:

> A development of the productive forces which diminished the absolute number of workers, i.e., enabled in fact a nation to carry out its total production in a lesser part of time, would bring about revolution because it would withdraw the majoirty of the population from circulation. In this appears again the specific limit of capitalist production and the fact that it is in no way an absolute form for the development of the productive forces and the creation of wealth, but rather collides with this latter at a certain point.[86]

The current labeling of this social process as "technological unemployment" testifies to the persistence with which this process yas been distorted into a "neutral" one. Keynes himself offers a particularly blatant example of the inability to recognize the societal form that a particular stage of productiveness can assume:

We are being afflicted with a new disease of which some readers may not yet have heard the name, but of which they will hear a great deal in the years to come—namely, *technological unemployment*. This means unemployment due to our discovery of means of economising the use of labour outrunning the pace at which we can find new uses for labour.

But this is only a temporary phase of maladjustment. All this means in the long run *that mankind is solving its economic problem.* [87]

Keynes is so absorbed in the technological aspect, or rather believes that technology has so absorbed capitalism, that in the greatest crisis of capitalism he can equate mass unemployment with long-run success *within* the capitalist mode of production; in other words, although it is true that such crises are expressions of increasing productiveness of labor which cannot be used to satisfy the wants of the workers and point to the need for a mode of production which "solves mankind's economic problem," Keynes insists on seeing this solution within the framework of a society that continues to give birth to such crises.

The central point here is that the capitalist form of the increasing productiveness of labor is expressed by a given amount of variable capital's ability to put into motion an ever larger amount of constant capital; this relation, which Marx called the organic composition of capital, rises with the accumulation of capital, which means that a given amount of capital will "employ" fewer workers. This implies the necessity to extract as much surplus labor as possible from as few workers as possible, a process which underlies the tendency for the rate of profit to fall. This increasing productivity does not of course mean that the commodities formerly consumed by the workers displaced by machines have disappeared; it merely means that the capitalists are no longer laying out sufficient variable capital for these workers to buy these commodities with their wages. As Ricardo recognized in a letter to McCulloch (June 30, 1821): "If machinery could do all the work that labour now does, there would be no demand for labour.

Nobody would be entitled to consume any thing who was not a capitalist, and who could not buy or hire a machine."[913] Taking this process of development one step further, Marx pointed out that revolutionizing the social relationship between workers and capitalists, of the capitalist mode of production, would alter this state of affairs:

> The workmen, if domineering, if allowed to produce for themselves, would only soon, and without any great exertion, bring up the capital (to use a phrase of the econ[omic] vulgarians) up [sic] to the standard of their wants. This is the very big difference: Whether the available means of production confront them as capital, and therefore can be applied by them *only* as far as necessary to the surplus value and surplus produce for their employers, whether these means of production employ *them,* or whether they, as subjects, apply the means of production—in the accusative—to create wealth for themselves.[88]

That the specter of mankind's failure to solve its economic problems within the capitalist mode of production continues to haunt non-Marxists despite the Keynesian revolution was made clear in a study of unemployment published during the height of the Vietnam War that realistically predicted a rise in unemployment once the war was over.[89]

B / MALTHUS

Keynes believed that "in the later phase of Malthus the notion of the insufficiency of effective demand takes a definite place as a scientific explanation of unemployment," but that afterward "the great puzzle of Effective Demand . . . vanished from economic literature."[90] There are definite similarities between Keynes' and Malthus' theories. In this context, it might be instructive to look at some of the major points of the debate carried on by Malthus and Ricardo in the early nineteenth century. Despite their sharp differences on the causes of crises, Ricardo and Malthus held a common view with respect to the working class. Both believed that it was not advisable that workers appropriate the whole of the product they produced, but rather that the capitalists should receive large enough revenues to ensure savings that could be reconverted into productive capital, which in turn would allow them to expand their production of wealth. Thus Malthus clearly sets forth the production of surplus value as the end of capitalist production: "All labour . . . might be stated to be productive of value to the amount of value paid for it, and in proportion to the degree in which the produce of the different kinds of labour, when sold at the price of free competition, exceeds in value the price of the labour employed upon them."[91] And he returns to this point: "To justify the employment of capital, there must be demand for the produce of it, beyond that which may be created by the demand of the workmen employed."[92]

This same notion, namely that capitalism is not oriented toward the satisfaction of the needs of the direct producers, that it is not even oriented toward any sort of consumption, also plays an important role in Keynes, although it contradicts his assertions that consumption is in fact the end of all economic activity. Both Keynes and Malthus contend that the working class chooses to consume less than it might. And Ricardo was no less insistent that the working class must not retain all of its product. But beyond this common belief, Ricardo and Malthus disagreed over what was to be done with part of the surplus value. Whereas Ricardo was a supporter of the industrial bourgeoisie, Malthus, a spokesman for landlords, maintained that part of the surplus value had to be realized through sale to a third class of unproductive consumers. In contrast to Ricardo's uninhibited defense of capitalist progress, Malthus' position was historically ambivalent. The value-theoretical foundations of his economic system also formed the crux of his debate with Ricardo concerning Say's Law:

> The inadequacy of effective demand which, in Malthus' view, made for the general glut, was fundamentally an inadequacy *built into his own theoretical system*. This is because of his very definition of value, which he measured by the labor which commodities could *command*, not as with Ricardo, by the labor which commodities *embodied*. According to Malthus' definition,

aggregate demand (subsistence wages, or labor "commanded") is defined in terms of the labor contained in commodities, and aggregate supply in terms of this quantity plus the surplus, or profit, created in production. Thus, given Malthus' particular theory of value, Say's Law *could* not hold, and, as Ricardo finally pointed out, Malthus' debates with Ricardo could lead nowhere because they started from different premises.[93]

Malthus explained profit as arising in the sphere of circulation—"profit upon alienation" (a theory that predates Malthus); profit arises when capitalists mark up their prices (this in part is due to Malthus' confusion of commodity and capital, value and self-expansion of value, for he incorporated the definition of profit into that of value) while paying the workers less than they produced (or "selling back" to them less than they produced). But at some point it becomes clear that profit cannot result from all the capitalists getting together to raise prices, and to this end Malthus introduces a class that would buy without selling, and thus without withdrawing the profit again. But this requires that these consumers not be producers yet represent effective demand:

> There must therefore be a considerable class of other consumers, or the mercantile classes could not continue extending their concerns and realizing their profits. In this class the landlords no doubt stand pre-eminent; but if the powers of production among capitalists are considerable, the consumption of the landlords, in addition to that of the capitalists themselves and of their workmen, may still be insufficient to keep up and increase the exchangeable value of the whole produce. . . .[94]

To supplement the effective demand of the landlords, Malthus includes the former's menial servants and the unproductive consumers supported by taxes.[95]

Malthus' recommendations with respect to letting the state compensate for failing effective demand are very similar to contemporary Keynesian policies. However, the shift of class interests makes for an essential social difference, for now it is the industrial bourgeoisie, threatened with obsolescence, which is forced to come to the defense of the "old" society. In this context it would be interesting to see how Keynesians assess Malthus' contribution to the question of effective demand.

Alvin Hansen, a leading American Keynesian, discusses one of Malthus' prescriptions for remedying deficient effective demand—namely " 'the employment of individuals in personal services, or the maintenance of an adequate proportion of consumers not directly productive of material objects'; in other words, the development of tertiary employment." Although Malthus distinguished these workers from others because they did not make material objects, according to Hansen, "a more useful classification is primary, secondary and tertiary production."[96] Hansen then applies Malthus' insights to the modern words:

> The history of all progressive countries reveals how sound Malthus was in his emphasis on the importance of an expansion of the service industries. As per capita productivity has increased, as standards of living have risen everywhere, a larger and larger proportion of the labor force are employed in the service industries, both public and private. Malthus, to be sure, had a limited conception of tertiary industries. . . . His "personal services" and other service industry activities relate for the most part to the comfort and living standards of the middle and upper classes. But he hoped for a sufficiently wide diffusion of property and income so that this group would be a fairly numerous one.[97]

This attempt to enlist Malthus in the ranks of present-day Keynesians rests on a misinterpretation of Malthus, the result of the failure of contemporary bourgeois economics to understand the peculiar societal qualities of capitalism. Hansen obviously is unaware of the difference between the self-expansion of value consequent upon the capitalist use of labor in the process of production and the use of labor "services" for the production of use values. The former is peculiar to capitalism, but the latter, which also existed in feudalism, appears in capitalism as a phenomenon which does not per se characterize classes. That is to say, one does not have to be a capitalist to purchase the labor "services" of domestic workers, although relatively few members of the working class could afford such a purchase. What is important here is that the consumer-domestic worker relationship is not a capitalistic one, since it is not directed at the production of surplus value.

Bourgeois economics may no longer recognize the presence of such fundamental differences in capitalism, and Malthus, to be sure, did not foresee the development of "service industries," but the type of industry Hansen is talking about not only does not correspond to Malthus' concept, it directly contradicts the purposes he set forth with respect to these services. The activities Malthus had in mind were not productive of surplus value, since the point he was making was that the workers could never buy back the entire value of their product. Malthus' conception of personal services corresponded to his understanding of the origin of crises. Whereas in Malthus' view the unproductive consumers merely were realizing surplus value through expending redistributed incomes, Hansen and other Keynesians believe that they create value and income. The inability of Keynesians to grasp such fundamental distinctions raises serious questions about their analysis of and proposed cures for capitalist crises.

Ricardo may have arrived at his insight into the effects of machinery on the working class too late to make it part of his theoretical systems, still his reply to Malthus is more than simply a recourse to Say's Law. The debate between the two was complicated inasmuch as each saw one aspect of the contradictory nature of capitalism without understanding the whole. Although Malthus believed that the contradictions of capitalist production found expression in the sphere of distribution, he severed the link to the source in the sphere of production. Ricardo, partly because he was blinded by his erroneous theory of the falling rate of profit and by the fact that in his lifetime he never experienced a serious purely capitalist crisis, fixed his sights on the speed of capital accumulation, thus neglecting the possibility of crises of overproduction and overaccumulation.

Because Ricardo formulated the reason for stagnation in an exaggerated fashion—"the people" have a great deal of effective demand which they refuse to spend—he found it difficult to take the doctrine seriously. Yet Keynes and many of his adherents still see the origins of stagnation in this light. What this theory—whether in its Malthusian or Keynesian form—does is to posit the surface phenomena during the low point of a crisis as its cause. Thus the source of stagnation is said to be insufficient demand: if only "the people" would spend their money.

It is true that the state can force or encourage people to part with money (in the last analysis through taxation or inflation). But what then? If the only purpose of such state intervention is to decrease unemployment, then Ricardo would certainly not deny its efficacy, for he himself pointed to unproductive employment as a way of absorbing those replaced by machines. Nor in fact would Marx contest this possibility. According to Marx, the relationship between capital and revenue fixes the ratio and the proportional growth of both classes as determined by the proportion in which increasing profits are transformed into capital or spent as revenue.

If one shifts the unproductive expenditures from the individual to the aggregate capitalist (the state), one can see the development which Marx understood as an inherent tendency in capitalism; however, in keeping with the increased need for protecting capital from its own contradictions, such state employment has asssumed new forms.

But Malthusian or Keynesian theory does not consider the mere absorption of unemployment the sole objective; the raising of profits from the stagnation level must also be assured, and it is here that mere effective demand will fail, for an upswing demands the improved profitability of capital based on the capital destruction, lowering of wages, and increased productivity characteristic of the depression or stagnation phase of the industrial cycle. To some extent state intervention can achieve "progress" here by regulating wage increases and lowering taxes and interest rates. But despite this ability to shorten depression phases, such policies have proved incapable of impeding the recurrence of the cycle and a renewed onset of stagnation, largely because the policies adopted during the boom phase to prevent "inflationary overheating" (i.e., price stability) serve to reduce profits when the boom could only be maintained by even larger profits. Keynes, unlike Malthus, favored increased production and was not content merely with raising the "propensity to consume."

Thus if one assumes that the Malthusian doctrine, even if correct, was a Sisyphean task, since at best it might prolong the interval between one crisis and the next, one can understand why the Ricardians did not consider it a particularly significant contribution.[98]

C / MARX'S CRITIQUE OF SAY'S LAW[99]

Since the Keynesian revolution tends to be celebrated in terms of having overcome the theoretical impasse on the impossibility of crises, it is important that before attempting an analysis of Keynes' critique we examine Marx's refutation of Say's Law which went largely unnoticed by bourgeois economics. However, once the Keynesians began to claim credit for this theoretical advance, they were also forced to come to grips with Marx's overall achievement, though they did not always represent his position adequately. As our point of departure let us consider a statement by a Keynesian familiar with *Capital* and sympathetic to Marx's theory. In her booklet on Marxist economics, Joan Robinson concludes a chapter on effective demand thus:

> Marx evidently failed to realise how much the orthodox theory stands and falls with Say's Law, and set himself the task of discovering a theory of crises which would apply to a world in which Say's Law was fulfilled, as well as the theory which arises when Say's Law is exploded. This dualism implants confusion in Marx's own argument, and, still more, in the arguments of his successors.[100]

According to Bernice Shoul, this "confusion" derives from the complex methodological structure of Marx's critique of

Say's Law: on the one hand Marx criticizes it for assuming away the commodity nature of exchange in capitalism and thus eliminating by definition the abstract possibility of crisis which lurks in the value form of production, and on the other hand, Marx tried "to demonstrate that the 'law of motion' of capitalist society produces not only a *tendency* to ultimate stagnation, or breakdown, but crises and business cycles as well, *even when the equilibrium conditions of Say's Law are fulfilled.*"[101]

Marx's main focus in the critique is on the assumption of barter inherent in Say's Law; with respect to Ricardo's formulation of it, Marx in Chapter 17 of the *Theories of Surplus Value* says the following.

> In order to prove that capitalist production cannot lead to general crises, all conditions and determining forms, all principles and *differentiae specificae,* in short, *capitalist production* itself, is denied, and in fact it is proved that if the capitalist mode of production, instead of being a specifically developed, peculiar form of societal production, were a mode of production chronologically prior to its crudest beginnings, then its peculiar antagonisms, contradictions, and hence their eruption in crises would not exist.[102]

He then proceeds to specify the manner in which Ricardo operated and the consequences of that methodology: in the first place the commodity

> in which the opposition of exchange value and value exists, is transformed into mere product (use value) and therefore the exchange of commodities into the bartering of products, mere use values. This is not only going back beyond capitalist production, but even beyond mere commodity production, and the most complicated phenomenon of capitalist production—the world market crisis—is denied outright by denying outright that the product must be commodity, must therefore represent itself as money and must go through the process of metamorphosis. . . . *Money* is then viewed consistently as a mere mediator of product exchange, not as an essential and necessary form of existence of the commodity which must represent itself as exchange value—universal societal labor. Inasmuch as

the essence of exchange value is erased through the transformation of the commodity into mere use value (product), *money* can just as easily be denied or rather must be denied as an essential form which in the process of the metamorphosis is an *autonomous* form vis à vis the original form of the commodity.[103]

As Shoul points out, it is important to grasp the difference between this critique and that offered by certain post-Ricardian economists (such as John Stuart Mill):

> lest it be concluded that Marx' opposition to Say's Law was a purely monetary one, and that he considered the structure and disruptions of the monetary system, or the "behavior of money" to be an independent cause of crises. Marx' criticism of Say's Law may be called "monetary criticism" only to the extent that it stresses the difficulties inherent in monetary exchange. But it must be made clear that this "monetary criticism" refers not simply to "unneutral money" (as opposed to the classical "money veil") but arises from Marx' theory of the dual nature of labor and of the commodity in the capitalist economy.[104]

Marx performs this critique with respect to Ricardo's understanding of the nature of money:[105]

> Money is not only "the medium by which the exchange is effected," but rather at the same time the medium by which the exchange of produce with produce becomes dissolved into two acts, independent of each other, in time and space. This false conception of money in Ricardo rests on the circumstance that in general he looks only at the *quantitative determination* of exchange value, namely that it = a certain quantity of labor time, but on the other hand forgets the *qualitative* determination that the individual labor must respresent itself as *abstract* universal societal labor only through its alienation. (That Ricardo [views] money merely as *means of circulation,* is the same that he [views] exchange value merely as an evanescent form, in general as something merely formal in bourgeois or capitalist production, which is also the reason why he does not consider the latter a specifically determined mode of production, but rather as *the* mode of production par excellence.)[106]

But these abstract possibilities of crisis grounded in the sphere of simple money circulation are not the explanation of crises, for this sphere often "runs smoothly" without crises. Why these forms of crises at times show their critical sides is not be to discovered from these forms alone. Marx knew that crises took the form of crises of overproduction, but what was necessary was to discover the cause of this phenomenal form. At this point Marx offers the second of his criticisms of the classical theory of the impossibility of crises. The purpose of this aspect of the attack is to show that crises are the result of inadequate profits, regardless of the state of demand; Marx called this process the tendency of the rate of profit to fall. And it is this process that is responsible for the reserve army of unemployed without which we would have neither rapid capital accumulation nor industrial cycles.

It is not our purpose here to offer a detailed exposition of Marx's theory of cycles or crises. We merely have attempted to put forth the central aspect of Marx's critique of the classical formulations of Say's Law so as to place the "revolutionary" nature of Keynes' theories in the proper historical perspective as well as to establish the counterpositions for our critique of Keynesianism.

D / KEYNES' CRITIQUE OF SAY'S LAW

As we have had occasion to remark, Keynes considered Malthus a forerunner as regards the notion of effective demand. In fact, striking similarities in their approach to Say's Law can be found, and to that extent Keynes' theory is subject to the same criticism as Malthus' on effective demand. However, we will attempt to go beyond this.

The "contemporary thought" which "is still deeply steeped in the notion that if people do not spend their money one way they will spend it in another"[108] is cited by Keynes as an example of the sort of economic thinking that has to be done away with. More specifically, he objects to the assumption that "an act of individual saving inevitably leads to a parallel act of investment,"[109] and surmising that such reasoning may be rooted in false analogies to "some kind of non-exchange Robinson Crusoe economy," he then offers this analysis:

> Those who think in this way are deceived, nevertheless, by an optical illusion, which makes two essentially different activities appear to be the same. They are fallaciously supposing that there is a nexus which unites decisions to abstain from present consumption with decisions to provide for future consumption; whereas the motives which determine the latter are not linked in any simple way with the motives which determine the former. [110]

This is the same dichotomy between saving and investment S makes so much of in Chapter 11, which we will discuss at that point. Instead of ferreting out the actual contradictions underlying this alleged dichotomy, Keynes apparently is content with remaining on a descriptive institutional level, for he refers to "our social and business organisation" that "separates financial provision for the future from physical provision for the future so that efforts to secure the former do not necessarily carry the latter with them." [111] To the extent that this is true it finds its justification in the capitalist development of the fundamental contradiction between use value and value ("physical" versus "financial" provision). But instead of investigating the source of this phenomenon Keynes limits his argument to the acceptance of this physical-financial dichotomy, on top of which a rather vague and crude psychology is invoked to reinforce the "paradoxical nature of capitalism.

With respect to the psychological explanation of the stagnation denied by Say's Law, Keynes places the proposition that increased aggregate income is not accompanied by an equal increase in aggregate consumption at the center of his doctrine of inadequate effective demand. As this gap widens, full employment will become more and more remote. Here again Keynes makes explicit the political relevance of the gap at this particular juncture:

The richer the community, the wider will tend to be the gap between its actual and its potential production; and therefore the more obvious and outrageous the defects of the economic system.[112]

As far as Keynes was concerned, this gap was largely due to the consumption habits of the "wealthier members" of capitalist society. "The key to our practical problem," he said, "is to be found in this psychological law."[113]

Although the Keynesians as well as all other bourgeois economists start out from the assertion that consumption is quite simply the end of production,[114] they wind up with an entirely different conclusion. One Keynesian summarized the reasoning involved as follows:

> In a society characterized by great inequality of wealth and income, the economic ability of the community to consume is limited. The rich have more income than they wish to consume currently and the poor have so little income that their ability to consume is narrowly restricted. As a consequence, there is a sizable potential surplus of resources in excess of what is needed to produce consumers goods. This surplus, if it is to be used at all, must be devoted to producing things that are not to be currently consumed. This production in excess of what is currently consumed is called investment.[115]

This view of investment conveys the impression that the *raison d'être* of investment is filling the gap between income and consumption in order to maintain full employment.[116] But it should be obvious that this cannot provide a long-term solution to the problem of effective demand since profitable investment would merely lead to an even greater reproduction of the contradictions Keynes is trying to deal with.

Although the Keynesians do think of investment in this light, they also recognize that the accompanying increase in income will only aggravate "the difficulty of securing equilibrium to-morrow."[117]

In point of fact, Keynes was not very optimistic about investment filling the gap between consumption and income:

> But worse still. Not only is the marginal propensity to consume weaker in a wealthy community, but, owing to its accumulation of capital being already larger, the opportunities for further investment are less attractive unless the rate of interest falls at a sufficiently rapid rate. . . .[118]

For Keynes, its scarcity determined the profitability of capital, so that increasing capital accumulation was bound to lead to a decline in its marginal efficiency.[119] Although Keynes does not make this explicit, he seems to imply that in the twentieth century a tendency toward stagnation replaced the cyclical crises of the nineteenth century. At the same time, however, Keynes holds that the "slump" caused by an overabundance of capital can be overcome by the cessation of investment which would contribute to a growing scarcity of capital; he mentions "the interval of time, which will have to elapse before the shortage of capital through use, decay and obsolescence causes a sufficiently obvious scarcity to increase the marginal efficiency."[120]

Waiting out this interval, a period marked by capital destruction and unemployment would however involve the very social upheavals Keynes wished to avoid, and that is why state intervention becomes necessary within the Keynesian framework. Marx sees the social antagonisms released by the periodic fall of the rate of profit as the struggle by the working class against the attempts of capital to counteract the relative diminution of the surplus-value-creating labor vis-à-vis constant capital

> by reducing the allotment made to necessary labour and by still more expanding the quantity of surplus labor with regard to the whole labour employed. Hence the highest development of productive power together with the greatest expansion of existing wealth will coincide with depreciation of capital, degradation of the labourer, and a most straightened exhaustion of his vital powers. These contradictions lead to explosions, cata-

clysms, crises, in which by momentaneous suspension of labour and annihilation of a great portion of capital the latter is violently reduced to the point where it can go on . . . fully employing its productive powers without committing suicide. Yet these regularly recurring catastrophes lead to their repetition on a higher scale, and finally to its violent overthrow.[121]

Although according to Joan Robinson "the theory of the falling rate of profit is a red herring across the trail, and prevented Marx from running the theory of effective demand to earth,"[122] it is not difficult to imagine a "model" without any classes other than workers and capitalists, so that the latter would retain all the surplus value created and would reinvest (accumulate) if conditions of profitability warranted such a "decision." This is in fact the method Marx developed by temporarily abstracting from the less fundamental problem of realization of surplus value to which Keynes assigned prime significance; for Marx this meant abstracting temporarily from

the real constitution of the society which in no way merely consists of the classes of the laborers and industrial capitalists, where hence consumers and producers are not identical, the former category (whose revenues in part are secondary, derived from profit and wages, not primitive revenues) of the consumers is much wider than the second and therefore the way in which it spends its revenues and the magnitude of the latter produces very great modifications in the economic household and particularly in the process of circulation and reproduction of capital.[123]

Moreover, a glance at the empirical reality of the process of retransformation of savings of these third classes (as well as those of workers and capitalists as individual consumers/savers) into accumulable productive capital indicates that the fundamental problem does not lie in the sphere of circulation as posited by Keynes' distinction between "industry" and "finance," between "physical" and "financial" provision.

This abstraction from more superficial phenomena is not

peculiar to Marx. We can detect a strand of Keynes' thinking, which acknowledges this as the proper methodology without being able to divorce it from the otherwise superficial approach characteristic of effective demand. Keynes makes the expansion of production dependent on (the expectation of) profit by the entrepreneur.[124] Once he has allowed the validity of such reasoning, Keynes forces the implication that effective demand is merely a subordinate relationship.

The question remains why the absence of effective demand is invoked as an explanation of stagnation by Keynes. The reason for this is largely connected with his circulation sphere approach, which seeks the origin of profit in the sale of the output, a particularly ironic method in the case of Keynes since he sought to reunite microeconomic theory with an aggregate view.[125] And although he did reintroduce aggregate categories,[126] he never overcame the tendency to confuse the individual capital in competition with other individual capitals with that of aggregate capital, something he had criticized in his neoclassical predecessors.[127]

But it is this very inability to transcend the point of view of the individual capitalist that makes it impossible to grasp the superficial phenomena of the competitive capitals as expressions of more fundamental aspects of capitalism.

In concluding this discussion of Keynes' theory of effective demand as refutation of Say's Law we would like to repeat that as far as capital is concerned, the "problem" is the outgrowth of surplus value creation and not of realization. This becomes very clear when we consider the two major components of effective demand—the workers' demand for consumption and the capitalists' demand for means of production. When the individual capitalist sells his commodities, i.e., when he changes the commodity form of his capitals into the money form—on the aggregate capital level, money capital at the same time is retransformed into functioning productive capital (some capitalists realize the commodity values of other capitalists by buying means of production) and the purchase of means of consumption by the working class (following the purchase of their labor power and its use in the sphere of production). But this latter process is in turn dependent on the conditions of profitability, a connection which does not elude the individual capitalist.

Let us look at one last aspect of Keynes' relation to bourgeois economic theory, namely the classical contention that the accumulation of capital can be blocked only by a rise in wages. When he wrote his *General Theory*, Keynes was dealing with the neoclassical theory that posited wage reductions as the proper method of increasing employment.[128] In entering the discussion, Keynes was reacting to the failure of these practical policies based on the classical and/or neoclassical theories. In this context his principal insight consisted in the view that although wage reductions might prove useful in increasing profits, this traditional method will remain limited in a period of great stagnation, given the enormous amount of unrealized surplus value, which is an obstacle to an upswing.

We must be cautious in our evaluation of the differences between Keynes and his predecessors. Keynes was not in principle opposed to money wage reduction, he merely doubted its efficacy. His acceptance of the marginal productivity theory of wages forms the major link between him and the classical theorists. Where Keynes diverged from his predecessors was on the relation between real wages and money wages. On this point he followed in the footsteps of those classical and neoclassical writers who posited an inverse relation between the number of workers and the size of total real wages—the so-called wages fund. Despite the clear and important similarities on this issue between Keynes and his predecessors the significance of Keynes' position lay precisely in his recognition that even the strategy of "demand management" could not put an end to the stagnating capital accumulation, and he therefore stressed the need for state intervention in the form of public utilization of idle capital and labor.

We have given this brief outline of the rise of Keynesianism because S has failed to provide any background material to prepare the reader for an understanding of Keynesianism as a part of traditional attempts to deal with the critical problems of capitalism. Lacking such an understanding, the reader cannot evaluate the "success" and limits of this newer trend in bourgeois economics, particularly in view of S's sparse information on the reality of contemporary capitalism.

Returning to the analysis of S's text, we have organized it into subsections on saving, investment, the propensities to consume and save, income determination, the multiplier, and state intervention.

III / "SAVING"

Keynesian theory places special emphasis on the alleged dichotomy between saving and investment. In fact, this point is central to Keynes' refutation of Say's Law. And that is why S opens his discussion of Keynesian theory with this topic.

S formulated the dichotomy in particularly strong terms: "The most important single fact about saving and investment activities is that in our industrial society they are generally done *by different people* and done *for different reasons*" (206). Taking this statement as our point of departure, let us proceed first to an empirical analysis of the underlying reality (Keynesians are not unaware of the "deviations" of their "model" from reality); here the emphasis rests on the overwhelming share of "saving" done by capital itself directly in the form of so-called undistributed profits and capital-consumption allowances, as well as on the class nature of that portion of "saving" that falls under the heading of personal saving. In the second part of our critique we will take up the concept of "saving" itself and the failure of S to mediate the superficial phenomenon of saving in national-income accounts with its base in the production and circulation of capital.

A / EMPIRICAL ASPECTS

1/ *"Internal financing" as the tendential overcoming of the "cleavage between saving and investment"* Although S admits that "when a corporation or a small business has great investment opportunities, its owners will be tempted to plow back much of its earnings into the business," he insists that "nevertheless, saving is *primarily* done by an entirely different group: by individuals, by families, by households" (206). In a later chapter he reintroduces the matter as a "qualification" to the powers attributed to the central banks to regulate investment via interest-rate changes; but even here he tries to give the impression that we are dealing with an obscure, recondite, peripheral point which it took experts to discover: "We must notice a point raised by experts in corporate finance. They point out that many firms, particularly large ones, finance their investments *out of retained earnings* and the cash flow generated by their own operations. Many avoid going to the banks or outside markets for borrowings or stock flotations" (337). More methodologically, Romney Robinson, in his *Study Guide* to S, after mentioning that firms do "most" of the investing and consumers "much" of the saving, concedes that "some saving is done by corporations. . . . Because most corporate saving is done in order to finance investment projects, it is an exception to the 'different groups' idea. Begin by assuming that such corporate saving is zero. It can easily be fitted into the analysis after you have mastered the all-important basic relationships."[129] Aside from the minor oddity that it is "the 'different groups' idea" that is the "exception" (and would thus cast some suspicion on a theory that bases itself on "exceptions" only to incorporate the "rule" at some subsequent point), the attention devoted to this supposed cleavage stems from the Keynesian rootedness in the sphere of circulation, which militates against its development into an incipient awareness that crises originate in the sphere of surplus-value production. Keynes himself was conscious of the specific weight of corporate saving within national saving.[130]

Industrial capital historically has tended toward independence of "outside" sources of money capital; in other words, it produces the overwhelming proportion of surplus value which is accumulated (i.e., productively reinvested) within its own sphere. This contrasts with other periods of capitalism, when insufficient accumulation made for greater dependence on banks which could redistribute potential money capital from other sources. Although with the progressive concentration and centralization of capital, this holds true in particular for large individual capitals. It is also become true of industrial capital as a whole, largely because, as a result of the fusion of industrial and bank capital into finance capital, even bank loans and many stocks and bonds issues have become a new type of internal financing in the sense that many of the industrial firms and banks belong to the same finance-capital group.

Had Keynes devoted himself as assiduously to understanding the objective workings of capitalism as he did to the dissection of the mind of the bourgeoisie and the proletariat, he might have discovered that his witty paradoxes are rooted in the assumtpion that "consumption—to repeat the obvious—is the sole end object of all economic activity."[131] However, if one proceeds from the theoretical insight that in fact consumption is only the mediate "goal" of the capitalist mode of production (it is a subjective goal of the workers) and that it is constantly "interfered" with by the production of surplus value, then one can see that in a relative sense capital is the very "self-subsistent entity" that Keynes so tenaciously attacked.[132]

As to the other aspect of saving, the relation of "business" to "personal" saving, here we also note that over the years the "personal" share has consistently been much the smaller one. The following table shows the breakdown of "private" savings (in billions of dollars) since 1950:

Year	total	Personal saving	Gross business saving
1950	42.5	13.1	29.4
1951	50.3	17.3	33.1

1952	53.3	18.1	35.1
1953	54.4	18.3	36.1
1954	55.6	16.4	39.2
1955	62.1	15.8	46.3
1956	67.8	20.6	47.3
1957	70.5	20.7	49.8
1958	71.7	22.3	49.4
1959	75.9	19.1	56.8
1960	73.9	17.0	56.8
1961	79.8	21.2	58.7
1962	87.9	21.6	66.3
1963	88.7	19.9	68.8
1964	102.4	26.2	76.2
1965	113.1	28.4	84.7
1966	123.8	32.5	91.3
1967	133.4	40.4	93.0
1968	135.2	39.8	95.4
1969	135.2	38.2	97.0
1970	153.2	56.2	97.0
1971	171.9	60.2	111.8
1972	174.2	49.7	124.4
1973	188.6	53.8	134.7

Thus until 1970, "business" saving consistently accounted for more than 70 percent of total private saving in the United States, approximately the same result obtained with respect to internal financing as a share of all investment sources. We also find a similar decline in the business share during the latest recession. Although this trend has begun to subside and hence is not a significant indicator, still the relative upswing in personal saving is at least in part due to "statistical definitions." That capital provides the source of most of its accumulation directly is neither novel nor is it unknown to Keynesians. Thus at the end of World War II, Alvin Hansen wrote that "the first thing to note is that almost the whole of business investment in plant, equipment and inventories is financed from depreciation and other reserves, and from the retained earnings of business,"[133] For the Keynesians the problem resolves into how to find "investment outlets" "to absorb the flow of savings" "without destroying existing property values," "without creating vast excess capacity."[134]

2/ *Class distribution of saving*   Although we have already offered some material on the distribution of savings,[135] some supplementary material will prove useful at this point. Our main purpose here is to show the nonexistence of an empirical basis for the supraclass and suprahistorical "psychological laws" that play so important a role within the Keynesian theory, and this despite the fact that a close reading of S's own figures clearly indicates that most U.S. families have no savings whatsoever. Thus his Table 11-1 (210) shows that families with annual incomes below $8,000 (after taxes) are in debt. In the text he contents himself with the vague statement that "the very poor are unable to save at all" (210). But if we turn back to Chapter 5 (Table 5-2; 83), S's own figures indicate that in 1967, 32 percent of all U.S. families had incomes below $7,500.[136] Furthermore, if we add the families whose small positive savings compensate for the negative savings of the still poorer ones, we see that in the aggregate considerably more than one half of all U.S. families save nothing—that is to say, their savings and debts cancel each other out. This might be compared with S's assertion in the first edition that "everyone will encounter, each day of his life, the problem of . . . investing his savings so as to afford maximum protection against the vicissitudes of life" (p. 201). Aside from the fact that S does not interpret the statistics, the table does not pretend to be a compilation of absolute or relative saving or its distribution; rather, it is presented as an example of saving propensities (of course, without sources). This constitutes a step backward from the comparative realism of the first edition, where, following the determination that "as a result of the war, the American people have accumulated more savings than ever before in our history," S notes that "a quarter of all families (or spending units) had no liquid savings at all in 1946: no savings accounts, no checking accounts, no governments bonds. Half the families had less than $400 of savings. On the other hand, the 10 percent of families with the highest savings averaged more than $10,000 of liquid assets apiece and had 60% of the total liquid assets" (pp. 211-13).

Two decades later, one sixth of all families still had no "liquid assets," and when we take into consideration a 50 percent drop in the domestic purchasing power of the dollar between 1946 and 1971, we see that more than half of all U.S. families still had less than the 1946 equivalent of $400 in such assets.[137] Since data on net savings comparable to earlier studies are not available for the post-1950 period, but since apparently not much has changed in the intervening years,[138] we feel we may compare that situation with that of 1929. In 1950, approximately three-quarters of the "spending units" showed no net saving inasmuch as the debt of one portion of that group canceled out the relatively small savings of the other. In 1929, the last pre-Depression year, we find a similar "break-even" point with respect to savings.[139] If we ignore the "dissaving" of the lowest income group, we find that about one half of all families had no savings. At the other end we find that whereas in 1929 2.3 percent of all families accounted for about two-thirds of all saving, by 1950, 4 percent of spending units accounted for about 55 percent of all savings.

This would seem to indicate that the two extremes developed in similar directions: both lost ground, but the gap between them widened. The relative gain by the intermediate income groups may not be that significant inasmuch as the relative decrease for the highest group may merely represent the continuing decline of the pensioner element. The richest capitalists are not likely to hold much of their personal wealth in the form of savings and checking accounts or U.S. savings bonds, but in stocks, and these would not appear in these tabulations.

To demonstrate the correlation between income and saving let us look at the following table which shows the percentage of before-tax money income and net "spending-unit" savings accruing to each income quintile for the year 1948:

		Before-tax Income	Net Family Saving
lowest	20%	4%	−24%
next	20%	11%	−3%
next	20%	16%	7%
next	20%	22%	21%
highest	20%	47%	99%
		100	100 [140]

Thus the richest one-fifth accounted for virtually all of net saving, whereas the lowest two-fifths had debts in excess of savings. The fact that the third and fourth quintiles show some net saving indicates that the working class does do some saving (this holds true even more for doctors, lawyers, and other "professionals" as well as for small capitalists), which would appear to form the rational kernel for the Keynesian thesis about the cleavage between saving and investment. For as soon as the mass of the population has been separated from the means of production, and to the extent that it can do any saving at all, that saving by definition cannot be identical with the net capital formation taking place. At this point savings must go through banks if they are to reenter capital circulation in the form of money capital (in this case, loan capital) that can be productively utilized by industrial capitalists. By this time, however, the small savers have lost control over what has become capital and receive a mere fraction of what the bank capitalists receive for mobilizing credit, and they in turn receive only part of the surplus value appropriated by the industrial capitalist.

In conclusion, we must entertain the possibility that savings held by the working class do exist. However, even though these furnish the justification for the alleged cleavage between saving and investment, they represent only a very minor portion of saving and merely accentuate the cleavage between the means of production and labor. There is no real cleavage between saving and investment, although there is one between the reasons workers save and the reasons capitalists do; the former are merely forgoing present consumption in order to provide for the future, while the latter never intend to consume their savings.

B / CONCEPTUAL ASPECTS

1/ *"Cleavage between saving and business motivations"* In proving S's assertions on the personal dichotomy between savers and investors wrong, we have by implication also demonstrated that the motives for saving and investing are not divergent. Yet we nonetheless wish to pursue this point, because it forms a link in the Keynesian theory of income determination. In listing the various reasons why "an individual may wish to save" (206), S merely seems to be concretizing the "eight main motives or objects of a subjective character which lead individuals to refrain from spending out of their incomes" enumerated in Chapter 9 of Keynes' *General Theory,* namely "Precaution, Foresight, Calculation, Improvement, Independence, Enterprise, Pride and Avarice."[141] On closer inspection, however, we find that S has conveniently omitted one of these "motives"— Enterprise—that is, saving "to carry out speculative or business projects."[142] This omission is vital to S's argument, since he would like to make atypical noncapitalistic saving motives appear as typical. In this way he has managed to sever any connection between saving and investment "motives" (except for the admission that "some business saving does still get motivated directly by business investment" [206]). Once this is done saving can then be safely relegated to the realm of psychology, and one can pretend that the difference in consumption levels in an otherwise homogeneous nonclass society are merely quantitative.

S's approach distorts the social framework essential to an understanding of the problem, so that instead of mediating saving with the production and circulation of capital, S in effect reduces the framework to that of simple commodity and money circulation. Having safely tucked the process of saving away in the sphere of circulation, S is prepared to deliver the coup de grace: "Whatever the individual's motivations to save, it often has little to do with the investment opportunities of society and business" (206). It is remarkable how he has managed to transform what was originally seen as a cleavage between saving and investment motivations into a differentiation between motivations on the one hand and "opportunities" on the other. Yet if we are to take this new "cleavage" seriously, then it is by no means peculiar to "our modern economy," for it is just as valid for Robinson Crusoe; that is to say, his motivation to save ("he may feel insecure and wish to guard against a rainy day" [206]) has just as little to do with the ability to "invest" his savings productively. Perhaps, as S contends, he would not save if he knew he could not invest, but that is another matter, for then we would no longer be dealing with motivations. By the same token, it is clear that the same situation holds true for the "modern" corporation, for its "motivation" for making a profit has little to do with its ability to realize it. This aspect of the critique is important because it refutes S's contention that the fundamental problems of the modern economy derive from the heterogeneity of motivations about saving and investment, in contrast to earlier (unspecified) economies. The rational kernel of this argument, however, is to be sought elsewhere—namely in the dichotomy between use value and exchange value in the "modern" economy, which did not hold true for Crusoe and others inasmuch as they saved and invested to increase their consumption. That the "modern" economy is not subject to the "problem" stressed by S becomes evident when we look at our "model," which shows no cleavage between saving and investment: there is one identical, homogeneous "motivation," and that is profit; yet this does not prevent capital from developing its contradictions (in S's view less than full employment and no investment opportunities for saving), rather, it causes them.

2/ *The use of precapitalist relations as the basis for understanding capitalism*   In his exposition of the Keynesian theory of saving and investment, S refers to noncapitalistic relations of production to elucidate those aspects of capitalism peculiar to it, and which thus presumably lie at the base of its "problems," in contrast to those which it shares with other modes of production. Upon closer examination, however, we find that in doing so he merely manages to confuse the two categories.

By way of illustrating the Keynesian thesis that the savings-investment mechanism holds the key to the refutation of Say's Law, S introduces a situation in "our industrial society" in which there is no "cleavage." This "was not always so, even today, when a farmer devotes his time to draining a field instead of planting and harvesting a crop, he is saving and at the same time investing" (206). The phrase "was not always so" would indicate that in times past there were societies where this cleavage did not exist. But instead of dealing with them, S turns to today's farmer, and since in the course of the paragraph this farmer is transformed into "a primitive farmer," we do not know whether S is talking about all farmers, including large-scale capitalist farmers, or about a natural economy in which a family provides for all its needs without any exchange. (In the 9th edition "primitive" is replaced by "self-sufficient.")

In addition to lack of clarity S's argument suffers from the failure to spell out what is meant by saving and investment. First of all he confuses the issue by speaking of a farmer devoting his *time* to improving his means of production—in this case land—rather than to producing means of consumption. Is this supposed to mean that a crop that had already been planted was left to rot so that the farmer could use the time to drain the field? Or that he forwent producing a portion of the crop altogether so as to gain extra time? To prove his point, S would have done better to use as his example a farmer taking part of his crop set aside for personal consumption and feeding it to his livestock so as to increase their "productivity." This would thus be an example of a farmer actually "abstaining" and simultaneously utilizing the "sacrificed" use values to improve his productivity.

By insisting on the identity of saving and investment, S ignores the fact that productivity can be increased by working longer hours, without a parallel reduction of consumption. (The possible objection that the farmer's level of consumption would not allow such an increase is not valid, since the same would then be said for any explanation based on unchanged labor-time with reduced consumption.) The farmer can do the normal amount of planting and harvesting and in addition drain his field; in that case investment would take place without any saving.

Similarly, saving can take place without any concomitant investment; for example, the farmer can take part of the harvest and store it for later use (reserve fund, etc.) without doing any investing whatsoever. This is also consistent with S's definition in Chapter 3: "to save—to abstain from present consumption and wait for future consumption" (51). S manages to salvage his equation of investment and saving in Chapter 11 by inserting one of his famous magic little words: "abstaining from *present* consumption in order to provide for larger consumption in the *future*" (206). The inserted word is "larger," which within S's framework turns the equation of saving and investment into a tautology; by neglecting productivity increases resulting from additional labor not at the expense of consumption, S has injected the definition of investment into that of saving inasmuch as the former means "improving the productive capacity of his farm." We are not quibbling with words or citing atypical examples, since most worker savings in "our modern industrial society" are not directed at increasing total consumption but merely represent deferred consumption, and this, when we abstract from its mediation through money, is materially no different from the farmer's storing up for winter.

It is S's intention to describe the differences between, as well as the common properties shared by, "primitive" ("self-sufficient") and "modern" societies. Before examining those differences more closely let us turn to the ideological purpose behind this assertion of certain nonexistent common properties. In Chapter 3 S had already sought to obliterate most of the essential differences of various modes of production. What he attempts here is to emphasize the universal content of certain categories. Investment is identified with net-capital formation, and net-capital formation in turn is equated with improving productivity. This sequence of identities is the product of S's inability to distinguish between the social form in which the means of production appear in various modes of production and their physical aspect. Because capital is not simply a means of production it does not serve merely to increase production; capital formation is oriented toward increasing surplus value by lowering the cost of production to the capitalist. But since this latter process periodically conflicts with the reduction of the total surplus value which can be appropriated from a given number of workers, the production of use values itself is cut back or stopped.

Although under the artificial conditions posited by S increased production would bring about a reduction of consumption, the attempt to shift this arrangement to "modern industrial society" fails on several grounds. First of all, it is extremely rare for anyone in "modern" society to abstain from consumption so as to increase production. Capitalists as individual investors-savers do not abstain from consumption, nor is it their intention to increase production by not consuming what they could not consume anyway: their purpose is to increase profits. The abstention that is taking place is the involuntary abstinence on the part of the working class.

Before leaving this subject we should once again make clear that S's assertions do contain a rational kernel, namely, that a Crusoe or any planned, natural economy can abstain from consumption (i.e., saving in S's terminology) with or without the intention of increasing production (investment or reserve building, respectively) without causing a crisis. But the fact that crises do not result stems not from a marginal propensity equal to one (for in the case of reserve-building this is not the case) and not merely from the fact that saving is directly investment (for this may also be the case within the "modern" capitalist corporation); but rather from the fact that the producing units do not relate to one another only indirectly on the basis of the value of their commodities. Production is not private; it is planned, and thus by definition social. There is thus only one producing unit and—thus to use bourgeois terminology—there can be no external effects.

3/ *Neglect of the reproduction of constant capital* The following set of equations or identities (see also S, 204) plays an important role within Keynesian theory and constitutes an important link to the field of national-income accounting:

Income = value of output = consumption + investment
Saving = income-consumption
Therefore saving = investment.[143]

According to Keynes, "The equality of saving and investment necessarily follows"

provided it is agreed that income is equal to the value of current output, that current investment is equal to the value of that part of current output which is not consumed, and that saving is equal to the excess of income over consumption. . . . Thus *any* set of definitions which satisfy the above conditions leads to the same conclusion. It is only by denying the validity of one or the other of them that the conclusion can be avoided.[144]

The validity of these "definitions" is, however, highly questionable.

The basic feature of bourgeois theories of national accounting—namely the sphere of circulation as the point of departure—also forms the basis for Keynes' equations: the problem of the formation or production of national income is replaced by that of its distribution between consumption and investment. Connected with this is the inability to distinguish consistently and systematically between national income and the total social product. Keynes' contention that income equals the value of output reflects this inability. If it were so it would mean that either the latter is equal to value added (in Marxist terms wages plus surplus value), or that the former (income) is equal to GNP (wages plus surplus value plus "depreciation," that is, the constant capital reproduced each year).

The first interpretation is tantamount to the assumption that no constant capital is used in production; the second, that depreciation represents income on an aggregate social level. Both exemplify the inability of bourgeois economics to come to grips with the reproduction of constant capital. In his effort to establish equality or identity of investment and saving, Keynes further assumes that all saving is done out of national income, while in fact part of it is formed from the amortization fund (depreciation allowance), hence part of investment also derives from this source. This in turn means that income does not equal consumption plus investment. As a result of these income-theoretical considerations Keynes finds himself in the ironic position of defending the underlying assumptions of Say's Law, for under effective demand Keynes programmatically includes only national income and ignores the replacement of the used-up constant capital. This becomes even more ironic in view of Keynes' empirical awareness of the untoward effects of the nonrenewal of the constant capital on "effective demand" during the stagnation of the 1930s.

IV / INVESTMENT

Having adequately explained the forces operating on the saving side, S feels free to turn his attention to the investment side: "The extreme variability of investment is the next important fact to be emphasized" (207). Doubtless this is important—so important, in fact, that it deserves an explanation. Instead, we are offered circumlocution. We are given the assurance that "this capricious volatile behavior is understandable when we come to realize that profitable investment opportunities depend on new discoveries, new products, new territories and frontiers, *new* resources, *new* population, *higher* production and income. . . . Investment depends largely on the *dynamic* and relatively unpredictable elements of *growth* in the system and on elements outside the economic system itself. . ." (207).

But what is this "system"? As far as we know, it is "our modern economy" as opposed to the "primitive" farmer and others like him. This would have to encompass both the socialist and the capitalist economies, but in fact the "system" turns out to be capitalism. The key to S's "explanation" is semantic, for without any apparent justification he has identified "variable" with "capricious, volatile" and "dynamic" with "unpredictable growth." But there is no justification for this identification, there is no essential connection between change and caprice. Cannot growth be planned? Of course it can, but not in an unplanned economy. That change in capitalism takes place anarchically is hardly the discovery of the Keynesian revolution. Furthermore, S's formulation appears to mark a backward step. First, his choice of words—"capricious, volatile"—is indicative of the subjectivistic thrust nurtured by Keynesianism. These are terms ordinarily used in a personal sense. S's choice is not a fortuitous one, nor is our criticism of that use gratuitous, for S speaks of investment as being "desired" by "individuals" and of "how much entrepreneurs can indulge their desire to invest" (207). Moreover, his choice of words implies that this variability is not only unplanned but also incapable of being subsumed under scientifically formulated categories; yet capitalism, though anarchic, is nonetheless subject to inherent developmental laws. Some of our confusion may disappear when we find that S is talking about "profitable investment opportunities." But before we sigh in relief over finally grasping what he is getting at, we must recognize that what first appears to be a rather banal reference to the peculiarities connected with the profit requirements of investment assumes significance once we determine its systematic function within S's reasoning. To be more explicit, the mere reference to profit as a condition of investment is both more and less banal than it appears at first glance, for S does not restrict this condition to capitalism; rather he regards profit (under the name of interest) as a fixed category associated with the net productivity resulting from "investment projects." Thus on the one hand one might conclude that capricious behavior could be common to all "progressive" societies (i.e., those undertaking "net capital formation"); on the other, since this "theoretical possibility" is in fact untenable, we would expect some explanation of why it is limited to one economic formation. S of course does not bother with such peripheral matters, and we are offered no explanation whatsoever at this point. Whatever explanation he chooses to offer is reserved for that branch of economic theory known as the study of business cycles (Chapter 14), which largely antedates the Keynesian revolution.

At this juncture S is solely interested in confirming or emphasizing certain surface phenomena. But he does leave the realm of psychology long enough to make a few general remarks concerning the consequences of the (capitalistic) variability of investment. He reminds us that laissez faire cannot guarantee that investment will be such as to ensure full employment. But lest the reader jump to the hasty conclusion that something is amiss, he prefaces this warning with praise for "an industrial system such as our own"—namely that it can do "many wonderful things," e.g., "respond to any given demand for goods" (207). S omits the little word "solvent" before demand, for obviously if capitalism were merely responding to a "demand for goods" it could guarantee full employment for generations to come. S fails to explain how the requirements for profitability manage to insert themselves between needs and fulfillment. In the end he admits that "the system is somewhat in the lap of the gods" as far as the stimulus to investment is concerned (208). Solace is offered in the form of "perfectly sensible public and private policies"; yet although he concedes that the "one thing" laissez faire "cannot always do" is guarantee full employment, we know that neither can our "mixed economy." And perhaps that is not its purpose, for in a very significant passage (expunged from the 8th edition) S confides that these "sensible policies" "cannot expect to wipe out business fluctuations

100 per cent. We would not want them to, even if they could. But they can try to reduce the range of wild fluctuations in prices and employment. . ." (7th ed., p. 198). Now who is the "we"? Certainly not those who are made unemployed by the less than "wild fluctuations" guaranteed by the mixed economy.

We have seen that the absorption of the reserve army of the unemployed creates definite dangers for capitalist production. Although economists are wont to describe this situation in terms of a trade-off between inflation and unemployment, a more pertinent description would refer to the "dilemma" confronting the bourgeoisie in the form of the "trade-off" between increased "social unrest" (greater unemployment) and "artificial" barriers to capital accumulation (less unemployment). Even though S manages to avoid the term capitalism by substituting such code words as "laissez faire" and "mixed economy," capitalism apparently has not managed to avoid this contradiction.

In his textbook S carefully avoids coming to grips with this issue. In Chapter 29 he even goes so far as to pooh-pooh the (Marxist) notion that the reserve army can have a "beneficial" effect on work "discipline," productivity and wage demands. However, in an article published in the early 1950s, S exhibited a much less cavalier attitude toward the potential problems generated by "full employment."[145] In it he examined the notion seriously and, while coming to no definitive conclusions on the merits of the argument, he acknowledged that no one had as yet devised a perfect formula for the appropriate mixture of carrot and stick in the area of production.

The 8th and 9th editions contain an important addendum to this section in the form of two "qualifications" on the alleged independence of the forces operating on saving and investment. We are already familiar with one—namely that corporate investment decisions are "often . . . closely related" to the magnitude of retained profits (which S insists on calling "savings," as though this could possibly have anything to do with "abstaining from consumption"). The second relates to the influence exerted by the availability of "people's savings"—"particularly in times of tight money and high interest rates"—on "how much entrepreneurs can indulge their desire to invest in new profitable opportunities" (207). This second qualification is to be sure not new either, although it had not yet been formulated this clearly. According to S, "saving and investment decisions are resolved by what happens to the level of income and employment and to interest rates" (207). This does not agree with the original Keynesian formulation, which held that "saving and investment . . . are the twin results of the system's determinants, namely, the propensity to consume, the schedule of the marginal efficiency of capital and the rate of interest."[146] Subsequently Keynes explicitly characterizes the volume of employment and national income as "our dependent variable" while refining the above-mentioned determinants into the "ultimate independent variable . . . consisting of (1) the three fundamental psychological factors, namely, the psychological propensity to consume, the psychological attitude to liquidity and the psychological expectation of future yield from capital-assets, (2) the wage-unit . . . and (3) the quantity of money as determined by the action of the central bank. . . ."[147]

To a large extent, these deviations are the result of S's propensity to weed out the subjective elements from the Keynesian theory and to graft more objective ones into it.

We will come back to the question of income determination. At this stage we merely wish to point out that the two "qualifications" inserted by S, taken together with our empirical information, show that saving and investment are merely superficial and misunderstood aspects of the process of capital accumulation.

V / THE PROSPENSITIES TO SAVE AND TO CONSUME

This section, perhaps more clearly than anything before, reveals the highly eclectic basis of S's methodology. However, given the absence of a consciously formulated methodology, the term "eclectic" implies greater methodological sophistication on S's part than the facts would warrant.

S cavalierly dismisses that which Keynes deemed the firm psychological foundations of the above topic. Thus although S devotes several subsections of Chapter 11 to various aspects of the propensities to save and consume, he encloses the references to them in quotation marks and labels them "so-called" (210). Yet despite his tendency to discard the psychological base in favor of "behavioralistic" criteria, he finds significant ideological value in retaining the psychological trappings. This emerges most clearly when he passes from the individual or family propensities to "the community's over-all consumption schedule" (215 ff.). In fact "society's" propensity to save or consume derives its plausibility from the "decisions" taking place on the individual or family level. With respect to the latter, we find this theoretical grounding in the original Keynesian, version:

> The fundamental psychological law, upon which we are entitled to depend with great confidence both *a priori* from our knowledge of human nature and from the detailed facts of experience, is that men are disposed, as a rule and on the average, to increase their consumption as their income increases, but not by as much as the increase in their income.[148]

While backing off from determining whether this proportion saved will increase, Keynes claims that the "fundamental psychological rule of any modern community" must obtain—otherwise the regularity "characteristic of the economic system in which we live," namely that its "severe fluctuations" are "not violently unstable," could not obtain.[149] And then he jumps to the conclusion that "since these facts of experience do not follow of logical necessity, one must suppose that the environment and the psychological propensities of the modern world must be of such a character as to produce these results."[150]

Since S himself is apparently loath to claim the existence of a psychological entity like an individual's marginal propensity to consume, we will not devote much space to this point. For the bulk of the members of capitalist society, "propensities" to consume and save can have little meaning; for if, as we know, that for the majority of the population the question of choice does not exist, that it is living on a level that permits only the propensity to survive, then the basis of Keynes' "psychological law" begins to crumble. For some, namely those with above-average even though not extremely high incomes who do actually make choices between consumption and saving, Keynes' "laws" do have some relevance. Finally there is the relatively small group of capitalists with disproportionately large incomes who also are not subject to the contraints underlying Keynes' laws, since their income was never meant to be consumed in the first place.

The notion of the individul or family decision-making process provides the plausibility for the aggregate propensity to consume and save. The irony here is that the prototypical microeconomic activity hardly represents the sound basis for its macroeconomic analog which it is supposed to supply. But this methodological consideration recedes into the background in favor of an overriding ideological one: namely, that by building on the image of family decision-making (in itself already a distortion of reality), S fosters the illusion that society as a whole is also deciding to consume part and save part of "its" yearly income. In fact, in the self-image of this theory the societal decision is supposedly a result of these individual decisions, which leads to the very desirable ideological result that our mixed economy contains a democratic element.

With reference to the propensity to consume, S says that "it is a basic, important concept whose general properties we must study" (211). Yet the pages that follow are devoted to mathematical and/or geometrical operations without ever developing what most serious social scientists would consider a "concept."

Now if such methodological problems arise even on the relatively straightforward level of individual propensities, they become compounded once they are "aggregated." True, during any given period of production a part of the newly produced commodity is consumed, and the relevant mathematical operations would yield a fractional figure, but whether the mere existence of such a fraction—which S persistently confuses with a "concept"—permits us to draw any conclusion about the existence of a "comunity's overall propensity to consume" is a crucial methodological consideration which S apparently does not consider problematic.

As we have repeatedly said, on a concrete level we are not denying the relevance of such factors as the division of net income into consumption and investment. But aside from the fundamental objection that Keynesianism fails to recognize the determination of this division in the relations of capitalist production, we must also note that its fixation on the sphere of circulation and the accompanying absence of a theory of reproduction are reponsible for a central weakness of the theory of income determination.

VI / INCOME DETERMINATION

Let us begin by summarizing some of the most important "simplifying assumptions" underlying "the modern theory of income determination." The two on which we have placed greatest stress and which play the biggest methodological role here are family-propensity schedules and the exclusion of undistributed corporate profits (220 f.).

As far as community consumption and saving schedules are concerned, "They are drawn up on the basis of our knowledge of the thriftiness of different families," income distribution, and several other "qualifications" which complicate but in no way are supposed to devastate the "aggregating" operations (216 ff., 220).

The second assumption, the neglect of internally generated profits, fits in quite nicely with the first, since it diverts attention from the objective laws governing the production and utilization of profit and focuses it on the allegedly dominant subjective factors relating to saving and consumption, and later to investment as well.

This psychological orientation finds unambiguous expression in phrases like "everyone will be content to go on doing"; "business firms will be willing"; "desired saving"; "desired investment"; firms "feel safe" (222); business "wants" (224); "the public will wish" (231); "make people feel poor enough" (236); etc. It is no coincidence that by and large these words are used in the context of circulation-sphere spending, for a major thrust of Keynesian theory is directed toward the analysis of spending and the practical efficacy of spending to increase production (income, or more accurately profits). Although neither Keynes nor S asserts that spending in itself leads to increased profits without increased production, they are remiss about showing the mediating links. Keynes emphasized the role of expectations; and even though S appears to eschew such blatant psychologizing when he can find a ready behavioralistic substitute, he is not at all reticent about resorting to a somewhat weaker subjectivism.

Thus in Chapter 12, he assigns a crucial role to changes in the rate of depletion or accumulation of inventory; in fact, one might say that he makes changes in production a function of these inventory changes (222-26). Now it is clear that on a practical level the relation between sales and inventory is bound to be a decisive indicator to the capitalist economic agents on making output decisions for their firms; and even on a very concrete analytical level the conclusions that can be drawn about the development of mass consumption power from the demand for means of consumption and production as expressed in sales and inventory can be important. What is not clear is why the analysis must remain on the level of subjective motives imposed upon the practicing capitalist by the forces of competition.

The income-determination analysis S offers is a three-tiered composite: (1) an arithmetic and geometric formulation of what appears on the surface of economic events; (2) a distortion of the deeper processes caused in part by this superficial view and in part by "simplifying assumptions";

and (3) an unintended refutation of the assertion that capitalism is not divided into classes and that consumption is the sole end of economic activity.

Although in Keynes' and S's model actual savings must equal actual investment ("by definition"), there is a cleavage between the motivations for saving and investing: individual consumers decide to save to provide for future consumption, whereas individual entrepreneurs decide to invest to provide for a "satisfactory profit position." Since the latter decisions are clearly contingent upon profitability conditions, while the former are not, what consumers want to save may not parallel what entrepreneurs want to invest. In Keynes' main "case" the tension generated by the level of savings in excess of that of investment is resolved by a reduction of total income, and thus of total consumption, to a level below that of the preceding period.

The Keynesian model argues as follows: the community chooses a certain level of consumption based on the expected level of income; profitability requirements, however, force modification of this level of consumption. The crucial point here is that these are economic, not technological requirements: though it may be technologically possible to produce for a certain level of consumption, it can be unprofitable for entrepreneurs to do so: hence, under these circumstances this level will not be achieved. This also means that Keynes and S have contradicted themselves, for their own analysis indicates that in capitalist society consumption cannot be the sole end of economic activity.

By positing this conflict between consumers and entrepreneurs, Keynesian theory rather confusedly and from the point of view of the circulation sphere is pointing to the existence of classes and class struggle under capitalism; for workers, as opposed to entrepreneurs, are primarily consumers, while capitalists by definition are primarily "entrepreneurs" and only secondarily consumers. In conjunction with the savings and investment statistics that showed that the same class of persons by and large controls savings and investment decisions, these considerations demonstrate that workers do not have any "real say" in determining the level of consumption of society through their savings and consumption decisions. Thus on this level Keynesian theory reflects the social contradictions of capitalist production in a very distorted fashion; the theory can do this because it has taken into consideration certain striking features on the surface of depressions, crises, stagnation periods, and of the industrial cycle in general. Yet the very fact that the theory sticks to these surface phenomena militates against a comprehensive formulation of *all* the contradictions of the capitalist mode of production, a weakness exemplified in S's description of a segment of the income-determination chain of events. When business firms as a whole are temporarily producing a high total product, higher than the sum of what consumers will buy and what business as a whole wants to be investing . . . their total sales revenue will be so low as to be putting disagreeable downward pressure on their profit position" and thus firms will cut back their production (226). This is empirically true, but in this vague formulation the lack of effective demand is merely another term for the lack of adequate conditions for the accumulation of capital; it properly points to the lack of mass-consumption power as a critical factor in the road to crisis and stagnation, but it is not able to explain the connections between this lack and the absence of conditions of sufficient profitability.

But even this relatively critical approach sacrifices its more promising possibilities by putting the central problem in the framework of a class-undifferentiated concept of oversaving. In other words, as long as all income is spent by consumers, there are no difficulties. But: "Realistically, we must recognize that the public will wish to save some of its income. . . . Hence businesses cannot expect their consumption sales to be as large as the total of wages, interest, rents and profits" (231). Left to its own devices—that is, if for the time being we abstract from monetary and fiscal policy—the economy provides two basic responses to this situation. One is the "investment offset": *"If there happen to be* sufficently profitable investment opportunities, business firms will be paying out wages, interest and other costs *in part for new investments goods* rather than 100 per cent for consumption goods. Hence to continue to be happy, business needs to receive back in consumption sales only *part* of the total income paid out to the public. . ." (ibid.). The second possible response centers on the question of what will happen "if business will not unwillingly invest more"—namely that production must be cut "until so much national income has been destroyed as to make people feel poor enough that they will finally end up not trying to save more than business will go on investing" (236). Let us begin by examining the latter of these two possibilities. In the original Keynesian formulation:

> If . . . the inducement to invest is weak, then . . . the working of the principle of effective demand will compel it ["a potentially wealthy community"] to reduce its actual output, until, in spite of its potential wealth, it has become so poor that its surplus over its consumption is sufficiently diminished to correspond to the weakness of the inducement to invest.[151]

Or, as Keynes rephrases it:

> So, failing some novel expedient . . . there must be sufficient unemployment to keep us so poor that our consumption falls short of our income by no more than the equivalent of the physical provision for future consumption which it pays to produce to-day.[152]

The most striking feature in all these formulations is the class-undifferentiated notion of saving and oversaving. A careful examination of the Keynesian reasoning will show that neither a class-specific "disaggregation" of the macroeconomic savings analysis nor the so-called aggregation itself contributes to an understanding of the underlying processes. Thus any attempt at disaggregating is vitiated by the fact that by and large those who "feel" poor *are* poor and do not save at either the higher or reduced levels of national income; and similarly, by and large the big savers are not made (to feel) poor by drops in national income, since "its surplus over its consumption" is almost always sufficient to force it to "save." If we look at the "community's" saving processes, the picture would seem to become even more distorted, for the Keynesian theory contends that the crisis is mastered by diminishing income until the level of savings becomes compatible with the level of investment corresponding to a weakened inducement to invest. But in point of fact the crisis is not mastered by destroying surplus value (i.e., savings); on the contrary, one of the prime mechanisms for restoring conditions of profitability is the destruction of capital—that is to say, the idling of some parts of the capital "stock," the depreciation of another, and the obsolescence of still a third. Paper titles to parts of total profit are destroyed via bankruptcies, etc.; and the relation of prices upon which money as means of payment rests is also thoroughly revolutionized.

Now let us return to the first of the two responses of the mechanism determining income to a situation in which "the public will wish to save some of its income" and thus withdraw that part from consumption sales. To begin with, this approach rather than being "simple" turns out to be convoluted. The reason S raises this possibility is connected with his methodological assumption of no "undistributed corporate profits"; for if instead he had assumed that profits were not distributed to the public (as dividends), but rather were internally generated and reinvested (accumulated), then it would become clear that "savings decisions" are in fact dependent on the contradictory process at work in determining the mass of surplus value produced. Instead, S starts from the assumption of an atypical state of affairs—namely, simple reproduction, in which the total annual product is consumed and not part productively accumulated. But even this notion of simple reproduction is distorted, insofar as it posits consumption as the determining factor, with savings (i.e., investment) as a sort of residual (238), the result of seeing investment as an offset "to absorb the excess of total output over what the community chooses to consume."[153] Furthermore, even within the bounds of simple reproduction S fails to take into consideration the various complications arising from the simple reproduction of constant capital.

Finally, connected with this distorted formulation of the

process of reproduction is S's failure to distinguish between problems of realization for individual capitals and for capital as a whole. Obviously, if all profits were distributed to "the public" in the form of dividends, and these were not consumed (or lent back to the corporations or used to buy newly issued shares, etc.), we would be faced with a severe case of overproduction. But even if we accept S's assumptions, it remains a fact that in the beginning at least this problem would not affect certain individual capitals— namely those mass production branches generating means of consumption for the working class which by and large has no net savings; in the first instance it would affect those branches producing luxury goods purchased largely by capitalists. This in turn would result in a reduction in demand for means of production by the producers of these luxury goods, with further effects on all interdependent reproductive relations.

Thus ultimately we are dealing with the complicated conditions of equilibrium between the two large departments of production: the producers of means of production and the producers of means of consumption. However this is obscrued in S's analysis (earlier he has spoken of "business firms as a whole" [226]) because his basic assumptions distort rather than reproduce the basic features of capitalist production.

VII / THE MULTIPLIER DOCTRINE

In this section, dealing with the more theoretical aspects of the theory of income determination, the extraordinary significance Keynesians attribute to spending per se—that is to say, regardless of its place within the capitalist mode of production—takes on particular importance.

Are the Keynesians able to prove that additional spending will lead to additional production, that is, that incremental spending will not turn out to be merely inflationary or inventory-depleting in nature? In case of the former, we have no increase in income and the multiplier cannot serve its reputed practical function of leading the way out of a period of stagnation; and if the effect of the multiplier is inventory-depleting, then, under certain conditions, it might ameliorate the problem of surplus-value realization but it would not solve the problem of surplus-value production.

To what extent does the "doctrine" of the multiplier come to grips with links that connect additional spending and increased production"? Given the "common sense and arithmetic" relation between the marginal propensities to consume and save and the multiplier (230), we can at this point turn back to the unreflected use to which S puts the marginal propensity to consume.

One major difficulty with using the marginal propensity to consume in the way Keynes and S attempt to is that their application rests on the false assumption that every time the increment in spending changes hands it is divided between saving and consumption spending without any intervening steps. In point of fact, however, at least every other change of hands brings money into the hands of a capitalist, which is then divided among replacement of the constant capital, wages, and surplus value (whereby the last in turn is subdivided into the various concrete phenomenal forms of surplus value such as interest, profit, rent, dividends, etc.).

Let us consider S's example illustrating the workings of the multiplier "by using ordinary common sense." This is how he proves that his hiring of "unemployed resources to build a $1,000 garage" will lead to "a *secondary* expansion of national income and production, over above" his *"primary* investment":

> My carpenters and lumber producers will get an extra $1,000 of income. But that is not the end of the story. If they all have a marginal propensity to consume of 2/3, they will now spend $666.67 on new consumption goods. The producers of these goods will now have an extra income of $666.67. If their MPC is also 2/3, they in turn will spend $444.44, or 2/3 of $666.67 (or 2/3 of 2/3 of $1,000). So the process will go on, with each new round of spending being 2/3 of the previous round [229].

To begin with, in characteristic fashion he has selected an atypical example. A developed capitalist economy is not a system of independent small commodity producers (S's carpenters) who merely receive in exchange the money form of the commodities (and/or "services") which they sell, as opposed to a society of capitalist producers for whom there is a difference between costs (namely constant plus variable capital) and the value of the commodities produced (namely constant capital plus the total value added by the workers).

S's example clearly assumes that the entire $1,000 accrues as income to individuals, and for that matter that at each successive spending step the entire amount accrues as income. Since by S's own assumptions we can disregard transactions between two consumers as consumers (e.g., the purchase of a used car from its previous owner), at least every other change of hands brings the money into the hands of a capitalist. We say "at least," because capitalists buy from one another in order to replace and/or expand their constant capital—and this does not constitute spending on consumer goods, new or otherwise.

Now if at least every other stage brings the money into the hands of a capitalist, it becomes inappropriate to speak of a marginal propensity to consume at each stage, for this is a property for consumers, not of corporations. True, some of the money of corporations goes toward wages and personal incomes, but at least part of it goes for replacement and expansion of constant capital. The share of income devoted to renewing and extending the constant capital depends largely on the organic composition of capital in the branches of industry involved (that is to say, how "capital or labor intensive" they are). Thus, if one wanted to trace the "flow of incremental spending," the organic composition of capital would be a more relevant criterion than the marginal propensity to consume. The more critical bourgeois economists have also found certain weaknesses in the multiplier theory, in particular with respect to the marginal propensity to consume. Thus one European economist, Hugo Hegeland, wrote in the early 1950s:

There is *no* connection between the given income and the increment of income. The two streams are merely aggregated as two numerical quantities without any causal relations. This presumes a peculiar behavior of the individual income earner, namely that he distinguishes between his original income and the additional stream which he will receive as a result from the new outlays on capital construction. The monetary saving from his original income will be transformed into capital outlays but the saving from his additional income will leak away. . . . The change in total income takes place without influencing the entrepreneurs, in spite of their given amount of capital outlays constituting, after all, the larger part of the total stream of capital outlays. These are the consequences of Keynes' proposition of a marginal propensity to invest equal to zero. It means that *all* economic unities of the given society will act only as consumers when they receive an increment in income. The producers and sellers of consumer goods will thus increase their outlays, *not as entrepreneurs* and sellers, whose activities are mainly based on the search for profit, *but as consumers,* and in a ratio determined by the given marginal propensity to consume. The whole process of income creation from one equilibrium situation to another is wholly governed by one individual activity, founded on utilitarian assumptions: the marginal propensity to consume. . . . In the multiplier model the behavior of corporations, of special groups of interest, of power blocks, or of human beings acting as entrepreneurs is entirely ruled out . . .[154]

And again focusing on the circulation-sphere orientation of Keynesian theory, Hegeland notes that in the multiplier theory

economic activities are considered mainly from the banking viewpoint: cash holdings, liquidity preference, saving, etc., are concepts playing a dominant role in this system, whereas the characteristic features of production, such as the technical development, the accumulation of capital equipment, the profit-motive, the presence of monopolies, etc., are generally neglected.[155]

Two types of answers have been made to the critique we have presented here. One points out that empirically the multiplier does not turn out to be anywhere near so large as one might expect on the basis of an aggregate propensity to consume of about 9/10, because the MPC is out of disposable personal income; thus in addition to the traditional "leakages" such as saving, foreign trade, taxes, etc., the very significant "withdrawals from GNP" represented by "business depreciation allowances and undistributed profits" must also be taken into consideration.[156]

The other type of answer, a hypothetical one, might hold that in S's example, the $1,000 does eventually accrue as income of individuals, although it would take more than one transaction for this process to reach its end. Accordingly, the MPC can be used to determine that after the $1,000 accrues as income, 1/3 of it will be saved and 2/3 spent, and this 2/3 will eventually also accrue as income, and so on for 2/3 of that income. Thus the multiplier still works as described, although with many intervening steps.

To concretize this rebuttal, according to which the $1,000 does after all accrue as income: let us say that the $1,000 is paid to a carpenter to bulid S's garage. The carpenter keeps only part of this sum as personal income; the rest he pays out for building equipment and materials. But the people from whom he buys these commodities must in turn use part of the purchase money to pay for labor, and so on until the entire $1,000 is spent as payment for labor, that is to say, until it accrues as income to individuals.

This argument is not new: Adam Smith used it two hundred years ago, and it has not improved with age. But just as Smith and the Keynesians contend that the entire annual product accrues as income to individuals, the same argument might be used to show that the entire $1,000 accrues not as income to individuals but as payment for means of production. After all, that portion of the $1,000 not spent by the carpenter for means of production will eventually be spent for other commodities, the person from whom he buys these commodities will spend a portion of the money received on means of production, and so on, until the entire $1,000 is spent on means of production.

There is obviously something fishy about an argument

that permits one to dissolve this spending increment into just about anything one chooses. We do not of course mean that the phenomenon in part described by the multiplier does not exist; in a way it is common sense to say that if S hires unemployed resources the end result *may* be the expansion of demand for means of consumption, and, consequently, for means of production. Whether such an expansion actually takes place is another matter (depending for example on the depth of the stagnation in question, that is to say, how much debt has accumulated whose repayment will not have a multiplier effect, on the size of the "backlog" of surplus value that because of overproduction remains to be realized, etc.).

In order to gain a better understanding of the distorted relation between consumption and production that typifies the multiplier "doctrine," let us examine S's other approach to the multiplier, which takes consumption rather than investment as its point of departure: "Just as investment spending is 'high-powered spending' with multiplier effects on income, consumption spending that represents a genuine *shift* in the propensity to consume and save will also be 'high-powered'!" (236). This notion is connected with a conception of economic growth that received much attention in immediate post-World War II discussions how to develop an economic policy able to eliminate stagnation periods such as that of the 1930s. This particular conception was known as "a high consumption . . . high-wage, low-profit economy."[157] According to this view:

> This is the goal that modern industrial communities need to reach in order to ensure adequate aggregate demand . . . because private consumption expenditures in all industrialized societies [!] fall below what they might be . . . owing to conditions arising in part from the *normal* functioning of the price system and in part from the *malfunctioning* of the system. The normal functioning of the price system inevitably produces an almost incredible inequality in the distribution of income.[158]

Both these authors are acutely aware of the contradictions involved in the attempt to put the multiplier into effect on the basis of a "genuine shift in the propensity to consume." Thus Williams remarks that "the great difficulty about rising wage rates as a means of raising national income is the conflict between wages as income and wages as cost. . . . This is a particularly difficult aspect of our problem. We must not lose sight of the fact that ours is a profit-seeking economy."[159] And Hansen speaks of "a wage-profit dilemma. . . . It must be recognized . . . that there are certain limitations on how far profits can be encroached upon."[160] Since they are also aware of dangers involved in the traditionally volatile "business" cycles, they try to arrive at some sort of compromise: "A lower rate of profits in a more stable economy would be preferable, even from the standpoint of business itself, if it did not impair long-run growth."[161] We are still waiting for the "decision" on the part of the capitalist class to accept, or rather enforce, a *permanently* reduced global rate of surplus value in order to preserve capitalism for the future. Until that time, "high-powered spending" via permanent income shifts from capital to labor will have to remain buried in the pages of textbooks.

VIII / FISCAL POLICY IN INCOME DETERMINATION

If at the beginning of this chapter sequence S could still maintain that "the income analysis described here is itself neutral: it can be used as well to defend private enterprise as to limit it" (8th ed., p. 193), by the time he gets around to introducing government fiscal policy "explicitly" (243) this seeming neutrality has evaporated. In a now-deleted passage in the 7th edition, S conceded that at this point "we stop being the detached observers of whatever it is that happens. Like the doctor who puts to work the objective findings of physiological science, we put to work the theory of income determination to show how government fiscal policy . . . can influence and stabilize the level of national income" (p. 222). Being aware of the "objectivity" of the analysis up to this point, we can well imagine with which class the now no longer "detached observer" will idenfity.

To return to the discussion of the practical aspects of the consumption-induced multiplier: As we know, Keynes attached great significance to programs aimed at increasing the propensity to consume: "For it is unlikely that full employment can be maintained, whatever we may do about investment, with the existing propensity to consume."[162] And although "Keynes' theory is not oriented to changes in the social structure, but is primarily concerned with how to make capitalism work, given the existing social structure,"[163] the so-called left-wing Keynesians in particular (Joan Robinson, Michael Kalecki, et al.) have placed great stress on income redistribution via progressive taxation as a means of raising the propensity to consume. In fact, well over three decedes ago even S espoused such views:

> A new canon of taxation can be enunciated as follows: *private income being given, any amount of revenue should be raised by taxation of income with the lowest marginal propensity to consume up to the point where marginal propensities to consume are equalized.* This will maximize national income.[164]

Unfortunately, S's fiscal imperative has not been implemented. In the words of one economist describing S's development since the first edition of his textbook, "a good deal of the boldness, originality, and activism of the early Keynesians has been modified or abandoned altogether."[165]

The reasons for his discarding of serious schemes to increase the propensity to consume via income redistribution are not hard to find. As Dillard explains:

> An inevitable limitation on the extent to which progressive taxes can be used arises from the fact that the money which is taxed away from the rich can hardly [!] be given directly to the poor, although to some extent this is possible in the form of pensions, relief payments, et cetera. Therefore, the government which collects taxes for purposes of redistribution must either pay subsidies to private citizens or expand the scope of its activities in order to provide social services for lower-income

groups. . . . Although services of this type are of great social significance, they do not enable the low-income groups to increase the money income out of which they must feed, clothe, and house themselves. Subsidies for housing, or low-cost government housing, of course, are possible but tend to be strongly opposed by private interest groups. A further limitation to redistributing income by means of progressive taxation is the danger that high rates on large incomes may discourage private investment, upon which the private capitalist economy primarily depends for filling the gap between income and consumption at high levels of unemployment. If progressive taxation increases the community's propensity to consume at the expense of weakening the inducement to invest, the losses in employment from the latter may more than cancel the gains from the former.[166]

It should come as no surprise to us that a redistribution of the yearly value created in favor of the working class, in other words a reduction of surplus value in favor of wages, would reduce the rate of profit and could hardly be suitable to the task of overcoming periods of stagnation by fostering the accumulation of capital.

Let us then examine the other methods available to Keynesian fiscal policy, primarily the various state investments and subsidies to private investment. In this connection S states that "public road building is economically no different from private railroad building" and that in general "government expenditure . . . has a multiplier effect upon income just like that of private investment." This is based on the "chain of *respending*" described by the multiplier theory (244).

It is crucial to determine the relevance of the type of spending as far as S's proclaimed goal of "stabilizing" capitalism is concerned.

Nothing in the history of economic theory makes the equation of "private" and state economic activities self-evident. Although the groundwork for the contemporary bourgeois view had been laid long before the triumph of Keynesianism, it fell to Alvin Hansen to recapitulate the arguments for the identification of private and state investment and to strengthen the theoretical underpinnings in anticipation of the possible counterarguments from "conservative" business quarters. Hansen seeks to establish a parallel between Adam Smith's treatment of the physiocrats and the treatment contemporary bourgeois economics accords the classical economists, or rather, he seeks to demonstrate that Smith's critique did not go far enough. And he also believes that Smith fell into the basic physiocratic error of remaining fixated on material production:

> It is remarkable that once he had taken the first step in the right direction, he should have made this error. If manufacturing is productive, since it no less than agriculture satisfies human wants, surely the opera singer, the servant, the teacher are equally productive.[167]

Since most economists accept this reasoning, Hansen is puzzled by their rejection of it with respect to government expenditures:

> It is sometimes said that there is an important difference between business expenditures and government expenditures, in that the former are self-sustaining while the latter are not. But this is not true. No private business can sustain its sales volume, unless the outlays of other businesses and the government continue to feed the income stream. . . . When it is said that public expenditures are "sustained out of" private income, it will be disclosed . . . that the reasoning is precisely similar to that of the Physiocrats. . . . In like manner, under modern conditions, many wants can be satisfied at all only by governmental action. . . . Just as the manufacturing population buys the surplus of agriculture in exchange for its products, so also the services of government enter into the exchange process and enrich the income stream. It is true that part of the exchange payment is in the form of taxes, but this in no way alters the fundamental fact of exchange. The income of the population attached to any private enterprise is derived not merely from the sale of its product to other private industries, but also from the sale of its product to the population attached to governmental projects. . . . In this process of exchange it is not true that any one segment of the exchange economy supports out of its surplus any other segment.[168]

The central confusion of Hansen's reasoning is connected with his attempt to explain the development of a specific mode of production with categories not specific to that mode. In methodological terms, this is tantamount to an inversion of Smith's historical approach toward the economic development of his era.

More specifically, Hansen is able to establish an identity between "business" and governmental activity because he views both from the point of view of circulation and/or immediate labor process removed from the societal form under which production takes place. According to him, a public park or concert hall would be a utility-creating governmental expenditure, while soil-preservation programs of public schools would be examples of efficiency-creating expenditures.[169] Although it is obvious that "under modern [capitalist] conditions, many wants can be satisfied . . . only by governmental action," Hansen has confused the specific need for this state "intervention" and the specific form which it assumes with its underlying material content (e.g., "infrastructure"); this in turn is linked to his failure to recognize the fundamental differences between the state in capitalism and in precapitalist class societies. Thus although it is true that the state has undergone marked changes since the days of Adam Smith, the specific qualitative role which *any* capitalist state can fulfill is delimited by the essential characteristics of capitalist accumulation which have not changed conceptually since Smith; and whereas Smith was consciously engaged in a class and historical struggle against the remnants of a prior mode of production, and thus was justified in his strictures on the physiocrats, Hansen bases his theoretical innovations upon the implication that the self-expansion of value is no longer the objective end of the capitalist mode of production.

This brings us to the multiplier effect of government expenditures on income. Keynesian theory sees the mass of profit as determined by the aggregate effective demand, and the expansion of demand brought about by incremental expenditures, as leading to increased total profits. Thus Hansen speaks of some government projects as being "genuinely profitable in the sense that they enlarge total national income by an amount at least equal to their cost."[170] The Keynesian misconception of the real processes characterizing capitalist production is due to the failure to recognize that "the economy can be stabilized" in accordance with the needs of a "healthy" capitalism only if money is spent as capital—that is, the purchase of means of production and labor power—and only if subsequently the labor power is expended in a capitalistically productive manner—that is, produces surplus value which can be accumulated.

Thus it is not the paid labor of the workers employed by the state investments that leads to increased total income, but only the increase of the productively employed workers. On the other hand, total income cannot exceed the increase of paid labor if only government expenditures take place, for these are by their very nature not surplus-value producing. It is true of course that through these state expenditures a rising demand for means of consumption and/or production can help with the realization problem of the surplus value represented by the overproduction characteristic of stagnation periods.[171]

We have touched upon state inducement to private investment only peripherally because S divides his treatment of fiscal policy into government deficit spending and reduced taxes to encourage private investment. Without being very clear about it, he gives the impression that these are interchangeable and, in effect, almost identical procedures. Yet Keynesians have long recognized that mere reliance on support of private investment is self-defeating.

Keynesian fiscal policy is able to come to grips with certain "difficulties" only by shifting the expression of underlying contradictions either to another sphere or to the future. This is a built-in contradiction in Keynesian policy itself, for to the extent that it is successful in its real—if often unproclaimed—task of recreating conditions of profitability it must at the same time lay the groundwork for the next cycle deriving from the contradictions inherent in the self-expansion of value.

9 The Capitalist Industrial Cycle
S's Chapter 14

During the 1960s the Depression nightmare was fading into history. The economy had nine years of almost uninterrupted prosperity, and long-run planning became very fashionable. The planning frequently wasn't very sophisticated, though, sometimes amounting to little more than "one good year deserves another."

Businessmen in the 1960s became so euphoric that many decided it was smart to keep on expanding during any slowdown—that it was important to "look beyond the valley." Then came the recession of 1969-70. . . . The recession reminded businessmen of the business cycle, of the fact that every year would not necessarily be a repetition of the past one.
—*The Wall Street Journal,* September 20, 1972

Considering that the contradictions of capitalist production find their clearest expression in the cyclical movements of economic activity, and considering also the enormous immediate impact of the capitalist industrial cycle on the daily life of the members of capitalist society, one might expect an introductory economics text to stress its significance. However, not so S: the effects of the cyclical development on the people living under capitalism are practically ignored, while the theoretical questions underlying the phenomenon are not assigned a key role in the science of economics—they merely form one of many branches of investigation.

This failure is due largely to the basic inability of contemporary bourgeois economics to understand the cycle; a superficially more plausible reason is to be found in the attitude adopted by bourgeois economics in the post-World War II period toward the cycle as an empirical phenomenon.

We will therefore begin our discussion with a review of this empirical reality and then proceed to an analysis of the theories presented by S.

I / HISTORY AND PRESENT EMPIRICAL REALITY OF CAPITALIST INDUSTRIALIST CYCLES

S's sustained effort to persuade the reader that we are here dealing with rather innocuous material is the most interesting feature of the empirical approach to "business" cycles: "We now turn to the related problems of how the level of national income has fluctuated, and how economists try to forecast the future" (249). But although the chapter ostensibly seeks to determine whether the cycle is "a thing of the past, a museum piece," S has prejudiced the search for the truth from the outset by reducing the phenomenon to the rather neutral term "business fluctuations," which in turn are characterized as "simply one further aspect of the economic problem of achieving and maintaining high levels of jobs, production, and progressive growth along with reasonable price stability" (250). If on the one hand S tries to minimize the significance of cycles, on the other he drops hints at strategic intervals that tend to absolve society of responsibility, describing the phenomenon as a natural dysfunction. Thus he compares cycles to "the fluctuations of disease epidemics, of the weather, or of a child's temperature" (250). And again in the concluding section of the chapter he repeats the analogy to natural catastrophes, asking whether the neoclassical synthesis has put "this curse of capitalism" to rest "in the same way that modern medicine has ended such scourges as polio and smallpox" (266).

Turning from the ideological climate S has established to his empirical treatment, we are struck by the focus on the Great Depression of 1929-41. It is given the dual task of warning us about the dangers confronting the "forces of democracy" among "the electorate in a mixed economy" if it slackens in its "new attitude" toward the "economic science' which "knows how . . . to keep any recessions that break out from snowballing into *lasting* chronic slumps" (266 f.), and of implying how well off we are today by comparison.

This longest and deepest stagnation period in the history of capitalism is taken as the gauge against which all subsequent cyclical movements are to be measured. As to post-World War II cyclical movements, S gives us only the skimpiest information; in essence it consists of one figure showing "business activity" as a "per cent of long-term trend" (250 f.). Although the figure shows very striking features during the period from 1902 to 1972, it is nonetheless deficient for a variety of reasons. To begin with, the reader is never told how the chart was constructed—that is, which economic "activity" is being measured; secondly, S does not even tell us what he means by a "long-term trend" (251, 253 n.1). As far as the post-World War II period is concerned, the figure 14-2 (252) offers a much more useful set of statistics. How does S interpret this material? "Let us first stick to the facts and statistics," he says. "Later we can attempt to devise hypotheses and explanatory theories to account for the facts" (251). From a pedagogical standpoint one must agree that the beginning student should be given this sort of useful information before being offered an explanatory theory. However, the material should be based on theoretical criteria, so that what follows makes sense to the student. However, because bourgeois economics has failed to develop any coherent theory of cycles, we are left with certain striking observable phenomena, which in turn lead back to theoretical pluralism. As happens so often, S fails to take an unambiguous stand; at best he ventures the statement that others "believe that the business cycle has finally been tamed" (266). In support of this view he contends that his graphs show "that the American mixed economy has reduced recessions in the post-World War II period to brief and infrequent punctuations in the progress of sustained growth" (266). Or, alternatively, he points out that a statistical series such as personal income "did not decline in any recent recession. It rears its ugly head in the form of a *slowing down of the rate of growth* . . . as compared with its normal or long-term 'secular trend' " (253).

And although he concedes that it is "premature" to relegate the business cycle to the museum, "nevertheless," with the help of the neoclassical synthesis, "expansion periods tend to be longer and fuller than in the past: the periods of recession . . . tend to be less frequent and shorter. Perhaps only half the customary number of recessions will take place; and many of them will last scarcely a year. . . . And mixed economies like West Germany have gone two decades without a single recession. . ." (7th edition, p. 255.). But that was back in the mid-1960s, when it was fashionable to define recessions as a slower rate of growth rather than as an absolute drop of production.

But then came the recessions of the late 1960s and early 1970s—"the 27th full-fledged slump in U.S. business history" since 1854—and more sober talk was heard:

> Back in the mid-1960s, some economists and politicians in Washington declared that the U.S. economy had entered a "new era" in which the traditional business cycle of expansion-recession-expansion was dead. Henceforth, these optimists proclaimed, business activity would perpetually expand, under the deft "fine-tuning" of federal experts, without any nasty old recessions to spoil the fun. Events since 1969, of course, have made painfully clear that the business cycle remains very much alive.[1]

If instead of looking at statistical series such as personal income which, particularly in view of the recent high rates of inflation, are not likely to register absolute drops, we look at the various "synthetic" indices of (physical) industrial production, we find that absolute drops have indeed taken place. Thus a look at 1966-67 figures in West Germany show that industrial production fell from 117.4 in 1966 to 114.2 in 1967 (1963 = 100), with consumer-goods production dropping from 117.3 to 11.8. (IMF, *International Financial Statistics*, XXV/8 [August, 1972], 148.) Similarly, indices for the U.S. also show absolute declines. Thus according to the *Business Week* index (1967 = 100) industrial production peaked at 113.0 the week of October 11, 1969, reached bottom at 102.0 the week of November 14, 1970, and did not regain the previous peak until the week of May 20, 1972; after several more weeks of fluctuations, the index finally broke through the old mark toward the middle of July, 1972.[2] Thus, as the accompanying chart shows, it took almost three years for industrial production to take off from a previously attained level.[3] And looking at the chart comparing the development of industrial production during four post-World War II cycles, we see that the latest "recovery" has by far proved to be the most "stubborn."[4]

Was it hindsight or a slip of the pen when, in the 8th edition, S inverted his formulation and said that "expansion periods tend to be frequent and shorter" (p. 250)? In summary we can say that S has not given us a "survey of business-cycle history" (246) but rather a misinterpretation of useful statistical material on the current period. Ulti-

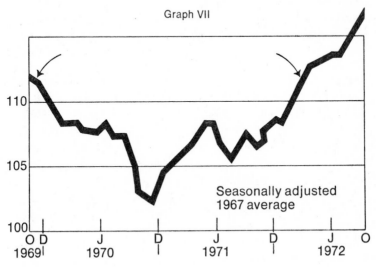

Graph VII

Seasonally adjusted
1967 average

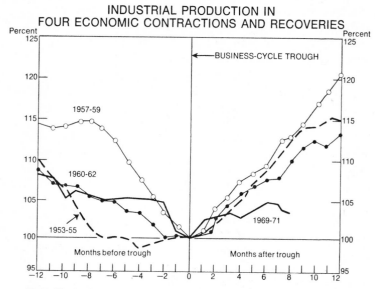

Graph VIII

INDUSTRIAL PRODUCTION IN
FOUR ECONOMIC CONTRACTIONS AND RECOVERIES

Note: The business-cycle troughs, as identified by the National Bureau of Economic Research, are August 1954, April 1958, February 1961, and November 1970 (tentative).

Source: Board of Governors of the Federal Reserve System.

mately S agrees that "the business cycle has been tamed" (267), although "changes in cold-war spending can have initially destabilizing effects upon general business activity" (266). "Tamed" for whose benefit? S gives the impression that it is "the electorate" or, in other words, the mass of the working people who have decided to ward off their own revolution by reducing unemployment. And in Chapter 41 S himself admits that although "there is nothing special about G spending on jet bombers, intercontinental missiles" etc., in point of fact that is what G is being spent on. Why? "It lies inside the realm of politics, not economics. An economically illiterate electorate may less reluctantly use the tools of the new economics for war than for peace purposes" (8th ed., p. 804).

On the one hand S admits that the fluctuations of the cycle have been reduced by military spending, while on the other he tries to take a critical stance against military spending as one of the few "destabilizing" factors still to be conquered. And most remarkable of all, he claims that "the electorate" has chosen to concentrate on warfare expenditures at the expense of schools, hospitals, housing, etc.

II / DESCRIPTION OF THE CYCLE

We now turn to S's general characterization of the cycle as opposed to the empirical presentation of the previous section and his attempt at theoretical explanation in the last section. For S it seems almost self-evident that "business conditions rarely stand still," that "prosperity may be followed by a panic or a crash." (249). But then he seems to change course, saying that "such . . . was the so-called 'business cycle' that used to characterize the industrialized nations of the world for the last century and a half at least—ever since an elaborate, interdependent *money economy* began to replace a relatively self-sufficient pre-commercial society" (249).

Thus rather than being a characteristic of economic activity per se, cyclical movements now appear to be peculiar to money economies. We know from the previous chapter that money played an important role in the controversy over Say's Law. How is it used here? The point S hints at is not new, it has been treated in detail by one of the founders of modern business-cycle resarch, Wesley C. Mitchell, who raises the issue in the context of a discussion of the disagreement in the first quarter of this century over the causes of cycles, namely whether they are related to capitalism or the money economy. Mitchell propounded the following view:

> The feature of modern economic organization which throws most light upon business cycles is that economic activities are now carried on mainly by making and spending money. This condition is characteristic of capitalism; but that term puts its stress upon other features of the present scheme of institutions—such as the ownership of the means of

production—features of primary importance in certain problems, and not to be neglected here, but features of less service in the effort to understand alternations of business prosperity and depression than the feature stressed by the term "money economy. . . ."

One reason why the connection between business cycles and pecuniary organization was long overlooked is that the difference between the use of money in communities which do not and in communities which do suffer from business cycles is a difference in degree, not a difference in kind. . . . Capitalism seemed to many men in the nineteenth century, men not versed in economic history, a new portent in economic life. They fastened upon it as an explanation of many phenomena which seemed to them equally new—commercial crises among others.[5]

This represents an objectively complex view. On the one hand it offers an unhistorical way of regarding the development of social relations, and on the other, there is "something" to the emphasis on money. But the contradictions inherent in the sphere of commodity and the sphere of circulation can resolve themselves in crises only in the presence of other concrete phenomena unique to capitalism. It is only under capitalism that commodities and money exist as dominant elementary forms of economic activity. But there is an important difference between Mitchell and S. S, when referring to a "money economy," is not interested in any essential distinctions between it and a "barter economy." For him, the key word is "interdependent," which in this context is supposed to mean that inherent in any complex economic society is the possibility of socially caused fluctuations. But Mitchell means something else when he speaks of a money economy:

Modern economic activity is immediately animated and guided, not by the quest of satisfactions, but by the quest of profits. Therefore business cycles are distinctly phenomena of a *pecuniary as opposed to* an *industrial* character.[6]

By emphasizing the value aspect of money in its concrete social form ("profits"), Mitchell in effect attacks the thesis of interdependence and indicates that cycles are specific to one society alone—capitalism.

S seeks to strengthen the impression that we are dealing with a technological phenomenon of "modern industrial society" by subordinating the cycle to the "trend line" both empirically and methodologically. We know that he views the "tamed" cycle as a temporary interruption of the normal upward trend of economic activity; now we are told that the trend line is the basis for grasping the cycle: "If we draw a smooth trend line or curve . . . through the strongly growing components of GNP, we discover the business cycle in the twistings of the data above and below the trend line" (253). This approach unfortunately confuses the real—namely the contradictory process of the self-expansion of capital—with the fictional average or "normal" rate of growth. Joseph Schumpeter, in his monumental study of cycles, comes close to this insight when he remarks that the trend

> carries realistic meaning only in discrete points or intervals. If we connect them by straight lines or fit a smooth curve to them, it must be borne in mind that the stretches between the neighborhoods are nothing but a visual help and devoid of realistic meaning without facts corresponding to them. Real is only the cycle itself.[7]

S continues along the lines of stressing the "modern industrial" nature of cycles by criticizing certain nameless "early writers" who, "possessing little quantitative information, tended to attach disproportionate attention to *panics* and *crises*" like those of 1720, 1837, 1873, 1893, 1904, and 1929 (253). This statement is both revealing and confusing. First of all, by joining such different crises as those of 1720 and 1929, S not only falls into his wonted ahistorical approach to modes of production, but also makes it obvious that in a substantive context he does not or cannot take his own thesis about the connection between cycles and "the money economy" seriously.

The rational kernel of the "money economy" thesis lies in the fact that once a sphere of commodity and money circulation has established itself, and in particular once the function of money as means of payment and its derivative concrete expression in credit relations have developed, crises become possible. Thus the crises of the eighteenth century, though generally touched off by political events, were examples of such monetary, credit, and speculative crises. But we must draw a distinction between these crises and those of the nineteenth and twentieth centuries, which, though at times seemingly speculative, were periodic industrial crises, at other times had the surface appearance of speculative crises. Secondly, by his loaded reference to "panics and crises," S prejudices the examination of the phases of the cycle. Perhaps the most striking aspect of his description is its undifferentiated approach to the phases: they just seem to keep going from one phase to the next with no laws governing their overall direction. The phases have even been given innocuous-sounding names (expansion, peak, recession, trough) that tend to conceal the social upheavals that mark both the cycle and the intervals between cycles.

This approach deters an understanding of the objective function of the cyclical development as a whole and of each of the phases. According to S, "no two business cycles are quite the same. Yet they have much in common" (249). True, but what is it that they do have in common other than minor deviations from the trend? In the past, bourgeois economists were less reluctant to examine the aggregate economic function of cycles. Thus Hubert D. Henderson, in a book written in the 1920s, and cited by S himself in another context (389 n. 8),[8] implied that "fluctuations" were neither simple deviations from a norm nor rectifiable deficiencies, but that the cycle was an inherent part of capitalist production through which certain fundamental forces had to express themselves. Once we understand why these forces express themselves in this way we can see that the emphasis on the cycles themselves as an almost timeless succession of qualitatively similar processes hides the fact that "the new cycle is not a mere repetition of the previous one: Every cycle is at the same time a stage in the history of capitalism which drives it a bit closer to its end."[9]

Similarly we must understand that although "each phase requires special explanatory principles" (253—which S never gets around to), their relative value within the cycle itself is determined by the objective function of the cycle as a whole within capitalist production. As we have pointed out, the function of crisis is to destroy enough capital to reduce the amount which has to be self-expanded; to create enough unemployment so that wages can be reduced; to cause enough bankruptcies, and hence centralization, and hence increased competition, so that productivity can be increased: in short, to act on the factors affecting the rate and mass of surplus value so as to restore conditions of profitability. But every new upswing, every new wave of accumulation, brings with it an increase in the organic composition of capital, and the reproduction of the contradictory forces leading to the cyclical fall in the rate of profit.

S might say that some of this reasoning did perhaps have relevance in Marx's time, and also that it is precisely the realization in practice of the "new economics" that has brought forth a new reality, and hence the need for a new theory or theories. Yet there is vague acknowledgment on the part of S of the continued existence of the fundamental forces when he says that "today it is recognized that not every period of improving business need take us all the way to full employment and true prosperity" (253). This serves as a further illustration of a phenomenon which we have touched on repeatedly, namely, that the apparent Keynesian successes are usually the result of a shift in the form of appearance of a basic capitalist contradiction either temporally onto another national capital, or onto another economic area. In this case, the state's ability to shorten the depression or stagnation phase of the cycle was made possible by curtailing the capital destruction and unemployment brought on by the crisis phase; but by preventing these self-healing forces from working themselves out, so that the conditions of profitability can be restored, state intervention simultaneously works against the traditionally "explosive" boom.

The last aspect of the cycle touched on by S, which he calls "a first clue to business fluctuations: capital formation" (255), will bring us to the next section on business-cycle theories. From the outset confusion reigns here, since S groups so-called consumer-durables (cars, washing machines, etc.) and capitalist "investment goods" (Marx's Department I—means of production), thus making it impossible to differentiate between the effects of the cycle on the reproduction of capital with respect to means of production and means of consumption.

The causes of cyclical development cannot be understood without taking into account the differential effect of the purchase of a residential house or an automobile and that of a new steel mill. The acquisition of new means of production (as well as of new labor power) represents part of the process of capital accumulation, and its development lies at the root of the intensity of upswings and crises. Consumer-durables purchases—especially since they tend to be bought on credit—can help in the realization of surplus value and extend a boom (even if only seemingly), but they are in no sense the basic factor.

S's confusion and/or identification of the two stems from the Keynesian circulation-sphere approach stressing spending regardless of its socioeconomic function. But even where S does single out capital investment in the stricter bourgeois sense of the term, he does so from a technological point of view; that is to say, he points to the fundamental *material* role of pig iron, etc., in the production process (255). This is an important factor and part of the rational kernel of the "accelerator" theory. But the one-sided emphasis of the technological aspect deprives the theory of a comprehensive grasp of the social entity represented by capital, and ultimately prevents it from contributing to the explanation of cycles.

S's attempt to account for the fluctuations in the demand for "durable goods" (which he equates with the "capital-goods sector of the economy") demonstrates how technological theories degenerate into ideology:

> By their nature, durable goods are subject to violently erratic patterns of demand. In bad times their new purchase can be indefinitely postponed; in a good year, everyone may suddenly decide to stock up on a 10-year supply of the services of durable goods at the same time [253].

Now there is nothing inherent in the means of production (or at least S has failed to prove the contrary) to make demand for them more erratic than demand for means of consumption. But then of course S is not really talking about what is inherent but about "good" and "bad" times; this becomes clear when we read the small print, which informs us that "profit fluctuations coincide with investment fluctuations" (255). But then this means that cycles are not only bound up with the "money economy," but more specifically with an economy which produces for profit and stops producing when profit is not forthcoming. But S has failed to specify these factors, and as a result, his theory is bound to suffer.

III / THEORIES

The practice of bourgeois economics to fasten on superficial observable and measurable phenomena has led to the postulating of a number of causes of cycles, and hence to a number of theories. This kind of "theoretical pluralism" finds expression in S's emphasis on "investment" and in his eclectic approach. Without a comprehensive theory of capitalist production as a whole, a modern economist has no other alternative but to point out the variety of forms in which cycles appear and to lend plausibility to theories which try to make sense of such seemingly disparate phenomena.

The distinction S draws between so-called internal and external theories has validity for the history of economic theory. The question arises, however, whether a different interpretation of S's distinction might not lead to other conclusions. For the time being we can accept his description of internal theories as discovering (self-generating) cycles, because in its generality it can apply to a Marxist theory of crises as an aspect of the self-reproducing contradictions of capitalist production. It is the so-called external factors such as technology and population which we must look at more critically. On the one hand, these factors are not external insofar as the development of capitalism brings forth both the specific technological advances (e.g., "labor-saving" machines) and the conditions which allow or inhibit the use of such innovations. Similarly, it is not changes in population as such, but rather the constraints which capitalist production forces on population growth that is the relevant factor in explaining economic development. In part S acknowledges these considerations when he speaks of technological inventions as acting "on business through net investment" or "the economic system . . . feed[ing] back on the so-called 'external factors' " (257); but he reverts to his empirical, untheoretical approach when he refers to investment "fluctuations" as "capricious and volatile" in their dependency on technology and population (259).

On the other hand, to the extent that these factors do have relative autonomy, they may modify the length or intensify a phase of a cycle, but they cannot form the foundation of the cyclical movements of capitalist production, they cannot be the cause of the cycles. We can illustrate this in the following way: in conjunction with so-called Kuznets cycles, S mentions labor supply and supply of other resources as important factors (8th ed., p. 239). Cyclical movements are characterized by sudden spurts of expansion and contradiction; this means that sudden expansions are possible only if a sufficiently large reserve army of unemployed is readily available. If the cycle were dependent on the natural growth of the population (or of the labor force), then it would not start in the first place, because the new upswing would have to wait for a generation of workers to grow up. But capitalism provides for itself in this respect by its reserve army of unemployed and its methods for increasing the production of relative surplus value and absolute surplus value, proof enough that cycles have their origin in a specific societal organization of production and not in nature or technology.

Let us now look at S's critique of Marx's theory of the "business" cycle (incidentally, the 8th edition is the first to say specifically that it is directed against Marx), offered in the context of a discussion of "some simple examples of possible, crude internal theories" (257). It is ironic that the crudeness attributed to Marx in fact inheres in S's explanation of cycles.

S has succumbed to a basic error, namely he has confused the cause of crises with the cause of their periodicity. In Marx's view, the turnover of the fixed capital is not the cause of the crisis but merely explains why the contradictions underlying the crises find their "solution" in crises marked by a certain regularity or periodicity. According to S, Marx and some bourgeois economists reason as follows: *If* all durables had the same lifespan, the business cycle would be explained by the bunching of new purchases at one time (upswing) and stagnation of business activity until the durable goods wore out (depression). But, S interjects, neither equipment bought at the same time nor identical cars produced at the same time will be replaced at the same time (257 f.). This is the sum total of S's critique. His revealing statement "never mind how" the boom gets started, prejudices the analysis from the outset, because Marx explains how it gets started, just as he explains that the crisis must also get started, on the basis of social features peculiar to capitalist production.

Marx does not reduce cycles to any sort of alleged production conditions of modern industry; he merely points to the increasing proportion of total social capital bound up in fixed capital as the "material foundation of periodic crises."[10] The fixed capital (not to be confused with constant capital, which is a category of the sphere of production), comprising basically the machinery and buildings of capitalist enterprises, unlike the circulating capital (raw materials plus variable capital), is not used up all at once; that is to say, it enters into the process of production and remains there as use value, while its exchange value is gradually transferred to the new commodities produced by these machines and in these buildings. With the wearing-out of the machine, the whole value of the original machines is transferred to the new commodities produced, the value is realized in the price of the products sold, and a new machine can be bought. At this point, Marx says, the fixed capital—(so called because only the value of the machine circulates, whereas the use values themselves are fixed in the sphere of production) has turned over. While the fixed capital may turn over once very five to ten years (a building may be amortized over fifty years), the circulating capital may turn over several times a year. Now S objects that not all durables wear out simultaneously. First of all, "consumer" automobiles are not capital (although trucks, etc., used by capitalist enterprises are), and hence of no interest here. Secondly, the wearing-out of capital equipment is only in part due to "natural" wear and tear; in large part the replacement of machinery is forced upon capitalists by competition; if their competitors have more efficient machines, then older machines will have to be junked before they have worn out. S himself concedes this when he says that "in a good year, everyone may suddenly decide to stock up on a 10-year supply of durable goods at the same time" (255). And finally, it is not at all necessary that all equipment wear out or be replaced at the same time. It is enough that the fixed capital in crucial branches (such as machine tools for heavy industry, or even pig iron, to use S's example) have approximately the same turnover period in order to impose cyclical form on a whole industry and the entire national capital. As we have seen, the need for "rationalization" of production following the crisis phase to keep from going under or to capture the largest possible share of the extra profits assures a certain uniformity in the renewal of fixed capital.

THE "ACCELERATION PRINCIPLE"

This brings us to the central theoretical point of this chapter. Since this section offers the only systematic explanation of cycles, one can only marvel at S's suggestion to instructors that "the material on the accelerator can be soft-pedaled."[11] But then one becomes a little less perplexed when one learns that S also believes that the entire chapter "could be skipped."[12] But regardless of the peripheral significance S attaches to cycles and their theoretical investigation, let us analyze the accelerator. Various bourgeois economists have raised objections to the accelerator principle largely on empirical or methodological grounds. S cannot be ignorant of them, since he has done some of the leading work in the field. Yet some of them are serious enough to merit mention by S, at least in the form of his customary "modifying" or "qualifying" factors, which in effect wind up undermining the theories they relate to; S's failure to do so is a serious omission.

In a widely used macroeconomics text, Barry N. Siegel summarizes some of the commonly criticized weaknesses of the accelerator:

A word of warning is appropriate here. The acceleration principle, even though it has explanatory value in the field of business-cycle analysis, is as yet an unconfirmed hypothesis, despite some fairly elaborate attempts to demonstrate its validity. That it has not been confirmed should not be surprising. The mechanical model . . . contains a number of assumptions which, if not realized in fact, will seriously impair the precision with which the acceleration effect works. First, the model assumed that businessmen were working with plant and equipment which were fully utilized before the process began. This assumption will rarely be realized in fact, especially for the economy as a whole. A further assumption was that each increase in demand for finished goods is regarded as permanent by entrepreneurs. Businessmen may prefer to press their equipment at an overcapacity rate of use until they are sure that the increase in demand is permanent enough to justify additional capital facilities. . . . A final assumption was that the technical capital-output relation was constant, that the new equipment designed to provide additional productive capacity, as well as to replace the depreciated facilities, was the same as the old. Actually, many businessmen use different and technologically superior equipment in their expansions and replacements.[13]

One of the studies referred to by Siegel, which attempt to verify the accelerator empirically, concluded "that the acceleration principle cannot help very much in the explanation of the details in real investment fluctuations, with the possible exception of railroad rolling stock."[14]

A more fundamental criticism, in particular of the accelerator-multiplier model, has been offered by Hegeland:

> When the multiplier principle can be meaningfully employed, as is the case just before a recovery is started, it will be completely meaningless to apply the acceleration principle since all industries can be expected to have excess capacity; whereas, on the other hand, when the use of the acceleration principle, in connection with the disappearance of excess capacity, may make sense, the multiplying effects of autonomous expenditure will be of a very limited reach.[15]

Hegeland proceeds to stress the superficial nature of these models:

> By combining the multiplier and acceleration principles neat models have been worked out that are subjected to regular variations, which numerically resemble the proportionate variations of some relevant magnitudes during the course of a business cycle. Such a model, however, reduces the business cycle problem to a mere question of disproportionate development of various quantities by concentrating on the indications only of changes, and refrains from any thorough analysis of the structural and qualitative processes below the surface of quantitative changes which actually determine the whole process.[16]

Common to most of the objections to the accelerator is the opinion that, whatever its defects, it nonetheless makes a contribution to business-cycle theory. We would say that despite some rational content, the accelerator in its present form contributes little to an understanding of the fundamental forces that regulate capitalist development.

First of all, the accelerator is largely based on technological considerations. It places primary emphasis on the fact that tooling up for increased demand takes so long that the backlog of unsatisfied demand results in an enormous increase in the production of means of production; the second "technological fact" refers to the lifetime of the means of production themselves: the longer their life, the longer the period over which they depreciate, the smaller the amount of yearly wear and tear that has to be replaced. (Interestingly enough, S's illustration [261] shows only simple reproduction; there is no capital accumulation at the initial point of departure.) The smaller the yearly replacement investment, the larger the fluctuations of gross investment brought about by the new investment needed to supply the producers of means of consumption—and vice versa in a downswing.

The irony here of course lies in the fact that this is more or less the "crude" internal theory falsely attributed to Marx. The emphasis on technology conceals great ideological advantages, by claiming that cycles and crises are rooted in "our modern industrial society." In a very distorted manner the accelerator reflects the fact that a given rate of growth of production of means of consumption (Department II) requires a higher rate of growth of the production of means of production (Department I); for "the *rapidity* of economic growth is determined by the margin by which the output of Department I exceeds the replacement requirements for the means of production of Departments I and II."[17]

Since capitalism expresses the growing productivity of labor through the more rapid growth of constant capital as against variable capital and surplus value, the only way in which the variable capital and surplus value in Department I can overtake the constant capital in Department II (the precondition for expanded reproduction) is for Department I to expand more rapidly than Department II.[18]

The ideological fruit of the accelerator once again is the projection of consumption as the driving force behind production in capitalism. The accelerator makes things easy for itself by starting us off in the middle of the process: we see extra demand in action. But where did the additional demand come from? If it merely represents a shift in demand from one commodity to another, then we cannot expect an increase in total production. If it represents an increase in total demand, then one would have to determine why the previous "round" of production resulted in such an increase of solvent demand. The solution to this would become difficult in S's model since he presupposes simple reproduction. Why the capitalists should suddenly use part of their revenue for, or rather transform it into, capital accumulation, remains unclear. What the accelerator reflects—and here we come to the second of the rational kernels—are the different conditions for realization in the departments of production devoted to means of production and consumption. The realization of the value embodied in the means of consumption is dependent by and large on wages (plus capitalist personal consumption revenue); realization of the commodities produced by producers of means of production depends on demand from within this Department I and from the producers of means of consumption. The latter will require more means of production only when demand exceeds their present output facilities; in large part, then Department I producers are dependent on prior expansion of Department II. Thus the "volatile fluctuations" of Department I are not so much due to the technological longevity of the machinery as to the understandable social fact that capitalists are loath to produce "ahead of the market."

The basic difficulty in the accelerator model seems to be that demand for means of consumption does not rise at a constant rate, with resultant fluctuations in Department I. But rather than being some kind of technical problem, this relation reveals the ultimate connection of the production of means of production to the "buying power" of the mass of the population—the working class. The accelerator theory merely accepts as given the contradiction between the limited purchasing power of the working class and the unlimited development of productive capacities. Although it can make some quantitative statements about this contradiction in the form of the disproportionalities between Departments I and II, it literally does not know what it is saying, and by shifting attention to technical and technological considerations, it actually buries the explanation of social contradictions under ideology.

Bourgeois economics attempts to transform the contradictions of capitalist production into external limitations of scarcity. S claims that the "law" of the accelerator decrees that "society's needed stock of capital . . . depends primarily upon the level of income or production. . . . *Net* investment, will take place only when income is growing" (260). The word "or" in the first sentence makes for ambiguity: if we are talking about production in the abstract, then obviously there is some relevance to establishing what Marx calls the technical composition of capital—that is, the relation of machines to workers needed to produce some given mass of use values. But when S talks about "income," he is becoming involved in a value category that conceals class contradictions—namely, that between wages and surplus value. If for some reason income were to grow as a result of wages rising more than profits fall, it is unlikely that investment would increase. On the other hand, if income rose because profits rose faster than wages fell, then investment would be sure to increase, but the bottom would soon drop out of the market because the flagging mass consumption power would make itself felt.

Or again, S explains a "downturn" by asking how can "a system grow forever at 6 or 7 per cent if its labor force grows only at 1 or 2 per cent and workers' productivity grows only at 2 or 3 per cent?" (262). If it were really a matter of such use-value considerations, then cyclical crises would be common to every "industrial" economy; yet S himself has admitted that socialist countries need not fear business cycles.[19] In any case, S's presentation does not deal with the specific crises of *capital* accumulation which cannot be explained on the basis of use-value "bottlenecks."

In the final analysis, the only solution to the problems revealed by the accelerator is comprehensive planning, but if bourgeois economists wait for capitalism to develop such planning on the basis of the neoclassical synthesis, they will wait in vain.

Notes and References

PREFACE

1. In an article entitled "Econ. 101: An Increase in 'Relevance' Demand Causes Rise in Supply" *The Wall Street Journal* outlined this development:

> Student impatience and boredom with standard macro-economics. . .have encouraged new course content. "The student is a restive fellow today," says Mr. Samuelson. . ."He's uptight with the environment and the war."
>
> To accomodate the trend. . .Mr. Samuelson of MIT has put new sections on the economic aspects of pollution, racial discrimination and the military-industrial complex in the eighth edition. (22 March 1971 1:4; cf. "Leader of Economic Mainstream. Paul Anthony Samuelson," in *New York Times*, 27 October 1970.)

2. As *Business Week,* published by the same corporation (McGraw-Hill) which publishes S's textbook, remarked with respect to "the ninth edition, a lavishly diagrammed, 42- [sic] chapter, four-color production selling for $11.50" which "is now the central feature of a marketing package that includes a study guide, programmed text, outside readings, instructor's manual, test bank, and transparency masters":

> The extra effort is becoming a necessity in an increasingly competitive market, "Samuelson's dominance won't continue indefinitely," says Charles R. Wade, marketing manager for McGraw-Hill's business and economics texts. "How long he can keep his book high on the charts depends upon how well he keeps up with the needs of the field." ("Samuelson's text never grows old," 24 March 1973, pp. 58 f.)

S. himself, on the other hand, with "annual royalties well into six figures" (ibid.), can afford to neglect profit considerations and claim that all that "effort" has no other function than to satisfy the consumer:

> Publishing has its economics and the fact that so many use this text permits an up-to-dateness that is invaluable in a subject like economics. . . . McGraw-Hill has cooperated magnificently in producing a book whose print, color diagrams, and layout have been designed with the *sole purpose of aiding in mastery of the economics subject matter.* (5th ed. 1961, p. vi.)

In reality, of course, the economics of publishing encompasses another aspect—it is a sphere of investment which, for instance, in 1971 offered a 10.7 percent rate of profit on stockholders' equity (*Statistical Abstract of the United States: 1972*, p. 483); in 1970 the value of shipments of the printing and publishing industry amounted to more than $25 billion (ibid., p. 711); and in 1967 the four largest book publishers accounted for one-fifth of total industry shipments by value (ibid., p. 705). McGraw-Hill itself was the 292nd largest industrial corporation in the U.S. in 1972 with sales of about $430 million and profits of approximately $22.5 million. (*Fortune*, LXXXVII/5 May, 1973, p. 232) and although it is considerably larger—in part because it is "diversified"—than its major competitors in the traditional economics textbook field such as Prentice-Hall (1971: net income of $16.5 million on sales of about $134 million [*Moody's Industrial Manual* 1972 (N.Y., 1972) II, 2859]) and Harper & Row (1971: profits of $1.7 million on sales of $59 million [ibid., I, 71f.]), it too must contend with RCA, the 19th largest industrial corporation in 1972 with sales of almost $4 billion (*Fortune*, op. cit., p. 222), which has acquired the far-flung publishing empire of Random House.

These data serve merely to indicate that in this industrial branch as in all others, nothing is produced which does not represent a potential profit to the capitalist producers.

3. We have no further interest in these various "put-up jobs." Our concern in this connection is with numerous attempts by individuals and groups, understanding themselves explicitly as left-wing or socialist in political intent, to present an attack on "orthodox" economics. As a result of the student-movement and professional-economist origins of most of these authors, their work has been characterized, despite their forthright opposition to U.S. capitalism, by a certain adherence to bourgeois theories and uncritical political-economic views of students, the working class, imperialism, the Soviet Union and other phenomena. (Perhaps the most significant effort in this direction to date is E. K. Hunt and Howard J. Sherman, *Economics: an Introduction to traditional and radical views* (N.Y., 1972). This book is meant not so much as a critique of the standard economics texts as a replacement; this has its good marketing grounds, for unless it "covers the same material" as S it cannot gain Harper and Row, the publisher, entry into "the lucrative book market in economic principles courses." (The authors of the present book are aware of this strategy from personal dealings with Prentice-Hall.) Partly as a result of this constriction, but no doubt also partly as a result of the theoretical convictions of the authors, this arrangement leads to a degradation of the notion of critique, for the book is so constructed that the teachers using it are offered a take-it-or-leave-it proposition with respect to the radical critique of capitalism and of "traditional" economics. (See, for example, Hunt and Sherman, *Instructor's Manual to Accompany*. . .[N.Y., 1972], p. 45).

Despite these limitations, we regard the rise of intellectual endeavors in opposition to capitalism—endeavors manifested, for example, in the activities of the Union for Radical Political economics—as a significant phenomenon indicative of profound changes in society which have begun to surface. As Engels noted almost a century ago:

> The wakening insight that the existing societal arrangements are irrational and unjust, that reason has become nonsense and benefit torment, is only an indication of the fact that silently in the methods of production and forms of exchange changes have taken place with which the social order which was tailored to earlier economic conditions no longer agrees. This also means that the means for the elimination of the abuses which have been discovered must similarly be present—more or less developed—in the changed relations of production themselves. These means are not say to be *invented* out of the head, but are rather to be discovered by means of the head in the material facts of production in question. (*Anti-Dühring*, Section 3, part II; German ed., *Marx-Engels Werke* [MEW], XX, 249.)

4. A noteworthy attempt to come to grips with such a problem was undertaken by Bertolt Brecht in some notes made toward the end of the 1920s; although specifically written with regard to intellectuals in Germany at the time, they have a certain wider relevance which merits examination:

> The legitimate distrust of the proletariat brings the intellectuals into their difficult position. They often undertake the attempt to coalesce with the proletariat, and precisely this proves not that there are different intellectuals, two sorts of intellectuals, such who are proletarian and such who are bourgeois, but rather that there is only one sort of them, for did they not in the past always try to coalesce with the ruling class? Was this not the reason why the intellect assumed its commodity character?

> If the intellectuals want to take part in the class struggle, then it is necessary to grasp intellectually their sociological constitution as a unified one and one determined by material conditions.

Their view which has often come to light, namely it is necessary to go under in the proletariat, is counterrevolutionary. . . . The real revolutions are not (as in bourgeois historiography) produced by feelings, but rather by interests.

The interest of the proletariat in the class struggle is clear and unambiguous, the interest of intellectuals, which is historically established, is harder to explain. The only explanation is that the intellectuals can hope for an unfolding of their (intellectual) activity only through the revolution. Their role in the revolution is determined by this: It is an intellectual role.

Revolutionary intellect distinguishes itself from reactionary intellect by being a dynamic, politically speaking, a liquidating intellect. ("Schwierige Lage der deutschen Intellektuellen," in Bertolt Brecht, *Schriften zur Politik und Gesellschaft, Gesammelte Werke,* XX [Frankfurt, 1967], 52 f.)

CHAPTER 2

1. See Marx, *Capital,* I, Ch. 3, Sect. 3a. (New York: International Publishers, 1970.). All references in English to *Capital,* Vols. I-III, are to this edition. German ed., *MEW,* XXIII, 147.

2. It is crucial to realize that the thrust of S's argumentation unreflectingly presupposes that this reproduction, that is, presupposes that "every economy must somehow solve the three fundamental economic problems." (38) In other words, the possibility that the "problems" will not be solved is not even included for consideration. This means that no explanation is offered for why certain societies (or whole modes of production) fail to "solve" the "problems" and what the consequences of this failure are. Just as the rise of no "economic society" is even described, so too the possible decline and/or overthrow of one is avoided. This aspect does not belong to economic theory, but rather to the branch of economics called economic history which only specialists are concerned with—so the methodology of bourgeois economics. When the occasion arises to mention such historical transformations—see for instance the discussion of U.S. slavery in ch. 39—recourse is had to technology and other "external" factors. No analysis of the societal changes taking place is offered. Although such a procedure might be considered unfortunate but at only peripheral interest since the decline of slavery or feudalism is "ancient

history" and thus has no bearing on modern economic analysis, it is precisely here that this approach becomes most pernicious; for S's analysis does not allow for the possibility that capitalism will not "solve" the "problems." But more important here is that S, by limiting his criteria for the problem and the solution almost exclusively to technological considerations, in effect declares the eternal nature of capitalism since the successor economy is not defined by social relations—or, alternatively, the end of history altogether is implied since man would have become incapable of dealing with the material reproduction of human society.

3. (Letter of 11 July 1868, in *MEW*, XXXII, 552f.)
4. Ibid.
5. Ibid., p. 554.
6. *Principles of Economics* (8th ed.; London, 1969), p. 129 n. 2.
7. *Capital*, I, Ch. 7, Sect. 1; German ed., pp. 194 f.
8. See the motto to Ch. 5 below with a passage from Samuelson's "Foreword" to Riva Poor (ed.), *4 Days 50 Hours* (Cambridge, 1970), p. 8.
9. Marx, "Introduction" to *Grundrisse* (Harmondsworth, 1973). p. 17.
10. *Statistical Abstract of the United States,* 1972, pp. 803-05.
11. It is of some ideological interest that in the just-cited footnote the 9th edition no longer includes S's gratuitous reference to "giv[ing] the country back to the Indians; similarly in the 8th edition the reference to "Southern hillbilly" was changed to "white people in Appalachia."
12. *The Common Sense of Political Economy* (London, 1910), p. 212.
13. John Strachey, *The Coming Struggle For Power* (New York, 1935), p. 52. Strachey was a British Revisionist.
14. See Marx, "Introduction" to *Grundrisse, Capital,* III, Ch. 51; German ed., p. 886.
15. *Capital,* I, Ch. 24; German ed., p. 742. For data on the proletarianization of the work force in the major Western capitalist countries in the post-World War II period see Edward F. Denison, *Why Growth Rates Differ* (Washington, D.C., 1967), pp. 46-50. We will present more detailed statistics on these trends in various places in the book.
16. *Capital,* I, Ch. 4; German ed., p. 189.
17. Of course S prejudices the matter by speaking of "revolutions' with respect to these factors and the changes called forth by the response of the economic system to them. Changes of this

kind are in fact associated with an unplanned mode of production. It must be noted that it is in fact claimed that any "rational" economic activity will be guided by the same principles which underlie the price system; furthermore, although this is not always clearly distinguished in S, other authors, working with a conception of supply and demand superordinate to prices, do very openly claim universality: "The profound adjustments of supply and demand will work themselves out and work themselves out again for so long as the lot of man is darkened by the course of Adam." H.D. Henderson, *Supply and Demand* (New York, 1922), p. 17.

18. *Grundrisse*, p. 74.
19. *Capital*, I, Ch. 17; German ed., p. 562.
20. *Capital*, I, Ch. 5; German ed., p. 194.
21. See *Capital*, I, Ch. 15, Sect. 2; German ed., Ch. 13, p. 414.
22. See Aristotle, *Nicomachean Ethics*, Book V, Ch. 5.
23. *Theories of Surplus Value*, III, Ch. 21, Sect. 3b; German ed., MEW, XXVI:3, 264 f.
24. *Capital*, I, Ch. 14, Sect. 5; German ed., Ch. 12, p. 386.
25. Article "Arbeit, Arbeiter," in *Handwörterbuch der Staatswissenschaften*, I (2nd ed.; Jena, 1898), p. 456.
26. Cf. *Contribution to the Critique of Political Economy*, Ch. I; German ed., *Zur Kritik der Politischen Okonomie*, MEW, XIII, p. 16.)
27. J.W. Galbraith, *The New Industrial State* (N.Y., 1968), chs. 18-20; in more popular format this thesis was presented in the bestseller by Vance Packard *The Hidden Persuaders* and has since been given wide coverage in all the media including a recent prime time one hour report on network TV advertising. A brief essay at applying a Galbraith-type critique to many of the "ideological" notions of neo-classical economics as presented in S' textbook was recently published by the Austrian bourgeois economist Friedrich Romig, *Die ideologischen Elemente in der neo-klassischen Theorie: Eine kritische Auseinandersetzung mit Paul A. Samuelson* (West Berlin, 1971).
28. Alexander Balinsky, "Problems and Issues in Soviet Economic Reform," in Balinky et al. (eds.) *Planning and the Market in the U.S.S.R.: The 1960's* (New Brunswick, 1967), p. 31.
29. Ibid., pp. 31f.
30. Ibid., p. 32.
31. Ibid., pp. 34 f.
32. Ibid., p. 35.
33. Joseph McKenna, *The Logic of Price* (Hinsdale, 1973), p. 285.
34. *Grundrisse*, p. 15.

35. Ibid., p. 7.
36. Ibid., p. 13.
37. Ibid., p. 15.
38. A. Allan Bates, "Low Cost Housing in the Soviet Union," in U.S. Congress, Joint Economic Committee, Subcommittee on Urban Affairs, *Industrialized Housing,* 91st Cong., 1st Sess. (Washington, D.C., 1969), p. 4.
39. "An appraisal of the Availability of Funds for Housing Needs 1969-78," in *The Report of the President's Committee on Urban Housing, Technical Studies* (Washington, D.C., 1968), II, 213.
40. "A Study of Comparative Time and Cost for Building Five Selected Types of Low-Cost Housing," in ibid., II, 9.
41. Paul A. Samuelson et al., *Instructor's Manual to Accompany Samuelson: Economics* (6th ed.; New York, 1964), p. 10.
42. *Capital,* III, Ch. 10; German ed., pp. 184, 204 f.
43. *Capital,* III, Ch. 10; German ed., p. 206.
44. Samuelson et al., *Instructor's Manual. . .,* p. 10.

CHAPTER 3

1. Marx, *Capital,* I; German ed., *MEW,* pp. 185 f.
2. Ibid., p. 647.
3. See R. Lampmann, *The Share of Top Wealth-Holders in National Wealth 1922-1956* (New York, 1962); For the United Kingdom: A. B. Atkinson, *Unequal Shares: Wealth in Britain* (Harmondsworth, 1974).
4. Source: Irwin Friend and Stanley Schor, "Who Saves?," in *Review of Economics and Statistics,* XLVI/2, Part 2 (May, 1959), p. 216.
5. Joseph Pechman and Benjamin Okner, "Simulation of the Carter Commission Tax Proposals for the United States," in *National Tax Journal,* XXII/1 (March, 1969), 21.
6. Methodologically it must be taken into consideration that the depression phase of the industrial cycle increases the relative share of the working class. Since on the whole the poor did not pay income taxes in the 1930s, S's figures are doubtless pre-tax. However, we can also compare them with the after-tax figures for 1966, in which case the lowest 10 percent of the population raises its share by a miniscule share to 1.36 percent, still lower than that for 1936.
7. See *Business Week,* April 1, 1972, pp. 56 f.
8. See for example T. Morgan, "Distribution of Income in Ceylon, Puerto Rico, United States and United Kingdom," *Economic*

Journal, LXIII/252 (Dec., 1953), esp. the Lorenz curve at p. 827; H. Oshima, "A Note on Income Distribution in Developed and Underdeveloped Countries," in Economic Journal, LXVI/266 (March, 1956), 156-60.

9. Taken from: G. Myrdal, Asian Drama, I (New York, 1968), 564.

10. Source: Bericht der Bundesregierung und Materialien zur Lage der Nation 1971. Ed. by the Federal Ministry for Inner German Relations, n.p., n.d., p. 138.

11. Der Spiegel, No. 24, June, 11 1973, p. 79.

12. Source: U.N. Economic Commission for Europe, Incomes in Postwar Europe (Geneva, 1967), Table 6.10.

13. The relation of the area above the Lorenz curve to the total area below the 45-degree line; O represents complete equality, 1 complete inequality. For those interested in the mathematical derivations of the Lorenz curve and Gini coefficient, see Joseph L. Gastwirth, "The Estimation of the Lorenz Curve and Gini Index," in Review of Economics and Statistics, LIV/3 (August, 1972), 306-16.

14. Schnitzer, The Economy of Sweden (New York, 1970), pp. 130 f.

15. This of course does not rule out the possibility that in certain professions, for instance medicine, which in the U.S. are still largely noncapitalist in nature, prices for "services rendered" may be paid on the basis of supply and demand and/or partial monopoly, and may vastly exceed education and other costs of reproduction, thus allowing for a large "profit."

16. In Journal of Political Economy, LXVI (April, 1958), 95-130 (here quoted according to the reprint in Conrad and Meyer, The Economics of Slavery and other studies in econometric history (Chicago, 1964).

17. The New Industrial State, (New York, 1967), p. 16. The highpoint of the nonsensical separation
J.K. Galbraith, The New Industrial State (New York, 1967), p. 16. The highpoint of the nonsensical separation of education and capital accumulation is S' suggestion all black servants and barbers could be re-educated to become (e.g.) French teachers at state universities. (8th ed., p. 783.) What irony that the government reports that unemployment rates among blacks are not affected by higher education. (Manpower Report of the President, Washington, D.C., 1971, p. 93).

18. David Cohen and Marvin Lazerson, "Education and the Corporate Order," in Socialist Revolution, II/3 May-June, 1971; cit. acc. reprint in The Capitalist System (Englewood Cliffs, 1972), pp. 185, 187.

19. Sources: *Statistical Abstract of the United States, 1967*, p. 116; *Statistical Abstract of the United States, 1972*, p. 111, *Manpower Report of the President*, Washington, D.C., 1972, p. 207. Or looked at from another point of view: from 1960 to 1970 craftsmen with four or more years of college as a percentage of all craftsmen rose from 2.1% to 2.2%; the figures for operatives are 0.6% and 0.8%; for laborers 0.6% and 1.2%. (Source: W. Deutermann, "Educational Attainment of Workers, March 1973," in *Monthly Labor Review*, [Jan. 1974], p. 60.)

20. *Manpower Report of the President*, Washington, D.C., March 1972, p. 115.

21. "The job gap for college graduates in the '70s," *Business Week* September 23, 1972, pp. 48, 49.

22. *Manpower Report of the President*, op. cit., p. 103.

23. *Business Week*, Sept. 23, 1972, p. 50

24 Fred M. Hechinger, "Suddenly Ph.D.'s are A Glut on the Market," Sunday *New York Times*, 4 Jan. 1970, sect. 4, p. 9. Similar fears were expressed about England after 12% of 1971's graduates remained unemployed. See "Die Gefahr eines Akademiker-Proletariats," in *Handelsblatt*, 14 March 1972, p. 7. See also, International Labor Office, *Some Growing Employment Problems in Europe*, Geneva, 1973, ch. 3; "Arbeitslose Raumfahrtspezialisten," in *Neue Zürcher Zeitung*, Dec. 2, 1973, pp. 5 f.; "Manche müssen auf der Strecke bleiben," in *Stuttgarter Zeitung*, Feb. 2, 1974, p. 2.

CHAPTER 4

1. K. Marx, *Capital*, V. II, Ch. 15.

2. R. Hilferding, *Das Finanzkapital* (Frankfurt, 1968 [1909]), pp. 107 f.

3. C. Wright Mills, *White Collar*, (New York, 1967), p. 102).

4 Ibid., p. 103. See here for instance the part a university "education" plays in forming this "utterly reliable committee for managing the affairs and pushing the common interests of the entire big-property class", p. 105.

5. Source: *Statistical Abstract of the United States*, 1969, p. 725.

6. *Capital*, III, Ch. 1, p. 34.

7. Most of the following was taken from Ottomar Kratsch, "Bürgerliche betriebswirtschaftliche Apologetik zu den aktuellen Abschreibungsproblemen in Westdeutschland," in *Probleme der Politischen Ökonomie*, V. III [Berlin (DDR), 1960], pp. 210-260.

CHAPTER 5

1. R. Lester, *Economics of Labor* (New York, 1941), pp. 4 f., 12 f.; our emphasis.
2. Paul A. Samuelson et al., *Instructor's Manual to Accompany Samuelson: Economics* (New York, 1964).
3. *MEW*, XXXIII, 332.
4. Ibid., p. 333.
5. William Haber, *Industrial Relations in the Building Industry* (Cambridge, 1930), pp. 198f. Our underlining. Since the construction industry is usually singled out for criticism in this area, we refer to a study which develops the hypothesis that on the whole unions increase productivity; see Allan B. Mandelstramm, "The Effects of Unions on Efficiency in the Residential Construction Industry: A Case Study," *Industrial and Labor Relations Review*, XVIII/4 (July, 1965), 503-21.
6. Thomas R. Brooks, "Job Satisfaction: An Elusive Goal," *The American Federationist*, LXXIX/10 (1972, October,) p. 5.

CHAPTER 6

1. Marx, *Zur Kritik der Hegelschen Rechtsphilosphie. Kritik des Hegelschen Staatsrechts*, in *Marx-Engels-Werke*, I, pp. 304 f.
2. J. K. Galbraith, *The Great Crash* (Boston, 1955), p. 171.
3. Arthur M. Schlesinger, *Political and Social History of the United States, 1829-1925* (New York, 1928), p. 360.
4. Ibid., p. 364.
5. Ibid., p. 366; this is a recurrent theme: cf. the statement by a tax lawyer on the effects of a 1962 law to close loopholes for siphoning profits overseas to avoid taxes: " 'Before 1962, we had a license to steal. The '62 law, by its sheer complexity, stopped some of that. But there hasn't really been much change—we just work harder to achieve the same thing.' " *Wall Street Journal*, Oct. 16, 1972, p. 26.
6. Schlesinger, op. cit., pp. 370 f.
7. Cf. *Statistical Abstract of the United States*, 1972, p. 278. Federal social welfare non-trust expenditures as a percentage of federal non-trust fund expenditures amounted to 30.2 percent in 1929 and 30.7 percent in 1972. See A. Skolnik and S. Dales, "Social Welfare Expenditures," *Social Security Bulletin*, XXVII/1 (Jan., 1974), p. 12.
8. M. Weidenbaum and D. Larkins, *The Federal Budget for 1973* (Washington, D.C., 1972), pp. 8, 24.

9. W. Müller and C. Neusüss, "Die Socialstaatsillusion und der Widerspruch von Lohnarbeit und Kapital," in *Sozialistische Politik*, No. 6-7 June, 1970, p. 9, n. 13.

10. For the 1950s: See U.N. Economic Commission for Europe, *Incomes in Postwar Europe* (Geneva, 1967), Table 6.1.

11. Andrew Shonfield, *Modern Capitalism* (London, 1969), pp. 265 f.

12. Sources: *Incomes in Postwar Europe*, op. cit., Table 6.1; Angus Maddison, *Economic Growth in the West* (New York, 1967), Table I-1; *Statistical Abstract*, 1967, 1967, p. 870.

13. *Capital*, I, Ch. 10, Sect. 7; German ed., p. 320. Cf.

14. Source: *Statistical Abstract of the United States*, 1972, p. 312. (Cf. below Ch. 12 for the intervening years.)

15. *Anti-Dühring*, Part III, Sect. 2; German ed., *MEW*, XX, 259 n.

16. Günter Zenk, *Konzentrationspolitik in Schweden*, Tübingen 1971, p. 139.

17 *Statistical Abstract*, 1972, pp. 278, 299. Now these latter categories are collected under the heading public assistance; in the requested budget authority for 1973, insurance and retirement payments amounted to ca. 5½ as much as public assistance expenditures. (Weidenbaum and Larkins, op. cit., p. 42.)

18 Source: U.S. Congress, Joint Economic Committee, Subcommittee on Fiscal Policy, *Studies in Public Welfare, Paper No. 2: Handbook on Income Transfer Programs*, 92nd Cong., 2nd Sess., 16, October 1972, p. 9. This volume presents a detailed overview of the entire welfare system. See also A. Skolnik and S. Dales, "Social Welfare Expenditures, 1972-73," in *Social Security Bulletin*, January, 1974. For the development of Federal payments from 1940 to 1973 see ibid., XXXVII/9 (Sept., 1974), Tables M-26 and M-27.

19. Charles Schultze et al., *Setting National Priorities: The 1973 Budget* (Washington, D.C., 1972).

20. First National City Bank, *Monthly Economic Letter*, August, 1972, p. 15.; see also Malcolm Cohen, "The Direct Effects of Federal Manpower Programs in Reducing Unemployment," *Journal of Human Resources*, IV/4 (Fall, 1969), 491-507; Sylvia Small, "Statistical effect of work-training programs on the unemployment rate," in *Monthly Labor Review*, XCV/9 (Sept., 1972), 7-13; see also a report on a criticism of the program by the capitalist National Urban Coalition which points out that "the program was not primarily used to help the 'chronically unemployed, difficult-to-place persons,' who have trouble competing in the labor market." *New York Times*, Oct. 22, 1972, p. 72, cols. 3-5.

21. *Statistical Abstract of the United States, 1972*, op. cit., p. 386; *New*

York Times, January 7, 1973. See Federal Reserve Bank of Chicago, Business Conditions, June, 1973, p. 7.

22. Pechman, Aaron and Taussig, Social Security (Washington, 1968), pp. 6 f.

23 Handbook on Income Transfer Programs, op. cit., p. 28. Certain improvements were made by recent legislation, but the trends remain unchanged.

24. Richard Edwards, "Who Fares Well in the Welfare State?" in Edwards, Reich and Weiskopf (eds.), The Capitalist System (Englewood Cliffs, 1972), p. 248.

25. Manpower Report of the President (Washington, D.C., 1968), p. 43.

26. Business Week, Sept. 16, 1972, p. 95; capital has already announced that any increases would not be at the expense of profit: the N.A.M. stated that "too much liberalization would be 'just another burden on consumers, just so much more inflation.' " Ibid. See also WSJ, July 31, 1972, p. 3, cols. 2-3. See F. Johnson, "Changes in workmen's compensation laws in 1973," in Monthly Labor Review, Jan., 1971, pp. 32-38.

27. "Das Arbeiterprogram" (Labor's Program), in Gesammelte Reden und Schriften, II, ed. E. Bernstein (Berlin, 1919), p. 181. This was written in 1862.

28. "Instructions for the Delegates of the Provisional General Council. The Different Questions," in Institute of Marxism-Leninsim of the C.C., C.P.S.U., The General Council of the First International 1864-1866 (Moscow, n.d. [ca. 1964]), p. 349.

29. Source: OECD, Revenue Statistics of OECD Member Countries, 1968-1970 (Paris, 1972), p. 27.

30. Incomes in Postwar Europe, op. cit., Ch. 6, p. 26; although the U.S. relies relatively less on indirect taxes than other countries, it does "compensate" for this by using ones called by this report "rather more marked" with respect to degree of regression than the other countries reported on. Ibid., p. 27.

31. Business Week, August 12, 1972, p. 83.

32. Source: Statistical Abstract, 1972, p. 412.

33. Joseph Pechman, Federal Tax Policy (Washington, D.C.: Brookings, 1971), p. 187.

34. Lundberg, The Rich and the Super-Rich, (New York, 1969), p. 388; see in general chs. 9 and 10 of Lundberg on the tax evasiveness of the capitalist class. Of interest is also Louis Eisenstein, The Ideologies of Taxation (New York, 1961), Cf. O'Connor, The Fiscal Crisis of the State (New York, 1973), Ch. 8.

35. Source: WSJ, 9 May 1972, p. 24, col. 5.

36. Ibid.
37. Ibid.
38. *Wall Street Journal* June 5, 1972, p. 25, cols. 4-5.
39. *Wall Street Journal* April 1, 1972, pp. 56 f. Cf. P. Henle, "Exploring the Distribution of Earned Income," in *Monthly Labor Review*, XCV/12 (Dec., 1972), 16-27.
40. Source: Woytinsky and Woytinsky, *World Population and Production*, NY 1953, p. 408, fig. 131.
41. Source: Joseph Pechman and Benjamin Okner, "Simulation of the Carter Commission Tax Proposals for the United States," in *National Tax Journal*, XXII/1 (March, 1969), 21.
42. *Incomes in Postwar Europe*, op. cit., Ch. 6, p. 17.
43. Ibid.; our emphasis.
44. Ibid., p. 41; our emphasis.
45. Ibid., Ch. 9, p. 26, Table 9.20; Ch. 6, p. 15, Table 6.10.
46. Ibid., Ch. 8, p. 41, Table 8.20; Ch. 6, p. 18, Table 6.11; cf. also Tables 9.19 and 6.13. "World Bank" statistics for Poland, Hungary and Czechoslovakia show that the income shares of the "lowest" 40 percent of the population are higher and those of the "highest" 20% are lower than those of any other countries. (S. Jain and A. Tiemann, *Size Distribution of Income: A Compilation of Data*, Development Research Center Discussion Paper No. 4, World Bank, Washington, D.C., 1973. Cited acc. to M. Ahluwalia, "Ungleichheit der Einkommen: Einige Dimensionen des Problems," in: *Finanzierung und Entwicklung*, XI/3 (Sept., 1974), p. 4.) That the socialist countries are characterized by the lowest degree of income distribution inequality did not surprise the researchers, since there is no income from capital in these countries. (Ibid., p. 3. The abovementioned article is taken from chapter 1 of Chenery et al., *Redistribution without Growth (Oxford, 1974), which was unfortunately not yet available at the time this manuscript was being prepared.)*

CHAPTER 7

1 Marx, *Capital*, II, Ch. 20, Sect. I, pp. 394 f.; German ed., pp. 393 f.
2. A. Smith *The Wealth of Nations*, Modern Library ed., p. 314; Book II, Ch. III.
3. Ibid., p. 315.
4. P. Samuelson et al., *Instructor's Manual to Accompany Samuelson: Economics* (6th ed.; New York, 1964), p. 34.

5.   A. Smith, op. cit., Book I, Ch. 6.

6.   Lionel Robbins, *An Essay on the Nature and Significance of Economic Science* (2nd. ed., revised and extended; London, 1940 [1930], p. 4).

7.   Ibid., p. 9.

8.   D. Ricardo, *The Principles of Political Economy and Taxation*, Everyman ed., op. cit., p. 1; for Lord Robbins' most recent views on Ricardo see his jejune article "The Bicentenary of David Ricardo," in *The Financial Times*, April 17, 1972, p. 27.

9.   John McCulloch, *The Principles of Political Economy* (5th ed.; Edinburgh, 1864 [reprinted, N.Y., 1965]), p. 1.

10.   Ibid., p. 504.

11.   Marshall considers "economics" a "better" description of the science than the "narrower term" political economy since economics "shuns many political issues, which the practical man cannot ignore." Alfred Marshall, *Principles of Economics* (London, 1969 [1920]), p. 36.

12.   Ibid., pp. 12f.

13.   A. Pigou, *The Economics of Welfare* (4th ed.; London, 1962 [1932], p. 10.

14.   Ibid., p. 31.

15.   Ibid.

16.   John Hicks, *Value and Capital* (2nd ed.; Oxford, 1965 [1946; lst ed.: 1939]), pp. 176-78.

17.   L. Robbins, op. cit., pp. 56f.)

18.   Ibid., pp. 15, 14.

19.   Ibid., p. 15.

20.   Samuelson et al., *Instructor's Manuel. . .*, op cit., p. 1.

21.   S. Kuznets, *National Income. A Summary of Findings* (New York, 1946), p. 114.

22.   Ibid., pp. 115, 114.

23.   Ibid., pp. 115 f.

24.   Kuznets, *National Income*, op. cit., p. 114.

25.   A. C. Pigou, *Income. An Introduction to Economics* (London, 1948), p. 15. Cf. John W. Kendrick, *Economic Accounts and Their Uses* (New York, 1972), p. 22, who reports that the U.S. Department of Commerce "regards people as the end, and not just a means of production. That is, no attempt is made to exclude expenditures for 'maintenance' of (or 'investment' in) human capital, since the daily living of people is taken as an end in itself."

26.   *Capital*, I, Ch. 8; German ed., Ch. 6, p. 214.

27.   Ibid., p. 221.

28. Ibid., Ch. 24, Sect. 4; German ed., pp. 633 f.
29. *Grundrisse,* op. cit., p. 17.
30. Cf. below, Ch. 16.
31. J. M. Keynes, *The General Theory of Employment, Interest and Money* (London, 1967 [1936]), p. 39.
32. Ibid., pp. 98 f.
33. Ibid., p. 104.
34. Ibid., p. 106.
35. See below, Ch. 16.
36. S. Kuznets, *National Income,* op. cit., p. 126; our emphasis.
37. S. Kuznets *National Product in Wartime* (New York, 1945), p. vii.
38. S. Kuznets, "On the Valuation of Social Income—Reflections on Professor Hicks' Articles," *Economica,* New Series, XV/57 (Feb., 1948), pp. 115-18.
39. Ibid., pp. 7 f.
40. Keynes, *The General Theory. . .,* op. cit., p. 220; cf. also ibid., p. 131.
41. Federal Reserve *Bulletin,* July, 1972, Table A70.

CHAPTER 8

1. J. Robinson, *Economic Philosophy* (Garden City, 1964), p. 77.
2. It must be stated here programmatically that we are not implying that unemployment is the essence of capitalist crisis. On the contrary, unemployment is a necessary and "healthy" aspect of the capitalist reproduction process. The emphasis on employment derives from an attempt to deal with the rise of Keynesianism in an immanent manner. Keynes' esoteric side, as it were, is the set of theories and programs of state intervention designed to improve the conditions of profitability. A contradiction arises, however, between the political necessity of avoiding mass unemployment and the economic necessities of capital accumulation which the state can in the last analysis not override. (Cf. C. Deutschmann, *Der linke Keynesianismus* [Frankfurt, 1973], pp. 208-10.)
3. J. M. Keynes, *General Theory of Employment, Interest and Money* (London, 1967 [1936]), p. 308.
4. Ellis W. Hawley, *The New Deal and the Problem of Monopoly* (Princeton, 1966), pp. 141 f.
5. Ibid., pp. 277-79.
6. Source: U.S. Congress, Joint Economic Committee, *1962 Supplement to Economic Indicators,* 87th Congress, 2nd Sess. (Washington, D.C., 1962), p. 117.

7. Ibid., pp. 22, 13.
8. Ibid., pp. 11, 13, 53, 22, 36.
9. J. K. Galbraith, *American Capitalism* (Boston, 1956), p. 65.
10. Rene Erbe, *Die nationalsozialistische Wirtschaftspolitik 1933-1939 im licht der modernen Theorie* (Zurich, 1958), p. 179.
11. Arthur Schweitzer, *Big Business in the Third Reich*, Indiana University Social Science Series No. 21 (Bloomington, 1964), p. 333.
12. Source: Charles Bettelheim, *L'economie allemande sous le nazisme*, (Paris, 1971 [1945]), II, 84; for similar statistics of industrial production for several other capitalist countries and for all capitalist countries taken together through 1933, see Eugen Varga, *Die grosse Krise und ihre politischen Folgen*, in E. Altvater (ed.), Eugen Varga, *Die Krise des Kapitalismus und ihre politische Folgen*, (Frankfurt, 1969), pp. 239 f.; *1962 Supplement. . .*, op. cit., p. 53, while indicating that the breakdown between "consumer goods" and "equipment" is unavailable before 1947, does show that "durable" manufacturing output still lagged considerably behind the output reached in 1929 as late as 1939 whereas "non-durables" had reached the 1929 level already by 1935-36. This is a good indicator of the failure of a genuine "recovery" period to appear before World War II. It should be noted that the exact positional value of armaments production within the Marxist schema of reproduction is still a matter of controversy; we would agree with the view presented by Hans Wagner, "Die zyklischen Uberproduktionskrisen der Industrieproduktion in den USA in den ersten beiden Etappen der allgemeinen Krise des Kapitalismus (1914-1958)," in *Jahrbuch für Wirtschaftsgeschichte*, 1964, Part 4, pp. 80-82, according to which such production must fall into the category of social consumption (for the purpose of stabilizing class rule) and thus becomes a subdepartment of department II which produces consumption commodities. In this sense then most Keynesian economies have "statistically" bloated department I's.
13. For a study of conditions of the working class in general under fascism see Jürgen Kuczynski, *Germany: Economic and Labor Conditions Under Fascism* (New York, 1945). Cf. J. Kuczynski, *Die Geschichte der Lage der Arbeiter under dem Kapitalismus*, Vol. 6 (Berlin, 1964).
14. A. Schweitzer, op. cit., p. x.
15. Keynes, *General Theory. . .*, op. cit., pp. 380 f.
16. *General Theory. . .*, op. cit., p. 376.
17. (Neumann, *Behemoth*, (New York 1966 [1942], p. 316; in general

18. Richard Caves et al., *Britain's Economic Prospects* (Washington, D. C.: Brookings, 1968), p. 156.
see ibid., pp. 316-17; and Schweitzer, op. cit., p. 469.

19. Sources: Stanley Lebergott, "Annual Estimates of Unemployment in the United States, 1900-1954," in National Bureau of Economic Research, *The Measurement and Behavior of Unemployment* (Princeton, 1957), p. 216; Walter Galenson and Arnold Zeller, "International Comparisons of Unemployment Rates," in ibid., p. 456.

20. A. G. B. Fisher, *International Aspects of Full Employment in Great Britain*, London: Royal Institute of International Affairs, 1946), p. 19.

21. "The Problem of Economic Instability," in *American Economic Review*, XL/4 (Sept., 1950), 506.

22. Robert Lekachman, *The Age of Keynes* (New York, 1968), p. 171.

23. Ibid., p. 167.

24. Richard Gardner, *Sterling-Dollar Diplomacy* (Oxford, 1956), p. 272. For a further discussion of the rejection see Congress' self-congratulatory celebration, *Twentieth Anniversary of the Employment Act of 1946,* Joint Economic Committee, 89th Cong., 2nd Sess., February 23, 1966, pp. 133 ff.

25. Samuelson, "Lord Keynes and the General Theory," in *Econometrica,* July, 1946; cit. acc. reprint in Seymour Harris (ed.), *The New Economics* (New York, 1948), pp. 145, 147 f.

26. P. Sweezy, "John Maynard Kaynes," in *Science & Society,* Fall, 1946; cit. acc. reprint in Harris (ed.), *The New Economics,* op. cit., p. 106, n. 4.

27. See R. V. Gilbert et al., *An Economic Program for American Democracy* (New York, 1938).

28. *The Theory of Capitalist Development* (New York, 1968 [1942]), pp. 348 f.

29. P. Baran and P. Sweezy, *Monopoly Capital,* (New York, 1966); we do not mean to diminish the importance of this political critique; rather our purpose is to point out how influential Keynesianism has been among the left—so much so that it has led to the abandonment of a large part of the theoretical field to the class enemy.

30. For a broad but superficial survey see Carl Turner, *An Analysis of Soviet Views on John Maynard Keynes* (Durham, N.C., 1969).

31. Keynes, *General Theory. . .*, op. cit., pp. 347 f.

32. Ibid., p. 377.

33. Ibid., pp. 220 f.; Hansen, *A Guide to Keynes,* op. cit., p. 159,

regards this as "a kind of 'freewheeling' detour by Keynes in his less responsible moments."

34. *General Theory. . .,* op. cit., pp. 373, 372.
35. Ibid., p. 373.
36. Ibid., p. 9.
37. Paul Mattick, *Marx and Keynes,* (Boston, 1969), p. 7.
38. Summer Rosen, "Keynes Without Gadflies," in Theodore Roszak (ed.), *The Dissenting Academy* (New York, 1968), p. 68. *The New York Times,* October 27, 1970, in reporting on S' winning the Nobel Prize, estimated that the text is "perhaps the world's best-selling textbook."
39. Source: Federal Reserve *Bulletin,* LVII/10 (Oct., 1971), 780; LVIII/8 (July, 1972), Table A64.)
40. C. L. Shultze, "Is Economics Obsolete? No, Underemployed," in *Saturday Review,* January 22, 1972; here according to Brookings *Reprints,* No. 233, May, 1972, n.p.
41. *Economic Report of the President* (Washington, D.C., 1972), p. 114.
42. See *Annual Report of the Council of Economic Advisers* (Washington, D.C., 1962), pp. 44-48.
43. First printed in *Challenge,* May-June, 1966; cit. acc. to reprint as "How Good are Government Statistics?," in P. Samuelson et al. (eds.), *Readings in Economics* (5th ed.; New York, 1967), p. 132.
44. Eleanor Gilpatrick, *Structural Unemployment and Adequate Demand* (Baltimore, 1966), pp. 218 f.
45. *Business Week,* July 3, 1971, p. 15.
46. "The Debate Over Public Jobs for the Jobless," in *Business Week* (Dec. 9, 1972), p. 106.
47. Andrew Shonfield, *Modern Capitalism* (London, 1969), p. 288.
48. *WSJ,* December 18, 1972, 1:5.
49. By 1971 U.S. investment in Canada reached ca. $35 billion; the U.S. accounts for 80% of all foreign investment in Canada which in turn accounts for but 4% of corporate profits. (See *Economic Notes,* June, 1972, p. 7; August, 1972, p. 3; October, 1972, p. 10; *Neue Zürcher Zeitung,* Oct. 24, 1973, p. 15.)
50. See S.F. Kaliski, "Structural Unemployment in Canada: Towards a Definition of the Geographic Dimension," in *Canadian Journal of Economics/Revue canadienne d'Economique,* I/3 (August 1968), 551-65.
51. See Donald Streever, "Capacity Utilization and Business Investment," University of Illinois *Bulletin,* LVII/55 (March, 1960), 64; cit. acc. Paul Baran and Paul Sweezy, *Monopoly Capital*

(Penguin, 1968), p. 237. Ironically this situation also reconstructs that of the pre-1930s period inasmuch as capacity utilization even then was low; thus during the 1925-29 period manufacturing plant utilization averaged 80%. (See Edwin Nourse and associates, *America's Capacity to Produce* ([New York, 1934], p. 301.) The fact that unemployment was relatively low at this time reveals that the overaccumulation of capital is not a particularly efficacious method of maintaining "full employment." We will return to this point below in discussing the limits of state intervention along Keynesian lines.)

52. *Business Week,* "Why the Big Deficits Fail to Stimulate," (March 4, 1972), p. 66.

53. Federal Reserve *Bulletin,* LVII/8 (August, 1971), 661 f. Our underlining. Several months previous to that Nixon's Council of Economic Advisers struck a similar note with respect to increased union militance. (*Economic Report of the President,* [Washington, D.C., 1971], p. 61.)

54. David C. Smith, "Incomes Policy," in Caves et al., *Britain's Economic Prospects* (Washington, D.C., 1968), p. 116.

55. F. Hirsch, *Money International* (Harmondsworth, 1969), pp. 137 f.

56. Barry Bosworth, "Phase II: The U.S. Experiment with an Incomes Policy," in *Brookings Papers on Economic Activity,* 2:1972, p. 353.

57. *Monthly Labor Review,* XCV/12 (December, 1972), 2; 20 percent of executives labored under the same "misunderstanding."

58. See Alvin Hansen, *A Guide to Keynes* (New York, 1953), pp. 3-11 on "pre-Keynesian dissenters."

59. Keynes, *General Theory. . .,* op. cit., pp. 18, 26.

60. Ibid., p. 33.

61. See Ricardo's letters to Malthus of 9 July 1921 and 21 July 1921 in *The Works and Correspondence of David Ricardo,* IX (Cambridge, 1962), 16, 26, in which he, despite his theoretical disagreements with Malthus, appeals to the lack of empirical evidence of the type of stagnation which Malthus theorized about.

62. Keynes, *General Theory. . .,* op. cit., p. 32.

63. Ibid., p. 355.

64. R. F. Harrod, *The Life of John Maynard Keynes* (London, 1951), p. 462.

65. Keynes, *General Theory. . .,* op. cit., p. 355.

66. These three aspects emerge even more explicitly in Say: (2) "money is but the agent of the transfer of values"; "the silver coin you will have received on the sale of your own products,

and given in the purchase of those of other people, will the next moment execute the same office between other contracting parties, and so on from one to another to infinity; just as a public vehicle successively transports objects one after the other"; (1) "a product is no sooner created, than it, from that instant, affords a market for other products to the full extent of its own value"; (3) "precisely at the same time that one commodity makes a loss, another commodity is making excessive profit. And, since such profits must operate as a powerful stimulus to the cultivation of that particular kind of products, there must needs be some violent means, or some extraordinary cause, a political or natural convulsion. . . . to perpetuate this scarcity on the one hand, and consequent glut on the other. No sooner is the cause of this political disease removed, than the means of production feel a natural impulse towards the vacant channels, the replenishment of which restores activity to all the others." (*A Treatise of Political Economy* (5th American ed.; Philadelphia, 1832), ch. 15; pp. 133, 134, 135.

67. *Theories of Surplus Value,* II, Ch. 17, Sect. 8; *MEW,* 26:2:502.

68. Keynes, *General Theory. . .,* op. cit., p. 20.)

69. D. Ricardo, *The Principles of Political Economy and Taxation* (London, n.d.), Ch. 21, pp. 193, 197.

70. J. S. Mill, *Principles of Political Economy* (New York, 1909), p. 73. According to this definition, capitalism will exist forever since it will never fulfil such needs. In contrast to such reasoning as well as to the demagogic appeals of Keynes and certain of his disciples to the need to increase consumption in order to overcome crises, we may quote the rather realistic statement of Alvin Hansen which indicates why Keynesian policies always seem to reduce to "public works" of some sort rather than a higher marginal propensity to consume for the population at large which would be tantamount to redistribution from "rich" to "poor": "It is not easy to solve the problem of full employment by raising consumption. It is true that there are untold consumer wants waiting to be satisfied. But it is not possible to leap from this fact to the conclusion that unemployed resources can, therefore, be readily absorbed in the consumer goods industries. The fact is that, at moderately high income levels, persistent institutional factors determine within rather rigid limits the ratio of consumption to income" (*Fiscal Policy and Business Cycles* [New York, 1941], p. 248.)

71. Keynes, *General Theory. . .,* op. cit., p. 4.

72. Ibid.
73. Ibid., p. 54; cf. also ibid., pp. 23 f.
74. Leonard G. Bower, "Unemployment Rate—Recent Trends Follow Movement in GNP Gap," in Federal Reserve Bank of Dallas *Business Review*, November, 1972, p. 1.
75. D. Dillard, *The Economics of John Maynard Keynes*, (New York, 1955), p. 105.
76. Ricardo, *Principles*. . ., Ch. 31, p. 267.
77. It is only consistent that Malthus, whom Keynes praised so highly for having anticipated the doctrine of effective demand, rejected Ricardo's views of net and gross revenue while adopting the "modern" approach which "democratically" elevates wages to equal status. (See Malthus *Principles of Political Economy* (London, 1820), pp. 423-26.)
78. Ricardo, See *Works and Correspondence*. . ., I (Cambridge, 1951), lvii-lx; also the correspondence between Ricardo and McCulloch from April to June 1821 in op. cit., III (Cambridge, 1952), 364-400.)
79. Ricardo, *Principles*. . ., op. cit., p. 267.
80. Ibid., p. 271.
81. Ibid., p. 270, n. 1.
82. Ibid., pp. 267 f. Ricardo devotes some space to discussing what modes of spending by the landlords and capitalists as consumers and the state—wars—will have the most effect on employment, concluding that since luxury commodities purchased by "those who are fairly entitled to. . .gratification and enjoyments" lead to no further employment, workers "must naturally desire that as much of the revenue as possible should be diverted from expenditures on luxuries to be expended in the support of menial servants."
83. For Ricardo's own estimate see *Works and Correspondence*. . ., op. cit., VIII, 387.
84. Ricardo, *Principles*. . ., op. cit., pp. 269 f.
85. Malthus, op. cit., p. 425, n.
86. *Capital*, III, Ch. 15, Sect. 4; German ed., p. 274. Cf. also Marx' sarcastic comments on the future which Ricardo describes for the working class in capitalism as luxury producers and menial servants: namely "that to win their necessaries, the same amount of them, the same number of labourers will enable the higher classes to extend, refine, and varify the circle of their enjoyments, and thus to widen the economical, social, and political gulf separating them from their betters. Fine pros-

pects, these, and very desirable results, for the labourer, of the development of the productive powers of his labour." *Theories of Surplus Value*, II, Ch. 18, Sect. B 1 d; German ed., *MEW*, 26-:2:574.

87. Keynes, "Economic Possibilities for our Grandchildren," in *The Nation and Athenaeum*, October 11, 1930; cit. acc. to reprint in *Essays in Persuasion*, (New York, 1932), p. 364.

88. *Theories of Surplus Value*, Ch. 18, Sect. B2a; German ed., *MEW*, 26:2:583.

89. Eleanor Gilpatrick, *Structural Unemployment and Aggregate Demand* (Baltimore, 1966), p. 229. Jürgen Kuczynski, "Kann die wissenschaftlichtechnische Revolution unter den Bedingungen des staatsmonopolistischen Kapitalismus durchgeführt werden?," in *Wirtschaftswissenschaft*, XX/11 (November, 1972), 1691-99, tries to explain the impossibility of complete automation in capitalism from a Marxist viewpoint.

90. Keynes, *General Theory. . .*, op. cit., pp. 362, 32. Cf. also Keynes' essay "Robert Malthus: The First of the Cambridge Economists," in *Essays in Biography*, new edition, edited by Geoffrey Keynes, (New York, 1963 [1951]), pp. 81-124, especially pp. 115-23.

91. T. Malthus, *Principles of Political Economy* (London, 1830), p. 38.

92. Ibid., p. 349; our emphasis.

93. Shoul, "Karl Marx and Say's Law," *Quarterly Journal of Economics*, LXXI (1957), pp. 617 f.

94. Malthus, op. cit., p. 466.

95. Ibid., pp. 479 ff.

96. A. Hansen, *Business Cycles and National Income* (New York, 1951), pp. 252, 253.

97. Ibid., pp. 252 f.

98. As late as 1912 Joseph Schumpeter could write that Malthus' proposition "that the consumption of unproductive, especially of luxury goods, was necessary" "appears very strange to us today but was very common at the time." See *Economic Doctrine and Method* (New York, 1967 [1954]), p. 150 (=*Epochen der Dogmen- und Methodengeschichte* [Tübingen, 1912]).

99. Some of these arguments can best be understood by looking over the exposition of Marx' theory of value below Ch. 10.

100. J. Robinson, *An Essay on Marxian Economics* (2nd ed.; London, 1967 [1942]), p. 51. For a Marxist reply to this tract see Roman Rosdolsky, *Zur Entstehungsgeschichte des Marxschen "Kapital"* (Frankfurt, 1968), pp. 626-52.

101. Shoul, op. cit., p. 614.
102. Sect. 8; *MEW,* 26:2:501.
103. Ibid.; 26:2:501f.
104. Shoul, op. cit., p. 620.
105. And as we shall see in Ch. 10 most bourgeois economists, including S, are still subject to this sort of criticism.
106. *Theories of Surplus Value,* Ch. 17, Sect. 8; *MEW,* 26:2:504 f.
107. It should be noted that Ricardo, despite his allegiance to Say's Law, also entertained a vision of capital stagnation in the form of a falling rate of profit; but with Ricardo this latter did not flow from his labor theory of value; rather it was derived from Ricardo's non-comprehension of the difference between profit and surplus value, of the grounding of the organic composition of capital in the sphere of production, and of the difference between value and price of production; since for Ricardo there was no difference between the rate of surplus value and the rate of profit, or rather, because he ignored the constant capital and examined only wages, and since he looked only at the rate of surplus value (and here he knew only relative surplus value stemming from productivity increases' lowering the value of labor power and neglected absolute surplus value driving from a lengthened working day), he could derive a falling rate of profit only from rising wages. In fact, Ricardo took as his starting point here the alleged diminishing fertility of land which would lead to rising prices of the food constituting the wage commodities of the working class; hence profits would fall. (See *Theories of Surplus Value,* II, chs. 15 and 16.)
108. Keynes, *General Theory. . .,* op. cit., p. 20.
109. Ibid., p. 21.
110. Ibid.
111. Ibid., pp. 104 f.
112. Ibid., p. 31.
113. Ibid., pp. 29 f. Although in general Keynes consistently adhered to this realistic judgment as we shall see in the discussion below of savings and investment, he sometimes slipped back into a rather shallow and vulgar view. Thus in a 1929 pamphlet entitled *Can Lloyd George do It?,* written together with H.D. Henderson, which supported the Liberal Party's public works program, Keynes said: "Individual saving means that some individuals are *producing* more than they are *consuming.* This surplus may, and should, be used to increase capital equipment. But, unfortunately, this is not the only way in

which it can be used. It can also be used to enable other individuals to *consume* more than they *produce*. This is what happens when there is unemployment. We are using our savings to pay for unemployment instead of using them to equip the country." (Cit. acc. reprint in *Essays in Persuasion,* op. cit., p. 123.) The overwhelming proportion of saving—and particularly during a period of stagnation such as the 1920s in the UK—is done by people who have never produced anything and whose entire consumption represents a deduction—not from the savings of those who work, to be sure, but from the product they have produced. This cannot be otherwise in capitalism: "In order to produce 'productively,' production must be such that the mass of the producers is excluded from a part of the demand for the produce; production must take place in opposition to a class whose consumption stands in no relation to its production—since the profit of capital consists precisely in the excess of its production over its consumption. On the other hand, production must take place for classes which consume without producing." (*Theories of Surplus Value,* III, Ch. 20, Sect. 3b; *MEW,* 26:3:117.)

114. A. Hansen, *A Guide to Keynes,* op. cit., p. 29, n. continued from p. 28: "Investment has no purpose except to provide consumers' goods."

115. Dillard, *The Economics of John Maynard Keynes* (New York, 1955), p. 7.

116. See *General Theory. . .,* op. cit., p. 27; as we shall see in a later section, Keynes ignores the rising organic composition of capital which leads to the "employment" of less labor by a capital of a given size.

117. Ibid., p. 105.

118. Ibid., p. 31.

119. See ibid., pp. 164, 213, 219 f., 308 f.

120. Ibid., pp. 317 f.

121. *Grundrisse. . .,* op. cit., p. 636. It must be kept in mind that Marx was not ignorant of the factors working to halt the fall in the rate of profit; he was even aware of such "modern" methods elimination of taxes on profits, unproductive waste of a large parts of capital, etc. See ibid., pp. 636 f.

122 J. Robinson *An Essay on Marxian Economics* (London, 1967 [1942], p. 51.

123. *Theories of Surplus Value,* II, Ch. 17, Sect. 6; *MEW,* 26:2:493.

124. *General Theory. . .,* op. cit., pp. 23 f., 53 f.; aside from the

psychological element involved here, it must be kept in mind that Keynes defined profit as "profit upon alienation"—that is, as the excess of income above cost; in other words, profit is interpreted as stemming from the sale of the commodities and is thus determined by total effective demand in the sphere of circulation.

125. Ibid., p. 293.

126. Ibid., pp. 258-60.

127. See ibid., pp. 5, 17, on Keynes' allegiance to marginal productivity theory; cf. Deutschmann, *Der linke Keynesianismus* (Frankfurt/Main, 1973), p. 33.

128. The text which Keynes chose for scrutiny was A. C. Pigou, *The Theory of Unemployment* (London, 1933), because it "is the only attempt with which I am acquainted to write down the classical theory of unemployment precisely." (*General Theory. . .,* op. cit., p. 279.) Despite the greater realism which Keynes exhibited with respect to practical solutions, both he and Pigou displayed a certain cynicism towards the misery of the working class. Thus in answer to suggestions of sharing the work, Keynes stated that "at present the evidence is, I think, strong that the great majority of individuals would prefer increased income to increased leisure. . . ." (Ibid., p. 326.) Since tens of millions of workers were already enjoying "leisure" twenty-four hours a day, this statement is meaningless; but if the suggestion is meant that wages are not reduced—that is profits are—then Keynes might be offered other "evidence." Pigou, on the other hand, emphasizes exclusively the other aspect so that he can say that "*prima facie,* when account is taken of the fact that an unemployed man escapes the dissatisfaction involved in work, it might seem doubtful whether there is any net subjective cost at all" in unemployment. (*The Theory of Unemployment,* op. cit., pp. 13 f.)

129. Op. cit., p. 83 and ibid., n. 4.

130. R. Robinson, *Study Guide to Accompany Samuelson, Economics* (New York, 1967), p. 83, and ibid., n. 4.

131. Keynes, *General Theory. . .,* op. cit., p. 104.

132. Ibid., p. 106; we say relative because in the last analysis the production of means of production is limited by the ability of producers of consumption commodities to realize their capital in sales to the working class.

133. A. Hansen, "Stability and Expansion," in Homan and Machlup (eds.), *Financing American Prosperity,* (New York, 1945), p. 222.

134. Ibid., pp. 220, 221, 224.

135. See above, Ch. 3.

136. It must be noted that the latter income is pre-tax so that a post-tax income of ca. $10,000 would have to be used for comparison; this would mean that ca. 50 percent of all families had no savings.

137. (Source: *Statistical Abstract, 1972,* p. 340.

138. Cf. Galbraith, The *New Industrial State,* (New York, 1963), p. 48: "There is no reason to suppose that saving has become more democratic since that time" (i.e., 1950).

139. Maurice Leven, Harold G. Moulton, and Clark Warburton, *American's Capacity to Consume* (New York, 1934), pp. 93-96.

140. Source: *Economic Report of the President to the Congress* (Washington, D.C., 1950), pp. 146 f.

141. Keynes, *General Theory. . .,* op. cit., p. 107 f.

142. Ibid., p. 108.

143. *General Theory. . .,* op. cit., p. 63.

144. Ibid.

145. Samuelson, See "Full Employment versus Progress and other Economic Goals," in Max Millikan (ed.), *Income Stabilization for a Developing Democracy. A Study of the Politics and Economics of High Employment without Inflation* (New Haven, 1953), pp. 547-82, esp. 549-54. This article was written at a time when various postwar plans for avoiding a repetition of the depression of the magnitude of the 1930s were still being debated.

146. Keynes, *General Theory. . .,* op. cit., pp. 183f.

147. Ibid., pp. 245-47.

148. Ibid., p. 96.

149. Ibid., p. 249.

150. Ibid., p. 250. In the debate which the publication of Keynes' *General Theory* provoked, Keynes himself was not at all reticent about emphasizing the fact that the psychological law of consumption "was of the utmost importance in the development of my own thought, and it is, I think, absolutely fundamental to the theory of effective demand as set forth in my book." ("The General Theory of Employment," *OJE,* LI/2 [Feb., 1937], 220.) Then again in a letter to a critic Keynes wrote: " 'My theory itself does not require my so-called psychological law as a premise. What the theory shows is that if the psychological law is *not* fulfilled, then we have a condition of complete instability.' " (Quoted in E. Gilboy, "Reply," *QJE,* LIII/4 [August, 1939], 634.)

151. Keynes, *General Theory*, op. cit., p. 31.
152. Ibid., p. 105.
153. Ibid., p. 27.
154. Hugo Hegeland, *The Multiplier Theory* (Lund, 1954), pp. 62 f.
155. Ibid., p. 69.
156. Bach, *Economics* (3rd ed., Englewood Cliffs, 1958), p. 186.)
157. John H. Williams, "Free Enterprise and Full Employment," in *Financing American Prosperity*, op. cit., p. 369.
158. Alvin Hansen, *Economic Policy and Full Employment* (New York-London, 1947), pp. 48, 46. We will forgo elaborating on the reasons Hansen adduces for this inequality such as: "the inequality of native capacities produces an unequal marginal value product among different individuals" such as "the opera singer or the movie actor." (Ibid., p. 46.)
159. Williams, op. cit., pp. 369¹ f.
160. A. Hansen, *Economic Policy. . .*, op. cit., pp. 48, 50.
161. Williams, op. cit., p. 371; see Hansen, *Economic Policy. . .*, op. cit., pp. 49 f.
162. Keynes, *General Theory. . .*, op cit., p. 325. Cf. also ibid., pp. 321, 372-74.
163. Dillard, *The Economics of John Maynard Keynes*, op. cit., p. 82.
164. Samuelson, "The Theory of Pump-Priming Reexamined," *American Economic Review*, XXX/3 (Sept., 1940), p. 504.
165. Sumner Rosen, "Keynes Without Gadflies," in Theodore Roszak (ed.), *The Dissenting Academy* (New York, 1968), p. 69. For S' personal life, on the other, practice what you preach is alleged to be reality; thus in a recent television interview, when asked in conjunction with his defense of Presidential candidate McGovern, whether anyone pays the 70 percent income tax rate, S replied: "I do, many people do." ("Wall Street Week," October 28, 1972, 6:30-7:00 P.M., Channel 52, Trenton, N.J.)
166. Dillard, *The Economics of John Maynard Keynes*, op. cit., p. 83.
167. *Fiscal Policy and Business Cycles* (New York, 1941), p. 149. Cf. our discussion of Hansen on Malthus above p. 78 f.
168. Ibid., pp. 150-52.
169. A. Hansen, *Fiscal Policy and Business Cycles*, op. cit., pp. 149 f.
170. A. Hansen, *Economic Policy and Full Employment*, op. cit., p. 189.
171. See Willi Semmler and Jürgen Hoffmann, "Kapitalakkumulation, Staatseingriffe und Lohnbewegung," in: *Probleme des Klossenkampfs*, No. 2 (Feb., 1972), pp. 58-64.

CHAPTER 9

1. Alfred Malabre Jr., *WSJ,* June 7, 1971, 1:5.

2. *Business Week,* October 21, 1972, p. 53.

3. Source: *BW,* November 18, 1972, p. 6; cf. Federal Reserve Bank of New York, *Annual Report 1972,* p. 12.

4. Source: Federal Reserve Bank of New York, *Monthly Review,* LIII/9 (Sept. 1971), 200. Cf. ibid., LIII/11 (Nov., 1971), 253, for a chart showing analogous developments for manufacturing capacity utilization for these cycles.

5. W. Mitchell, *Business Cycles,* Vol. I: *The Problem and Its Setting* (New York, 1927), p. 62.

6. W. Mitchell, *Business Cycles and Their Causes* (Berkeley and Los Angeles, 1941), pp. 187 f. Cf. also *Business Cycles,* Vol. I, op. cit., p. 107. Our emphasis.

7. W. Mitchell, *Business Cycles,* I (New York, 1939), 206 f. Cf. J. Kuczynski, *Propheten der Wirtschaft* (Berlin, 1970), pp. 43 ff.

8. Hubert D. Henderson, *Supply and Demand* (New York, 1922), pp. 35 f.

9. Eugen Varga, "Die Krisentheorie von Marx und die Probleme der Weltwirtschaftskrise," in E. Varga, *Die Krise des Kapitalismus und ihre politische Folgen,* ed. by E. Altvater (Frankfurt, 1969), p. 208.

10. *Capital,* II, Ch. 9; English ed., p. 186; German ed., p. 185.

11. Samuelson, *Instructor's Manual* (6th ed.; New York, 1964), p. 50.

12. Ibid.

13. Barry N. Siegel, *Aggregate Economics and Public Policy* (3rd ed., Homewood, Ill., 1970), pp. 195 f.

14. Jan Tinbergen, "Statistical Evidence on the Acceleration Principle," *Economica,* V (New Series) (May, 1938), 176. Cf. also James S. Duesenberry, *Business Cycles and Economic Growth* (New York, 1958), pp. 38 ff. For some interesting methodological remarks concerning the construction of the usual illustrations of the accelerator such as S', see William Baumol, "Acceleration Without Magnification," *AER,* XLVI/3 1956, 409-12.

15. H. Hegeland, *The Multiplier Theory* p. 209. The whole passage is italicized in the original.

16. Ibid., p. 255; for another critique of S' accelerator-multiplier model see R. Richter, "Uber die Grenzen der Multiplikator-theorie," in H. Giersch and R. Richter, *Beiträge zur Multip-likatortheorie* (West Berlin, 1954), pp. 37-45, esp. 43 f.

17. A. Evenitsky, "Marx' Model of Expanded Reproduction," *Science and Society*, XXVII/2 (Spring, 1963), 168.

18. See L.B. Al'ter, *Burzhuaznaia politicheskaia ekonomiia SShA* (Moscow, 1961), pp. 593-99. Although as we shall see below the accelerator reflects societal contradictions peculiar to capitalism, Marx too saw a need for planned continuous relative over-production of fixed capital in post-capitalist society to take care of the requirements of reproduction. See *Capital*, II, Ch. 20, Sect. XI, p. 3; English ed., pp. 468 f.; German ed., pp. 464 f.

19. See Ch. 8.